THE BOOK OF
BRITISH
BIRTHPLACES

The 'who was born where' guide to the famous and infamous

THE BOOK OF BRITISH BIRTHPLACES

The 'who was born where' guide to the famous and infamous

A. J. & Marilyn Mullay

breedon **books**
PUBLISHING

First published in Great Britain in 2002 by
The Breedon Books Publishing Company Limited
Breedon House, 3 The Parker Centre,
Derby, DE21 4SZ.

Second edition.

First edition published by Wherewithal Publishing, 1997.

ISBN 1 85983 312 8

Printed and bound by Butler & Tanner, Frome, Somerset,
England.

Cover printing by Lawrence-Allen Colour Printers,
Weston-super-Mare, Somerset.

CONTENTS

INTRODUCTION

British Birthplaces is believed to be the first-ever A to Z listing of cities, towns and villages matched with the names of the most illustrious, notorious, or just downright interesting, people who were born there.

Why is a book like this necessary? The answer is that many communities are unaware of the existence of former townspeople who have gone on to fame and fortune elsewhere. For example, one Midlothian village has nothing to mark the achievements of a famous bird illustrator born there, but he is celebrated by an art gallery exclusively dedicated to him in Cornwall, 500 miles away!

Researching birthplaces is not easy. The registration of births was traditionally the preserve of either church or town hall, before a standardised procedure was adopted in the 19th century, and, if anything, was even later in Scotland. The task of research is made no easier by the inaccurate reporting of their own birthplaces by the eminent and famous.

Some were genuinely mistaken about where they were born – Sir Harry Lauder, for example, was happy to escort bemused admirers around his hometown until even the most enthusiastic of them was forced to conclude that the great man had no clear idea of where in the town he was actually born, if he was born there at all. Others have claimed to be born in a particular location because it seems more 'fashionable' than their real birthplace. A well-known present-day classical dancer has claimed to be born in the Outer Hebrides rather than his own (presumably unfashionable) city in the Midlands, while the comedy celebrity Will Hay found an Aberdeen birthplace more appropriate to his stage persona than his real birthplace of Stockton-on-Tees. The American film actor Robin Williams claimed to have been born in Edinburgh; when challenged, the Chicago-born actor admitted that this was a joke. Biographical researchers are not amused!

The book throws up some extraordinary anomalies. Why has Northampton produced three major composers? What accident of birth has caused the Kent village of Tenterden to produce two colossi of media communication – William Caxton and Sir David Frost? How many larger communities can equal the achievement of two comparatively small Scottish towns – Dunfermline and Linlithgow – in producing five monarchs between them – four Scottish and one British? Why have the

Pennine valleys between Lancashire and Yorkshire proved such fertile ground for Nobel Laureates? Do the present-day villagers of Groton in Suffolk know that their community has produced governors of both Connecticut and Massachusetts?

Rules for inclusion

Subjects have been included if they are listed in any one of nine major biographical dictionaries, provided their birthplace is not subject to query. For this reason, for example, Hereward the Wake is not listed under 'Bourne, Lincolnshire', as this birthplace reference is apocryphal; similarly Marie Stopes and Sir Malcolm Sargent are claimed by more than one community, and have only been included after considerable additional research.

Individuals are listed with their birth and, where applicable, death dates, along with a brief explanation for their fame or notoriety. Thus:

Anthony [Tony] Charles Lynton Blair (Prime Minister [1997–], 1953–)

Further details should be obtained from biographical works. The inclusion of a birthplace in this list does not imply that it is in, or on, public property.

This reference work, like all others, is subject to the changes dictated by time, and it is hoped that new editions will be published at suitable intervals. The publisher would welcome additional information on any birthplace reference.

All the place names which follow have been checked in the Ordnance Survey Gazetteers. Northern Ireland and the Isle of Man are included in this survey, but not the Republic of Ireland or Channel Islands. Geographical descriptors are usually the local authority place name, but not invariably; such labels as 'Avon', 'Cleveland', and 'Strathclyde' are not helpfully specific, and are not used. No county is given if the town is the county town, or its name the same as the county, so, no: CHESTER, Cheshire.

[Parentheses] indicate a familiar or alternative name. '[b.]' indicates name at birth.

The compilers gratefully acknowledge assistance given by Richard Lacey, Alison Lonie, Rupert Harding, Susan Last, and biographers everywhere!

ABBOTS LANGLEY Hertfordshire

Adrian IV [Nicolas Breakspear] (Only English Pope, 1100-1159)

ABERAVON West Glamorgan

Richard Lewis [Dic Penderyn] (Rioter executed for allegedly wounding a soldier, c.1807-1831)

ABERCWMBOI Mid Glamorgan

Stephen Davies (Socialist politician and Welsh nationalist, 1886-1972)

ABERDALGIE Perthshire

James Lorimer (International jurist, wrote *The Institutes of the Laws of Nations*, 1818-1890)

ABERDEEN

Marion Angus (Poet, wrote lament for Mary Stewart ['Alas poor queen'], 1866-1946)

John Barbour (Poet and scholar, author of *The Brus*, 1316-1396)

Alexander Blackwell (Adventurer, executed in Sweden for political intrigue, c.1700-1747)

John Hill Burton (Historian [*History of Scotland* 9 vols], 1809-1881)

Alexander Chalmers (Publisher of *General Biographical Dictionary* in 32 vols between 1812 and 1817, 1759-1834)

Michael Clark (Dancer and choreographer, 1962-)

Alexander Cruden (Scholar and London bookseller, 1701-1770)

Andrew Cruickshank (Actor, played Dr Cameron in TV's *Dr Finlay's Casebook*, 1907-1988)

George Dalgarno (Educationalist, devised language for the deaf and dumb, c.1626-1687)

Sir James Donaldson (University administrator, 1831-1915)

William Dyce (Artist, executed frescoes in Buckingham Palace and the House of Lords, 1806-1864)

Sir David Ferrier (Neurologist, contributed to the 'mapping' of the human brain, 1843-1928)

Graeme Garden (TV actor and comedian [*The Goodies*], 1943-)

Mary Garden (Outstanding operatic soprano at beginning of 20th century, 1874-1967)

James Gibbs (Architect, designer of St Martin-in-the-Fields, 1682-1754)

Sir David Gill (Pioneer of photographic astronomy, 1843-1914)

Evelyn Glennie (Percussionist, 1965-)

David Gregory (Mathematician and astronomical theorist, 1659-1708)

James Gregory (Physician, created 'Gregory's Mixture' [laxative], 1753-1821)

George Grub (Ecclesiastical historian, 1812-1892)

George Jamesone (Portrait artist, c.1588-1644)

David Patrick Kilmuir, [1st Earl] (Jurist, prosecutor at Nuremburg trials, 1900-1967)

Denis Law (International footballer, played for Scotland and both Manchester teams, 1940-)

Annie Lennox (Singer, achieved recognition with the Eurythmics, 1954-)

David Masson (Historian and biographer, 1822-1907)

Robert Morison (Botanist, appointed 'Botanist Royal' by Charles II, 1620-1683)

Sir George Nares (Commander of HMS *Challenger* on its 1872-4 expedition, 1831-1915)

John Phillip (Artist, famous for his Spanish scenes, 1817-1867)

Edward Bannerman Ramsay (Theologian, 1793-1872)

George Croom Robertson (Philosopher, 1842-1892)

Jeannie Robertson (Folk singer, 1908-1975)

Joseph Robertson (Historian, 1810-1866)

Flora Munro Sadler (First female astronomer at Royal Observatory, Greenwich, 1912-)

Mary Slessor (Missionary, known as 'Great Mother' in Nigeria, 1848-1915)

Charles Hamilton Sorley (Poet killed in battle, 1895-1915)

Sir John Steell (Sculptor ['Alexander taming Bucephalus' at Edinburgh's City Chambers], 1804-1891)

Douglas Strachan (Artist, worked with stained glass, 1875-1950)

ABERSYCHAN Near Pontypool, Gwent

Roy Jenkins [Baron] (Statesman, co-founder of the Social Democratic Party, 1920-)

ABINGDON Berkshire

Charles Colchester [1st Baron] (Speaker of House of Commons, 1757-1829)

St Edmund [Edmund Rich] (Ecclesiastic, d.1240)

Edward Moore (Playwright [*The Gamester*], 1712-1757)

Dorothy Miller Richardson (Author of 12 novels including *Painted Roofs* and *Clear Horizon*, 1873-1957)

ABINGER Surrey

Prunella Scales (Actor, star of TV's *Marriage Lines* and *Fawlty Towers*, 1945-)

ACCRINGTON Lancashire

Sir Harrison Birtwhistle (Operatic composer [*The Masque of Orpheus* and *Gawain*], 1934-)

Graeme Fowler (Former Test cricketer [Lancashire and England] and broadcaster, 1957-)

David Lloyd (Former Test cricketer [Lancashire and England] and broadcaster, 1947-)

ACTON Clwyd

George Jeffreys [1st Baron] (Hanging judge, 1648-1689)

AINSDALE Lancashire

Sir Anthony Quayle (Actor and director of Shakespeare Memorial Theatre [1948-56], 1913-1989)

AIRDRIE Lanarkshire

Ian Bannen (Actor, Oscar-nominated for *The Flight of the Phoenix*, 1928-1999)

AIRTH Stirlingshire

Robert Bruce (Churchman, banished for opposing bishops in Scotland, 1554-1631)

ALBOURNE Sussex

James Starley (Cycling manufacturer, produced Ariel geared bicycle in 1871, 1831-1881)

ALBURY Surrey

Henry Drummond (Politician and religious leader, established chair of economics at Oxford, 1786-1860)

ALDEBURGH Suffolk

George Crabbe (Poet whose work inspired Britten's *Peter Grimes*, 1754-1832)

Dame Millicent Fawcett (Suffragette and social reformer, 1847-1929)

ALDERLEY Gloucestershire

Sir Matthew Hale (Jurist, wrote *A History of the Common Law*, 1609-1676)

ALDERSHOT Hampshire

Maud Gonne (Irish political activist,
    1865–1953)
Terence Hands (Stage director, co-founded
    Everyman Theatre, Liverpool, 1941–)
Maud MacBride (Co-founder of Sinn Fein,
    1865–1953)
Myrtle Lillias Simpson (Arctic explorer, first
    woman to ski across Greenland ice-
    cap,1931–)

ALDERSTONE Surrey

Julian Rossi Ashton (Artist, founder of the
    Sydney Art School, 1851–1942)

ALDERTON Suffolk

Sir Robert Naunton (Author and Secretary
    of State to James I, 1563–1635)

ALDFIELD Yorkshire

William Powell Frith (Artist who painted
    huge canvases showing crowd scenes
    such as 'The Railway Station' [1862],
    1819–1909)

ALDWINCLE Northamptonshire

John Dryden (Poet ['All for Love'] who held
    post of Poet Laureate for 20 years until
    the Glorious Revolution [1688],
    1631–1700)
Thomas Fuller (Cleric and historian
    [*Histories of the Worthies of Britain* – left
    unfinished at his death], 1608–1661)

ALFORD Aberdeenshire

Charles Murray (Poet who became South
    African Director of Defence, 1864–1941)

ALFORD Lincolnshire

Anne Hutchinson (Religious leader in
    American colonies, 1591–1643)

ALFORD Somerset

Edward Thring (Educationalist, wrote

Theory and Practice of Teaching,
    1821–1887)
Lord Henry Thring (Legislature draftsman,
    1818–1907)

ALLER Somerset

Ralph Cudworth (Philosopher, wrote *The
    True Intellectual System of the Universe*,
    1617–1688)

ALLESTREE Derbyshire

Alan Bates (Actor, starred in *The Go-
    Between* and *Women in Love*, 1934–)

ALLINGTON Near Maidstone, Kent

Sir Thomas Wyatt (Poet, introduced Italian
    sonnet into English literature,
    1503–1542)

ALLOA Clackmannanshire

David Allan (Artist known as the 'Scottish
    Hogarth', 1744–1796)
John Erskine Mar [Earl] (Military
    commander exiled after heading the
    1715 Jacobite Rebellion, 1675–1732)

ALLOWAY Ayrshire

Robert Burns (Poet, Scotland's national
    bard, 1759–1796)

ALNWICK Northumberland

Sir George Airy (Astronomer, promoted
    acceptance of Greenwich zero meridian,
    1801–1892)
Thomas Cobden Sanderson (Artistic printer
    and bookbinder, 1840–1922)
Prideaux John Selby (Naturalist, co-founder
    of *Magazine of Zoology and Botany*,
    1788–1857)

ALRESFORD Hampshire

Sir Frank Benson (Theatre manager and
    actor, knighted by George V on stage,
    during a matinée, 1858–1939)

Mary Mitford (Poet and author of plays on the lives of Mary Stewart and Charles I, 1787-1855)

ALSTON Cumbria
Hugh Lee Pattinson (Metallurgist who devised economic way to extract silver from lead, 1796-1858)

ALTOFTS Wakefield, Yorkshire
Sir Martin Frobisher (Explorer who sought North West Passage and who died fighting the Spanish, c.1535-1594)

ALTON Hampshire
William Curtis (Founded *Botanical Magazine*, 1746-1799)

ALTRINCHAM Cheshire
Paul Allott (Former Test cricketer [Lancashire and England] and broadcaster, 1956-)
Eileen Postan [b.Power] (Economic historian, founder of *Economic History Review*, 1889-1940)

ALVA Clackmannanshire
John Eadie (Biblical scholar, 1810-1876)
William Alexander Stirling [1st Earl] (Poet and printer, c.1567-1640)

ALVECHURCH Worcestershire
Fay Weldon (Author and TV playwright [*The Life and Loves of a She-Devil*], 1931-)

ALVINGHAM Lincolnshire
Barnabe Googe (Early English pastoral poet, 1540-1594)

ALWALTON Cambridgeshire
Sir Frederick Henry Royce (Motor manufacturer, co-founded Rolls-Royce with Charles Rolls in 1906, 1863-1933)

AMBERLEY Sussex
Noel Streatfield (Children's author [*Ballet Shoes, The Circus is Coming*], 1895-1986)

ANCRUM Roxburghshire
William Buchan (Medical author [*Domestic Medicine*], 1729-1805)

ANDERTON Cheshire
Eaton Hodgkinson (Engineer, co-designed Britannia Bridge over Menai Strait, 1789-1861)

ANNALONG County Down
Francis Rawdon Chesney (Explorer, surveyed Suez isthmus and possible rail route to India, 1789-1872)

ANNAN Dumfriesshire
Thomas Blacklock (Poet and minister [at Kirkcudbright] blind from infancy, 1721-1791)
Hugh Clapperton (Explorer, sought source of the Niger, 1788-1827)
Edward Irving (Mystical preacher, predicted Second Coming, 1792-1834)

ANNERY Devon
Walter De Stapledon (Edward II's Treasurer, 1261-1326)

ANSTRUTHER Fife
Thomas Chalmers (Theologian, pioneer of Scotland's free church, 1780-1847)
John Goodsir (Anatomist, also researched cell biology, 1814-1867)
William Tennant (Poet ['Anster Fair'] and linguist [*Syriac and Chaldee Grammar*], 1784-1848)

APPLETREE Northamptonshire
Alban Butler (Hagiographer and Chaplain to the Duke of Norfolk, 1710-1773)

ARBROATH Angus

James Chalmers (Inventor of adhesive postage stamp, 1782–1853)

Lynda Myles (Film producer, [*The Commitments*], 1947–)

Kathleen Whyte (Embroiderer, taught at Glasgow School of Art, 1909–)

ARBURY Warwickshire

Sir Roger Newdigate (Antiquarian, founder of Newdigate Prize for poetry at Oxford, 1719–1806)

ARDROSSAN Ayrshire

Dugald Drummond (Locomotive engineer for the Caledonian, North British and London & South Western railways, 1840–1912)

William Henry Gairdner (Missionary, 1873–1928)

John Kerr (Physicist, researched passage of light through electromagnetic fields, 1824–1907)

ARDSLEY Near Wakefield, Yorkshire

(See also EAST ARDSLEY)

James Nayler (Preacher condemned for blasphemy, c.1617–1660)

ARMTHORPE Yorkshire

Kevin Keegan (International footballer and manager at club and national levels, 1951–)

ARNESBY Near Leicester

Robert Hall (Ecclesiastical author who began preaching aged 11 and who later wrote *Modern Infidelity...*, 1764–1831)

ASHBURTON Devon

Richard Carlile (Radical journalist, imprisoned for his beliefs, 1790–1843)

William Gifford (Editor and translator [of Juvenal], 1756–1826)

ASHBY-DE-LA-ZOUCH Leicestershire

Sir Frank Watson Dyson (Astronomer Royal for Scotland [1905–10] and England [1910–33], 1868–1939)

Joseph Hall (Ecclesiastic, held bishoprics of Exeter and Norwich in succession, 1574–1656)

ASHE Hampshire

Sir John Henry Lefroy (Military commander, wrote *Handbook of Field Ordnance*, 1817–1890)

ASHFORD Kent

Patsy Byrne (TV character actor, 1933–)

Mark Alan Ealham (Test cricketer [Kent and England], 1969–)

Frederick Forsyth (Author [*The Day of the Jackal*], 1938–)

Sir Malcolm Sargent (Orchestral conductor, 1895–1967)

John Wallis (Mathematician who deciphered enemy messages for the Roundheads and, later, William III, 1616–1703)

ASHINGTON Northumberland

Jack Charlton (International footballer and manager of Ireland side, 1935–)

Sir Robert [Bobby] Charlton (International footballer with Manchester United, 1937–)

ASHLEY Gloucestershire

Thomas Bowdler (Prudish adaptor of Shakespeare, 1754–1825)

ASHTON Somerset

Sir Ferdinando Gorges (American colonist, c.1566–1647)

ASHTON-UNDER-LYNE Lancashire

Dawn Acton (TV actor [*Coronation Street*], 1977–)

Amanda Barrie [b.Shirley Ann Broadbent] (Film [*Carry on Cleo*] and TV [*Coronation Street*] actor, 1939–)

Margaret Mary Beckett (Politician and cabinet minister [1997–], 1943–)

Sir Geoff Hurst (Footballer, scored 3 goals in 1966 World Cup Final, 1941–)

ASHTON-UPON-MERSEY Near Manchester

Lascelles Abercrombie (Poet and author of *Principles of Literary Criticism*, 1881–1938)

William Stanley Houghton (Playwright [*The Dear Departed*], 1881–1913)

ASLOCKTON Nottinghamshire

Thomas Cranmer (Martyred Archbishop of Canterbury, burnt at the stake for treason, 1489–1556)

ASTLEY Warwickshire

Marian Evans (Author better known as George Eliot [*Mill on the Floss*], 1819–1880)

ASTON Staffordshire

John Rogers (Martyred religious reformer, c.1500–1555)

ASWARBY Lincolnshire

George Bass (Explorer after whom Bass Strait is named, 1771–1803)

ATCHAM Shropshire

Ordericus Vitalis (Historian, 1075–1143)

ATHERSTONE Warwickshire

Nehemiah Grew (Botanist and physician, 1641–1712)

ATHERTON Lancashire

Eric Roberts Laithwaite (Innovative engineer, researched magnetic levitation as means of transport, 1921–1997)

Nigel Short (Britain's youngest chess Grandmaster, 1965–)

ATTENBOROUGH Nottinghamshire

Henry Ireton (Civil War commander, Cromwell's son-in-law, 1611–1651)

AUCHTERARDER Perthshire

James Kennaway (Novelist [*Tunes of Glory*], 1928–1968)

AUCHTERHOUSE Angus

Patrick Bell (Inventor of mechanical reaper, 1799–1869)

AUCHTERMUCHTY Fife

John Glas (Founder of Sandemanian religious sect, 1695–1773)

AUSTHORPE Near Leeds

John Smeaton (Civil engineer [Ramsgate Harbour, Forth & Clyde Canal], 1724–1794)

AUSTERFIELD Yorkshire

William Bradford (Member of Pilgrim Fathers, 1590–1656)

AYLESBURY Buckinghamshire

Michael Apted (Film director [*Gorillas in the Mist*], 1941–)

Rutland Boughton (Composer, 1878–1960)

AYNHO Northamptonshire

Shackerley Marmion (Playwright [*A Fine Companion*], 1603–1639)

AYR

John Loudon McAdam ('Tarmacadam' inventor, 1756–1836)

Robert McBryde (Artist who worked in Cubist and Expressionist styles, 1913–1966)

William MacLure ('Father of American geology', 1763-1840)

Andrew Michael Ramsay ['Chevalier de Ramsay'] (Author, 1686-1743)

William Ross [Lord] (Politician, longest-serving Secretary of State for Scotland [1964-70, 1974-6], 1911-1988)

BACUP Lancashire
Betty Jackson (Fashion designer, 1949-)

BADMINTON Gloucestershire
Fitzroy James Henry Raglan [Baron] (Commander who ordered charge of the Light Brigade, 1788-1855)

BALBY Yorkshire
(See also DONCASTER)
Ethel Mary Turner (Australian-based novelist [*Seven Little Australians, The Family at Misrule*], 1870-1958)

BALFOUR Fife
David Beaton (Statesman, persecutor of Scottish protestants, 1494-1546)

BALFRON Stirlingshire
Alexander Thompson (Greek-influenced architect, his work best seen in Glasgow, 1817-1875)

BALLYMONEY County Antrim
Joey [William Joseph] Dunlop (Champion motorcyclist killed in action, 1952-2001)

BALLYRONEY County Down
Thomas Mayne Reid (Children's author, 1818-1883)

BALSARROCH Near Stranraer Wigtownshire
Sir John Ross (Polar explorer, attempted to discover fate of the Franklin Expedition, 1777-1856)

BAMBER BRIDGE Lancashire
George Woodcock (Trade union leader, 1904-1979)

BAMBURGH Northumberland
Grace Darling (Lifeboat heroine, saved lives from Farne Islands wreck in tumultuous seas, 1815-1842)

BAMPTON Cumbria
Edmund Gibson (Ecclesiastical jurist, 1669-1748)

BAMPTON Oxfordshire
John Philips (Poet commemorated in Westminster Abbey, 1676-1709)

BANBURY Oxfordshire
Richard Bevin Braithwaite (Philosopher, 1900-1990)

Gary Glitter [b.Paul Gadd] (Glam rock singer, 1940-)

Sir Alan Lloyd Hodgkin (Nobel Prize-winning physiologist, 1914-)

BANCHORY Aberdeenshire
James Scott Skinner (Fiddler known as the 'Strathspey King', 1843-1927)

BANFF
Katherine, Duchess of Atholl [b.Ramsay] (The 'Red Duchess', first female Conservative minister, 1874-1960)

Elspeth Buchan (Religious sect founder, 1738-1791)

St John Ogilvie (Jesuit martyr, 1580-1615)

James Sharp (Religious activist who betrayed Covenanters, 1613-1679)

BANGOR County Down
Keith Gillespie (International footballer [Blackburn Rovers and Northern Ireland], 1975-)

BANGOR Gwynedd
Sir Charles Warren (Archaeologist,
  researched mainly in Palestine and
  Jerusalem, 1840–1927)

BANGOUR West Lothian
William Hamilton (Poet who fled abroad
  after taking part in Second Jacobite
  Rebellion [1745], his later work edited by
  Adam Smith, 1704–1754)

BARDSEY Yorkshire
William Congreve (Dramatist and poet [*The
  Way of the World*], 1670–1729)

BARFORD Warwickshire
Joseph Arch (Religious activist,
  1826–1919)

BARGOED Mid Glamorgan
Alun Hoddinott (Composer and Director of
  the Cardiff Festival [1967–89], 1929–)
John Tripp (Journalist and poet,
  1927–1986)

BARNARD CASTLE County Durham
Cyril Northcote Parkinson (Economist and
  political scientist, 1932–1993)

BARNET Hertfordshire
Elaine Paige (Actor, played Evita on stage,
  1952–)
Dame Cicely Saunders (Founder of hospice
  movement, 1918–)
Philip Clive Roderick Tufnell (Test cricketer
  [Middlesex and England], 1966–)

BARNSLEY Yorkshire
John Arden (Playwright, [*Armstrong's Last
  Goodnight*], 1930–)
Darren Gough (Test cricketer [Yorkshire and
  England], 1970–)
Sir Michael Ernest Sadler (Educationalist,
  1861–1943)

BARNSTAPLE Devon
Sir Francis Chichester (Yachtsman,
  circumnavigated world solo in his sixties
  [1966–67], 1901–1972)
Richard Charles Eyre (Stage and film
  director, 1943–)
John Gay (Poet, wrote libretto for *Beggar's
  Opera*, 1685–1732)
Sir Francis Carruthers Gould (Cartoonist,
  1881–1925)
William Richard Lethaby (Architect and
  building conservationist, 1857–1931)
Ethel Mairet (Artistic weaver, 1872–1952)

BARNT GREEN Hereford and Worcester
Margaret Leighton (Actor, Oscar-
  nominated for *The Go-Between*,
  1922–1976)

BARNWELL Leicestershire
William Bradford (American-based
  publisher, 1663–1752)
John Montagu Sandwich [1st Earl]
  (Statesman and naval commander, killed
  when fighting the Dutch, 1625–1672)

BARRHEAD Renfrewshire
John Davidson (Author [*Fleet Street
  Eclogues*] who committed suicide,
  1857–1909)
Kenneth Mellanby (Environmental scientist,
  wrote *Pesticides and Pollution*, 1908–1993)

BARROW Suffolk
Mary Beale (Portrait painter, 1632–1699)

BARRY South Glamorgan
Glyn Edmund Daniel (Archaeologist, chair
  of TV panel game *Animal, Vegetable,
  Mineral*, 1914–1986)

BARTON SEAGRAVE Northamptonshire
Elizabeth Harwood (Operatic soprano,
  1938–1990)

BARTON-ON-SEA Hampshire
Jamie Redknapp (International footballer
[Liverpool and England], 1973–)

BARTON-UPON-HUMBER Lincolnshire
Benjamin Huntsman, (Inventor of crucible
steel making, 1704–1776)
Chad [Edward] Varah (Founder of the
Samaritans and children's storyteller,
1911–)

BASINGSTOKE Hampshire
Thomas Warton (Historian of poetry,
1728–1790)

BATH Somerset
William Pitt Amherst [1st Earl] (Governor-
General of India, 1773–1857)
Bill Bailey (TV comedian, 1964–)
George Earle Buckle (Editor of *The Times*
for 28 years, 1854–1935)
Sir Henry Cole (Designer and administrator,
1808–1882)
Richard Lovell Edgeworth (Irish-based
inventor and author of *Practical
Education*, 1744–1817)
David Hartley [The Younger] (Inventor and
legislator, 1731–1813)
William Hone (Author and bookseller,
1780–1842)
Caryll Houselander (Mystic and poet,
1901–1954)
William Lonsdale (Geologist who
considerably advanced palaeontological
knowledge through his study of fossils in
Devon, 1794–1871)
Robert Montgomery (Religious poet,
1807–1855)
Edward Vansittart Neale (Co-operative
pioneer, 1810–1892)
Sir William Edward Parry (Arctic explorer,
1790–1855)
Henry James Prince (Controversial cult
founder, 1811–1899)

Benjamin Robins (Mathematician and
ballistics expert, 1707–1751)
Charles Prestwich [C.P.] Scott (Editor,
Manchester Guardian, 1846–1932)
John Allsebrook Simon [1st Viscount]
(Home and Foreign Secretary, 1873–1954)
Daniel Terry (Actor, playwright,
c.1780–1829)

BATHGATE West Lothian
Catherine Blair (Artist and suffragist,
1872–1946)
Sir James Young Simpson (Pioneer of
anaesthesia, 1811–1870)

BATLEY Yorkshire
Robert Palmer (Pop singer [*Addicted to
Love*], 1949–)

BEARSDEN Dunbartonshire
Jessie King (Artist, 1875–1949)

BEARSTED Kent
Robert Fludd (Mystic philosopher,
1574–1637)

BEAUCHAMP COURT Warwickshire
Sir Fulke Greville [1st Baron Brooke] (Poet,
1554–1628)

BECCLES Suffolk
Joseph Arnold (Botanist, 1782–1818)
William Aldis Wright (Shakespearean
scholar, 1836–1914)

BECKENHAM Kent
Peter Frampton (Pop singer [*Show Me the
Way*], 1950–)
George Grote (Historian and political
reformist, 1794–1871)
Sir William Searle Holdsworth (Legal
historian, 1871–1944)
Bob Monkhouse (TV comedian and
presenter, 1928–)

BEDFORD

Ronnie [Ronald William George] Barker
  (Comedian, star of TV's *Two Ronnies* and
  Porridge, 1929–)
Frederick Gustavus Burnaby (Soldier and
  traveller, 1842–1885)
Ernest Urban Trevor Huddleston
  (Archbishop and anti-Apartheid
  campaigner, 1913–1998)
Dame Bertha Phillpotts (Educationalist,
  1877–1932)
William Hale White (Author, used 'Mark
  Rutherford' as pseudonym, 1831–1913)

BEDLINGTON Northumberland

Sir Daniel Gooch (Engineer, laid first trans-
  Atlantic telegraph cable, 1816–1889)

BEKESBOURNE Kent

Stephen Hales (Botanist, 1677–1761)
Michael Powell (Film director, collaborated
  with Emeric Pressburger on *Small Back
  Room*, *The Red Shoes*, 1905–1990)

BELFAST

Gerry [Gerald] Adams (Politician, 1948–)
Thomas Andrews (Chemist, 1813–1885)
Derek Bell (Harpist specialising in
  traditional folk music, 1935–)
John Stewart Bell (Physicist, 1928–1990)
George Best (International footballer, 1968
  European Footballer of the Year, 1946–)
Danny Blanchflower (International
  footballer, captained Spurs to League and
  Cup double in 1961, 1926–1993)
Kenneth Branagh (Actor/director, 1960–)
James Bryce [1st Viscount] (Statesman,
  1838–1922)
Mairead Corrigan-Maguire, (Nobel
  Peace Prize-winner for her attempts
  to bring stability to Northern Ireland,
  1944–)
James Craig [1st Viscount Craigavon]
  (Statesman, 1871–1940)

Joseph Devlin (Irish nationalist,
  1872–1934)
James Galway (Flautist, 1939–)
St John Greer Ervine (Playwright,
  1883–1971)
Sir Samuel Ferguson (Poet and scholar,
  1810–1886)
Gerry [Gerard] Fitt [Baron] (Politician,
  1926–)
Francis Fowke (Architect, designer of
  London's Albert Hall, 1823–1865)
Michael Gibson (Rugby player selected for
  five British Lions tours, 1947–)
Alex ['Hurricane'] Higgins (Snooker player,
  1949–)
Paddy Higson (Film producer, [*Gregory's
  Girl*], 1941–)
Lord Kelvin [William Thomson]
  (Outstanding physicist of his generation,
  1824–1907)
Sir John Lavery (Artist, 1856–1941)
Cecil Day Lewis (Poet, 1904–1972)
Clive Staples Lewis (Author, 1898–1963)
Robert Lynd (Essayist, 1879–1949)
Siobhan McKenna (Actor, 1923–1986)
Louis MacNeice (Poet, 1907–1963)
Derek Mahon (Poet, 1941–)
Brian Moore (Novelist [*The Lonely Passion
  of Judith Hearne*], 1921–)
Van Morrison (Rock singer [*Brown-eyed
  Girl*], 1945–)
Ruby Murray (Pop singer [*Softly, Softly*],
  1935–)
Osbourne Reynolds (Engineer, 1842–1912)
Robert Smillie (Miners' leader and
  politician, 1857–1940)
James Thomson (Hydraulics engineer,
  1822–1892)
Betty Williams (Peace activist, co-winner
  of 1976 Nobel Peace Prize, 1943–)

BELFORD Northumberland

Sir William Coldstream (Artist, 1908–1987)

BELLSHILL Lanarkshire
Sir Matt Busby (Football manager,
associated with Manchester United,
1909–1994)
Michael Denness (Captain of England
cricket team [1973–5], 1940–)
Sheena Easton (Singer, 1959–)
William [Billy] McNeill (International
footballer, first British captain to lift
European Cup [1967], 1940–)

BELPER Derbyshire
Alison Hargreaves (First British woman to
climb Eiger north face, 1962–1995)
Samuel Slater (Textile engineer,
1768–1835)
Sir Frank Swettenham (Administrator in
Malaya, 1850–1946)

BENTWORTH Hampshire
George Wither (Poet and satirist, 1588–1667)

BENVIE Angus
John Playfair (Mathematician and
geologist, 1748–1819)

BERKELEY Gloucestershire
Edward Jenner (Discoverer of vaccination,
1749–1823)

BERKHAMSTED Hertfordshire
William Cowper (Poet, 1731–1800)
Graham Henry Greene (Novelist, [*Our Man
in Havana, The Human Factor*],
1904–1991)
Hugh Carleton Greene (Television
administrator, BBC Director-General
[1960–9], 1910–1987)
Sir Michael Hordern (Actor, 1911–1994)
Esther Rantzen (Broadcaster, 1940–)

BERRYNARBOR Near Ilfracombe, Devon
John Jewel (Early Protestant churchman,
1522–1571)

BERWICK-ON-TWEED
James Redpath (American-based social
reformer, 1833–1891)

BETTON Shropshire
Sir Humphrey Mackworth (Politician and
educationalist, 1657–1727)

BETWS Near Ammanford, Dyfed
James Griffiths (Miners' leader and
politician, 1890–1975)

BEVERLEY Yorkshire
Ken Annakin (Film director, 1914–)
John Fisher (Theologian and saint,
1469–1535)

BEWDLEY Worcestershire
Stanley Baldwin (Prime Minister during
1936 abdication crisis, 1867–1947)

BEXHILL Sussex
Sir Angus Frank Wilson (Author [*Old Men in
the Zoo*], 1913–1991)
Sir David Hare (Playwright [*Licking Hitler,
Plenty*] and film director, 1947–)

BEXLEY Kent
Sir Edward Creasy (Historian, 1812–1878)

BIBURY Gloucestershire
Charles John Hyne (Author, created
'Captain Kettle', 1865–1944)

BIDEFORD Devon
Sir John William Nott (Defence Minister
during Falklands conflict, 1932–)
David Robert Shepherd (Test cricket
umpire, 1940–)

BIGGAR Lanarkshire
John Brown (Author, 1810–1882)
Anne Hunter McAllister (Speech therapist
pioneer, 1892–1983)

BILLINGE Near St Helens

Angus Robert Charles Fraser (Test cricketer [Middlesex and England], 1965–)

BILSTON West Midlands

Sir Henry John Newbolt (Poet, 1862–1938)

Tom Gilbert Thomas Webster (Sporting cartoonist, 1890–1962)

BINGHAM Nottinghamshire

Robert Lowe Sherbrooke [1st Viscount] (Chancellor of the Exchequer [1868–73], 1811–1892)

BINGLEY Yorkshire

Rodney Bewes [Film and TV actor [*The Likely Lads*], 1938–)

Sir Fred Hoyle (Astronomer and author, 1915–2001)

Harvey [Robert] Smith (Equestrian show jumper, gave his name to a two-fingered salute, 1938–)

THE BINNS West Lothian

Thomas Dalyell (Military commander, raised Royal Scots Greys, c.1615–1685)

BIRKENHEAD Cheshire

(See also ROCK FERRY and WALLASEY)

Edward John Bevan (Industrial chemist, 1856–1921)

Arthur John Briscoe (Marine etcher, 1873–1943)

Sir Lewis Casson (Actor-manager, 1875–1969)

William Ralph [Dixie] Dean (Footballer, scored record 60 goals in a season for Everton, 1907–1980)

Sir Thomas Douglas Forsyth (Administrator in India, 1827–1886)

Hugh Esmor Huxley (Biophysicist, 1924–)

Glenda Jackson (Actor and government minister, 1936–)

Jason McAteer (International footballer [Republic of Ireland], 1971–)

John Peter McGrath (Playwright and theatre-founder, 1935–2002)

Frederick Edwin Smith [1st Earl Birkenhead] (Statesman, 1872–1930)

Philip Wilson Steer (Artist, 1860–1942)

BIRKIN Yorkshire

Thomas Hill Green (Philosopher, 1836–1882)

BIRMINGHAM

Walter Allen (Novelist [*Dead Man Over All*, *Rogue Elephant*], 1911–1995)

Dennis Amiss (Test cricketer and administrator for Warwickshire CCC, 1943–)

Francis Aston (Nobel Prize-winning physicist, 1877–1945)

Eileen Atkins (Actor [*The Dresser, Gosford Park*], 1934–)

Francis Edward Bache (Violinist and composer, 1833–1858)

Sir Michael Balcon (Film producer [*The 39 Steps, Whisky Galore*], 1896–1977)

David Bomberg (Artist, noted for Abstract and Vortacist styles, 1890–1957)

Matthew Boulton (Engineer, partnered James Watt in building steam engines, 1728–1809)

Gerald Leslie Brockhurst (Artist [painted 'Adolescence', 1933], 1891–1979)

Sir Edward Coley Burne-Jones (Artist, specialised in Arthurian and Greek mythical subjects, 1833–1898)

George Cadbury (Chocolate manufacturer, 1839–1922)

Dame Barbara Hamilton Cartland (Novelist, 1901–1999)

Sir Austen Chamberlain (Nobel Peace Prize-winning statesman, 1863–1937)

Arthur Neville Chamberlain (Prime Minister [1937–40], 1869–1940)

Alexander Macomb Chance (Industrial chemist, 1844–1917)

John Michael Copley (Theatre producer for both Sadler's Wells and Covent Garden, 1933–)

John Anthony Curry (Ice skater, 1949–1994)

David Burman Edgar (Playwright [Destiny, 1976], 1948–)

George Richards Elkington (Pioneer of electroplating, 1801–1865)

Sir Francis Galton (Innovative scientist, devised finger-printing, 1822–1911)

Tony Garnett (Television producer [Cathy Come Home], 1936–)

James Louis Garvin (Encyclopaedist and biographer, 1868–1947)

Bernard Griffin (Ecclesiastic, Cardinal and Papal legate, 1899–1956)

Tony Hancock (Comedian [Hancock's Half Hour for radio and TV], 1924–1968)

Matthew Davenport Hill (Legal reformer, advocated enlightened alternatives to punishment, 1792–1872)

George Jacob Holyoake (Last atheist imprisoned in England, 1817–1906)

Clement Mansfield Ingleby (Philosopher and Shakespeare scholar, 1823–1886)

Elizabeth Jolley (Author of Australian-based novels, 1923–)

Albert William Ketelbey [Anton Vodorinski] (Composer, wrote piano sonata at age of 11, 1875–1959)

Ronald Arbuthnott Knox (Theologian, 1888–1957)

Felicity Kendal (Actor, star of TV's The Good Life, 1947–)

Ralph Robert Lingen [Baron] (Treasury administrator, 1819–1905)

Henry Vollam ['H.V.'] Morton (Travel author [In Search of... series], 1892–1979)

Charles Talbut Onions (Lexicographer, worked on Oxford dictionaries, 1873–1965)

Ozzy [b.John] Osbourne (Rock singer, [once with group Black Sabbath], 1948–)

Alexander Parkes (Chemist, pioneer of electroplating, 1813–1890)

Sir Max Pemberton (Novelist and journalist, 1863–1950)

William Pole (Engineer, 1814–1900)

Alfred Reginald Radcliffe-Brown (Social anthropologist, 1881–1955)

Sax Rohmer [Arthur Sarsfield Ward] (Novelist, created Fu Man Chu, 1886–1959)

Iain Murray Rose (Triple champion Olympic swimmer, 1939–)

Sir William Napier Shaw (Meteorologist, 1854–1945)

Joseph Henry Shorthouse (Novelist, 1834–1903)

Kenneth Tynan (Theatre critic, pioneered swearing on TV, 1927–1980)

Darius Vassell (International footballer [Aston Villa and England], 1966–)

Julie Walters (Actor [Educating Rita], 1950–)

Rex Warner (Author [Young Caesar], 1905–1986)

Brooke Foss Westcott (Scholar and Bishop of Durham, 1825–1901)

Steve Winwood (Singer and songwriter with Spencer Davis Group, 1948–)

William Wyon (Coinage designer, 1795–1851)

BIRSE Aberdeenshire
John Skinner (Ecclesiastical historian and songwriter, 1721–1807)

BIRTLEY County Durham
Sir Harold Jeffreys (Astronomer and mathematician, 1891–1989)

BIRTSMORTON Hereford and Worcester
William Huskisson (Statesman, 1770–1830)

BISHOP AUCKLAND County Durham
Henry George Liddell (Greek scholar and
lexicographer, 1811–1898)

BISHOP MIDDLEHAM County Durham
Sir Henry Taylor (Poet [St Clement's Eve],
1800–1886)

BISHOPSTOKE Hampshire
William Gilbert (Surgeon and novelist,
1804–1889)

BISHOP'S STORTFORD Hertfordshire
Frederick Scott Archer (Inventor of
improved photography process,
1813–1857)
Sir Walter Gilbey (Wine merchant,
1831–1914)
Cecil John Rhodes (Imperialist statesman,
after whom Rhodesia named,
1853–1902)

BISHOPTHORPE Yorkshire
George Sandys (Colonist in America and
classical scholar, 1578–1644)

BITTON Gloucestershire
Tom Cribb (Champion prize-fighter,
1781–1848)

BLACKBOURTON Oxfordshire
Maria Edgeworth (Irish-based novelist
[Castle Rackrent] and author of
educational works, 1767–1849)

BLACKBURN Lancashire
Teresa Billington Greig (Suffragette,
1877–1964)
Ian McShane (TV actor [Lovejoy], 1942–)
John Morley [1st Viscount] (Editor and
biographer, 1838–1923)
Ronald Stevenson (Composer and music
author, 1928–)

BLACK NOTLEY Essex
William Bedell (Irish-based churchman,
1571–1642)
John Ray (Naturalist, gave name to Ray
Society, 1627–1705)

BLACKPOOL Lancashire
George Eastham (Footballer [Arsenal],
1936–)

BLACKWOOD Gwent
Gwyn Jones (Author and expert on Viking
history, 1907–)
Dame Margaret Price (Operatic soprano
specialising in roles by Mozart and Verdi,
1941–)

BLAIRGOWRIE Perthshire
Hamish Henderson (Folklorist, founded
School of Scottish Studies, 1919–2002)

BLAIRHALL Fife
Sir William Bruce (Architect, rebuilt
Holyrood Palace in 1670s, 1630–1710)

BLAKELAW Roxburghshire
Thomas Pringle (Author and anti-slavery
campaigner, 1789–1834)

BLANDFORD FORUM Dorset
Thomas Creech (Classical scholar,
1659–1700)
Alfred Stevens (Artist and sculptor, worked
in St Paul's Cathedral, 1818–1875)
William Wake (Archbishop of Canterbury
[1716–37], 1657–1737)

BLANDFORD ST MARY Dorset
Thomas Pitt (Merchant venturer,
1653–1726)

BLANEFIELD Ayrshire
Sir Gilbert Blane (Antiscorbutic expert,
1749–1834)

BLANTYRE Lanarkshire
(See also LOW BLANTYRE)
Mary Nicol Armour (Artist, taught at
Glasgow School of Art, 1902–)

BLENHEIM PALACE Oxfordshire
Lord Randolph Churchill (Statesman,
1849–1895)
Sir Winston Spencer Churchill (War leader,
1874–1965)

BODMIN Cornwall
Sir Edward Bruce Hamley (Military
commander, 1824–1893)
Herman Cyril McNeile ['Sapper'] (Creator of
'Bulldog' Drummond, 1888–1937)
Sir Arthur Quiller-Couch (Poet, 1863–1944)

BOGNOR REGIS West Sussex
Russell Drysdale (Australian-based artist,
1912–1981)
Bruce Welch [b.Bruce Cripps] (Guitarist [with
The Shadows] and record producer, 1941–)

BOLLINGTON Cheshire
Terry [Terence Hardy] Waite (Ecclesiastical
representative held hostage in Beirut,
1939–)
Sir James Chadwick (Nobel Prize-winning
physicist, 1891–1974)

BOLTON Lancashire
Thomas Cole (Artist, 1801–1848)
William Lassell (Astronomer, discovered
moons of Saturn, Uranus and Neptune,
1799–1880)
Tommy Lawton (International footballer
[England], 1919–1996)
William Hesketh Leverhulme [1st Viscount]
(Soap manufacturer and philanthropist,
established Port Sunlight, 1851–1925)
Denis McLoughlin (Magazine cartoonist
dealing with Wild West and detective
subjects, 1918–2002)

Thomas Marin (US-based landscape artist,
1872–1953)
Thomas Sutcliffe Mort (Refrigeration
pioneer, 1816–1878)
Sir Charles Joseph Moses (Australian-based
broadcaster, 1900–1988)
James Riddick Partington (Historian of
science, 1886–1965)

BOOTLE Merseyside
Elaine Feinstein (Poet and novelist [*The
Circle*], 1930–)

BORDESLEY Worcestershire
Thomas Blount (Lexicographer, 1618–1679)

BORLUM Inverness-shire
William MacKintosh (Jacobite and
arboriculturist, 1662–1743)

BOROUGHBRIDGE Yorkshire
Isabella Bird (Travel writer [*Englishwoman
in America*], 1831–1904)

BORTHWICK Midlothian
William Robertson (Historian [*History of
America*], 1721–1793)

BOSTON Lincolnshire
John Foxe (Author of *Book of Martyrs*,
1516–1587)
Jean Ingelow (Novelist and poet,
1820–1897)
Herbert Ingram (Founder of *Illustrated
London News*, 1811–1860)
John Westland Marston (Poet, 1819–1890)
John Taverner (Musician accused of heresy,
c.1490–1545)

BOTHWELL Lanarkshire
Joanna Baillie (Poet and philanthropist,
1762–1851)

BOUGHTON MALHERBE Kent

Sir Henry Wotton (Diplomat, served James I for 20 years as ambassador in Venice and Austria, 1568-1639)

BOURNE Lincolnshire

William Cecil [1st Baron Burghley], Secretary of State to Elizabeth I, 1520-1598)

William Dodd (Forger hanged for his crimes, 1729-1777)

Robert Mannyng (Poet and historian, d.c.1338)

Charles Frederick Worth (Fashion designer to Empress of France, 1825-1895)

BOURNE END Buckinghamshire

Beatrix Lehmann (Actor and writer, 1903-1979)

John Frederick Lehmann (Poet and magazine publisher [London Magazine], 1907-1987)

BOURNEMOUTH Dorset

Peter Bellamy (Singer, interpreter of Rudyard Kipling's poems, 1944-1991)

Harold Sydney Geneen (US-based telecommunications director, 1910-)

Radclyffe Hall (Author [Well of Loneliness], 1880-1943)

Sir Charles Hubert Parry (Professor of music, composed Jerusalem as a unison chorus, 1848-1918)

Virginia Wade (Wimbledon Ladies tennis champion [1977], 1945-)

BOVINGDON Hertfordshire

Frances de la Tour (TV actor [Rising Damp], 1944-)

BOYNDIE Near Banff

Thomas Ruddiman (Latin scholar, 1674-1757)

BRACKENHURST Nottinghamshire

Edmund Henry Allenby [1st Viscount] (Military commander, liberated Jerusalem from the Turks in 1917, 1861-1936)

BRACON ASH Norfolk

Edward Thurlow [1st Baron] (Attorney General, 1731-1806)

BRADENHAM HALL Norfolk

Sir Henry Rider Haggard (Novelist [King Solomon's Mines], 1856-1925)

BRADFORD Yorkshire

(See also THORNTON)

Sir Edward Appleton (Nobel Prize-winning physicist, 1892-1965)

John Braine (Novelist, [Room at the Top], 1922-1986)

Gathorne Cranbrook [1st Earl] (Politician, 1814-1906)

Kiki Dee [b.Pauline Matthews] (First white UK singer to sign for Tamla Motown, 1947-)

Frederick Delius (Composer [Song of Summer], 1862-1934)

Adrian Edmondson (Actor in films [Guest House Paradiso] and on TV [Bottom, Comic Strip Presents...], 1957-)

David Hockney (Artist, 1937-)

Richard Keith Illingworth (Test cricketer [Worcestershire, Derbyshire and England], 1963 -)

James Charles Laker (Test cricketer, took 19 Australian wickets in 4th Test at Old Trafford in 1956, 1922-1986)

Samuel Cunliffe Lister [1st Baron Masham] (Textile inventor, 1815-1906)

Thomas Martin Lowry (Optical scientist, 1874-1936)

Sir Douglas Mawson (Geological explorer, discovered Magnetic South Pole, 1882-1958)

John Boynton [J.B.] Priestley (Novelist [*The Good Companions*] and playwright, 1894–1984)

Sir William Rothenstein (War artist in both world wars, 1872–1945)

Joseph Wright (Compiler of dialect dictionary, 1855–1930)

BRADFORD ON AVON Wiltshire

Henry Shrapnel (Inventor of anti-personnel weapon, 1761–1842)

Richard Bethell Westbury [Baron] (Legal reformer, 1800–1873)

BRADGATE Leicestershire

Lady Jane Grey (Queen of England for nine days, 1537–1554)

BRADLEY Yorkshire

Sir Henry Savile (Scholar who helped found Bodleian Library, 1549–1622)

BRADPOLE Dorset

William Edward Forster (Statesman, associated with 1870 Education Act, 1819–1886)

BRAEMAR Aberdeenshire

Johann von Lamont (Professor of Astronomy at Munich University, calculated mass of Uranus, 1805–1879)

BRAINTREE Essex

James Challis (Astronomer, published Cambridge 'observations' [1832–64], 1803–1882)

Sir Henry Evelyn Wood (Military commander, won VC in Indian Mutiny, 1838–1919)

BRAMHALL Cheshire

Dame Wendy Hiller (Oscar-winning actor [*Separate Tables*], 1912–)

BRAMPTON Cumberland

George Routledge (Publisher, 1812–1888)

BRANDON Near Durham

Thomas Tredgold (Carpentry author, and engineer, 1788–1929)

BRECHIN Angus

Thomas Guthrie (Theologian and reformer, 1803–1873)

Peter Spence (Industrial chemist, pioneer in dyeing technology, 1806–1863)

Sir Robert Watson-Watt (Pioneer of radar, made victory possible in Battle of Britain, 1892–1973)

BRECON Powys

Charles Kemble (Actor, Examiner of Plays, brother of Sarah Siddons, 1775–1854)

Sarah Siddons [b.Kemble] (Leading female actor of her day, 1755–1831)

BREDWARDINE Hereford and Worcester

Sir Charles Thomas Newton (Archaeologist, researched Greek history, 1816–1894)

BRENCHLEY Kent

Siegfried Sassoon (Poet [*Memoirs of a Fox-Hunting Man*], 1886–1967)

BRIDEKIRK Cumbria

Thomas Tickell (Poet, translated the *Iliad*, 1686–1740)

BRIDGE OF ALLAN Stirlingshire

Ian Fairweather (Australian-based artist and adventurer, 1891–1974)

BRIDGE OF EARN Tayside

John Tulloch (Theologian and principal of St Andrews University, 1823–1886)

BRIDGERULE Devon

Elizabeth MacArthur (Australian-based agriculturist, 1766–1850)

BRIDGNORTH West Midlands

Gerald Hugh Berners (Eccentric composer [*The Triumph of Neptune*], 1883–1950)

Francis Moore (Astrologer, originated *Old Moore's Almanac*, 1657–1715)

Thomas Percy (Antiquarian, promoted interest in early English poetry, 1729–1811)

BRIDGWATER Somerset

Robert Blake (Naval commander, victor at Battle of Santa Cruz, 1599–1657)

Harry [Breaker] Morant (Australian-based poet and soldier, 1865–1902)

BRIDLINGTON Yorkshire

William Kent (Architect, introduced Palladian style to Britain, 1685–1748)

Alfred Edward Matthews (Comedy actor, 1869–1960)

BRIGG Lincolnshire

Joan Ann Plowright [Lady Olivier] (Leading actor of stage, film, and TV, 1929–)

BRIGHTON Sussex

(See also HOVE)

Aubrey Vincent Beardsley (Influential illustrator, 1872–1898)

Stanley Thomas [Tim] Bindoff (Historian, author of *Tudor England*, 1908–1980)

Clementina Maria Black (Novelist, campaigned against 'sweated' industries, 1853–1922)

Frank Bridge (Composer and conductor, 1879–1941)

Ray Brooks (Actor in films [*The Knack*] and TV [*Cathy Come Home*], 1939–)

Edward Carpenter (Social reformer, 1844–1929)

Anson Dyer [b.Ernest Anson-Dyer] (Animation cartoonist, 1876–1962)

Constance Garnett (Translator and sister of Clementina Black, 1861–1946)

David Garnett (Novelist and RAF war historian, 1892–1981)

Eric Gill (Sculptor/typographer, 1882–1940)

Sir Edward Marshall Hall (Controversial defence barrister, 1858–1927)

Sir Thomas Erskine Holland (Legal author, 1835–1926)

Therese Lessore (Artist, specialised in theatrical subjects, 1884–1945)

Florence Marryat (Novelist and author of spiritualist works, 1838–1899)

Steve [Stephen Michael] Ovett (Olympic champion athlete, 1955–)

David Roger Pilbeam (Anthropologist [*Evolution of Man*], 1940–)

Roger Quilter (Composer [*Songs of the Sea*], 1877–1953)

Anita Lucia Roddick (Founder of Body Shop retailing, 1942–)

Gilbert Ryle (Philosopher, wrote *The Concept of Mind*, 1900–1976)

Sir Martin Ryle (Nobel Prize-winning radio astronomer, 1918–1984)

BRINKLEY Cambridgeshire

Christopher Anstey (Author, creator of 'Squire Blunderhead', 1724–1805)

BRISTOL

(See also CLIFTON, and SHIREHAMPTON)

Edward Hodges Baily (Sculptor of Nelson's statue, Trafalgar Square, 1788–1867)

Johnny Ball (TV presenter, 1938–)

Elizabeth Blackwell (Physician, founded women's hospitals in New York and London, 1821–1910)

Emily Blackwell (Physician, assistant to James Young Simpson and worker in women's hospitals founded by her sister, 1826–1910)

Thomas Edward Bowditch (Explorer of Africa's Gold Coast, 1791–1824)

Richard Bright (Physician to Queen Victoria, researched kidney disease now named after him, 1789–1858)

Rosemary Butcher (Choreographer of Michael Nyman's music, 1947–)

Thomas Chatterton (Poet whose suicide is better remembered than his poetry, 1752–1770)

William Child (Religious composer, c.1606–1697)

Edward Colston (Philanthropist, founded almshouses in London and Bristol, 1636–1721)

William Combe (Satirical author, creator of Dr Syntax, 1741–1823)

Russ Conway [b.Trevor Stanford] (Popular pianist [*Side-saddle*], 1927–2000)

Paul Adrien Dirac (Nobel Prize-winning mathematician, 1902–1984)

Lee Evans (Film and TV comedian, 1962–)

Sir Roy [Albert Hubert] Fedden (Aeronautical engineer who produced engines for such fighters as the Spitfire, 1885–1973)

William Friese-Greene (Cinematographic pioneer, 1855–1921)

Christopher Fry (Playwright [*The Lady's Not for Burning*], 1907–)

William Ernest Giles (Explorer of Australia, 1835–1897)

Edward William Godwin (Architect and designer, 1833–1886)

Cary Grant [b.Archibald Leach] (Leading Hollywood actor, 1904–1986)

Archibald Vivian Hill (Nobel Prize-winning physiologist, 1886–1977)

Sir Allen Lane (Publisher, pioneered Penguin books, 1902–1970)

Sir Thomas Lawrence (Artist appointed to George III, 1769–1830)

Richard Long (Landscape artist, won 1989 Turner Prize, 1945–)

Thomas Longman (Publisher, 1699–1755)

Sir [Alfred Charles] Bernard Lovell (Radio astronomer, 1913–)

Hannah More (Author and playwright [*The Fatal Falsehood*], 1745–1833)

William James Muller (Landscape artist, 1812–1845)

Sir Thomas Percy Nunn (Educationalist, 1870–1944)

Peregrine Phillips (Patented manufacturer of sulphuric acid, b.c.1800)

Samuel Plimsoll (Politician, created legislation for 'Plimsoll line' to improve ship safety, 1824–1898)

Sir Michael Redgrave (Actor, star of *The Lady Vanishes*, 1908–1985)

William Rees-Mogg [Baron] (Journalist and broadcaster, 1928–)

Mary 'Perdita' Robinson (Poet and novelist, mistress to the Prince of Wales until 1780, 1758–1800)

Isaac Rosenberg (Artist and poet, 1890–1918)

William Joseph Slim [1st Viscount] (Military commander, 1891–1970)

Robert Southey (Poet Laureate from 1813, 1774–1843)

William Stroud (Physicist and instrument maker, 1860–1938)

John Addington Symonds (Literary biographer [of Dante, Shelley etc], 1840–1893)

Benjamin Tillett (Trade union leader, 1860–1943)

Marcus Edward Trescothick (Test cricketer [Somerset and England], 1975–)

Frances Trollope (Novelist, author of 115 books, 1780–1863)

Edward Tyson (Physician, early promoter of evolutionary science, 1651–1708)

Samuel Wesley (Ecclesiastical composer, 1766–1837)

Sir Nathanael Wraxall (Historian and diplomat, 1751–1831)

Robert Wyatt (Pop singer and drummer, 1945–)

Ann Yearsley (Poet and playwright, 1753–1806)

BROADHEATH Hereford and Worcester
Sir Edward Elgar (Composer, 1857–1934)

BROADSTAIRS Kent
Richard Rodney Bennett (Composer for films and opera, 1936–)
Thomas Russell Crampton (Engineer, constructed locomotives and first successful cross-Channel cable, 1816–1888)
Sir Edward Richard Heath (Prime Minister [1970–4], 1916–)
Lionel Pigot Johnson (Poet and literary critic, 1867–1902)

BROKE HALL Suffolk
Sir Philip Broke (Naval commander in hostilities against US, 1776–1841)

BROMLEY Kent
Norman Cook [Fatboy Slim] (Pop singer [*Praise You*], 1963–)
Susan Dallion (Singer better known as Siouxsie Sioux, 1957–)
Gertrude Hermes (Printmaker and sculptor, 1901–1983)
David Edward Jenkins (Controversial Bishop of Durham [1974–84], 1925–)
Charles Langbridge Morgan (Novelist and essayist, 1894–1958)
Dame Antoinette Sibley (Ballerina, 1939–)
Derek Leslie Underwood (Test cricketer for Kent and England, 1945–)
Herbert George [H.G.] Wells (Novelist and popular author [*War of the Worlds*], 1866–1946)

BROMLEY CROSS Lancashire
Susan Brierley Isaacs (Educational psychologist, 1885–1948)

BROMSGROVE Worcestershire
Geoffrey William Hill (Poet ['For the Unfallen'], 1932–)
Laurence Housman (Novelist and playwright [*Victoria Regina*], 1865–1959)

BROOKE HALL Norfolk
Sir Astley Cooper (Surgeon to George IV, 1768–1841)

BROOKSBY Leicestershire
George Villiers Buckingham [1st Duke] (Statesman, 1592–1628)

BROSELEY Shropshire
Hermione Baddeley [b.Hermione Clinton-Baddeley] (Actor whose career spanned more than 70 years, 1906–1986)

BROUGHTON-IN-FURNESS Cumbria
Sir Robin Philipson (Artist and President of RSA [1973–83], 1916–1992)

BROUGHTY FERRY Angus
James Lewis Spence (Folklorist and poet, 1874–1955)

BROXBOURNE Hertfordshire
Dame Elizabeth Maconchy (Composer of chamber music and operas, 1907–1994)

BUCKLAND ABBEY Devon
Sir Richard Grenville (Naval commander killed when his ship engaged a superior Spanish force, c.1541–1591)

BUCKLEBURY Berkshire
Henry Octavius Coxe (Head of Bodleian Library, 1811–1881)

BUERTON Cheshire
Thomas Brassey (Engineer, employed 6,000
men to construct the Great Northern
Railway, 1805–1870)

BULWELL Nottinghamshire
Frank Cousins (Trade union leader and
government minister,
1904–1986)

BULWICK Northamptonshire
Sir George Tryon (Naval commander who
perished after ordering collision
manoeuvre during fleet exercises,
1832–1893)

BUNCHREW Inverness-shire
Duncan Forbes of Culloden (Judge, put to
flight by Bonnie Prince Charlie,
1685–1747)

BUNGAY Suffolk
Susanna Moodie [b.Strickland] (Canadian-
based author, 1803–1885)

BUNKLE Berwickshire
John Brown (Physician, opposed blood-
letting as a medical practice,
c.1735–1788)

BUNTINGFORD Hertfordshire
Reginald Cotterell Butler (Sculptor who
worked in iron and steel, 1913–1981)

BURBAGE Leicestershire
Roger Cotes (Mathematician, assisted Isaac
Newton with second edition of *Principia*,
1682–1716)

BURES Suffolk
Baroness Tessa Blackstone (Sociologist and
education minister, 1942–)

BURFORD Oxfordshire

Sir William Beechey (Artist appointed to
Queen Charlotte in 1793, 1753–1839)
Peter Heylin (Historian and Chaplain to
Charles I, 1599–1662)

BURGH ST PETER Norfolk
Charles Cunningham Boycott (Land agent
ostracised in business, 1832–1897)

BURLEY IN WHARFEDALE Yorkshire
Sir John William Watson (Poet ['Father of
the Forest'], 1858–1935)

BURNBANK Hamilton, Lanarkshire
Jock Stein (First British football manager to
win European Cup [in 1967], 1922–1985)

BURNLEY Lancashire
Dame Judith Hart (Politician and Labour
Cabinet Minister, 1924–1991)
Sir Ian McKellen (Actor whose range
extends from Shakespeare to Tolkein,
1939–)
Linus Roache (Film actor [*Priest, Wings of a
Dove*], 1964–)

BURNHAM THORPE Norfolk
Horatio Nelson [Viscount] (Killed during
victory at Trafalgar, 1758–1805)

**BURSLEDON Near Southampton,
Hampshire**
Claude Grahame White (Pioneering aviator,
1879–1959)

BURTON Cheshire
Thomas Wilson (Ecclesiastical author,
Bishop of Sodor and Man, 1663–1755)

BURTON CONSTABLE Staffordshire
James Wyatt (Architect, cathedral restorer
and designer of Royal Military College,
1746–1813)

BURTON JOYCE Nottinghamshire

Sherrie Hewson (TV character actor
[*Coronation Street, Lovejoy*], 1950–)

BURTON-ON-TRENT Derbyshire

Helen Allingham [b.Paterson] (Artist,
painted portraits of Thomas Carlyle,
1848–1926)

Michael Thomas Bass (Brewer, 1779–1884)

Joe Jackson (Pop singer and songwriter
[*Fools in Love*], 1955–)

Robert McElwee (TV weather forecaster,
1961–)

BURY Lancashire

Sir John Charnley (Orthopaedic surgeon,
1911–1982)

Richmal Crompton [Richmal Samuel
Lamburn] (Writer of *Just William* books,
1890–1969)

Reginald Hargreaves Harris (Cycling
champion, 1920–)

John Kay (Textile inventor of 'Flying
Shuttle', 1704–c.1764)

Gary and Phil Neville (International
footballing brothers [Manchester United
and England], 1975– and 1977–
respectively)

Sir Robert Peel (Prime Minister who
repealed Corn Laws in 1846, 1788–1850)

Molly Reibey (Australian-based ship-owner
and philanthropist, 1777–1855)

BURY ST EDMUNDS Suffolk

Richard Aungerville (Churchman and tutor
to Edward III, 1287–1345)

Charles James Blomfield (Classical scholar,
1786–1857)

Stephen Gardiner (Theologian and
persecutor of Protestants, c.1483–1555)

Sir Peter Reginald Hall (Theatre and film
director, 1930–)

Bob [Robert William] Hoskins (Actor [*The
Long Good Friday*], 1942–)

Elizabeth Inchbald [b.Simpson] (Novelist
and playwright [*Lovers' Vows* 1798],
1753–1821)

Ouida [Marie Louise de la Ramée] (Novelist
[*Under Two Flags*], 1839–1908)

Humphrey Repton (Landscape designer,
1752–1818)

Henry Crabb Robinson (Pioneering war
correspondent, 1775–1867)

BUSHEY Hertfordshire

George Michael [b.Yorgos Kyriatou
Panayiotou] (Pop singer, at one time with
group Wham!, 1963–)

Mark Ravindra Ramprakash (Test cricketer
[Middlesex, Surrey, and England], 1969–)

BUTTERLEY HALL Derbyshire

Sir James Outram (Indian administrator,
1803–1863)

BUTTINGTON Near Welshpool, Powys

Sir William Boyd Dawkins (Geologist and
prehistoric anthropologist, 1837–1929)

BUXTON Derbyshire

Tim Brooke-Taylor (TV comedian [*The
Goodies*] and writer, 1940–)

Lloyd Cole (Pop singer [sometimes with
group The Commotions], 1961–)

BUXTON Norfolk

Thomas Cubitt (Industrial builder, built
Belgravia and part of Buckingham Palace,
1788–1855)

**BYERS GREEN Near Bishop Auckland,
County Durham**

Thomas Wright (Philosophical
mathematician, 1711–1786)

CAERNARFON Gwynedd

Edward II [King of England] (1284–1327)

Sir William Henry Preece (Electrical

engineer, introduced telephones to UK,
1834–1913)

CAERPHILLY Mid-Glamorgan
Tommy Cooper (Comedian and magician,
1922–1984)

CAISTER ON SEA Norfolk
Sir John Fastolf (Military commander, built
Caister Castle, 1378–1459)

CALEDON County Tyrone
Sir Harold Alexander [1st Earl Alexander of
Tunis] (Soldier, last to leave France in
1940 Dunkirk evacuation, 1891–1969)

CALTON Near Settle, Yorkshire
John Lambert (Civil War commander,
overthrew Richard Cromwell,
1619–1684)

CALVERLEY Yorkshire
Frederick William Faber (Hymn writer, won
1836 Newdigate Poetry Prize, 1814–1863)

CAMBERLEY Surrey
Joan Violet Robinson [b.Maurice]
(Keynesian economist, 1903–1983)
Frederick William Twort (Bacteriologist,
studied effects of bacteria on viruses,
1877–1950)

CAMBORNE Cornwall
William Bickford (Inventor of slow-burning
fuse, 1774–1834)
Arthur Woolf (Steam-power engineer,
1766–1837)

CAMBRIDGE
Richard Attenborough [Lord] (Actor
[*Brighton Rock*] and film director
[*Gandhi*], 1923–)
Sir John Cheke (First regius professor of
Greek at Cambridge, 1514–1557)

Dame Margaret Cole (Socialist historian,
1893–1980)
Sir Christopher Cockerell (Hovercraft
inventor, 1910–1999)
Richard Cumberland (Playwright,
1732–1811)
George Fordham (Champion jockey,
1837–1887)
Robert Greene (Playwright, inspired
Shakespeare's *Winter's Tale*, 1558–1592)
Patrick Arthur Hadley (Composer and
Cambridge Professor of Music [1946–62],
1899–1973)
Douglas Rayner Hartree (Mathematician
and physicist, 1897–1958)
Jacquetta Hawkes (First woman to study
archaeology and anthropology to degree
level at Cambridge, 1901–1996)
Sir John Berry [Jack] Hobbs (First English
cricketer knighted, 1882–1963)
John Maynard Keynes [1st Baron]
(Economist who advocated full
employment through capital projects,
1883–1946)
Frank Raymond Leavis (Literary critic,
1895–1978)
Damaris Masham (Educationalist,
1658–1708)
Francis John Minton (Artist, noted for
watercolours and book illustrations,
1917–1957)
Olivia Newton-John (Pop singer raised in
Australia, successful in US, 1948–)
Ronald George Norrish (Nobel Prize-
winning chemist, 1897–1978)
Edward Henry Palmer (Oriental scholar,
1840–1882)
Frank Plumpton Ramsey (Mathematician
and philosopher, 1903–30)
Michael Ramsey [Baron] (Archbishop of
Canterbury [1961–74], 1904–1988)
Gwendolen Mary Raverat [b.Darwin]
(Landscape painter and book illustrator,
1885–1957)

Ronald William Searle (Cartoonist creator of 'St Trinian's', 1920–)

Max Stafford-Clark (Theatre director, 1941–)

Marjorie Stephenson (Microbiologist, one of first women to be FRS, 1885–1948)

Sir George Paget Thomson (Nobel Prize-winning physicist, 1892–1975)

Judith Weir (Operatic composer [*The Black Spider*], 1954–)

William Whitehead (Poet and playwright, 1715–1785)

Baroness Barbara Wootton of Abinger (Social scientist, 1897–1988)

CAMBUSLANG Lanarkshire

Claudius Buchanan (Missionary, translated Gospels into Persian and Hindustani, 1766–1815)

John Claudius Loudon (Horticultural author, 1783–1843)

CAMBUSNETHAN Lanarkshire

John Gibson Lockhart (Biographer [of Sir Walter Scott] and critic, 1794–1854)

CAMPBELTOWN Argyllshire

David Colville (Steel manufacturer, 1813–1898)

Norman McLeod (Theologian, chaplain to Queen Victoria [1857–72], 1812–1872)

CAMPSIE Stirlingshire

Annie Macpherson (Teacher and missionary, worked with under-privileged teenagers, c.1824–1904)

CANNOCK Staffordshire

William Duesbury (China manufacturer, 1725–1786)

CANTERBURY Kent

Eadmee [Edmer] (Historian and monk, c.1060–1128)

Richard Harris Barham (Humorist [wrote *The Ingoldsby Legends*], 1788–1845)

Richard Boyle [1st Earl of Cork] (Irish administrator, 1566–1643)

Stephen Hales (Botanist and chemist, 1677–1761)

Thomas Linacre (Founder of Royal College of Physicians, c.1460–1524)

Christopher Marlowe (Playwright, often attributed authorship of Shakespeare's plays, 1564–1593)

Isaac Nathan (First composer to harmonise Australian aboriginal music, 1790–1864)

John Arthur Robinson (Theologian, 1919–1983)

Charles Abbott Tenderton (Legal author, 1762–1832)

Mary Tourtel (Creator of cartoon character 'Rupert the Bear', 1874–1948)

CAPUTH Perthshire

Belle Stewart (Folksinger, born to 'travelling' people, 1906–1997)

CARDIFF

Dannie Abse (Physician and author, 1923–)

Shirley Bassey (Singer [*Goldfinger*, *Diamonds are Forever*], 1937–)

Jeremy Bowen (TV journalist and presenter, 1960–)

David Broome (Show jumper, 1940–)

Gillian Clarke (Poet ['Letter from a Far Country'], 1937–)

Dave Edmunds (Rock singer [*I Hear You Knocking*], 1944–)

Merlyn Evans (Artist, noted for anti-Nazi symbolism ['The Chess Players'] 1910–1973)

Ryan Giggs (International footballer [Manchester United and Wales], 1973–)

Brian David Josephson (Nobel Prize-winning physicist, 1940–)

Sir Thomas Lewis (Cardiac specialist and author, 1881–1945)

Ivor Novello [Ivor Novello Davies] (Songwriter and playwright [*The Dancing Years*], 1893–1951)

Howard Spring (Novelist [*Fame is the Spur*], 1889–1965)

James Sullivan (Rugby League player, once kicked 22 goals in a single game, 1903–1977)

Ronald Stuart Thomas (Poet ['Poetry for Supper'], 1913–)

CARDINGTON Bedfordshire

George Gascoigne (Satirical poet and dramatist, c.1525–1577)

CARDROSS Dunbartonshire

Archibald Joseph [A.J.] Cronin (Author, creator of 'Doctor Finlay', 1896–1981)

Tobias George Smollett (Novelist [*Humphrey Clinker*], 1721–1771)

CARLISLE Cumbria

Bernard Barton (Poet [*Household Verses*], 1784–1849)

Samuel Bough (Landscape artist, 1822–1878)

Mandell Creighton (Historian of Elizabethan Age, 1843–1901)

Margaret Forster (Novelist [*Georgy Girl*], 1938–)

Jancis Robinson (TV wine expert, 1950–)

CARLTON HALL Near Newark

Edmund Beckett Grimthorpe [1st Baron] (Lawyer and horologist, 1816–1905)

CARMARTHEN Dyfed

Tony Curtis (Poet, Chairman of Welsh Academy [1984–7], 1946–)

Hugh Price Hughes (Methodist and socialist, 1847–1902)

Sir Lewis Morris (Barrister and poet ['Songs of Two Worlds'], 1833–1907)

Henry Brinley Richards (Pianist and composer, 1819–1885)

CARNBEE Fife

Archibald Constable (Publisher of Scott and *Encyclopaedia Britannica*, 1774–1827)

CARPOW Perthshire

John Brown (Theologian, wrote *Self-interpreting Bible*, 1722–1787)

CARSKEOCH Ayrshire

James McCosh (Professor of Philosophy at Princeton [1868–94], 1811–1894)

CARSKERDO Fife

James Wilson ('Parent of United States constitution', 1742–1789)

CASKIEBEN Aberdeenshire

Arthur Johnston (Latin poet and physician, 1587–1641)

CASTLEDAWSON County Derry

Seamus Justin Heaney (Nobel Prize-winning poet, 1917–)

CASTLEFORD Yorkshire

Henry Spencer Moore (Sculptor, 1898–1986)

CASTLE HEDINGHAM Essex

Sir John de Hawkwood (Mercenary soldier in Italy, (d.1394)

CATTON Near Norwich

John Lindley (Botanist and horticulturist, 1799–1865)

CAVERSWALL Staffordshire

Robert Williams Buchanan (Poet, critic of Swinburne and the Pre-Raphaelites, 1841–1901)

CAWTHORNE Yorkshire
Thomas Whittlam Atkinson (Architect
   and traveller in Asiatic Russia,
   1799–1861)

CEFNEITHIN Dyfed
Barry John (International rugby player,
   1945–)

CHACEWATER Cornwall
Jonathan Carter Hornblower (Engineer,
   designed compound and rotary steam-
   engines, 1753–1815)

CHADLINGTON Oxfordshire
Sir Henry Creswicke Rawlinson (Diplomat
   and Middle East scholar, 1810–1895)

CHAPEL OF GARIOCH Aberdeenshire
William Alexander (Novelist and editor,
   1826–1894)

CHARD Somerset
Sheila Allen (TV and film [Pascali's Island]
   actor, 1932–)
Margaret Grace Bondfield (First British
   woman Cabinet member, 1873–1953)

CHARLBURY Oxfordshire
Arthur Albright (Industrial chemist,
   1811–1900)

CHARLTON Hertfordshire
Sir Henry Bessemer (Engineer, invented
   new steel-making process, 1813–1898)

CHARLTON Wiltshire
Stephen Duck (Ploughman poet,
   1705–1756)

CHATHAM Kent
Richard Dadd (Artist incarcerated for
   murder of his father, 1819–1887)
Sir William Jenner (Royal physician,

established difference between typhus
   and typhoid fever, 1815–1898)
Zandra Lindsey Rhodes (Fashion designer,
   1940–)
William Pett Ridge (Cockney humorist,
   author of 60 books, 1857–1930)

CHELMSFORD Essex
Ursula Bloom [Mrs Gower Robinson]
   (Novelist [The First Elizabeth] and
   playwright, 1892–1984)
Philemon Holland (Classical translator, [of
   Livy, Plutarch, Pliny], 1552–1637)

CHELSHAM Surrey
Victor [Edwin John] Pasmore (Artist,
   founder of 'Euston Road School', 1908–)

CHELTENHAM Gloucestershire
Frederick Archer (Champion jockey,
   1837–1886)
Sir Rowland Biffen (Botanist, researched
   rubber and wheat production,
   1874–1949)
Andrew Cecil Bradley (Literary critic and
   Oxford Professor of Poetry, 1851–1935)
Sir Arthur ['Bomber'] Harris (Head of
   wartime Bomber Command, 1892–1984)
Gustav Holst (Composer [Planets Suite],
   1874–1934)
Edith How-Martyn (Suffragette, c.1875–1954)
John Nevil Maskelyne (Stage magician,
   1839–1917)
Sir Frederick Handley Page (Aircraft
   designer, 1885–1962)
James Payn (Novelist and editor of Cornhill
   magazine, 1830–1898)
William Charles Renshaw (Champion tennis
   player, 1861–1904)
Sir Ralph Richardson (Stage and film actor,
   1902–1983)
Edward Adrian Wilson (Explorer, reached
   South Pole but perished with Scott on
   the return journey, 1872–1912)

CHEPSTOW Gwent

William Bedloe (Self-proclaimed conspirator in the 'Popish Plot', 1650–1680)

Richard [John Hannay] Meade (Equestrian athlete, 1938–)

CHERTSEY Surrey

Ashley Fraser Giles (Test cricketer [Warwickshire and England], 1973–)

CHESTER

Russ Abbot (TV comedian, 1947–)

Sir Adrian Boult (Conductor, 1889–1983)

Randolph Caldecott (Artist and book illustrator, 1846–1886)

Albert Sidney Hornby (Linguist and lexicographer, 1898–1978)

Sir John Hubert Marshall (Indian-based archaeologist, 1876–1958)

Samuel Molyneux (Astronomer, researched use of reflecting telescopes, 1689–1728)

Michael Owen (International footballer [Liverpool and England], 1979–)

Richard Laurence Synge (Nobel Prize-winning biochemist, shared 1952 prize for chemistry, 1914–1994)

CHESTERFIELD Derbyshire

Dame Barbara Castle [b.Betts] (Politician and Cabinet Minister, 1910–2002)

Francis Frith (Photographer who travelled widely from 1856, 1822–1898)

Charles Rivington (Theological publisher, 1688–1742)

Sir Robert Robinson (Nobel Prize-winning chemist, 1886–1975)

Peter Wright (Intelligence specialist, author of *Spycatcher* in 1987, 1916–1995)

CHICHESTER Sussex

Peter Baldwin (TV actor [*Coronation Street*], 1933–)

Thomas Bradwardine (Consecrated as Archbishop of Canterbury not long before his death, 1290–1349)

William Clowes (Pioneered steam-powered printing, 1779–1847)

William Collins (Lyricist and poet, 1721–1759)

Michael Elphick (Film and TV actor [*Private Shultz*], 1946–2002)

John Frederick Charles Fulton (Military commander who advocated mobile armoured warfare, 1878–1966)

William Hayley (Poet, and biographer of Milton and Cowper, 1745–1820)

William Juxon (Archbishop of Canterbury [1660–63], 1582–1663)

Edward Bradford Titchener (US-based exponent of experimental psychology, 1867–1927)

CHIGWELL Essex

Sally Gunnell (Champion hurdler at Olympic, Commonwealth, European and World levels in early 1990s, 1966–)

CHIPPING CAMPDEN Gloucestershire

Robert Payne-Smith (Middle East scholar, 1819–1895)

Ernest Henry Wilson (Botanist specialising in Chinese flora, 1876–1930)

CHIRNSIDE Berwickshire

Ebenezer Erskine (Ecclesiastic who led forces against Bonnie Prince Charlie, 1680–1754)

CHISLEHURST Kent

Sir Malcolm Campbell (Speedster on land and water, 1885–1949)

Friniwyd Tennyson Jesse (Novelist [*Moonraker*] and female war correspondent, 1889–1958)

Sir Francis Walsingham (Statesman and spymaster, fatally implicated Mary Stewart in treason plot, c.1530–1590)

CHORLEY Lancashire
Sir Walter Norman Haworth (Nobel Prize-
winning chemist, determined structure of
Vitamin C, 1883-1950)
Sir Henry Tate (Sugar refiner, 1819-1899)

CHORLEY WOOD Hertfordshire
Barbara Mills (First woman Director of
Public Prosecutions, 1940-)

CHURCHILL Oxfordshire
Warren Hastings (Administrator in India,
1732-1818)
William Smith (Geological map-maker,
'Father of English geology', 1769-1839)

CHURCHTOWN Lancashire
Sir Edward Frankland (Chemist and
researcher in water supply and
sanitation, 1825-1899)

CINDERFORD Gloucestershire
Sir Jimmy [b.Leslie Ronald] Young (Radio
presenter and former pop singer, 1921-)

CLAPHAM Yorkshire
(For CLAPHAM, London, see LONDON)
Reginald John Farrer (Botanist and plant
collector, 1880-1920)

CLAYPOLE Lincolnshire
Frances Brooke [b.Moore] (Author, wrote
first Canadian novel, 1723-1789)

CLEETHORPES Lincolnshire
Dame Madge Kendal [b.Margaret Brunton
Grimston] (Actor and theatre co-
manager, 1849-1935)

CLEVEDON Somerset
David Hartley Coleridge (Poet and
biographer, 1796-1849)

CLIFTON Cumbria
John Wilkinson (Ironmaster, supplied
cylinders to Boulton & Watt, 1728-1808)

CLIFTON Near Bristol
Thomas Lovell Beddoes (Poet and physician,
1803-1849)
Emmeline Pethick-Lawrence (Suffragette
and World War One peace campaigner,
1867-1954)

CLIFTONVILLE Kent
Trevor Wallace Howard (Actor [*Brief
Encounter, The Third Man*], 1916-1988)

CLIVE Shropshire
William Wycherley (Playwright [*The
Country Wife*], released from debtors'
prison by James II, c.1640-1716)

CLOAG Perthshire
Robert Stirling (Clergyman and air engine
pioneer, 1790-1878)

COALVILLE Leicestershire
Kathleen Fidler (Children's author,
established prize for child writers,
1899-1980)

COATBRIDGE Lanarkshire
Katherine Stewart MacPhail (Paediatrician,
practised in Balkans in peace and war,
1888-1974)
Peter Marshall (Chaplain to US Senate,
1902-1949)

COCKBURNSPATH Berwickshire
John Broadwood (Piano manufacturer,
1732-1812)

COCKERMOUTH Cumbria
Fletcher Christian (Mutineer on the *Bounty*,
c.1764-c.1794)

Dorothy Wordsworth (Author, 1771–1855)
William Wordsworth (Poet, 1770–1850)

CODSALL Staffordshire
Sir Charles Wheeler (Sculptor, President of
   Royal Academy for 10 years, 1892–1974)

COLCHESTER Essex
Margaret Cavendish, [Duchess of Newcastle]
   (Civil War author, 1623–1673)
Charles John Darling [Baron] (Judge and
   humorous poet, 1849–1936)
Thomas William Davids (Oriental scholar,
   1843–1922)
William Gilbert (Physician to Elizabeth I,
   and electrical pioneer, 1540–1603)

COLDINGHAM Berwickshire
David Bogue (Theologian, co-founder of
   London Missionary Society, 1750–1825)

COLEFORD Gloucestershire
Robert Forester Mushet (Metallurgist,
   improved steel-making techniques,
   1811–1891)

COLERNE Wiltshire
William Grocyn (Greek scholar,
   c.1446–1519)

COLESHILL Buckinghamshire
Edmund Waller (Politician and poet,
   banished after involvement in plot to
   assassinate Charles I, 1606–1687)

COLLESSIE Fife
Sir William Hutchison (Artist, Director of
   Glasgow School of Art [1932–43],
   1889–1970)

COLLINGBOURNE KINGSTON Wiltshire
John Norris (Religious philosopher,
   1657–1711)

COLLYWESTON Northamptonshire
John Stokesley (Chaplain to Henry VIII,
   c.1475–1539)

COLMONELL Ayrshire
John Snell (Benefactor to Oxford
   University, 1629–1679)

COMPTON BEAUCHAMP Berkshire
Nassau William Senior (Economist, involved
   in drafting Poor Laws, 1790–1864)

CONGREVE Staffordshire
Richard Hurd (Theological author,
   Preceptor to Prince of Wales,
   1720–1808)

CONISTON Cumbria
Robin George Collingwood (Philosopher
   and archaeological expert on Roman
   Britain, 1889–1943)

COOKHAM Berkshire
Sir Stanley Spencer (Artist, specialised in
   war and military subjects, 1891–1959)

CORNEY Cumbria
Edward Troughton (Designed instruments
   for surveying and astronomy,
   1753–1835)

COSGROVE Northamptonshire
Henry Longueville Mansel (Religious
   philosopher and Dean of St Paul's,
   1820–1871)

COTON Staffordshire
William Wollaston (Philosopher [*Religion of
   Nature Delineated*], 1659–1724)

COTTENHAM Cambridgeshire
Thomas Tenison (Theologian, Archbishop of
   Canterbury from 1694, 1636–1715)

COTTINGHAM Yorkshire

Jane Ellen Harrison (Classical scholar and
  Cambridge magistrate, 1850–1928)
Sir Brian Norman Roger Rix (Actor and
  theatre manager, 1924–)

COULSTON Wiltshire

Mary Delany [b.Granville] (Poet and
  historian, 1700–1788)

COVENTRY Warwickshire

Cyril Vernon Connolly (Author, founder of
  Horizon magazine, 1903–1974)
Laura Davies (Golfer, winner of both British
  and US Opens, 1964–)
Sir John Leopold Egan (Industrialist, chief
  executive of Jaguar and British Airports
  Authority, 1939–)
Frank Ifield (Pop singer who had four No.1
  hits within 12 months [1962–3], 1937–)
Vince Hill (Pop singer [*Edelweiss*], 1937–)
Philip Arthur Larkin (Poet [*High Windows*],
  1922–1985)
John Rastell (Printer and playwright,
  1475–1536)
Dame Ellen Terry (Actor and theatre
  manager, 1848–1928)
Billie Whitelaw (Actor, noted for her
  interpretation of Samuel Beckett's work,
  1932–)
Sir Frank Whittle (Jet engine inventor,
  1907–1996)
Nigel Winterburn (Former international
  footballer, 1963–)

COWDENBEATH Fife

Sir James Whyte Black (Nobel Prize-
  winning pharmacologist, 1924–)

COWDRAY West Sussex

Henry Wriothesley Southampton [3rd Earl]
  (Patron of Shakespeare, 1573–1624)

COXHOE County Durham

Elizabeth Barrett Browning (Poet,
  1806–1861)

CRADLEY Worcestershire

Jessica Blackburn [b.Thompson] (Pioneered
  aviation, helped establish British
  aerospace industry, 1894–1995)
William Caslon (Typeface designer,
  1692–1766)

CRANBORNE Dorset

Edward Stillingfleet (Theologian, Bishop of
  Worcester, 1635–1699)

CRANBROOK Kent

Sydney Thompson Dobell (Poet [*England in
  Time of War*], 1824–1874)

CRANLEIGH Surrey

Godfrey Harold Hardy (Mathematician,
  wrote *A Mathematician's Apology* [1940],
  1877–1947)

CRATHENAIRD Aberdeenshire

John Brown (Royal favourite, 1826–1883)

CRAYKE Yorkshire

William Ralph Inge (Theologian known as
  the 'Gloomy Dean' [of St Paul's
  Cathedral] owing to his pessimistic
  sermons, 1860–1954)

CREDITON Devon

Boniface (Missionary, killed bringing
  Christianity to German tribes,
  c.680–c.754)
Sir Redvers Henry Buller (Military
  commander, won VC in Zulu War,
  1839–1908)

CREETING MILL Suffolk

John Austin (Jurist [*Lectures in
  Jurisprudence*, 1863], 1790–1859)

CREICH Fife
Alexander Henderson (Covenanter leader,
c.1583–1646)

CRICCIETH Merioneth
Gwilym Lloyd-George of Dwyfor, [1st
Viscount Tenby] (Politician and cabinet
minister, 1894–1967)
Lady Megan Lloyd-George of Dwyfor
(Politician, 1902–1966)

CRIEFF Perthshire
James Stalker (Theologian, wrote
biographies of Christ and St Paul,
1848–1927)

CROFT Yorkshire
Thomas Burnet (Clergyman, Master of
Charterhouse [1685–1715],
c.1635–1715)

CROMARTY Ross & Cromarty
Hugh Miller (Anti-Darwin geologist and
author, 1802–1856)
David Urquhart (Diplomat, advocated
introduction of Turkish baths to UK,
1805–1877)
Sir Thomas Urquhart (Royalist author and
savant spared by Cromwell,
c.1611–1660)

CROMER HALL Norfolk
Evelyn Baring Cromer [Earl] (Colonial
administrator [Egypt], 1841–1917)

CROMFORD Derbyshire
Alison Uttley (Children's author [*The
Country Child*, 1931], 1884–1976)

CROPREDY Oxfordshire
Richard [Howard Stafford] Crossman
(Statesman and cabinet minister,
1907–1974)

CROSBY Lancashire
Sir Henry William Lucy (Political author
and journalist, 1845–1924)
Robert Alexander Runcie [Baron]
(Archbishop of Canterbury [1980–91],
1921–)

CROSSHOUSE Ayrshire
Andrew Fisher (Three times Prime Minister
of Australia, 1862–1928)

CROWBOROUGH Sussex
Sir Edward Evans-Pritchard
(Anthropologist, studied East African
indigenous cultures, 1902–1973)

CROWELL Oxfordshire
Thomas Ellwood (Quaker friend of John
Milton, 1639–1713)

CROWNDALE Dorset
Sir Francis Drake (Circumnavigator of
world, c.1540–1596)

CROYDON Surrey
Dame Peggy Ashcroft (Oscar-winning actor
[*Passage to India*], 1907–1991)
Lionel Atwill (Actor, particularly in horror
roles [*House of Frankenstein*, 1944]
1885–1946)
Lilian Braithwaite (Actor, starred in 3-year
theatre run of *Arsenic and Old Lace*
[1942–5], 1873–1948)
Richard David Briers (Actor [TV's *Marriage
Lines, The Good Life*], 1934–)
Helen Chadwick (Photographer and
performance artist, 1953–1996)
Mark Alan Butcher (Test cricketer [Surrey
and England], 1972–)
John Cunningham (Pilot of wartime night
fighters, later a test pilot, 1917–2002)
Henry Havelock Ellis (Physician and sex
therapist, 1859–1939)

Charles Burgess Fry (Test cricketer, athlete, football internationalist and director of sail training ship, 1872–1956)

Josef Holbrooke (Chamber music composer, 1878–1958)

Roy Hudd (TV and radio comedian [*News Huddlines*], 1937–)

Sir David Lean (Film director [*Lawrence of Arabia, Dr Zhivago*], 1908–1991)

Kate Moss (Supermodel, 1974–)

CUCKFIELD Sussex
Debra Beaumont (TV actor [*Birds of a Feather, Eastenders*], 1967–)

CULROSS Fife
St Mungo [St Kentigern] (Bishop of Cumbria, patron saint of the city of Glasgow, c.518–603)

CULTS Fife
Sir David Wilkie (Artist ['The Penny Wedding' 1818], 1785–1841)

CUMBERLOW GREEN Hertfordshire
Thomas Stanley (Historian of philosophy, 1625–1678)

CUPAR Fife
John Campbell [1st Baron Campbell] (Lord Chancellor [1859–61], 1779–1861)

CWMAMAN Mid Glamorgan
Alun Lewis (Author and soldier, killed during Burma campaign, 1915–1944)

CWMAVON Gwent
William Abraham (Miners' union leader and MP [1885–1920], 1842–1922)

CWMSYCHBANT Dyfed
Evan James Williams (Physicist, 1903–1945)

DAGENHAM Essex
Sir Alf Ramsey (Football manager who won 1966 World Cup for England, 1922–1999)

Sandie Shaw [b.Sandra Goodrich] (Pop singer [*Always Something There to Remind Me*], 1947–)

DALHOUSIE CASTLE Midlothian
James Andrew Dalhousie [Marquis] (Viceroy of India [1847–56], 1812–1860)

DALKEITH Midlothian
Archibald Campbell [9th Duke of Argyll] (Supporter of Duke of Monmouth, 1629–1685)

David Mushet (Innovative ironmaster, 1772–1847)

Peter Guthrie Tait (Mathematician and physicist, 1831–1901)

DALMALLY Argyllshire
John Smith (Leader of the Labour Party [1992–94], 1938–1994)

DALSWINTON Dumfriesshire
Allan Cunningham (Poet and collector of traditional ballads, 1784–1842)

DALTON IN FURNESS Cumbria
Margaret Fell [b.Askew] (Quaker imprisoned for her beliefs, 1614–1702)

George Romney (Society artist, 1734–1802)

DANE END Hertfordshire
Herbert John Gladstone [1st Viscount] (Statesman and Home Secretary [1905–10], 1854–1930)

DARESBURY Cheshire
Charles Lutwidge Dodgson (Author better known as Lewis Carroll [*Alice in Wonderland*], 1832–1898)

DARLINGTON County Durham

Joseph Mallaby Dent (Publisher,
1849–1926)

Maurice Elvey [b.William S. Folkard]
(Britain's most prolific film director,
[*Sally in Our Alley*, 1931], 1887–1967)

Dame Elizabeth Esteve-Coll (Former
museum director [Victoria and Albert],
1938–)

Edward Pease (Philanthropic industrialist
and promoter of Stockton & Darlington
Railway, 1767–1858)

DARTFORD Kent

Sir Peter Blake (Artist, designed Beatles'
'Sgt Pepper' LP cover [1967], 1932–)

Sydney Arthur Keyes (World War Two
poet, killed in action in Libya,
1922–1943)

Sir Mick [Michael Phillip] Jagger (Lead
singer in Rolling Stones, 1943–)

Keith Richards (Guitarist and songwriter
with Rolling Stones, 1943–)

DARTINGTON Devon

James Anthony Froude (Historian, wrote 12
vol. *History of England*, 1818–1894)

William Froude (Engineer, assistant to
Brunel, 1810–1879)

DARTMOUTH Devon

Thomas Newcomen (Engineer, invented
steam pumping engine for mining use,
1663–1729)

Sir Nicholas Nicolas (Antiquarian and
genealogist, 1799–1849)

John [Jack] Russell ('Sporting curate', gave
name to terrier breed, 1795–1883)

DARVEL Ayrshire

Sir Alexander Fleming (Nobel Prize-winning
discoverer of penicillin, 1881–1955)

DAWLEY Shropshire

Matthew Webb (First cross-Channel
swimmer, 1848–1883)

DEAL Kent

Elizabeth Carter ('Blue stocking' scholar
and poet, 1717–1806)

DEANSTON Perthshire

James Smith (Agricultural engineer,
invented subsoil plough, 1789–1850)

DEDDINGTON Oxfordshire

Sir William Scroggs (Judge, notorious for
his handling of 'Popish Plot' trials,
1623–1683)

DEER Aberdeenshire

Thomas Davidson (Author of works on
religious history, 1840–1900)

DEERNESS Orkney

Edwin Muir (Poet and essayist, 1887–1959)

DENBIGH Clwyd

Arthur Glyn Prys-Jones (Poet, President of
Welsh Academy [1970–87], 1888–1987)

Sir Henry Morton Stanley (Journalist and
explorer, uttered immortal question 'Dr
Livingstone, I presume?', 1841–1904)

DENBY Derbyshire

John Flamsteed (First Astronomer Royal,
1646–1719)

DENHAM Buckinghamshire

Ben Nicholson (Artist, 1894–1982)

DENHOLM Roxburghshire

William Johnstone (Artist, 1897–1981)

John Leyden (Poet and linguist,
1775–1811)

Sir James Augustus Murray (Editor of the
Oxford English Dictionary, 1837–1915)

DENT Cumbria

Adam Sedgwick (Cambridge-based geologist and palaeontologist, 1785–1873)

DENTON Cambridgeshire

Sir Robert Bruce Cotton (Antiquarian, imprisoned for his opposition to the Stewart kings, 1571–1631)

DENTON Yorkshire

Thomas Fairfax [3rd Baron] (Military commander, defeated Charles I at Battle of Naseby in 1645, 1612–1671)

DERBY

Sir William Abney (Chemist, improved photo-technology for all film users and also for stellar photography, 1844–1920)

Edward Blore (Architect, built Abbotsford for Sir Walter Scott, 1787–1879)

John Cotton (Puritan who fled to America to escape persecution, 1585–1652)

Sir Charles Fox (Civil engineer, built Crystal Palace for Great Exhibition of 1851, 1810–1874)

Judith Hann (TV presenter [*Tomorrow's World*], 1942–)

John Atkinson Hobson (Economist [*The Science of Wealth*], 1858–1940)

Sir George Clarke Simpson (Meteorologist, served on Scott's 1910 Antarctic Expedition, 1878–1965)

Herbert Spencer (Evolutionary philosopher, coined phrase 'survival of the fittest', 1820–1903)

Constance Spry (Author of books on cookery and flower-arranging, 1886–1960)

John Wood (Film actor [*Shadowlands, Madness of King George*], 1930–)

Joseph Wright (Artist, specialised in group portraiture ['Experiment with the Air Pump'], 1734–1797)

DEREHAM Norfolk

Brian Wilson Aldiss (Science fiction novelist, 1925–)

DETHICK Derbyshire

Antony Babington (Regicide plotter against Elizabeth I, tortured to death for his involvement, 1561–1586)

DEVONPORT Devon

Guy Burgess (Soviet agent, 1910–1963)

Thomas Holloway (Philanthropist, using funds accumulated from sales of patent medicine, 1800–1883)

Leslie Hore-Belisha [1st Baron] (Innovative Minister of Transport, gave name to 'Belisha beacons' at street crossings, 1893–1957)

William Jessop (Civil engineer, built canals and railways, 1745–1814)

Samuel Phelps (Actor and theatre manager, noted for his 'Shylock', 1804–1878)

Robert Falcon Scott (Polar explorer, perished in Antarctica, 1868–1912)

Alfred Wallis (St Ives-based fisherman and ice-cream seller celebrated for his paintings after taking up art aged 70, 1855–1942)

DEWSBURY Yorkshire

Sir Thomas Allbutt (Physician, devised modern clinical thermometer, 1836–1925)

Betty Boothroyd (First woman Speaker of House of Commons, 1929–)

Tom Kilburn (Computer pioneer, helped perfect Random Access Memory, 1921–)

Sir Owen Willans Richardson (Nobel Prize-winning physicist, 1879–1959)

DICKLEBOROUGH Norfolk

George Cattermole (Artist and illustrator, 1800–1868)

DILHAM Norfolk
Sir William Cubitt (Civil engineer, became
    Lord Mayor of London, 1785–1861)

DINTON Wiltshire
Edward Hyde Clarendon [1st Earl]
    (Statesman, banished abroad when held
    responsible for breach of English
    defences at Medway, 1609–1674)
Henry Lawes (Composer, set poetry by
    Milton and Herrick to music,
    1596–1662)

DISEWORTH Leicestershire
William Lilly (Astrologer, arrested on
    suspicion of being involved in Great Fire
    of London, 1602–1681)

DISHLEY Leicestershire
Robert Bakewell (Agriculturist, improved
    livestock breeding methods, 1725–1795)

DISLEY Cheshire
Christopher William Isherwood (Novelist
    [*Mr Norris Changes Trains*], 1904–1986)

DISS Norfolk
John Wilbye (Madrigal composer,
    1574–1638)

DITCHLEY Oxfordshire
John Wilmot Rochester [Earl] (Debauched
    poet, 1647–1680)

DITTISHAM Devon
William [Bill] Giles (TV weather forecaster,
    1939–)
Francis Rous (Hymn writer, produced
    metrical version of psalms, 1579–1659)

DOCKER Cumbria
William James Farrer (Agricultural pioneer,
    improved wheat strains, 1845–1906)

DODBROOKE Devon
John Wolcot [Peter Pindar] (Physician and
    satirist, 1738–1819)

DODINGTON Oxfordshire
Sir Edward Codrington (Naval commander,
    won 1827 Battle of Navarino,
    1770–1851)

DOLWAR-FECHAN Powys
Ann Griffiths [b.Thomas] (Hymn composer,
    died in childbirth, 1776–1805)

DONCASTER Yorkshire
(See also BALBY)
Jeremy Clarkson (TV presenter [*Top Gear*],
    1960–)
John McLaughlin (Guitarist, formerly with
    Miles Davis Group, 1942–)
Dame Diana Rigg (Actor and university
    chancellor [Stirling], 1938–)

DONINGTON Lincolnshire
Matthew Flinders (Explorer,
    circumnavigated Australia, 1774–1814)

DORCHESTER Dorset
John Endecott (American colonist,
    c.1588–1665)
Maurice Evans (Actor [*Rosemary's Baby*],
    1901–1989)
Llewelyn Powys (Novelist [*Ebony and Ivory*],
    1884–1939)
Thomas William Roberts (Australian-based
    artist, 1856–1931)
Sir Frederick Treves (Surgeon who treated
    'Elephant Man', 1853–1923)

DORKING Surrey
Thomas Robert Malthus (Economist and
    population theorist, 1766–1834)
Laurence Kerr Olivier [Baron] (Actor and
    director, 1907–1989)

DORRINGTON Shropshire
John Boydell (Illustrator who became Lord
Mayor of London, 1719–1804)

DOUGLAS Isle of Man
Edward Forbes (Biologist and
oceanographer, 1815–1854)

DOVER Kent
Walter Hammond (Test cricketer, captained
Gloucestershire and England,
1903–1965)
Edward Pellew [Viscount Exmouth] (Naval
commander in Napoleonic wars,
1757–1833)

DOWLAIS Mid Glamorgan
Sir Josiah John Guest (Ironmaster,
1785–1852)

DOWN AMPNEY Gloucestershire
Ralph Vaughan Williams (Composer,
1872–1958)

DOWNEND Gloucestershire
William Gilbert [W.G.] Grace (Test cricketer
regarded as pioneer of the sport,
1848–1915)

DOWNING Clwyd
Thomas Pennant (Travel author and
zoologist, 1726–1798)

DRAGLEY BECK Lancashire
Sir John Barrow (Naval administrator,
founder of Royal Geographical Society,
1764–1848)

DREGHORN Ayrshire
John Boyd Dunlop (Inventor, developed
R.W. Thomson's idea of pneumatic tyre,
1840–1912)

DREM East Lothian
Lord James Scott Reid (Lord Advocate
[1941–5], 1890–1975)

DRESDEN Staffordshire
William Havergal Brian (Composer of 32
symphonies, 1876–1972)

DRINKSTONE Suffolk
Sir Nicholas Bacon (Statesman at court of
Elizabeth I, 1510–1579)

DROITWICH Worcestershire
Edward Winslow (Member of the Pilgrim
Fathers, 1595–1655)

DROYLESDEN Lancashire
Harry Pollitt (Communist politician,
1890–1960)

DRUMOAK Aberdeenshire
James Gregory (Mathematician and
telescope designer, 1638–1675)

DUDLEY Northumberland
Robson Green (TV actor [*Soldier, Soldier*],
1964–)

DUDLEY West Midlands
Sir William Angliss (Australian-based
businessman and philanthropist,
1865–1957)
Charles Alfred Coulson (Theoretical chemist
and mathematician, 1910–1974)
Lenny Henry (TV comedian and actor [*Hope
and Glory*], 1958–)
Maurice Vincent Wilkes (Computer
scientist, worked on first stored-program
computer, 1913–)

DUFFIELD Derbyshire
John Heathcoat (Textile inventor, designed
machines to produce lace, ribbon and
net, 1783–1861)

DUFFRYN Glamorgan

Henry Austin Bruce Aberdare [1st Baron]
(Home Secretary [1868-73], 1815-1895)

DULVERTON Somerset

Sir George Williams (Founder of the YMCA,
1821-1905)

DUMBARTON

Patrick Colquhoun (Founder of first
Chamber of Commerce, 1745-1820)
Robert Napier (Shipbuilder and marine
engineer, 1791-1876)

DUMFRIES

Dougal Dixon (Dinosaur expert who also
predicted zoology of the future [in 1981
book *After Man*], 1947-)
John Laurie (Actor [played Fraser in TV's
Dad's Army], 1897-1980)
Dominic Matteo (International footballer,
Liverpool, Leeds United, and Scotland,
1974-)
Sir John Richardson (Arctic explorer, took
part in search for lost Franklin
expedition, 1787-1865)
Kirsty Wark (TV journalist and presenter,
1955-)

DUNBAR East Lothian

David Hume of Godscroft (Genealogist,
c.1560-1630)
John Muir (Environmentalist, created
concept of National Parks, 1838-1914)

DUNBEATH Caithness

Neil Miller Gunn (Novelist [*The Well at the
World's End*], 1891-1973)

DUNDEE

Hector Boece (Philosopher, wrote *History of
Scotland* [in Latin] in 1527, c.1465-1536)
Brian Cox (Actor, played Hannibal Lecter in
film *Manhunter*, 1946-)

Sir William Alexander Craigie
(Lexicographer, worked on *Oxford English
Dictionary* for 31 years, 1867-1957)
Adam Duncan [Viscount] (Naval
commander, victor at the Battle of
Camperdown in 1797, 1731-1804)
Sir James Alfred Ewing (Engineer and
Admiralty code breaker, 1855-1935)
Williamina Fleming [b.Stevens] (Harvard-
based astronomer, perfected
photographic interpretation of stellar
images, 1857-1911)
Thomas Henderson (First Astronomer Royal
for Scotland, 1798-1844)
Sir Richard Claverhouse Jebb (Greek
scholar and MP for Cambridge University
from 1891, 1841-1905)
Liz McColgan [b.Lynch] (Athlete, one-time
World Champion distance runner, 1964-)
Sir George MacKenzie of Rosehaugh
(Lawyer, persecutor of Covenanters,
1636-1691)
William Lyon MacKenzie (Canadian
politician, imprisoned after leading
insurrection at Toronto, 1795-1861)
James McIntosh Patrick (Landscape painter,
1907-1998)
David Couper Thomson (Publisher of
newspapers, magazines, and comics
[*Beano, Dandy*], 1861-1954)
William Turnbull (Artist and sculptor, 1922-)
Sir James Walker (Chemist, improved
explosives production in WWI,
1863-1935)
Elizabeth Mary Watt (Artist in ceramics
and wood, 1886-1954)
Fanny [Frances Darusmont] Wright (US-
based slavery abolitionist, 1795-1852)

DUNFERMLINE Fife

Andrew Carnegie (Philanthropist, endowed
many public libraries, 1835-1918)
Charles I [King of Scotland and England]
(Beheaded during Civil Wars, 1600-1649)

David II [King of Scotland] (Invaded England and was imprisoned for 11 years, 1324–1371)

Barbara Dickson (Singer, associated with Willy Russell stage shows, 1947–)

Dorothy Dunnett (Historical novelist, 1923–2001)

James I [King of Scotland] (First Scottish king to be assassinated in 400 years, 1394–1437)

Sir Kenneth MacMillan (Choreographer with Royal Ballet, 1929–)

Sir Peter Chalmers Mitchell (Zoologist and author, improved London Zoo, 1864–1945)

Sir Joseph Noel Paton (Artist appointed to Queen Victoria, 1821–1901)

Moira Shearer (Ballerina and film actress [*The Red Shoes*], 1926–)

DUNGLASS East Lothian

Sir James Hall (Experimental geologist, supported Hutton's theories, 1761–1832)

DUNMOW Essex

Sir George Beaumont (Artist, helped found National Gallery, 1753–1827)

DUNOON Argyllshire

Virginia Bottomley (Cabinet minister [1992–7], 1948–)

DUNS Berwickshire

John Duns Scotus (Scholar and philosopher, c.1265–1308)

Thomas McCrie (Ecclesiastical historian, 1772–1835)

George Allardice Riddell [1st Baron] (Newspaper proprietor [*News of the World*], 1865–1934)

DUNSFOLD Surrey

Joseph Warton (Poetry critic and translator of Virgil, 1722–1800)

DUNSTABLE Bedfordshire

Elkanah Settle (Playwright, organised pageants for City of London, 1648–1724)

DUNSTON Staffordshire

George Edward Thorneycroft [Baron] (Politician, resigned as Chancellor of the Exchequer after one year, 1909–1994)

DUNVANT West Glamorgan

John Ormond (Poet and film-maker [biographies of Welsh poets and artists], 1923–1990)

Ceri Richards (Artist and teacher, 1903–1971)

DUNWICH Suffolk

John Day (Printer imprisoned for his religious beliefs, 1522–1584)

DURHAM

George Henry Cadogan [5th Earl] (Statesman [Lord Privy Seal 1886–92], 1840–1915)

Violet Hunt (Novelist [*The Maiden's Progress*] and suffragist, 1866–1942)

Cyril Edwin Joad (Philosopher and broadcaster, member of 'Brains Trust', 1891–1953)

Thomas Morton (Playwright [*Speed the Plough*], 1764–1838)

Anna Maria Porter (Novelist [*The Hungarian Brothers*], 1780–1832)

Jane Porter (Romantic author [*Thaddeus of Warsaw*], 1776–1850)

Alan Price (Pop singer [*Don't Stop the Carnival*], 1942–)

Michael Scott (Scholar and 'wizard', c.1175–1230)

Granville Sharp (Anti-slavery campaigner, won freedom for all slaves on British soil, 1735–1813)

Robert Surtees (Historian of north of England, 1779–1834)

Robert Smith Surtees (Novelist, created 'John Jorrocks', 1803–1864)

DYSART Fife
John McDouall Stuart (Explorer in Australia, 1815–1866)

EAGLESFIELD Near Cockermouth, Cumbria
John Dalton (Chemist whose Atomic Theory proved seminal for the science, 1766–1844)

EARLS COLNE Essex
Thomas Audley [Baron] (Henry VIII's Lord Chancellor, 1488–1544)
Sir Thomas Buxton (Social reformer and slavery abolitionist, 1786–1845)

EARLSFERRY Fife
James Braid (Champion golfer, won the British Open five times, 1870–1950)

EARLSTON Berwickshire
Thomas the Rhymer (Balladeer, allegedly kidnapped by fairies, c.1220–1297)

EASINGTON County Durham
Tommy Simpson (Cyclist, killed during Tour de France, 1938–1967)

EAST ARDSLEY Wakefield, Yorkshire
Ernie Wise [b.Ernest Wiseman] (Comedian, partnered Eric Morecambe, 1925–1999)

EAST BERGHOLT Suffolk
William Branwhite Clarke (Geologist, 'Father of Australian geology', 1798–1878)
John Constable (Landscape painter ['The Haywain'], 1776–1837)

EASTBOURNE Sussex
Angela Olive Carter [b.Stalker] (Novelist [*The Magic Toyshop*], 1940–1992)

Michael Fish (TV weather forecaster, 1944–)
Margaret Rumer Godden (Novelist [*The Greengage Summer*], 1907–1998)
Sir Frederick Gowland Hopkins (Biochemist, won Nobel Prize for Medicine in 1929, 1861–1947)
Frederick Soddy (Nobel Prize-winning chemist, 1877–1956)

EAST COKER Somerset
William Dampier (Cross-Pacific navigator and buccaneer, 1652–1715)

EAST COWES Isle of Wight
Thomas Arnold (Educationalist, headmaster of Rugby School, 1795–1842)

EAST DEREHAM Norfolk
George Henry Borrow (Travel author, 1803–1881)
William Hyde Wollaston (Chemist, revealed secret of platinum manufacture shortly before his death, 1766–1828)

EAST DRAYTON Nottinghamshire
Nicholas Hawksmoor (Church architect, worked with Wren, 1661–1736)

EAST KILBRIDE Renfrewshire
John Hannah (Actor in films [*The Mummy*] and on TV [as 'Inspector Rebus'], 1962–)
John Hunter ('Father of scientific surgery', appointed to George III, 1728–1793)
William Hunter (Anatomist and obstetrician appointed to Queen Charlotte, 1718–1783)

EAST KNOYLE Wiltshire
Sir Christopher Wren (Architect of St Paul's Cathedral, 1632–1723)

EAST LINTON East Lothian
John Rennie (Bridge and dock builder [e.g.

Waterloo Bridge, docks at London and
Portsmouth], 1761–1821)

EAST RETFORD Nottinghamshire
Catherine Gore [b.Moody] (Novelist, wrote
more than 70 books, 1799–1861)

EAST RUSTON Norfolk
Richard Porson (Classical scholar and
Professor of Greek at Cambridge from
1792, 1759–1808)

EAST STOUR Dorset
Sarah Fielding (Sister of Henry Fielding and
one of the earliest authors to write
novels for children, 1710–1768)

EASTWOOD Nottinghamshire
David Herbert [D.H.] Lawrence (Novelist
[*Sons and Lovers, Lady Chatterley's
Lover*], 1885–1930)

EASTWOOD Renfrewshire
William Collins (Weaver who entered book
trade and founded the UK's biggest
independent publishing house,
1789–1853)

EBRINGTON Gloucestershire
William Henry Hadow (Educationalist who
recommended that 'all-age' schools be
replaced by primary and secondary
schools, 1859–1937)

ECCLEFECHAN Dumfriesshire
Thomas Carlyle (Author, historian [*The
French Revolution*], and campaigner
against slavery, 1795–1881)

ECCLESFIELD Yorkshire
Juliana Horatia Ewing [b.Gatty] (Children's
author, created characters who gave
name to the Brownie movement,
1841–1885)

ECCLESMACHAN West Lothian
Robert Liston (Surgical pioneer of
anaesthesia, 1794–1847)

ECCLESTON Lancashire
Richard John Seddon (Prime Minister of
New Zealand [from 1893], 1845–1906)

EDINBURGH (Includes LEITH)
Earl of Aberdeen [George Hamilton
Gordon] (Prime Minister who resigned
after taking UK into Crimean War,
1784–1860)
Alexander Alesius (Religious activist, twice
Rector of Leipzig University, 1500–1565)
Sir William Allan (Artist, appointed to
Queen Victoria in 1841, 1782–1850)
Thomas Anderson (Chemist, discoverer of
pyridine, 1819–1874)
Thomas Dickson Armour (Golfer, won both
British and US Opens, 1895–1968)
William Edmonstone Aytoun (Poet and
Sheriff of Orkney, 1818–1865)
Francis Balfour (Embryologist, died just
after appointment to Cambridge
professorship, 1851–1882)
James Ballantine (Artist and poet [*The
Gaberlunzie's Wallet* 1843], 1808–1877)
Robert Michael Ballantyne (Author [*Coral
Island*], 1825–1894)
George Bannatyne (Historian who compiled
his best work after fleeing plague in
Edinburgh, 1545–1608)
Helen Brodie Bannerman [b.Boog-Watson]
(Author of *Little Black Sambo*,
1862–1946)
John George Bartholomew (Cartographer,
1860–1920)
Sir George Beilby (Chemist who improved
method of extracting gold from ores and
founded Fuel Research Station,
1850–1924)
Alexander Graham Bell (Inventor of
telephone, 1847–1922)

Alexander Melville Bell (Educationalist, father of Alexander Graham Bell, 1819–1905)

Sir Charles Bell (Anatomist and surgeon, after whom 'Bell's Palsy' is named, 1774–1842)

Adam Black (Publisher of Sir Walter Scott and *Encyclopaedia Britannica*, became MP aged 72, 1784–1874)

Jemima Blackburn (Wildlife artist [*Birds From Nature*], 1823–1909)

William Blackwood (Publisher of the most popular magazine of the day, named after him, 1776–1834)

Anthony [Tony] Charles Lynton Blair (Prime Minister [1997–], 1953–)

Sir Robert Boothby (Politician and broadcaster, 1900–1986)

James Boswell (Biographer of Samuel Johnson, 1740–1795)

Thomas Braidwood (Pioneer teacher of disabled, 1715–1798)

Rory Bremner (TV comedian and impressionist, 1961–)

Henry Brougham [1st Baron] (Politician and slavery abolitionist, has carriage named after him, 1778–1868)

Alexander Crum Brown (Organic chemist, made study of vertigo, 1838–1922)

Ken Buchanan (World champion lightweight boxer, 1945–)

William Burn (Architect, designed Edinburgh Academy and Music Hall, 1789–1870)

John Stuart Bute [3rd Earl] (Prime Minister for one year [1762–3], 1713–1792)

Francis Campbell Cadell (Artist, member of the Scottish Colourists, 1883–1937)

Nicky Campbell (TV and radio presenter, 1961–)

Sir Robert Christison (Toxicologist, wrote *Treatise on Poisons*, 1797–1882)

Sir Sean [Thomas] Connery ('James Bond' actor, 1930–)

James Connolly (Irish freedom activist, 1868–1916)

Ronnie [Ronald Balfour] Corbett (Actor, partnered Ronnie Barker on TV, 1930–)

Thomas Coutts (Banker, founder of Coutts & Co., 1735–1822)

William Cunningham (Both a professor of economics and church archdeacon, 1849–1919)

Randall Thomas Davidson [Baron] (Archbishop of Canterbury [1903–28], 1848–1930)

Richard Demarco (Artist and exhibition organiser, 1930–)

Joan Dickson (Cellist, frequently appearing at London Prom concerts, 1921–)

James Donaldson (Philanthropist, bequeathed Hospital for the Deaf, a building believed coveted by Queen Victoria, 1751–1830)

Sir William Fettes Douglas (Artist, curator of National Gallery of Scotland, 1822–1891)

William Douglas-Home (Playwright [*The Chiltern Hundreds*], 1912–1992)

John Alexander Dowie (US-based religious leader, 1847–1907)

Sir Arthur Conan Doyle (Creator of 'Sherlock Holmes', 1859–1930)

Thomas Drummond (Engineer and Dublin-based magistrate, 1797–1840)

Henry Erskine (Jurist and Lord Advocate, 1746–1817)

Thomas Erskine [1st Baron] (Jurist and Lord Chancellor, 1750–1823)

William Falconer (Poet who drew on his shipwreck experience, 1732–1769)

Robert Fergusson (Poet greatly admired by Robert Burns, 1750–1774)

James Frederick Ferrier (Philosopher, wrote *The Institutes of Metaphysics*, 1808–1864)

Susan Edmonstone Ferrier (Novelist whose anonymous works were assumed to have been written by Sir Walter Scott, 1782–1854)

Robert Bannantyne Finlay [Viscount] (Lord Chancellor, 1842–1929)

Tom Fleming (Actor and broadcaster, particularly of royal occasions, 1927–)

Sir William Russell Flint (Artist, noted for erotic Spanish themes, 1880–1969)

George Forbes (Electrical engineer and astronomer, predicted discovery of Pluto, 1849–1936)

Brigit Forsyth (TV actor ['Thelma' in *The Likely Lads*], 1940–)

Robert Garioch [Robert Garioch Sutherland] (Poet, 1909–1981)

Sir Archibald Geikie (Director-General of Geological Survey [1882–1901], 1835–1924)

James Geikie (Geologist, expert on Ice Ages 1839–1915)

James Gillespie (School founder in Edinburgh, 1726–1797)

Hannah Gordon (Actor [TV's *My Wife Next Door*], 1941–)

Sir John Watson Gordon (Portrait painter, 1788–1864)

James Graham (Controversial medical practitioner described by DNB as a 'quack', 1745–1794)

Kenneth Grahame (Author of *Wind in the Willows*, 1859–1932)

Elizabeth Grant of Rothiemurcus (Diarist, and author who began writing when family was persecuted for debts, 1797–1885)

James Grant (Military historian and author of 56 novels, 1822–1887)

Sir Nigel Gresley (Designed *Flying Scotsman* and world's fastest steam locomotive [*Mallard*], 1876–1941)

Sir Douglas Haig [Earl] (Military commander, 1861–1928)

John Scott Haldane (Physiologist, researched mine ventilation, 1860–1936)

Elizabeth Sanderson Haldane (Author, Scotland's first female JP, 1862–1937)

Richard Burdon Haldane [1st Viscount] (Statesman, modernised British Army before World War One, 1856–1928)

George Heriot (Goldsmith and school founder, 1563–1624)

Joseph Hislop (Internationally acclaimed operatic tenor, 1884–1977)

John Home (Clergyman who resigned after writing play *Douglas*, 1722–1808)

Thomas Charles Hope (Chemist, discovered strontium, 1766–1844)

David Hume (Philosopher, 1711–1776)

John Hunter (Global circumnavigator, Governor of New South Wales, 1718–1783)

James Hutton ('Founder of modern geology', 1726–1797)

Frieda Inescort [b.Wightman] (Stage and Hollywood film actor [*A Place In The Sun*], 1900–1976)

Andrew Irvine (International rugby player for Heriots' and Scotland, 1951–)

James VI [of Scotland] and I [of England] (1566–1625)

Sir Leander Starr Jameson (South Africa-based statesman, led raid named after him, 1853–1917)

Francis Jeffrey [Lord] (Jurist and author, 1773–1850)

Dorothy Johnstone (Kirkcudbright-based artist, 1892–1980)

James Johnstone (Jacobite soldier, aide-de-camp to Bonnie Prince Charlie, 1719–c.1800)

James Keir (Chemist and industrialist, 1735–1820)

Sir Ludovic Kennedy (Author and broadcaster, 1919–)

Alison Kinnaird (Artist and glass engraver, 1949–)

Robert Knox (Surgeon supplied with 'specimens' by Burke and Hare, 1791–1862)

Alexander Gordon Laing (First European explorer to reach Timbuktu; murdered by hostile Africans, 1793–1826)

Sir Harry Lauder (Entertainer, 1870–1950)

Robert Scott Lauder (Artist, painted subjects from Scott's writings, 1803–1869)

John Law of Lauriston (Economist and adventurer who became Comptroller of France, 1671–1729)

James Lind (Antiscorbutic expert, devised lime juice as answer to seaboard scurvy, 1716–1794)

Joan Lingard (Author [The Prevailing Wind], 1932–)

Sir Robert Stodart Lorimer (Architect, specialist in mock-baronial style, 1864–1929)

Norman Alexander MacCaig (Poet, 1910–1995)

Sir Alexander Campbell MacKenzie (Composer and principal of the Royal College of Music for nearly 40 years, 1847–1935)

Henry MacKenzie (Novelist [The Man of Feeling], 1745–1831)

Agnes McLaren (Missionary, founded first women's hospital on the Indian sub-continent, 1837–1913)

Agnes MacLehose (Robert Burns's 'Clarinda', 1759–1841)

Chrystal MacMillan (Lawyer and feminist, 1882–1937)

William Calder Marshall (Sculptor, worked on Albert Memorial, 1813–1894)

Sir Theodore Martin (Author commissioned by Queen Victoria to write biography of Prince Albert, 1816–1909)

James Clerk Maxwell (Physicist and colour photography pioneer, 1831–1879)

Naomi [Mary Margaret] Mitchison [b.Haldane] (Author of more than 70 novels, 1897–1999)

Sir Alexander Moncrieff (Artillery inventor, 1829–1906)

Alexander [Secundus] Monro (Anatomist, described parts of the brain, 1733–1817)

John Murray (Founder of publishing company which produced books by Darwin, Disraeli, and David Livingstone, 1745–1793)

Thea Musgrave (Composer, 1928–)

Robert Mylne (Architect, designer of Blackfriars Bridge, 1734–1811)

John Napier (Inventor of logarithms, 1550–1617)

Alexander Nasmyth (Landscape painter, 1758–1840)

James Nasmyth (Steam-hammer inventor, 1808–1890)

Stephen Charles Neill (Ecumenical movement leader, 1900–1984)

Thomas Nelson (Founder of publishing company which produced educational works, and books by John Buchan, 1780–1861)

William Nicol (Physicist and mineralogist, worked on prisms, 1768–1851)

John Ogilby (Printer and publisher of maps, 1600–1676)

Sir William Quiller Orchardson (Artist, 1832–1910)

Sir Eduardo Luigi Paolozzi (Sculptor, 1924–)

Samuel John Peploe (Artist, member of the Scottish Colourists, 1871–1935)

Archibald Pitcairne (Medical author and satirist, 1652–1713)

John Porteous (Soldier lynched by Edinburgh mob, d.1736)

Barbara Rae (Artist, winner of Guthrie and Gillies awards, 1943–)

Sir Henry Raeburn (Portrait painter, 1756–1823)

Allan Ramsay (Portrait painter and pamphleteer, 1713–1784)

William John Rankine (Engineer, furthered science of thermodynamics, 1820–1872)

Jean Redpath (Ballad singer with more than 400 songs in repertoire, 1937–)

Jean Atkinson Ritchie (Nutritionist, served Food and Agriculture Organisation for over 30 years, 1913–)

David Roberts (Artist, painted striking studies of Biblical lands, 1796–1864)

Daniel Rutherford (Physician and botanist, 1749–1819)

David Scott (Artist, painted 'Traitors' Gate', 1806–1649)

Sir Walter Scott (Novelist and poet, known as 'Wizard of the North', 1771–1832)

William Bell Scott (Artist and poet, 1811–1890)

Richard Norman Shaw (Architect, designed New Scotland Yard, 1831–1912)

Sir Robert Sibbald (Co-founder of Edinburgh's Royal Botanic Garden, 1641–1722)

Alastair Sim (Elocution teacher who became outstanding character actor, 1900–1976)

William Smellie (First *Encyclopaedia Britannica* editor, 1740–1795)

Graeme Sounness (International footballer and manager [Rangers, Liverpool, Blackburn Rovers etc], 1955–)

Dame Muriel Spark (Author [*The Prime of Miss Jean Brodie*], 1918–)

John Dalrymple Stair [2nd Earl] (Military commander and Governor of Minorca, 1673–1747)

Joseph Rayner Stephens (Industrial and social reformer imprisoned for his beliefs, 1805–1879)

Robert Louis Stevenson (Novelist and storyteller, author of *Treasure Island* and creator of Jekyll and Hyde, 1850–1894)

Balfour Stewart (Physicist, studied aurorae, magnetic storms and solar phenomena, 1828–1887)

Dugald Stewart (Professor of Philosophy at Edinburgh for 25 years, 1753–1828)

Marie Charlotte Stopes (Birth control pioneer, 1880–1958)

John Stuart [b.John Croall] (Film actor [*Sink the Bismarck*], 1898–1979)

Alan Archibald Swinton (Engineer and inventor, published first X-ray picture in UK, 1863–1930)

James Syme (Surgeon and waterproofing inventor, 1799–1870)

Archibald Campbell Tait (First Scottish Archbishop of Canterbury, 1811–1882)

Sir D'Arcy Wentworth Thompson (Zoologist, studied animal morphology, 1860–1948)

Ernest and David Torrence [brothers] (Actors in silent films and early talkies, 1878–1933 and 1880–1942 respectively)

Fred Urquhart (Novelist [*Time Will Knit*], 1912–1996)

Dame Ethel Walker (Artist, impressionistic in later work, 1861–1951)

John James Waterston (Physicist whose Kinetic Theory of Gases was rejected until rediscovered by Lord Rayleigh, 1811–1883)

Robert Whytt (Neurologist who researched reflex action, 1714–1766)

Sir Daniel Wilson (Archaeologist who made important contribution to the organisation of Canadian education, 1816–1892)

EDNAM Roxburghshire

Henry Francis Lyte (Composer of *Abide With Me*, 1793–1847)

James Thomson (Poet, believed to have written *Rule Britannia*, 1700–1748)

EDROM Berwickshire

Robert Fortune (Botanist and plant collector in China, 1813–1880)

EDWORTH Bedfordshire

Agnes Beaumont (Religious activist, unjustly accused of having conspired with John Bunyan to kill her father, 1652–1720)

EGHAM Surrey
Frederick James Furnivall (Philologist, his studies leading to the establishment of the *Oxford English Dictionary*, 1825–1910)

EGLINGHAM Near Alnwick, Northumberland
Henry Baker Tristram (Travel author and naturalist in Palestine, 1822–1906)

ELBERTON Gloucestershire
Joseph Sturge (Anti-slavery campaigner and philanthropist, 1794–1859)

ELDERSLIE Renfrewshire
Sir William Wallace (Guardian of Scotland, killed by order of King Edward I, c.1274–1305)

ELEMORE HALL Durham
Lady Annabella Byron (Philanthropist, wife of Lord Byron, 1792–1860)

ELGIN Morayshire
Frederick Fyvie Bruce (Classical and Biblical scholar, 1910–1990)
William Grant (Lexicographer, editor of *Scottish National Dictionary*, 1863–1946)

ELLESMERE Shropshire
Eglantyne Jebb (Philanthropist, created 'Save the Children' fund in 1919, 1876–1928)

ELLESMERE PORT Cheshire
Joe [Joseph] Mercer (Footballer and England team manager, 1914–1990)

ELPHINSTONE TOWER Near Airth, Stirlingshire
George Keith Elphinstone [Viscount Keith] (Naval commander, captured Cape Town, Ceylon and Malta, 1746–1823)

ELSON Hampshire
Richard Chandler (Archaeologist, author of *Ionian Antiquities*, 1738–1810)

ELSTEAD Surrey
Sir Alan Patrick Herbert (Author [*Bless the Bride*] and politician who promoted Parliamentary Act to ease divorce laws, 1890–1971)

ELSTOW Bedfordshire
John Bunyan (Author of *Pilgrim's Progress*, 1628–1688)

ELTON Nottinghamshire
Erasmus Darwin (Scientist, grandfather of Charles Darwin, author of *Zoonomia*, 1731–1802)

EMBLETON Northumberland
William Thomas Stead (Campaigning journalist, imprisoned for demonstrating ease with which child prostitutes could be bought in London, 1849–1912)

ENDON Staffordshire
Thomas Ernest Hulme (Philosopher, killed in war action, 1883–1917)

ENGLEFIELD GREEN Surrey
Mary Siepman [b.Farmar] (Novelist better known as Mary Wesley, author of *The Camomile Lawn*, 1912–)
Sir Pierson John Dixon (Diplomat, held ambassadorial appointments in Prague and Paris, 1904–1965)

ENNISKILLEN County Fermanagh
Josias Christopher Gamble (Industrial chemist, produced bleach, sulphuric acid etc in quantity, 1776–1848)
Ciaran McMenamin (Actor in films [*Titanic Town*] and TV [title role in *David Copperfield*], 1974–)

William Conyngham Plunket [1st Baron]
(Irish Lord Chancellor [1830–41],
1764–1854)

EPSOM Surrey
Petula Clark (Actress and singer
[*Downtown*], 1932–)
James Chuter Ede [Baron] (Politician, Home
Secretary [1945–51], 1882–1965)
Spencer Frederick Gore (Artist, painted
theatrical subjects, 1878–1914)
John Egerton Christmas Piper (Artist,
designed stained glass for new Coventry
Cathedral, 1903–1992)

EPWORTH Lincolnshire
Charles Wesley (Evangelist, 1707–1788)
John Wesley (Evangelist, 1703–1791)

ESHER Surrey
Sir Terence Orby Conran (Furniture designer
and retailer, 1931–)

ESKBANK Near Dalkeith, Midlothian
John Anderson Waverley [Viscount] (Cabinet
minister, responsible for family air-raid
shelters in World War Two, 1882–1958)

ETON Berkshire
William Oughtred (Mathematician,
invented early slide-rule, 1575–1660)
Sir Donald Francis Tovey (Pianist and
composer better remembered for his
editing of works by Bach and Beethoven,
1873–1940)

ETTRICKHALL Selkirkshire
James Hogg ['Ettrick Shepherd'] (Poet and
novelist, 1770–1835)

EVERSHOT Dorset
William Fox Talbot (Inventor of negative-
positive photography, 1800–1877)

EVESHAM Hereford and Worcester
Conrad Hall Waddington (Geneticist and
science populariser [*Biology for the
Modern World*], 1905–1975)

EXETER Devon
Baldwin (Archbishop of Canterbury who
died on Crusade, d.1190)
Sabine Baring-Gould (Author and
churchman, wrote *Onward Christian
Soldiers*, 1834–1924)
Sir Thomas Bodley (Scholar, supporter of
Bodleian Library, 1545–1613)
Sir John Bowring (Diplomat, Governor of
Hong Kong, 1792–1872)
Eustace Budgell (Author who lost his
fortune in South Sea 'Bubble',
1686–1737)
Mary Carpenter (Educationalist, concerned
about child welfare and prison reform,
1807–1877)
William Carpenter (Doctor who studied
neurology and also zoological subjects,
1813–1885)
William Kingdon Clifford (Mathematician
and science populariser, 1845–1879)
Samuel Cousins (Engraver, 1801–1887)
Thomas D'Urfrey (Comedic playwright
whose plays were attacked as 'immoral',
1653–1723)
Sir Vicary Gibbs (Attorney-general
[1807–12], 1751–1820)
Francis Hayman (Artist, taught
Gainsborough and helped found Royal
Academy, 1708–1786)
Henrietta Anne [Duchess of Orléans] (Sister
of Charles II, assisted him in foreign
diplomacy, 1644–1670)
Nicholas Hilliard (Miniaturist artist,
1537–1619)
James Holman ('Blind traveller' who
published travel accounts, 1786–1857)
William George Hoskins (Historian and
broadcaster, 1908–1992)

Matthew Locke (Composer appointed to
  Charles II, c.1621–1677)
Lilly Martin-Spencer (US-based artist,
  1822–1902)
Thomas Mudge (Horologist appointed
  watchmaker to George III, 1717–1794)
Richard Parker (Mutiny ringleader at the
  Nore, c.1767–1797)
William Temple (Archbishop of Canterbury
  from 1942, 1881–1944)
Dame Irene Vanbrugh (Actor, specialised in
  roles by Barrie and Pinero, 1872–1949)
Violet Vanbrugh (Actor, specialised in
  Shakespearean roles, 1867–1942)
John Walker (Ecclesiastical historian,
  1674–1747)

EYAM Derbyshire
Anna Seward (Poet, her work published
  posthumously by Scott, 1747–1809)

EYTON Shropshire
Edward Herbert of Cherbury [1st Baron]
  (Soldier and statesman who wrote works
  on deism, 1583–1648)

FAIRFORD Gloucestershire
John Keble (Religious poet, published 12
  vols of parish sermons, 1792–1866)

FALKIRK Stirlingshire
(See also REDDING)
Elizabeth Blackadder (Artist, elected to full
  membership of both Royal and Royal
  Scottish academies, 1931–)
John Aitken (Physicist, researched natural
  phenomena – clouds, dew etc,
  1839–1919)
David Weir (International footballer
  [Everton and Scotland], 1970–)

FALKLAND Fife
Richard Cameron (Martyred covenanter,
  1648–1680)

FALLODON Northumberland
Charles Grey [2nd Earl] (Reforming Prime
  Minister [1830–4], 1764–1845)

FAREHAM Hampshire
Sir William Randal Cremer (Nobel Peace
  Prize-winner; co-founded International
  Parliamentary Union, 1838–1908)
Sir John Goss (Ecclesiastical composer and
  St Paul's organist for 44 years,
  1800–1880)

FARINGDON Oxfordshire
Charles Lapworth (Geologist and
  stratigraphist, 1842–1920)

FARNHAM Surrey
William Cobbett (Radical author, 1763–1835)
Sir Peter [Neville Luard] Pears (Operatic
  tenor, 1910–1986)
Helen Kemp Porter [b.Archbold]
  (Biochemist, researched food
  preservation methods, 1899–1987)
Graham Paul Thorpe (Test cricketer [Surrey
  and England], 1969–)
Augustus Montague Toplady (Clerical
  author of *Rock of Ages*, 1740–1778)
Robert Gilbert Vansittart [Baron]
  (Statesman who lost appointment
  because of his opposition to appeasing
  Nazi Germany, 1881–1957)
William Willett (Campaigner for daylight-
  saving in UK, 1856–1915)

FARNSFIELD Nottinghamshire
Augustus Charles Gregory (Explorer and
  surveyor in Australia, 1819–1905)

FARNWORTH Cheshire
Richard Bancroft (Archbishop of
  Canterbury from 1604, 1544–1610)
Roy Chadwick (Designer of Lancaster
  bomber, killed when testing a new
  aircraft, 1893–1947)

Alfred Moritz Mond [Baron Melchett]
(Industrialist and politician, 1868–1930)
Frank Holmes Tyson (Test cricketer, bowler
known as 'Typhoon' Tyson, 1930–)

FARSLEY Yorkshire
Samuel Marsden ['The Flogging Parson']
(Clerical disciplinarian and agriculturist
who began Australian woollen trade,
1764–1838)

FAVERSHAM Kent
George Finlay (Classical scholar who fought
in Greek War of Independence and wrote
History of Greece, 1799–1875)

FEARN Angus
James Tytler (Polymath and first balloonist
on mainland Britain, 1745–1804)

FEARN Ross and Cromarty
Peter Fraser (New Zealand Prime Minister
[1940–9], 1884–1950)

FELIXSTOWE Suffolk
Dawn Addams (Actor, starred in Chaplin's *A
King in New York*, 1930–1985)
Sir John Mills (Actor [*Ice Cold in Alex*,
Ryan's Daughter], 1908–)

FENNY DRAYTON Leicestershire
George Fox (Founder of Society of Friends,
1624–1691)

FENNY STRATFORD Buckinghamshire
Thomas Lake Harris (Spiritualist, claimed to
be immortal, 1823–1906)

FENWICK Ayrshire
John Paton (Covenanter martyr, d.1684)

FERNDALE Mid Glamorgan
Sir Stanley Baker (Actor [*Zulu*],
1927–1976)

FIFEHEAD MAGDALEN Dorset
Sir William Erle (Judge and legislator,
1793–1880)

FINCHINGFIELD Essex
Sir Evelyn John Ruggles-Brise (Penal reformer,
introduced borstal system to separate
children from adult prisoners, 1857–1935)

FITZWILLIAM Yorkshire
Geoffrey Boycott (Test cricketer and
broadcaster, 1940–)

FLEETWOOD Lancashire
Charles Kay Ogden (Linguistic expert,
created 'Basic English' consisting of only
850 words, 1889–1957)

FOCHABERS Morayshire
George Chalmers (Antiquarian, biographer
of Daniel Defoe and Tom Paine,
1742–1825)
William Marshall (Fiddle composer,
1748–1833)

FOCKBURY Hereford and Worcester
Alfred Edward Housman (Poet [*A
Shropshire Lad*], 1859–1936)

FOLKESTONE Kent
Alfred Edgar Coppard (Author on country
life despite leaving school aged nine,
1878–1957)
William Harvey (Discoverer of the
circulation of blood, 1578–1657)

FONTHILL Wiltshire
William Thomas Beckford (Author who
built his own abbey [at Fonthill] and
became a recluse, 1760–1844)

FORFAR Angus
Ritchie Calder [Baron] (Journalist and
educationalist, 1906–1982)

Joseph Henry Wedderburn (US-based mathematician, 1882–1948)

FORRES Moray
Alexander Adam (Teacher and author of works on Roman history, 1741–1809)
James Dick (Philanthropist, sponsored local education, 1743–1828)
Hugh Falconer (Botanist and palaeontologist, experimented with growing tea in India, 1808–1865)
Donald Alexander Strathcona [1st Baron] (Canadian High Commissioner from 1896, 1820–1914)

FORT GEORGE Inverness-shire
William Arbuthnot Lane (Innovative surgeon, 1856–1943)

FOTHERINGHAY CASTLE Northamptonshire
Richard III [King of England] (1452–1485)

FOULBY Near Pontefract, Yorkshire
John Harrison (Navigational instrument inventor, devised means of reckoning longitude at sea, 1693–1776)

FOULSHIELS Selkirkshire
Mungo Park (African explorer killed in Africa by hostile aboriginals, 1771–1806)

FOUNTAINHALL Midlothian
Sir Thomas Dick Lauder (Author of the *Wolf of Badenoch*, 1784–1848)

FOWEY Cornwall
Antony Hewish (Nobel Prize-winning radio astronomer, co-discovered existence of pulsars, 1924–)

FRAMPTON ON SEVERN Gloucestershire
Sir Edward John Russell (Soil and agricultural scientist, 1872–1965)

FRASERBURGH Aberdeenshire
Gordon Mitchell Forsyth (Ceramic designer, wrote *Art and Craft of the Potter*, 1879–1953)
Thomas Blake Glover (Promoted industrialism in Japan, his wife said to be the inspiration for *Madame Butterfly*, 1838–1911)
Charles Alfred Jarvis (Received first Victoria Cross of World War One, 1881–1948)
David Donald Murison (Editor of the *Scottish National Dictionary* for 30 years, 1914–1997)
Dennis Nilsen (Serial murderer, 1945–)

FRESHWATER Isle of Wight
Robert Hooke (Chemist and physicist, designed reflecting telescope, anticipated flight, steam power etc, 1635–1703)

FRESSINGFIELD Suffolk
William Sancroft (Archbishop of Canterbury imprisoned in Tower of London by James II, 1617–1693)

FROME Somerset
Sir Benjamin Baker (Civil engineer, co-designed Forth Rail Bridge, 1840–1907)
Sir Charles Oatley (Electronics engineer, applied techniques from wartime radar to making workable electron scanning microscope, 1904–1996)

FULFORD Yorkshire
James Eric Drummond [16th Earl of Perth] (Statesman, Secretary-General of the League of Nations for 14 years, 1876–1951)

FULMER Buckinghamshire
Michael York (Actor [*Logan's Run*, TV's *Forsyte Saga*], 1942–)

FULNECK West Yorkshire

Benjamin Henry Latrobe (US-based civil engineer, rebuilt buildings in Washington DC burned by British, 1764–1820)

FYVIE Aberdeenshire

Cosmo Gordon Lang (Archbishop of Canterbury [1928–42], 1864–1945)

GAINSBOROUGH Lincolnshire

John Alderton (Actor in films [*Please Sir*] and TV, 1940–)

Vic [Victor Grayson] Feather [Baron] (Trade union leader, 1908–1976)

Sir Halford John McKinder (Geographer and statesman, 1861–1947)

Dame Sybil Thorndyke (Actor, appeared as first Shaw heroine St Joan in UK, 1882–1976)

GAIRLOCH Ross and Cromarty

John Baillie (Theologian, wrote *Diary of Private Prayer*, 1886–1960)

GALASHIELS Selkirkshire

John Collins (International footballer [Fulham and Scotland], 1968–)

Andrew John Herbertson (Oxford-based geographer, 1865–1915)

Arthur Lapworth (Chemist, promoted study of physical organic chemistry, 1872–1941)

Anne Redpath (Artist, regarded as one of Scotland's most outstanding, 1895–1965)

GALCH HILL Clwyd

Sir Hugh Myddelton (Goldsmith and founder of London water supply, c.1560–1631)

GARDEN Stirlingshire

James Stirling (Mathematician and engineer, 1692–1770)

GARLET Clackmannan

Mary Erskine (Banker and benefactor of women's education, 1629–1707)

GARNANT Carmarthenshire

Hwyel Bennett (TV and film actor [*The Family Way, Virgin Soldiers*], 1944–)

GARTMORE Stirlingshire

Robert Cunninghame Graham (Bill of rights compiler, d.1797)

GASK Perthshire

Carolina Nairne [Baroness] (Songwriter and collector of such songs as *Will Ye No Come Back Again?*, 1766–1845)

GATESHEAD County Durham

Steve [Stephen] Cram (Athlete, competed at 1500m and mile distance, 1960–)

Paul Gascoigne (International footballer, 1967–)

Don Hutchison (International footballer [West Ham United and Scotland], 1971–)

GAWCOTT Buckinghamshire

Sir George Gilbert Scott (Architect [St Pancras Station and hotel], and promoter of architectural conservation, 1811–1878)

GAWSWORTH Cheshire

Mary Fitton (Maid of honour to Elizabeth I, believed to be the 'Black Lady' of Shakespeare's sonnet, c.1578–1647)

GAYHURST Buckinghamshire

Sir Kenelm Digby (Diplomat imprisoned during Civil War, 1603–1665)

GERRARD'S CROSS Buckinghamshire

Kenneth More (Film actor, star of *Reach For The Sky*, 1914–1982)

GIFFORD East Lothian

John Witherspoon (Theologian and teacher, 1723–1794)

GIGGLESWICK Yorkshire

Sir John Hare [b.Fairs] (Manager of Court and Garrick theatres, 1844–1921)

Henry Maudsley (Pioneering psychiatrist, 1835–1918)

GILLINGHAM Kent

William Adams (Navigator, first Englishman to visit Japan, 1564–1620)

Dame Kathleen Courtney (Suffragette, helped compile UN Charter, 1878–1974)

David Harvey (US-based geographer, 1935–)

Sir Henry Thomas Tizard (Chemist and wartime scientist [radar], 1885–1959)

GLAMIS CASTLE Angus

Princess Margaret Rose (1930–2002)

GLANTON Northumberland

Hugh Trevor-Roper [Baron Dacre] (Historian, edited Goebbels's diaries and wrongly authenticated those purported to be Hitler's, 1914–)

GLASBURY Powys

Francis Herbert Bradley (Philosopher, wrote *Appearance and Reality*, 1846–1924)

GLASGOW *(See also RUTHERGLEN)*

Eugen Charles d'Albert (Composer, best remembered for his music-drama *Tiefland* premiered in Prague in 1903, 1864–1932)

Hely Hutchinson Almond (Educationalist, believed in Spartan conditions for his pupils, 1832–1903)

Robert Baillie (Religious activist, marched with Covenanters but reconciled with Charles II, 1599–1662)

William Black (War correspondent in Franco-Prussian War and novelist, 1841–1898)

John Stuart Blackie (Professor of Greek at Edinburgh for 30 years, 1809–1895)

Sir Muirhead Bone (War artist and Trustee of National Gallery, 1876–1953)

James Boyle (Convicted murderer and artist, 1944–)

Mark Boyle (Artist, works in concrete and metal, 1934–)

James Bridie (Playwright [*The Anatomist*], 1888–1951)

Sir Arthur Whitten Brown (Aviator, knighted after flying Atlantic non-stop with John Alcock in 1919, 1886–1948)

James Gordon Brown (Chancellor of the Exchequer [1997–], 1951–)

Isobel Wilson Buchanan (Soprano, noted soloist with Australian Opera, 1954–)

Sir George Burns (Shipowner, co-founded Cunard Line, 1795–1890)

Sir William Burrell (Shipowner and art collector, 1861–1958)

Katherine Cameron (Watercolour artist, 1874–1965)

Charles Arthur Campbell (Philosopher, wrote *In Defence of Free Will*, 1897–1974)

Sir Colin Campbell [Baron Clyde] (Commander of the 'Thin Red Line' at Battle of Balaclava, 1792–1863)

Thomas Campbell (Poet [*Ye Mariners of England*], 1777–1844)

Sir Henry Campbell-Bannerman (Prime Minister [1905–8], 1836–1908)

Robert Carlyle (Film actor [*Trainspotting, Riff Raff*], 1961–)

William Carstares (Diplomat twice imprisoned but eased accession of William of Orange in Britain, 1649–1715)

Catherine Roxburgh Carswell (Novelist, wrote controversial life of Robert Burns, 1879–1946)

Erik Chisholm (South African-based composer, 1904–1965)

Sir Dugald Clerk (Engineer, worked on two-stroke gas engines, 1854–1932)

Catherine Cranston (Teashop proprietress who commissioned Charles Rennie Mackintosh to undertake decoration, 1850–1934)

Kenny Dalglish (International football player and manager, 1951–)

Donald Dewar (Politician, Scotland's first First Minister, 1937–2000)

Tommy [Thomas Henderson] Docherty (International footballer and manager [Scotland, Manchester United etc,] 1928–)

Lonnie [b.Anthony James] Donegan (Pop singer [My Old Man's a Dustman], 1931–)

Donovan [b.Donovan Phillip Leitch] (Folk and pop singer [Catch the Wind], 1946–)

Christopher Dresser (Designer, noted for work in metal, 1834–1904)

William Elphinstone (Ecclesiastic, founded Aberdeen University, 1431–1514)

Gavin Esler (TV journalist and presenter, 1953–)

Sir Alex Ferguson (Football manager knighted after winning treble of League, FA Cup and European Cup with Manchester United in 1999, 1941–)

Sir Harold Montague [Monty] Finniston (Industrialist, headed British Steel [1973–6], 1912–1991)

Sir Alexander Fleck [Baron] (Industrial chemist, headed ICI, 1889–1968)

Bill Forsyth (Film director [Gregory's Girl], 1946–)

Sir James George Frazer (Anthropologist, wrote The Golden Bough, 1854–1941)

Annie French (Artist, designed postcards and posters, 1872–1965)

Rikki Fulton (Comedian, one half of 'Francie and Josie', 1924–)

Thomas Graham (Chemist and Master of the Mint, 1805–1869)

James Grahame (Poet and ornithologist, 1765–1811)

Iain Ellis Hamilton (Composer of orchestral music and opera [The Cataline Conspiracy], 1922–2000)

Patrick Hamilton (Reformation martyr, 1503–1528)

Thomas Hamilton (Greek-influenced architect, 1784–1858)

Sir William Hamilton (Philosopher, 1788–1856)

Sir Ian Morris Heilbron (Organic chemist, 1886–1959)

Arthur Henderson (Nobel Peace Prize-winning statesman, 1863–1935)

James Herriot [James Alfred Wight] (Author [All Creatures Great and Small] and veterinary surgeon, 1916–1995)

Sir William Wilson Hunter (Statistician, carried out Census of India in 1872, 1840–1900)

Sir James Colquhoun Irvine (Carbohydrate chemist, 1877–1952)

Alick Isaacs (Discoverer of interferon, 1921–1967)

Jeremy Israel Isaacs (TV and opera-house administrator [1988–97], 1932–)

John Jamieson (Scholar and lexicographer, 1759–1838)

Helena Kennedy [Baroness] (Barrister and writer, 1950–)

William Paton Ker (Mediaeval scholar, 1855–1923)

Carol Kidd (Jazz singer, 1944–)

Stuart Oliver Knussen (Composer and co-director of Aldeburgh Festival, 1952–)

Ronald David Laing (Psychiatrist, wrote The Divided Self in 1960, 1927–1989)

Frederic Lamond (Pianist and composer, taught by Liszt, 1868–1948)

Sir William Boog Leishman (Discoverer of typhoid vaccine, 1865–1926)

Sir Thomas Johnstone Lipton (Grocery retailer and philanthropist, 1850–1931)

Frank Lloyd (Film director [Oscar-winning *Mutiny on the Bounty*, 1935], 1888–1960)

Lulu [b.Marie Lawrie] (Pop singer, 1948–)

Benny Lynch (Champion flyweight boxer, 1913–1946)

Mary Reid MacArthur (Trade union leader, campaigned for women's welfare in sweated and munitions industries, 1880–1921)

Frances MacDonald (Artist, 1873–1921)

Sharman MacDonald (Playwright [*When I Was A Girl I Used To Scream And Shout*], 1951–)

Dugald Sutherland McColl (Artist, 1859–1948)

John MacDonald MacCormick (Politician, 1904–1961)

Sir John Alexander MacDonald (Canadian-based statesman, 1815–1891)

James McGill (Founder of McGill University, Montreal, 1744–1813)

Charles MacIntosh (Inventor of waterproof clothing, 1766–1843)

Charles Rennie MacKintosh (Artist and architect, 1868–1928)

Alistair McLean (Novelist [*Ice Station Zebra*], 1922–1987)

Hugh Pattison MacMillan [Lord] (Lawyer and information minister at outbreak of World War Two, 1873–1952)

Herbert McNair (Architect and designer, 1868–1955)

Bessie McNicol (Portrait artist, 1869–1904)

James Maxton (Politician, imprisoned for his Socialist beliefs, 1885–1946)

Patrick Connolly [Paddy] Meehan (Unjustly convicted of murder, 1927–1994)

William Miller (Poet, author of 'Wee Willie Winkie', 1810–1872)

James Allan Mollison (Aviator husband of Amy Johnson, 1905–1959)

Sir John Moore (Military commander, killed in action at Corunna, 1761–1809)

Alan Lauder Morton (International footballer [Rangers], 1893–1971)

William Motherwell (Folklorist, 1797–1835)

John Muir (Sanskrit scholar, 1810–1882)

Thomas Muir (Radical activist transported to Australia, 1765–1799)

Sir William Muir (Indian administrator, 1819–1905)

McVey Napier (Lawyer and encyclopaedia editor [*Encyclopaedia Britannica*, 7th edn], 1776–1847)

James Beaumont Neilson (Inventor of hot blast iron production, 1792–1865)

Robert Dale Owen (Anti-slavery campaigner in US, 1801–1877)

Allan Pinkerton (Founder of American detective agency, 1819–1884)

Agnes Middleton Raeburn (Artist, 1872–1955)

Sir William Ramsay (Nobel Prize-winning chemist, 1852–1916)

Sir William Mitchell Ramsay (Archaeologist, expert on topography of ancient Asia Minor, 1851–1939)

Belinda Robertson (Fashion designer specialising in cashmere, 1959–)

Muriel Robertson (Microbiologist, researched parasites of human blood, 1883–1973)

John Gordon Sinclair (Actor in films [*Gregory's Girl*], TV, and theatre, 1962–)

Madeleine Hamilton Smith (Murder suspect found 'not proven', 1835–1928)

Sir William Spens (Educationalist, laid foundations for increased secondary education under 1944 Education Act, 1882–1962)

Robert Stevenson (Engineer, designed 23 lighthouses, 1772–1850)

Al Stewart (Pop singer and songwriter [*Year of the Cat*], 1945–)

James Hutchison Stewart (Philosopher, 1820–1909)

James Tassie (Fine arts engraver, 1735–1799)

Alexander Todd [Baron Trumpington] (Nobel Prize-winning chemist, 1907–1997)

Victor Witter Turner (African-based anthroplogist, 1920–1983)

Andrew Ure (Chemist, compiled *Dictionary of Chemistry* in 1821, 1778–1857)

Cecile Walton (Artist, became member of the Edinburgh Group of Artists, 1891–1956)

George Walton (Interior designer, 1867–1933)

Molly Weir (Actor, has written extensive autobiographical material, 1920–)

Sir Robert Mortimer Wheeler (Archaeologist who popularised his work in books and on TV, 1890–1976)

Sir Isaac Wolfson (Health philanthropist who endowed colleges in Oxford and Cambridge, 1897–1891)

James Young (Industrial chemist known as 'Paraffin Young' for his establishment of paraffin's industrial extraction from shale, 1811–1883)

GLENARM County Antrim
John MacNeill (Irish historian and nationalist, 1867–1945)

GLENCORSE Midlothian
Charles Thomson Rees Wilson (Nobel Prize-winning physicist who invented cloud chamber to trace extra-terrestrial particles, 1869–1959)

GLOSSOP Derbyshire
Eileen Cooper (Artist concerned with the human condition, 1933–)

GLOUCESTER
Winifred Cullis (Physiologist refused a degree because of her gender, later became a professor at London University, 1875–1956)

Ivor Gurney (Composer and poet psychologically damaged by his war experiences, 1890–1937)

William Ernest Henley (Poet, an amputee believed to have inspired Stevenson to base Long John Silver on him, 1849–1903)

Albert Mansbridge (Educationalist, established organisation which became the Workers' Educational Association, 1876–1952)

Robert Raikes (Newspaper proprietor and philanthropist, 1735–1811)

John Stafford Smith (Composer of *The Star Spangled Banner*, 1750–1836)

John Taylor ('Water Poet', drafted into Navy, later travelled widely, 1580–1653)

Herbert Alfred Vaughan (Archbishop of Westminster from 1892, 1832–1903)

Sir Charles Wheatstone (Physicist, pioneered wireless telegraphy and invented the concertina, 1802–1875)

George Whitefield (Evangelist, renowned for his open-air preaching, 1714–1770)

GODALMING Surrey
Aldous Leonard Huxley (Novelist [*Point Counter Point, Brave New World*], 1894–1963)

GODOLPHIN HALL Near Helston, Cornwall
Sidney Godolphin [1st Earl] (Lord High Treasurer [1702–10], 1645–1712)

GOFF'S OAK Hertfordshire
Victoria Beckham [b.Victoria Caroline Adams, also known as 'Posh'] (Singer, at one time with Spice Girls, 1974–)

GOODNESTONE Kent
Montague Rhodes James (Ghost story
author, 1862–1936)

GORING Berkshire
Sir John Soane (Architect, designed Bank of
England building [later destroyed],
1753–1837)

GOSPORT Hampshire
Sir Howard Douglas [3rd Baronet] (Military
commander, 1776–1861)
Edward Hammond Hargraves (Successful
gold prospector in Australia, 1815–1891)
Alexander Bryan Johnson (Philosopher,
wrote *The Meaning of Words*,
1786–1867)

GOUROCK Renfrewshire
Bet Low (Artist co-founder of New Charing
Cross Gallery, 1924–)

GRACEDIEU Leicestershire
Francis Beaumont (Dramatist and
satirist, worked with John Fletcher,
c.1584–1616)

GRANDBOROUGH Buckinghamshire
Henry Arthur Jones (Playwright [*The Silver
King, Saints & Sinners*], 1851–1929)

GRANGEMOUTH Stirlingshire
Alan Davie (Painter and jazz saxophonist,
1920–)

GRANTCHESTER Near Cambridge
Gregory Bateson (Anthropologist, studied
human and animal communication,
1904–1980)

GRANTHAM Lincolnshire
John Nicholas Maw (Composer, 1935–)
Henry More (Philosopher, corresponded
with Descartes, 1614–1687)

Margaret Hilda Thatcher [b.Roberts] (Prime
Minister [1979–90], 1925–)
John William Wand (Bishop of London,
expert on church history, 1885–1977)

GRAVESEND Kent
Sir Edwin Arnold (Poet and journalist,
became editor of *Daily Telegraph*,
1832–1904)
Sir Derek Barton (Nobel Prize-winning
chemist, 1918–)
Thomson Gunn (Poet, addresses modern
concerns such as AIDS, 1929–)
Katharine Hamnett (Fashion designer, uses
natural fibres, 1952–)
John MacGregor (Travel author, popularised
canoeing in UK, 1825–1892)
Thomas James Wise (Literary collector and
forger, 1859–1937)

GRAYSHOTT Hampshire
Colin Firth (Actor in films [*Bridget Jones's
Diary*] and on TV [Mr Darcy in *Pride and
Prejudice*], 1960–)

GREAT BEDWYN Wiltshire
Thomas Willis (Co-founder of the Royal
Society, 1621–1675)

GREAT HARLOW Essex
Sarah Adams [b.Flower] (Poet, wrote
Nearer My God to Thee, 1805–1848)

GREAT NESTON Cheshire
Lady Emma Hamilton [b.Amy Lyon]
(Nelson's mistress, c.1765–1815)

GREAT POTHERIDGE Devon
George Monk [1st Duke of Albemarle]
(Military commander in Civil Wars,
1608–1670)

GREAT SHELFORD Cambridgeshire

Philippa Pearce (Award-winning children's novelist [*Tom's Midnight Garden*], 1920–)

GREAT SNORING Norfolk

John Pearson (Theologian, wrote *Exposition of Creed*, 1613–1686)

GREAT YARMOUTH Norfolk

Joseph Ames (Bibliographer, 'Founder of English bibliography', 1689–1759)

Francis Turner Palgrave (Poet and educationalist, 1824–1897)

Anna Sewell (Author of *Black Beauty*, 1820–1878)

GREENHITHE Kent

George Malcolm Young (Historian, 1882–1959)

GREENOCK Renfrewshire

Margaret Bayne (Missionary, pioneered women's education in India, 1798–1835)

Bill Bryden (Dramatist [*Willie Rough*], 1942–)

Edward Caird (Philosopher, original Fellow of the British Academy, 1835–1908)

Sir James Guthrie (Artist, President of the Royal Scottish Academy, 1859–1930)

William Kidd [Captain Kidd] (Merchant sailor proclaimed a pirate, c.1645–1701)

MacGregor Laird (Explorer, first European to sail up Benue River, 1808–1861)

John Dunmore Lang (Missionary in Australia, 1799–1878)

Hamish McCunn (Composer [*Land of Mountain and the Flood*], 1868–1916)

William Scott (Artist, still-life painter, 1913–1989)

Ernest Archibald Taylor (Furniture and glass designer, 1874–1951)

William Wallace (Composer, pioneered symphonic poems, 1860–1940)

James Watt (Steam-engine pioneer, 1736–1819)

Richard Wilson (Actor, 'Victor Meldrew' in *One Foot in the Grave*, 1936–)

GRIFFITHSTOWN Gwent

Annabel Giles (TV actor and presenter [*Through the Keyhole*], 1959–)

GRIMSBY Lincolnshire

Anne Askew (Protestant martyr, tortured and burned for her faith, 1521–1546)

John Whitgift (Archbishop of Canterbury [1583–1604], c.1530–1604)

GROTON Suffolk

John Winthrop (Governor of Massachusetts, 1588–1649)

John Winthrop (Governor of Connecticut, founded New London, 1606–1676)

GUILDFORD Surrey

Mildred Cable (Missionary in China, 1878–1952)

John Russell (Portrait artist, wrote *Elements of Painting with Crayons*, 1745–1806)

John St Loe Strachey (Politician, Minister for Food [1946–50], 1901–1963)

Kate Westbrook (Jazz singer, 1937–)

Sir Pelham Grenville Wodehouse (Comic novelist, created 'Jeeves', 1881–1975)

GWAUN–CAE–GURWEN West Glamorgan

Gareth Owen Edwards (Rugby player, youngest-ever Welsh captain, 1947–)

GWERN VALE Powys

Sir George Everest (Military surveyor after whom Mt Everest is named, 1790–1866)

GYFFIN Gwynedd

John Gibson (Sculpted Queen Victoria statue in the House of Lords, 1790–1866)

HACKFORTH North Yorkshire
Cuthbert Tunstall (Bishop of Durham who
lost office twice because of
disagreements with successive monarchs,
1474–1559)

HADDINGTON East Lothian
Alexander II [King of Scotland],
(1198–1249)
Jane Baillie Carlyle [b.Welsh] (Wife of
Thomas Carlyle, 1801–1866)
Sir William Gillies (Outstanding Scottish
artist of his time, 1898–1973)
John Knox (Galley slave who became
Reformation leader in Scotland,
c.1513–1572)
Agnes Sampson (Folk healer executed for
witchcraft, d.1592)
Samuel Smiles (Biographer and author of
Self-Help, 1812–1904)

HADLEIGH Suffolk
Joseph Beaumont (Poet and chaplain to
Charles II, 1616–1699)

HADLEY Near Telford, Shropshire
Lionel [Len] Murray [Baron] (Trade union
leader, 1922–)

HADLOW Kent
Sir Henry Vane (Statesman executed after
Civil Wars, 1613–1662)

HAFOD Carmarthenshire
Timothy Richards Lewis (Pioneering
pathologist, 1841–1886)

HAGLEY Hereford and Worcester
George Lyttleton [1st Baron] (Politician and
poet, 1709–1773)

HALEWOOD Lancashire
Mary Elizabeth Peters (Olympic gold
medal-winner in 1972, 1939–)

HALESOWEN West Midlands
Francis Brett Young (Award-winning
novelist [*Portrait of Clare*], 1884–1954)

HALESWORTH Suffolk
Sir Joseph Dalton Hooker (Botanist and
plant collector, President of the Royal
Society [1872–7], 1817–1911)

HALIFAX Yorkshire
Henry Briggs (Mathematician, worked on
logarithms with John Napier,
1561–1631)
Sir Francis Crossley (Carpet manufacturer
and philanthropist, 1817–1872)
Sir Matthew Arnold Smith (Artist noted as
a colourist, 1879–1959)
John Henry Whitley (Politician, presided
over Whitley Councils to decide teachers'
pay, 1866–1935)
John Frederick Wolfenden [Baron] (Social
reformer and educationalist, 1906–1985)

HALSTEADS North Yorkshire
Felix Slade (Art collector and benefactor,
founded Slade School of Art, 1790–1868)

HAMBLEDEN Berkshire
James Thomas Brudenell [7th Earl of
Cardigan] (Leader of Charge of the Light
Brigade, 1797–1868)
St Cantelupe (Bishop of Hereford,
c.1218–1282)

HAMILTON Lanarkshire
William Cullen (Physician, coined term
'neurosis', 1710–1790)
William Cunningham (Theologian, taught
at Edinburgh and Princeton, 1805–1861)

HAMPTON COURT Surrey
Henry Flitcroft (Architect of London
churches, 1679–1769)

HANDSWORTH Staffordshire
Francis Asbury (Missionary, first Methodist
bishop in the US, 1745–1816)

HANNINGTON Northamptonshire
Francis Godwin (Bishop of Hereford who
wrote science-fiction classic, *Man in the
Moon*, 1562–1633)

HARBORNE Staffordshire
Edward Augustus Freeman (Historian [*The
Norman Conquest*], 1823–1892)

HARDENDALE Cumbria
Sir John Gardner Wilkinson (Egyptologist
and explorer, 1797–1875)

HAREWOOD Yorkshire
George Henry [7th Earl] Harewood (Music
administrator, 1923–)

HARPENDEN Hertfordshire
Michael Joseph Oakeshott (Political
philosopher, 1901–1990)
Sir Edward James Salisbury (Botanist,
Director of Royal Botanical Gardens at
Kew [1943–56], 1886–1978)

HARPHAM East Yorkshire
St John of Beverley (Saint, d.721)

HARROGATE Yorkshire
Sir Edward George Hulton (Publisher of
illustrated magazines [*Picture Post*], and
comics [*Eagle*], 1906–1988)

HARTFORD Cheshire
Geoffrey Cheshire (Bomber pilot who
established homes for the disabled,
1917–1992)

HARTLEPOOL County Durham
Christopher Furness [1st Baron] (Ship
owner, 1852–1912)

Sir Compton MacKenzie (Author,
1883–1972)
Sir Edward Mellanby (Physiologist,
1884–1955)
Reg Smythe [Reginald Smith] (Cartoonist
creator of 'Andy Capp', 1917–1998)

HARTSHILL Warwickshire
Michael Drayton (Poet ['Fair stood the
wind for France'], buried in Westminster
Abbey, 1563–1631)

HASLEMERE Surrey
Sir Geoffrey de Havilland (Aircraft designer
and manufacturer, 1882–1965)

HASLINGDEN Lancashire
John Cockerill (Industrialist, produced
manufacturing equipment, 1790–1840)
Alan Rawsthorne (Orchestral composer,
1905–1971)

HASTINGS Sussex
Jo Brand (TV comedian [*Through the
Cakehole*], 1957–)
Emma Bunton (Singer, formerly with the
Spice Girls, and TV presenter, 1979–)
Shirley Collins (Folk song collector and
performer, 1935–)
Sophia Jex-Blake (Medical education
pioneer who fought for female equality
in the teaching of medicine, 1840–1912)
Thomas Sturge Moore (Poet and bookplate
designer, 1870–1944)
Marianne North (Botanical artist who
undertook her own expeditions,
1830–1890)

HATFIELD Hertfordshire
(See also HATFIELD HOUSE, BELOW)
Martin Carthy (Folk music historian and
performer, 1940–)

HATFIELD South Yorkshire

Dame Janet Abbot Baker (Mezzo-soprano famed for concert and operatic performances, 1923–)

HATFIELD HOUSE Hertfordshire

Robert Arthur Cecil [3rd Marquis] (Prime Minister [1895–1902], 1830–1903)
Robert Arthur Cecil [5th Marquis] (Statesman, declined appointment as Viceroy of India, 1893–1972)

HATHEROP Gloucestershire

Hugh Langbourne Callendar (Physicist, standardised thermometer calibration, 1863–1930)

HAUXWELL Yorkshire

Dorothy Pattison (Philanthropist who took holy orders and ran smallpox hospital, 1832–1878)

HAVERFORDWEST Dyfed

Gwen John (Artist, mistress of Auguste Rodin, 1876–1939)
Waldo Williams (Poet, imprisoned twice for his pacifism, 1904–1971)

HAVERHILL Suffolk

Nathaniel Ward (Legal authority in American colonies, 1579–1652)

HAVERING-ATTE-BOWER Essex

Joan of Navarre [Queen of England, wife of Henry IV], (c.1370–1437)

HAWFORD Hereford and Worcester

Hesketh Pearson (Biographer [*Gilbert and Sullivan, Oscar Wilde*], 1887–1964)

HAWICK Roxburghshire

Dame Isobel Baillie (Soprano, gave more than 1,000 performances of Handel's *Messiah*, 1895–1983)

James Guthrie (Champion motorcyclist, 1897–1937)
James Paris Lee (Part-inventor of Lee-Enfield rifle, 1831–1904)
Sir John Blackwood McEwen (Composer and Principal of the Royal College of Music [1924–36], 1868–1948)
Francis George Scott (Composer of music to verses by Burns, Dunbar, and McDiarmid, 1880–1958)
James Wilson (Founded *The Economist* magazine, 1805–1860)

HAWTHORNDEN Near Roslin, Midlothian

William Drummond of Hawthornden (Poet and historian, 1585–1649)

HAYDON BRIDGE Northumberland

John Martin (Artist who painted Biblical scenes and landscapes on an awesome scale, 1789–1854)

HAYES BARTON Devon

Sir Walter Raleigh (Explorer, executed after expedition failure, 1552–1618)

HAYFIELD Derbyshire

Arthur Lowe (Actor ['Captain Mainwaring' in TV's *Dad's Army*], 1914–1982)

HAYLING ISLAND Hampshire

George Kennedy Bell (Theologian who attempted to maintain links with non-Nazis in Germany in World War Two, 1885–1958)
Simon Gray (Dramatist for stage [*Quartermaine's Terms*] and TV [*They Never Slept*], 1936–)

HEADLEY Surrey

Emily Faithfull (Publisher and feminist, established women's printing house, 1835–1895)

HEBBURN-ON-TYNE County Durham
Arthur Holmes (Geologist, specialised in researching age of the Earth, 1890–1965)

HECKMONDWIKE Yorkshire
John Curwen (Cleric who resigned to perfect his sol-fa music notation, 1816–1880)

HELENSBURGH Argyllshire
John Logie Baird (Inventor and TV pioneer, 1888–1946)
Deborah Kerr [Deborah Kerr Viertel] (Actor [*From Here to Eternity, The King and I*], 1921–)
David MacDonald (Film director, worked with Cecil B. De Mille, 1904–1983)
Peter Such (Test cricketer [Essex and England], 1964–)

HELMSLEY Yorkshire
Jane Glover (Musicologist and conductor at Glyndebourne and Covent Garden, 1949–)

HELPSTON Near Peterborough
John Clare (Poet [*The Shepherd's Calendar*], died insane, 1793–1864)

HELSTON Cornwall
Robert Fitzsimmons (Boxing champion, 1862–1917)

HEMEL HEMPSTEAD Hertfordshire
Sir Wilfrid Clark (Anatomist who exposed 'Piltdown Man' hoax, 1895–1971)

HEMPSTEAD Essex
Dick Turpin (Highwayman, executed for murder, 1705–1739)

HENFIELD Sussex
Thomas Stapleton (Controversial theologian and author, 1535–1598)

HEREFORD
John Blashford-Snell (Explorer, took part in more than 40 expeditions, 1936–)
Albert Walter Gamage (Founder of Gamage's retail store, 1855–1930)
David Garrick (Actor and theatre owner [Drury Lane], 1717–1779)
Nell Gwyn (Actor, royal mistress [to Charles II], c.1650–1687)
Henry James [1st Baron Hereford] (Attorney General [1880–5], once took 12 days to sum up a client's case, 1828–1911)
Edward William Lane (Middle East scholar, 1801–1876)
Beryl Reid (Comedic actor who moved on to more serious roles, e.g. *The Killing of Sister George*, 1920–1996)
Thomas Traherne (Poet whose major work was lost for many years, c.1636–1674)
Robert Welch (Designer working in ceramics, jewellery, and ironmongery 1929–)

HERMISTON Near Edinburgh
James Anderson (Agricultural economist, invented two-horse wheel-less plough, 1739–1808)

HERNE BAY Kent
Kevin Ayers (Rock musician, 1945–)

HERNE HILL Kent
Joseph Ackerley (Author and literary critic [for *The Listener* 1935–59], 1896–1967)
Sir George Robey (Stage comedian known as 'The Prime Minister of Mirth', 1869–1954)

HERSHAM Surrey
Edmund Gurney (Researcher of psychic phenomena, 1847–1888)

HERTFORD

William Earl Johns (Author of 'Biggles' books, 1893–1968)

HESKET NEWMARKET Cumbria

Edward [Eddie] Stobart (Transport tycoon whose truck fleet has gained cult following, 1955–)

HESWALL Cheshire

Ian Terence Botham (Test cricketer, now TV commentator, 1955–)

HETTON-LE-HOLE County Durham

Bob [Robert] Paisley (Football manager [Liverpool FC], 1919–1996)

HEVERSHAM Cumbria

Richard Watson (Theologian and agriculturist, 1737–1816)

HEXHAM Northumberland

Aethelred [or Ailred] (Chronicler, adviser to both English and Scottish kings, 1109–1166)

Wilfrid Wilson Gibson (Poet and playwright [*Daily Bread*], 1878–1962)

Joseph Parker (Religious author [*The People's Bible*], 1830–1902)

HEYSHOTT Sussex

Richard Cobden (Economist and politician, successfully opposed Corn Laws, 1804–1865)

HEYWOOD Lancashire

Julie Goodyear [b.Julie Kemp] (TV actor ['Bet Lynch' in *Coronation Street*], 1943–)

HIGH WYCOMBE Buckinghamshire

William Henry Havergal (Ecclesiastical composer, 1793–1870)

Rosamond Lehmann (Novelist [*Dusty Answer*], later became prominent spiritualist, 1901–1990)

Mike Westbrook (Jazz pianist and composer, 1936–)

HIGHAM-ON-THE-HILL Warwickshire

Geoffrey Francis Fisher [Baron] (Archbishop of Canterbury [1954–61], 1887–1972)

HIGHER BOCKHAMPTON Dorset

Thomas Hardy (Novelist [*Tess of the D'Urbervilles, Jude the Obscure*], 1840–1928)

HIGHER WALTON Lancashire

Kathleen Ferrier (Contralto, forever associated with the song *Blow the Wind Southerly*, 1912–1953)

HILLSBOROUGH County Down

Harry George Ferguson (Inventor of farm tractor with hydraulic linkage which revolutionised farming, 1884–1960)

Sir Herbert Hamilton Harty (Composer and conductor of the Hallé Orchestra [1920–33], 1880–1941)

HINDLIP Worcestershire

William Habington (Poet, wrote *Historie of Edward the Fourth*, 1605–1654)

HIPPERHOLME Yorkshire

Frank Lawrence Lucas (Poet and playwright [*Land's End*], 1894–1967)

HITCHIN Hertfordshire

Henry Hawkins [1st Baron Brampton] (Judge known as 'Hanging Hawkins', 1817–1907)

Kevin Phillips (International footballer [Sunderland and England], 1973–)

HOBY Leicestershire
Jenny Pitman [b.Harvey] (First woman
racehorse trainer to win Grand National
and Gold Cup races, 1946–)

HODDESDON Hertfordshire
William Christie Gosse (Explorer of
Australia, first white man to reach Ayers
Rock, 1842–1881)

HODDOM CASTLE Dumfriesshire
Charles Kirkpatrick Sharpe (Historian and
antiquarian, 1781–1851)

HOGSTHORPE Lincolnshire
Christopher Addison [Viscount] (Politician,
first Minister of Health [1919–21],
1869–1951)

HOLBEACH Lincolnshire
Sir Norman Angell [b.Angell Lane] (Nobel
Peace Prize-winner, author of *The Great
Illusion*, illustrating the futility of war,
1872–1967)
Susannah Centlivre [b.Freeman] Dramatist,
wrote 19 plays [*The Busie Body*],
c.1667–c.1723)

HOLDENBY Northamptonshire
Sir Christopher Hatton (Elizabethan Lord
Chancellor [1587–91], active in ensuring
the execution of Mary Stewart, Queen of
Scots, 1540–1591)

HOLKHAM Norfolk
Thomas William Coke of Holkham [1st Earl
of Leicester] (Agriculturist, and MP for 55
years, 1752–1842)

HOLMES CHAPEL Cheshire
Sir Henry Cotton (Golfer, won British Open
three times, 1907–1987)

HOLNE Devon
Charles Kingsley (Author of *The Water
Babies*, 1819–1875)

HOLNICOTE Somerset
Sir Arthur Acland (Politician, successfully
agitated for raising of school-leaving age
to 11, 1847–1926)

HOLYHEAD Gwynedd
Dawn French (Comedian, famously
partnered by Jennifer Saunders, 1957–)

HOLYWOOD County Down
John Joly (Physical geologist, calculated
age of the Earth and pioneered colour
photography, 1857–1933)

HONINGTON Suffolk
Robert Bloomfield (Poet and maker of
Aeolian harps, 1766–1823)

HOPTON Suffolk
John Bell (Sculptor of Guards' Crimean
Memorial in London, 1811–1895)

HORBURY Near Wakefield, Yorkshire
Stan Barstow (Novelist [*A Kind of Loving*],
1928–)

HORLEY Surrey
Donald Malcolm Campbell (Adventurer,
killed in attempt on world water speed
record on Lake Coniston, 1921–1967)

HORNBY Yorkshire
Mark Pattison (Author, journalist, and
biographer, 1813–1834)

HORNCASTLE Lincolnshire
Thomas Sully (US-based artist, painted over
2,000 portraits, 1783–1872)

HORNCHURCH Essex
Jilly Cooper (Author and journalist, 1937–)

HORNSEA Yorkshire
Edward John Eyre (Explorer of Australia,
and Governor of New Zealand, St
Vincent, and Jamaica, 1815–1891)

HORSEHAY Shropshire
Edith Pargeter (Historical novelist, creator
of 'Brother Cadfael' under pen name 'Ellis
Peters', 1913–1995)

HORSFORTH Yorkshire
Frazer Hines (TV actor [*Doctor Who*,
Emmerdale Farm], 1944–)

HORSHAM Sussex
Sir Cecil James Barrington Hurst (Founder
of International Courts of Justice,
1870–1963)
Barnaby Bernard Lintot (Literary publisher
of work by Pope, Gay, and Steele,
1675–1736)
Percy Bysshe Shelley (Poet ['Prometheus
Unbound', 'To a Skylark'], 1792–1822)

**HORTON Near Chipping Sodbury,
Gloucestershire**
William Prout (Physiologist, first to divide
foodstuffs into carbohydrates, fats and
proteins, 1785–1850)

HORTON Northamptonshire
Charles Montagu Halifax [1st Earl] (Prime
Minister [1697–9] who also established
the Bank of England, and the National
Debt, 1661–1715)

HOUSTON Renfrewshire
Sir William Arrol (Engineer, builder of the
second Tay Bridge, and the Forth Rail
Bridge, 1839–1913)

HOVE Sussex
Alexandra Bastedo (Actor [*Casino Royale*]
and writer, 1946–)

HOVETON Norfolk
Henry Calthorpe Blofeld (Cricket
commentator [BBC Radio's *Test Match
Special*], 1939–)

HOWDEN Yorkshire
Sir William Empson (Poet and critic [*The
Structure of Complex Words*], 1906–1984)
Henry Bernard Kettlewell (Entomologist
and geneticist who researched colour
changes in insects, caused by pollution,
1907–1979)
Roger of Hovedon (Historian and envoy to
Galloway for Henry II, d.c.1201)

HOYLAKE Cheshire
William Swainson (Zoological illustrator,
employing lithographic techniques to
improve accuracy, 1789–1855)

HUCKNALL Nottinghamshire
Eric Coates (Composer [*The Three
Elizabeths*], 1886–1957)

HUDDERSFIELD Yorkshire
James Mason (Actor [*A Star is Born, 20,000
Leagues Under the Sea*], 1909–1984)
James Harold Wilson [Baron] (Twice Prime
Minister [1964–70, 1974–6], 1916–1995)

HULL [KINGSTON–UPON–HULL]
(See also COTTINGHAM)
Nick Barmby (International footballer
[Everton and England], 1974–)
Tom [Thomas Daniel] Courteney (Actor
[*Billy Liar, Loneliness of the Long Distance
Runner*], 1937–)
Robert Hartley Cromek (Engraver,
illustrated works by Robert Burns,
1770–1812)

Henry Dawson (Artist ['The wooden walls of Old England'], 1811–1878)

Joseph Duveen [Baron] (Art collector, gifted gallery to British Museum to house Elgin Marbles, 1869–1939)

Sir Joseph Henry Gilbert (Agricultural chemist, researched nitrogen fertilisers, 1817–1901)

Ronnie Hilton [b.Adrian Hill] (Singer, 1926–)

Amy Johnson (Pioneer aviator, first woman to fly solo UK-Australia, killed on wartime service, 1903–1941)

Maureen Lipman (Actor, star of theatre, TV and film, 1946–)

Edward Arthur Milne (Astrophysicist, researched age of the universe, 1896–1950)

James Arthur Rank [1st Baron] (Film company chairman, 1888–1972)

Jean Rook (Journalist known as 'The First Lady of Fleet Street', 1931–1991)

Florence Margaret Smith (Novelist and poet better known as Stevie Smith, [poem 'Not Waving But Drowning'], 1902–1971)

John Venn (Logician, wrote *Logic of Chance*, 1834–1923)

James Ward (Psychologist philosopher, 1843–1925)

William Wilberforce (Anti-slavery campaigner, 1759–1833)

HUNGERFORD Berkshire
Charles Frederick Portal [1st Viscount] (Chief of RAF Air Staff in World War Two, 1893–1971)

HUNSDON Hertfordshire
Henry Howard Surrey [Earl] (Pioneer of blank verse, c.1517–1547)

HUNSTANTON Norfolk
William [Bill] Alexander (Theatre director, Birmingham 'Rep', 1948–)

Sir Roger L'estrange (Restoration pamphleteer, imprisoned for four years as a Royalist spy, 1616–1704)

HUNTINGDON Cambridgeshire
Oliver Cromwell (Military commander and statesman, 1599–1658)

Sir Michael Foster (Physiologist [*Textbook of Physiology*], 1836–1907)

HUNTLY Aberdeenshire
James Hastings (Ecclesiastical author [*Dictionary of the Bible*], 1852–1922)

James Legge (Missionary in China, 1815–1897)

George MacDonald (Controversial preacher and novelist [*At the Back of the North Wind*], 1824–1905)

HUNTWORTH Somerset
Sir John Popham (Judge at trial of Guy Fawkes, c.1531–1607)

HURSTPIERPOINT Sussex
James Hannington (Missionary murdered in Uganda, 1847–1885)

Paul [David] Scofield (Oscar-winning actor [*A Man for all Seasons*], 1922–)

HURSTWOOD Lancashire
Richard Tattersall (Racehorse auctioneer, 1724–1795)

ILCHESTER Somerset
Roger Bacon (Philosopher and scientist, predicted motorised transport, c.1214–1292)

ILFORD Essex
John Carmel Heenan [Cardinal] (Roman Catholic Archbishop of Westminster [1963–75], 1905–1975)

Ian Holm (Actor [*Alien, Chariots of Fire*], 1931–)

Paul Ince (International footballer
[Middlesbrough and England], 1967–)
Denise Levertov (US-based poet and
essayist ['Evening Train'], 1923–)
Ruth Pitter (Poet ['A Trophy of Arms'],
1897–1992)
Dame Maggie [Margaret Natalie] Smith
(Actor [*Prime of Miss Jean Brodie*], 1934–)

ILFRACOMBE Devon
Emily Dilke (Writer, campaigned for
women's rights, 1840–1904)

ILKESTON Derbyshire
Roland Bainton (American-based religious
activist, 1894–1984)
William Roache (TV actor ['Ken Barlow' in
Coronation Street], 1932–)

ILKLEY Yorkshire
Alan Titchmarsh (TV gardening expert,
1949–)

ILLOGAN Near Redruth, Cornwall
Richard Trevithick (Steam locomotive
pioneer, 1771–1833)

ILMINSTER Somerset
John Hanning Speke (Explorer, accidentally
shot himself when hunting, 1827–1864)
John Edward Taylor (Founder of *The
Guardian* newspaper, 1791–1844)

ILSINGTON Devon
John Ford (Dramatist [*Tis Pity She's a
Whore*], c.1586–1640)

INGOLDISTHORPE Norfolk
Sir William Hoste (Naval commander,
defeated French at Lissa, 1780–1828)

INVERARAY Argyllshire
Neil Munro (Novelist, creator of 'Para
Handy', 1864–1930)

INVERBERVIE Kincardineshire
John Arbuthnot (Royal physician and
author, created 'John Bull', 1667–1735)

INVERIE Inverness-shire
William Forbes Skene (Highland historian,
wrote *Celtic Scotland*, 1809–1892)

INVERKEITHING Fife
Andrew Martin Fairbairn (Theologian,
wrote *Christ in Modern Theology*,
1838–1912)
Sir Samuel Greig (Admiral in Russian navy,
1735–1788)

INVERNESS
Jessie Kesson (Novelist [*The White Bird
Passes, Glitter of Mica*], 1915–1994)
Elizabeth MacKintosh (Author also known
as Josephine Tey [*The Daughter of Time*],
1896–1952)
John Ferguson McLennan (Lawyer and
sociologist, wrote *The Patriarchal Theory*,
1827–1881)
Sir James Swinburne (Inventor, 'Father of
British plastics', co-founded the Bakelite
Company, 1858–1958)
Jane Elizabeth Waterston (Missionary in
South Africa, 1843–1933)

INVERUGIE CASTLE Aberdeenshire
James Keith (Commander of Prussian army
and Governor of Berlin [in 1749],
1696–1758)

INVERURIE Aberdeenshire
James Pittendrigh MacGillivray (Sculptor,
appointed to George V, 1856–1938)

IPSWICH Suffolk
Margaret Catchpole (Australian pioneer,
1762–1819)
Richard Cobbold (Novelist, also edited letters
by Margaret Catchpole, 1797–1877)

Edward Byles Cowell (Sanskrit scholar, 1826–1903)

Kieron Dyer (International footballer [Newcastle United and England], 1978–)

Frederick John Jackson (Theologian, author of *The Christian Church*, 1855–1941)

Frank Leslie [b.Henry Carter] (Magazine proprietor in US, 1821–1880)

Sir Trevor Nunn (Stage and film director [*Cats, Starlight Express*], 1940–)

Sir Victor Sawdon Pritchett (Novelist [*Claire Drummer* 1929] and biographer, 1900–1997)

Clara Reeve (Gothic novelist [*School for Widows*], 1729–1807)

Sarah Trimmer (Promoter of Sunday schools, 1741–1810)

Thomas Wolsey [Cardinal] (Statesman during reign of Henry VIII, c.1475–1530)

IRONBRIDGE Shropshire

Jonathan Barlow (TV actor [*Casualty, Coronation Street*], 1956–)

IRONSIDE Aberdeenshire

William Edmund Ironside [1st Baron] (Commander of British Home Forces during invasion scare 1940, 1880–1959)

IRVINE Ayrshire

Harry Eckford (Designer of early steamships, 1775–1832)

John Galt (Novelist [*Annals of the Parish*], 1779–1839)

Agnes Smith Lewis (Biblical scholar, discovered old Syriac Gospel Manuscripts, 1843–1926)

James Montgomery (Poet twice imprisoned for libel, 1771–1854)

Agnes Miller Parker (Artist and printmaker, 1895–1980)

ISLAY Argyllshire

John Francis Campbell (Folklorist, wrote

Popular Tales of the West Highlands, 1822–1885)

John Crawfurd (Oriental scholar, wrote *History of the Indian Archipelago*, 1783–1868)

ISLIP Oxfordshire

Edward The Confessor [King of England] (c.1003–1066)

Simon Islip (Archbishop of Canterbury [1349–66], d.1366)

JEDBURGH Roxburghshire

Sir David Brewster (Optical scientist [perfected theory of lighthouse illumination], and inventor [the kaleidoscope], 1781–1868)

Mary Greig Somerville [b.Fairfax] (Self-taught mathematician after whom an Oxford college is named, 1780–1872)

JOHNSTONE Renfrewshire

Renée Houston [b.Katerina Gribbin] (Actor, of more than 40 films, 1902–1980)

Sir George Houstoun Reid (Australian statesman, 1845–1918)

JUNIPER HILL Oxfordshire

Flora June Thompson [b.Timms] (Rural historian, wrote trilogy *Lark Rise to Candleford*, 1876–1947)

KAMES Berwickshire

Henry Home Kames [Lord] (Philosopher and legal historian, 1696–1782)

KEADY County Armagh

Tommy Makem (Folksinger, often sang with the Clancy Brothers, 1932–)

KEDLESTON HALL Derbyshire

George Nathaniel Curzon [Marquis] (Viceroy of India [1898–1905], Foreign Secretary [1919–24], 1859–1925)

KEIG Aberdeenshire

William Robertson Smith (Theologian and Arabic scholar, 1846–1894)

KEIGHLEY Yorkshire

Gordon Bottomley (Poet and playwright [*King Lear's Wife*], 1874–1948)

John Rupert Firth (Linguistic scholar, wrote *The Tongues of Men*, 1890–1960)

KEINTON-MANDEVILLE Somerset

Sir Henry Irving [b.John Henry Brodribb] (First actor to be knighted, 1838–1905)

KEITH Banffshire

James Gordon Bennett (US-based newspaper editor, created *New York Herald*, 1795–1872)

Colin Hendry (International footballer, 1965–)

KELSO Roxburghshire

James (1772–1833) and John Ballantyne (1774–1821) (Brothers in printing partnership with Sir Walter Scott, whose work they published).

Sir James Brunlees (Designer of bridges [Solway Viaduct] and piers [including those at Southend and Southport], 1816–1892)

Sir William Fairbairn (Engineer, built hundreds of locomotives and boats, 1789–1874)

KELSTON Near Bath

Sir John Harington (Author and satirist, designed early water closet, 1561–1612)

KELVEDON Essex

Charles Haddon Spurgeon (Preacher, wrote 50 volumes of sermons, 1834–1892)

KENDAL Cumbria

Ephraim Chambers (Pioneering encyclopaedist, c.1680–1740)

Sir Arthur Stanley Eddington (Astronomer, specialised in stellar observations, and wrote popularising books on subject, 1882–1944)

William Hudson (First British botanist to adopt Linnean classification [in *Flora Anglica*], 1734–1793)

KENILWORTH Warwickshire

John Bird Sumner (Archbishop of Canterbury [1848–62], 1780–1862)

KENLEY Shropshire

Sir Archibald Alison (Historian, wrote *History of Europe* over a 26-year period, 1792–1867)

William Farr (Statistician, served Registrar-General's Office for over 50 years, 1807–1883)

KENNOWAY Fife

George Lillie Craik (Literary scholar [*The Pictorial History of England*], 1798–1866)

KESWICK Cumbria

Sara Coleridge (Writer and scholar, edited works of her father Samuel Coleridge-Taylor, possibly to the detriment of her own career, 1902–1952)

Robley Dunglison (US-based physician, 1798–1869)

Eliza Lynn Linton [b.Lynn] (Novelist [*Joshua Davidson*] who opposed female enfranchisement, 1822–1898)

Frederic William Myers (Poet and psychic researcher, 1843–1901)

KETTERING Northamptonshire

Sir Alfred East (Artist noted for his Japanese landscapes, 1849–1913)

Henry Nettleship (Classical scholar, 1839–1893)

Roy [Royston] Wilson (Comic strip artist, mainly for children's publications, 1900–1965)

KIBWORTH-HARCOURT Leicestershire
Anna Laetitia Barbauld [b.Aikin] (Children's
author [*Early Lessons for Children*],
1743-1825)

KIDDERMINSTER Hereford & Worcester
Edward Bradley (Author [*Adventures of Mr
Verdant Green*], 1827-1889)
Sir Rowland Hill (Post Office moderniser,
1795-1879)
Sir Josiah Mason (Industrialist [making
pens] and philanthropist, 1775-1881)
Sir Walter Nash (New Zealand Prime
Minister [1957-60], 1882-1968)

KILGRASTON Perthshire
Sir James Hope Grant (Military commander,
introduced war games and lectures into
military education, 1808-1875)

KILLEARN Stirlingshire
Colin Blackburn [Lord] (Judge,
1813-1896)
George Buchanan (Scholar, survived
Inquisition to become tutor to James VI,
c.1506-1582)

KILLYCLOGHER County Tyrone
Brian Friel (Playwright [*Dancing at
Lughnasa*], 1929-)

KILLYLEAGH County Down
Sir Hans Sloane (Naturalist and physician,
whose collections formed core of the
British Museum, 1660-1753)

KILMANY Fife
Jim Clark (World champion racing driver [in
1963 and 1965], killed in practice,
1936-1968)

KILMARNOCK Ayrshire
Robert Colquhoun (Artist, employed circus
themes, 1914-1962)

Alexander Smith (Poet and author [*Sonnets
on the War*], 1830-1867)
Patrick Stirling (Locomotive engineer,
famed for his 8ft 'Single' for the Great
Northern Railway, 1820-1895)

KILMAURS Ayrshire
John Boyd-Orr (Nobel Prize-winning
nutritionist, 1880-1971)

KILNINVER Argyll
John McLeod Campbell (Theologian, once
regarded as heretical by the Church of
Scotland, 1800-1872)

**KINCARDINE-ON-FORTH
Clackmannanshire**
Sir James Dewar (Scientist, inventor of the
vacuum flask, 1842-1923)

KINCLAVEN Perthshire
Thomas Duncan (Artist who painted
Jacobite themes, 1807-1845)

KINGARTH Bute
John William MacKail (Classical scholar,
translated *The Odyssey*, 1859-1945)

KINGLASSIE Fife
Sir William Reid (Colonial governor and
meteorologist, wrote *An Attempt to
Develop the Law of Storms*, 1791-1858)

KINGSBRIDGE Devon
William Cookworthy (Porcelain
manufacturer, built china factory in
Portsmouth, 1705-1780)
Sir Courtenay Ilbert (Parliamentary
historian, 1841-1924)

KINGSCLIFFE Northamptonshire
William Law (Religious author, tutor to
historian Edward Gibbon, 1686-1761)

KING'S LYNN Norfolk
Fanny Burney (Novelist [*Evelina*] and
diarist, 1752–1840)
Stanley Arthur Cook (Theologian, Professor
of Hebrew at Cambridge, 1873–1949)
George Gordon Coulton (Historian, wrote
Life in the Middle Ages, 1858–1947)
George Vancouver (Explorer, charted the
west coast of North America,
1757–1798)

KINGSMUIR Angus
Alexander Sutherland [A.S.] Neill
(Reforming educationalist, founded
Summerhill School, 1883–1973)

KING'S NORTON Warwickshire
Brian Aherne (Actor, played 'gentleman
cad' parts, 1902–1986)

KING'S SUTTON Northamptonshire
William Lisle Bowles (Romantic poet ['The
Missionary of the Andes'], 1762–1850)

KINGSTON-UPON-HULL see HULL

KINGSTON-ON-THAMES Surrey
Eadweard Muybridge [Edward James
Muggeridge] (Photographic inventor,
conducted pioneering studies to record
motion, 1830–1904)
Robert Cedric Sherriff (Playwright
[*Journey's End*], 1896–1975)

KINGTON Hereford and Worcester
Stephen Kemble (Actor and litigious
theatre manager, 1758–1822)

KINGUSSIE Inverness-shire
John Leslie (Scottish historian,
ecclesiastical adviser to Mary Stewart,
Queen of Scots, 1527–1596)

KINLOCHLEVEN Argyllshire
Sir Ian Kinloch McGregor (Business
manager, headed National Coal Board,
1912–1998)

**KINNAIRD HOUSE Near Larbert,
Stirlingshire**
James Bruce (Explorer whose accounts of
Abyssinia were widely disbelieved
[although true], 1730–1794)

KINNESSWOOD Kinross
Alexander Buchan (Meteorologist,
established cyclic nature of weather
patterns, 1829–1907)

KINNORDY Angus
Sir Charles Lyell (Prominent geologist,
author of *Principles of Geology*,
1797–1875)

KIPLIN North Yorkshire
George Calvert Baltimore [Baron] (Founder
of Maryland, c.1580–1632)

KIRBY MUXLOE Leicestershire
Tina Baker (TV 'showbiz' presenter, 1958–)

KIRBY WISKE Yorkshire
Roger Ascham (Scholar, wrote *The
Scholemaster*, 1515–1568)

KIRKBEAN Kirkcudbrightshire
John Paul Jones (Naval commander,
regarded as founder of US Navy,
1747–1792)

KIRKBY LONSDALE Cumbria
Edward Bickersteth (Theologian, co-founder
of the Parker Society, 1786–1850)

KIRKBYMOORSIDE Yorkshire
Sir Herbert Read (Art historian and critic,
1893–1968)

KIRKCALDY Fife
Robert Adam (Architect [Edinburgh's Register House], 1728–1792)
Henry Balnaves (Reformer, wrote *The Confession of Faith*, 1512–1579)
Sir Thomas Elder (Australian-based agriculturist, 1818–1897)
Marjorie Fleming (Child author [*Pet Marjorie*], 1803–1811)
Sir Sandford Fleming (Builder of Canadian railways, 1827–1915)
George Gillespie (Clergyman who opposed Episcopalianism, 1613–1648)
Adam Smith (Economist who wrote *Wealth of Nations*, 1723–1790)

KIRKCONNEL Dumfriesshire
James Hyslop (Shepherd poet, later a teacher, 1798–1827)

KIRKHAM Lancashire
Sir Vincent Wigglesworth (Experimental entomologist, 1899–1994)

KIRKHARLE Northumberland
Lancelot ['Capability'] Brown (Landscape gardener, 1716–1783)

KIRKHEATON Yorkshire
Wilfred Rhodes (World's oldest Test cricketer, played for England in his 53rd year, 1877–1973)

KIRKINTILLOCH Dunbartonshire
Archibald Scott Couper (Organic chemist whose research was originally ignored, 1831–1892)

KIRKPATRICK-FLEMING Dumfriesshire
James Currie (Controversial biographer of Burns, 1756–1805)

KIRKWALL Orkney
William Balfour Baikie (Explorer and founder of colony on the river Niger, 1825–1864)
Sir Robert Strange (Jacobite engraver, 1721–1792)

KIRRIEMUIR Angus
Sir James Barrie (Playwright, creator of 'Peter Pan', 1860–1937)

KNARESBOROUGH Yorkshire
Mother Shipton (Alleged witch, 1488–c.1560)
William Stubbs (Ecclesiastical historian, wrote *Constitutional History of England*, 1825–1901)

KNOLE Kent
Sir William Waller (Civil War commander for Parliamentarians, imprisoned for suspected Royalist sympathies, c.1598–1688)

KNOWLE Warwickshire
John Wyndham [John Wyndham Harris] (Science-fiction author, [*The Day of the Triffids*], 1903–1969)

KNOWSLEY HALL Lancashire
Edward Geoffrey Derby [14th Earl] (Three times Prime Minister, 1799–1869)
Edward Henry Derby [15th Earl] (Politician, twice Foreign Secretary, 1826–1893)

LADYKIRK Berwickshire
George Ridpath (Historian whose *Border History of England and Scotland* was published four years after his death, c.1717–1772)

LALEHAM Middlesex
Matthew Arnold (Poet ['Dover Beach'], 1822–1888)

LANCASTER
Sir John Ambrose (Physicist, 1849–1945)

John Langsham Austin (Philosopher, wrote *Sense and Sensibilia*, 1911–1960)

Laurence Binyon (Poet, elegy 'For the Fallen' to remember war dead, 1869–1943)

Henry Cort (Ironmaster, ruined in business but pensioned in recognition of naval service, 1740–1800)

Sir Richard Owen (Zoologist, coined the word 'dinosaur', 1804–1892)

Sir Albert Charles Seward (Palaeobotanist, wrote *Jurassic Flora*, 1863–1941)

William Whewell (Polymath scholar, Vice-Chancellor of Cambridge, 1794–1866)

LANEAST Cornwall

John Couch Adams (Astronomer, calculated existence of Neptune, 1819–1892)

LANGAR Nottinghamshire

Samuel Butler (Artist and author of *Way of All Flesh*, 1835–1902)

LANGHAM Leicestershire

Simon Langham [Cardinal] (Archbishop of Canterbury [1366–76], d.1376)

LANGLEY Near Macclesfield

Charles Frederick Tunnicliffe (Ornithological artist, 1901–1979)

LANGHOLM Dumfriesshire

Hugh McDiarmid [Christopher Grieve] (Poet ['A Drunk Man Looks at the Thistle'], 1892–1978)

William Julius Mickle (Poet ['Cumnor Hall'], 1735–1788)

LANGPORT Somerset

Walter Bagehot (Constitutional historian, argued for introduction of life peers, 1826–1877)

LAPWORTH Warwickshire

Robert Catesby (Gunpowder plotter, 1573–1605)

LARGO Fife

Sir John Leslie (Physicist, invented numerous laboratory instruments, including pyrometer, and created first artificial ice, 1766–1832)

Alexander Selkirk (Sailor original of 'Robinson Crusoe', 1676–1721)

Sir Andrew Wood (Leading commander in Scottish navy, c.1455–1539)

LARGS Ayrshire

Sir Thomas Makdougall Brisbane (Colonial adminstrator for whom Brisbane is named, also astronomer, 1773–1860)

LASSWADE Midlothian

Archibald Thorburn (Ornithological artist whose work is still being reproduced in modern bird books, 1860–1935)

LAUGHARNE Dyfed

Reginald Pecock (Theologian [*Book of Faith*], c.1395–1460)

LAURENCEKIRK Kincardineshire

James Beattie (Poet and minstrel, 1735–1803)

LAXFIELD Suffolk

William Dowsing (Puritan iconoclast active in Suffolk and Cambridgeshire, c.1576–1679)

LEADHILLS Lanarkshire

Allan Ramsay (Poet and playwright, wrote *The Gentle Shepherd*, c.1685–1758)

William Symington (Pioneering steamboat builder, also patented road locomotive, 1763–1831)

**LEAMINGTON (Royal Leamington Spa)
Warwickshire**

Ethel Anderson (Author [*The Little Ghosts*], 1883–1958)

Ernest Belfort Bax (Co-founder of Socialist League, 1854–1926)

Dennis Joseph Enright (Novelist and poet, 1920–)

Terry Frost (Artist, specialises in abstract works, 1915–)

Sir John Richard Hicks (Nobel Prize-winning economist, 1904–1989)

Robert Wilfred Simpson (Composer and musicologist, specialises in atonal composition, 1921–)

Randolph Turpin (World middleweight boxing champion for just 64 days after beating Sugar Ray Robinson, 1925–1966)

**LEAMINGTON HASTINGS Near Royal
Leamington Spa, Warwickshire**

Sir Bernard Henry Spilsbury (Crown pathologist involved in the Crippen trial, 1877–1947)

LEATHERHEAD Surrey

Sir John Thomas Duckworth (Naval commander who captured Caribbean colonies from Sweden and Denmark, 1748–1817)

Susan Howatch (Novelist [*Penmarric*], 1940–)

LEDBURY Hereford and Worcester

Henry Scott Holland (Theologian, Canon of St Paul's, 1847–1918)

John Edward Masefield (Poet Laureate [1930–67] ['Sea Fever'], 1878–1967)

LEEDS see also AUSTHORPE

Henry Hinchcliffe Ainley (Actor, specialised in Shakespearean roles, 1879–1945)

Kenneth Armitage (Sculptor, uses semi-abstract figures united into groups by stylised clothing, 1916–)

Joseph Aspdin (Inventor, patented Portland cement, 1779–1855)

Alfred Austin (Controversial appointment as Poet Laureate [1896–1923], 1835–1913)

David Batty (International footballer [Leeds United and England], 1968–)

Alan Bennett (Author and playwright [*Forty Years On, The Madness of George III*], 1934–)

Robert Blackburn (Aircraft designer and founder of aerospace company, 1885–1955)

Barbara Taylor Bradford (Novelist [*A Woman of Substance*], 1933–)

Frank Dunlop (Stage director and administrator [Edinburgh Festival 1983–91], 1927–)

Arthur Greenwood (Politician, became Lord Privy Seal, 1880–1954)

Michael Alexander Kirkwood Halliday (Language scholar [*Breakthrough to Literacy*], 1925–)

Tony Harrison (Poet who takes contemporary problems for his themes, 1937–)

Sir John Hawkshaw (Engineer, built Charing Cross station and bridge, and the Amsterdam Ship Canal, 1811–1891)

Patrick Heron (Artist and textile designer, 1920–1999)

Sir Henry Stuart Jones (Classical scholar, worked on a Greek-English lexicon, 1867–1939)

Stuart McCall (International footballer [Bradford City and Scotland], 1964–)

Dame Anne Loughlin (Trade union leader and first woman President of the TUC, 1894–1979)

Simon Marks [Baron] (Co-founder of Marks & Spencer, 1888–1964)

Sir Nevill Francis Mott (Nobel Prize-winning physicist, 1905–1996)

Richard Oastler (Factory welfare reformer

who campaigned against industrial exploitation of children but was imprisoned for debt, 1789–1861)

Jeremy Paxman (TV journalist [*Newsnight*] and author [*The English*], 1950–)

Gordon [Douglas Alastair] Pirie (Athlete, former world record holder at 3,000 and 5,000 metre distances, 1931–)

Joseph Priestley (Chemist and ecclesiastic, 1733–1804)

Bryan Waller Procter [Barry Cornwall] (Barrister and poet ['Mirandola'], 1787–1874)

Arthur Mitchell Ransome (Author of *Swallows and Amazons*, 1884–1967)

Sheila Rowbotham (Social historian, wrote *Women, Resistance, and Revolution*, 1943–)

Baroness Sue Ryder (Philanthropist, concerned with refugee welfare, 1923–)

Sir Jimmy [James Wilson Vincent] Savile (Broadcaster, 1926–)

Arthur Scargill (Miners' union leader, 1938–)

Percy Alfred Scholes (Musicologist, edited *Oxford Companion to Music*, 1877–1958)

John Sheepshanks (Art enthusiast who left his collection of British Masters to the nation, 1787–1863)

Samuel Sugden (Chemist, worked on military applications of his science, 1892–1950)

Keith Spencer Waterhouse (Novelist creator of 'Billy Liar', 1929–)

LEEK Staffordshire

Elizabeth Wardle (Embroiderer, founded Leek Embroidery Society, 1834–1902)

LEICESTER

Henry Walter Bates (Naturalist, brought back 8,000 insect specimens from the Amazon Basin, 1825–1892)

Christopher Bruce (Dancer and choreographer working in both UK and US, 1945–)

Deryck Victor Cooke (Musical author, 1919–1976)

Thomas Cooper (Chartist poet, completed Mahler's 10th Symphony, 1805–1892)

Richard Farmer (Author and ecclesiastic, twice Vice-Chancellor of Cambridge, 1735–1797)

Ernest William Gimson (Architect and furniture designer who preferred to use untreated native timbers, 1864–1919)

Emile Heskey (International footballer [Liverpool and England], 1978–)

William Inman (Ship owner, began weekly sailing to New York in 1860, 1825–1881)

Henry Woodd Nevinson (Campaigning journalist & war correspondent, 1856–1941)

Joe [John Kingsley] Orton (Playwright, wrote *Loot* and *Entertaining Mr Sloan*, 1933–1967)

Peter Shilton (Goalkeeper with record number of England caps, 1949–)

Charles Percy Snow (Novelist [*Corridors of Power*] and scientist, 1905–1980)

Sue Townsend (Author, creator of 'Adrian Mole', 1946–)

Colin Henry Wilson (Author of occult books and novels, 1931–)

LEIGH Lancashire

James Hilton (Novelist, author of *Lost Horizon* and *Goodbye Mr Chips*, 1900–1954)

Ronald Charles Irani (Test cricketer [Lancashire, Essex, and England], 1971–)

LEIGH-ON-SEA Essex

John Fowles (Novelist, author of *The Collector* and *The French Lieutenant's Woman*, 1926–)

LEIGHTON Shropshire
Mary Gladys Webb [b.Meredith] (Novelist [*Precious Bane*], 1881-1927)

LEIGHTON BUZZARD Bedfordshire
Mary Norton [b.Pearson] (Children's novelist, created 'The Borrowers', 1903-1992)

LELANT Cornwall
Rosamunde Pilcher (Novelist [*The Shell Seekers*], 1924-)

LENHAM Kent
Hugh Christopher Longuett-Higgins (Chemist and neurophysicist, researching music perception and mechanics of language, 1923-)

LENNOXLOVE East Lothian
John Maitland [Duke of Lauderdale] (Statesman, imprisoned for nine years for his religious beliefs, became the 'L' of the first Cabal, 1616-1682)

LEOMINSTER Hereford and Worcester
Sir George Newman (Pioneering medical officer, raised health standards in schools, 1870-1948)

LERWICK Shetland
Sir Herbert John Grierson (Poetic scholar [*Milton and Wordsworth*], 1866-1960)

LEVENS Cumbria
Harold Stabler (Designer who worked in ceramics, enamels and jewellery, 1872-1945)

LEWES Sussex
George Baxter (Engraver, patented colour printing process, 1804-1867)
Richard Challoner (Religious author [*The Garden of the Soul*], 1691-1718)

Gideon Algernon Mantell (Palaeontologist, introduced idea of a prehistoric 'Age of Reptiles', 1790-1852)

LICHFIELD Staffordshire
Elias Ashmole (Antiquarian whose benevolence to Oxford University created the Ashmolean Museum, 1617-1692)
Richard Garnett (Author and biographer of Shelley, Carlyle and Dryden, 1835-1906)
Samuel Johnson [Dr Johnson] (Author and lexicographer [*Dictionary of the English Language*], 1709-1784)

LIDGATE Suffolk
John Lydgate (Poetic monk, wrote 'The Siege of Thebes', 'The Fall of Princes', c.1370-1451)

LIMAVADY County Londonderry
William Ferguson Massey (Prime Minister of New Zealand [1912-25], 1856-1925)

LIMEKILNS Fife
George Thomson (Folklorist whose works were set to music by Haydn and Beethoven, 1757-1851)

LIMPSFIELD Surrey
Graham Anthony [Tony] Lock (Test cricketer for Surrey and England, 1929-1995)

LINCOLN
George Boole (Mathematician after whom Boolean symbolic logic is named, 1815-1864)
William Byrd (Cathedral organist who became one of England's finest composers of ecclesiastical music, 1543-1623)
Penelope Mary Fitzgerald (Biographer who wrote Booker Prize-winning novel [*Offshore*], 1916-)
William Fulbecke (Legal textbook author, 1560-c.1603)

Sir Neville Marriner (Orchestral conductor, 1924–)

Foster Watson (Educational historian [*The English Grammar Schools to 1660*], 1860–1929)

LINDFIELD Sussex

Sir Charles Blake Cochran (Theatrical impresario, produced *Bless the Bride* for nearly 900 performances, 1872–1951)

Philip Henslowe (Theatre manager in Shakespeare's time, c.1550–1616)

LINLITHGOW West Lothian

James V [King of Scotland] (Father of Mary, died after defeat at Solway Moss, 1512–1542)

Mary Stewart [Queen of Scots] (Executed in England on the order of Queen Elizabeth I, 1542–1587)

Sir Charles Wyville-Thomson (Marine scientist, led Challenger Expedition to survey world's oceans, 1830–1882)

LISSANOURE Near Belfast

George Macartney [1st Earl] (Statesman, ambassador to China and Governor of Cape of Good Hope, 1737–1806)

LITTLE BARFORD Bedfordshire

Nicholas Rowe (Playwright [*Tamarlane*] and Poet Laureate from 1715, 1674–1718)

Mabel Alington Royds (Artist and printmaker, 1874–1941)

LITTLE BERKHAMSTED Hertfordshire

Thomas Ken (Bishop of Bath and Wells who was imprisoned for his principles, 1631–1711)

LITTLE DUCHRAE Dumfriesshire

Samuel Rutherford Crockett (Minister who retired from clergy to write full-time [*The Rivals*], 1859–1914)

LITTLE HADHAM Hertfordshire

Hannah Bolton Barlow (Ceramic decorator, enhanced Doulton pottery, c.1870–1913)

LITTLE MISSENDEN Buckinghamshire

Herbert Austin [Baron] (Motor manufacturer who produced Wolseley and 'Baby' Austin 7 car designs, 1866–1941)

LITTLE WHITEFIELD Near Coupar Angus, Perthshire

James Croll (Physicist, researched landscape effect on weather, 1821–1890)

LITTLEHAM-CUM-EXMOUTH Devon

Jesse Collings (Politician, promoted ideas of smallholdings and allotments for those unable to own gardens or farms, 1831–1920)

LIVERPOOL *(See also WALLASEY)*

Jean Alexander (TV actor, best known as 'Hilda Ogden' in *Coronation Street*, 1925–)

Arthur Askey (Comedian renowned in the age of radio, 1900–1982)

Sir John Aspinall (Locomotive engineer, [Lancashire & Yorkshire Railway], 1851–1937)

Dame Beryl Margaret Bainbridge (Novelist, author of *An Awfully Big Adventure*, 1934–)

Joan Benesh (Choreographer, created dance notation system [Choreology], 1920–)

Augustine Birrell (Politician, Secretary for Ireland who resigned following Easter Rising of 1916, 1850–1933)

John Birt [Baron] (Broadcasting executive, BBC Director-General [1993–8], 1944–)

Cilla Black (Singer and TV compère, originally Priscilla White, 1943–)

Alan Bleasdale (Author of *Boys from the Blackstuff*, 1946–)

Charles Booth (Ship owner and social reformer, wrote *Life and Labour of the People in London* [in 17 volumes], 1840–1916)

Bessie Braddock [b.Bamber] (Politician famed for her outspokenness, 1899–1970)

Sir John Tomlinson Brunner (Industrial chemist who was Pro-Chancellor of Liverpool University for nine years, 1842–1919)

Craig Charles (TV actor [*Red Dwarf*] and presenter, 1964–)

Anne Jemima Clough (Educationalist, campaigned for higher education for women, 1820–1892)

Arthur Hugh Clough (Poet whose best work 'Say Not the Struggle Not Availeth' was published posthumously, 1819–1861)

William Gershom Collingwood (Artist and archaeologist, expert on Vikings, 1854–1932)

Elvis Costello (Singer-songwriter [*Watching the Detectives*], 1955–)

Walter Crane (Artist, leader of the Arts & Crafts Movement, 1845–1915)

Ken Dodd (Comedian, 1929–)

Stephen Dowling (Strip cartoonist, creator of 'Tich' and 'Garth', 1904–1986)

William Earle (Military commander killed in war in Sudan, 1833–1885)

Charles Sutherland Elton (Biologist, author of *Animal Ecology*, 1900–1991)

William Ewart (Politician [an MP for 40 years] and humanitarian reformer [campaigned for abolition of capital punishment for minor offences], 1798–1869)

Sebastian Ziani de Ferranti (Electronics inventor, established Ferranti company in 1905, 1864–1930)

Sir [Samuel] Luke Fildes (Artist, painted state portraits of royal family, 1844–1927)

Frederic Franklin (Dancer with companies in Monte Carlo and US, 1914–)

William Ewart Gladstone (Four times Prime Minister, 1809–1898)

Sir Richard Tetley Glazebrook (Physicist, first Director of National Physical Laboratory [1899–1919], 1854–1935)

Leon Goossens (Orchestral oboist who turned to teaching, 1897–1988)

Tommy Handley (Radio entertainer, [*It's That Man again*], 1892–1949)

George Harrison (Beatles singer-guitarist, later film producer, 1943–2002)

Sir Rex [Reginald Carey] Harrison (Actor, starred in *My Fair Lady*, 1908–1990)

John Liptrot Hatton (Composer of 300 songs, operas [*Rose*] and cantatas [*Robin Hood*], 1809–1886)

Felicia Hemans [b.Browne] (Poet ['The Boy Stood on the Burning Deck'], 1793–1835)

Frank Hornby (Toy and model manufacturer [Meccano, Dinky Toys etc], 1863–1936)

Jeremiah Horrocks (Astronomer, made first recorded observation of the Transit of Venus, 1619–1641)

George Holbrook Jackson (Literary historian, wrote *On Art and Socialism*, 1874–1948)

William Stanley Jevons (Economist, wrote *Pure Logic* and *Theory of Political Economy*, 1835–1882)

Jack [James Larkin] Jones (Trade union leader, 1913–1993)

Lynda La Plante (Writer [TV series *Prime Suspect*], 1946–)

James Larkin (Irish-based labour leader, 1876–1947)

Sir John Knox Laughton (Naval historian, founded Navy Records Society, 1830–1915)

James Laver (Art author, wrote history of English costume *Taste and Fashion*, 1899–1975)

Richard Le Gallienne (Poet and author [*Quest of the Golden Girl*], 1866–1947)

John Lennon (Beatles singer-guitarist/songwriter, murdered by stalker in New York City, 1940–1980)

Sir James Paul McCartney (Beatles singer and composer, 1942–)

John Milne (Seismologist, inventor of the seismograph, 1859–1913)

Nicholas John Turney Monsarrat (Novelist [*The Cruel Sea*], 1910–1979)

Robert Morris (American revolutionary leader and founder of the Bank of North America, 1734–1806)

Ernest Newman (Music critic and author of studies of Wagner, 1868–1959)

Mary Winifred Parke (Botanist, specialist on algae, 1908–1989)

John Bede Polding (Australian-based ecclesiastic, Archbishop of Sydney [1842–77], 1794–1877)

Sir Simon Rattle (Orchestral conductor [Birmingham and Berlin], 1955–)

Eleanor Florence Rathbone (Feminist MP who advocated family allowances, wrote *The Disinherited Family*, 1872–1946)

James Renwick (US-based physicist, wrote *Outlines of Natural Philosophy*, 1790–1863)

William Roscoe (Historian who was declared bankrupt and took to writing children's stories [*The Butterfly's Ball and Grasshopper's Feast*], 1753–1831)

Leonard Rossiter (Actor, played 'Rigsby' in *Rising Damp*, 1926–1984)

Agnes Maude Royden (Social worker and feminist, wrote *Woman and the Sovereign State*, 1876–1956)

William [Willy] Henry Russell (Playwright [*Educating Rita, Blood Brothers*], 1947–)

Herbert Louis Samuel [1st Viscount] (Statesman, twice appointed Home Secretary, 1870–1963)

Sir Charles Santley (Operatic baritone, sang in first UK production of *Faust*, 1834–1922)

John Selwyn-Lloyd [Baron] (Statesman who served as Foreign Secretary and Chancellor of the Exchequer, 1904–1978)

Peter Shaffer (Playwright [*Equus, Amadeus*], 1926–)

Edward Askew Sothern (Actor, described by DNB as receiving 'slender encouragement', 1826–1881)

Kate [Catherine Wilson] Sheppard [b.Malcolm] (New Zealand-based feminist who campaigned successfully for female enfranchisement, 1848–1943)

Ringo Starr [b.Richard Starkey] (Beatles drummer and singer, 1940–)

George Stubbs (Artist, specialised in animal studies, wrote *The Anatomy of the Horse*, 1724–1806)

Sir Banastre Tarleton (Military commander in American colonies, 1754–1833)

Brandon Thomas (Actor-playwright [*Charley's Aunt*], 1849–1914)

Bill [William Edward] Tidy (Cartoonist [*The Fosdyke Saga*], 1933–)

Steve Tilston (Folk singer and guitarist, 1950–)

Frankie [b.Frank Abelson] Vaughan (Singer and entertainer [*The Garden of Eden, The Green Door*], 1928–1999)

Alfred Waterhouse (Architect, designed London's Natural History Museum, 1830–1905)

Colin Welland (Actor and playwright, scripted *Chariots of Fire*, 1934–)

Frederick James Woolton [1st Baron] (Wartime Minister of Food, 1883–1964)

Sir Charles Wyndham (Actor and theatre manager, who enlisted as a surgeon on the Union side in the American Civil War, 1837–1919)

LLANARMON Gwynedd

John Owen (Epigrammatic poet, popular on the Continent, c.1560–1622)

LLANCARFAN South Glamorgan
Edward Williams (Poet, published
supposedly 14th century poetry which
was in fact his own, 1747–1826)

LLANDAFF South Glamorgan
Roald Dahl (Author of children's books
[*Charlie and the Chocolate Factory*] and
stories for adults, 1916–1990)

LLANDINAM Powys
David Davies (Industrialist and politician,
built Barry Docks, 1818–1890)
David Davies [1st Baron] (Philanthropist,
founded New Commonwealth Society,
1880–1944)

LLANDOGO Gwent
Edmee Dashwood [E.M. Delafield] (Novelist
[*Diary of a Provincial Lady*], 1890–1943)

LLANDUDNO Gwynedd
William Morris Hughes (Australian-based
statesman, 1864–1952)
Hywel David Lewis (Religious philosopher,
author of *The Elusive Mind*, 1910–1992)

LLANELLI Dyfed
John Graham Chambers (Athletics and
boxing administrator, helped compile
Queensberry Rules, 1843–1883)
Donald Swann (Popular song composer [*I'm
a Gnu*], 1923–1994)

LLANFIHANGEL-AR-ARTH Dyfed
Caradoc [David] Evans (Poet, attacked Welsh
culture in his writings, 1878–1945)

LLANFYLLIN Powys
Clement Edward Davies (Politician, led
Liberal Party [1945–56], 1884–1962)

LLANFYNYDD Dyfed
John Dyer (Poet and artist ['Grongar Hill'],
1699–1757)

LLANRUMNEY South Glamorgan
Sir Henry Morgan (Buccaneer who was
knighted and became Governor of
Jamaica, c.1635–1688)

LOCHEARNHEAD Perthshire
Jane Findlater (Novelist [*A Daughter of
Strife*] and co-author of *Crossrigs*,
1866–1946)
Mary Findlater (Novelist [*Betty Musgrave*]
and co-author of *Crossrigs*, 1865–1963)

LOCHGELLY Fife
Jennie Lee [Baroness] (UK's first Arts
minister and instrumental in creating the
Open University, 1904–1988)

LOCHRUTTON Dumfriesshire
Henry Duncan (Minister of Ruthwell parish
for 48 years, where he established the
world's first savings bank, 1774–1846)

LOCHWINNOCH Renfrewshire
Robert Barr Smith (Australian-based wool
merchant, 1824–1915)

LOGIE PERT Angus
James Mill (Philosopher, wrote *Analysis of
the Phenomenon of the Human Mind*, and
historian [*History of British India*],
1773–1836)

LOGIERAIT Perthshire
Adam Ferguson (Philosopher, wrote
Principles of Moral and Political Science,
1723–1816)
Alexander MacKenzie (First Liberal Prime
Minister of Canada [1873–8],
1822–1892)

LONDON

(See also PINNER, RICHMOND [Surrey] and TEDDINGTON)

John Abernethy (Eccentric surgeon, 1764–1831)

Joss Ackland (Actor [*White Mischief*], 1928–)

Peter Ackroyd (Novelist and biographer [*Hawksmoor, London – the Biography*], 1949–)

Richard Addinsell (Film-music composer [*Warsaw Concerto* from *Dangerous Moonlight*], 1904–1977)

Edgar Adrian [Baron] (Physiologist, 1889–1977)

Anna Airy (Painter, wrote *The Art of Pastel*, 1882–1964)

John Alcott (Cinematographer, worked with Stanley Kubrick, 1931–1986)

Eric Ambler (Novelist, pioneer of spy genre, 1909–1998)

Michael Anderson (Film director, [*The Dam Busters*], 1920–)

Henry William Paget, [1st Marquis of Anglesey] (Soldier, lost a leg when commanding cavalry at the Battle of Waterloo, 1768–1854)

Agnes Arber [b.Robertson] (Author of 84 papers on botany, 1879–1960)

George Arliss (Oscar-winning actor [*Disraeli*], 1868–1946)

Edward Armitage (Artist, decorated House of Lords, 1817–1896)

Henry Armstrong (Chemist, reformed teaching of advanced science, 1848–1937)

Charles Robert Ashbee (Architect and designer, 1863–1942)

Sir Eric Ashby (Botanist, chaired Royal Commission on Environmental Pollution, 1904–1992)

Daisy Ashford (Children's author, wrote *The Young Visitors* aged nine, 1881–1972)

Winifred Ashton (Dramatist and novelist best known as Clemence Dane, 1888–1965)

Anthony Asquith (Film director, [*The Winslow Boy, The V.I.P.s*], 1902–1968)

Sir Michael Atiyah (Mathematician, author of *Geometry and Science of Knots*, 1929–)

Sir David Attenborough (Naturalist and broadcaster, [*Zoo Quest, Life on Earth*], 1926–)

Clement Attlee (Prime Minister [1945–51], 1883–1967)

Sir Alfred Ayer (Philosopher, Oxford professor of logic [1959–78], 1910–1989)

Michael Ayrton (Artist and novelist [*The Midas Consequence*], 1920–1975)

William Edward Ayrton (Co-invented electric tricycle, 1847–1908)

Charles Babbage (Designer of calculating machines and science critic [*Decline of Science in England*], 1791–1871)

Francis Bacon (Philosopher, 1561–1626)

John Bacon (Sculptor, executed statues in London of Pitt the Elder and Dr Johnson, 1740–1799)

Robert Baden-Powell (Boy Scout founder, 1857–1941)

Sir Douglas Bader (Air ace, subject of the film *Reach for the Sky*, 1910–1982)

William Baffin (Explorer, sought North-West Passage, c.1584–1622)

David Royston Bailey (Fashion and portrait photographer, 1938–)

Edgar Leslie Bainton (Australian-based composer, 1880–1956)

Richard [Douglas James] Baker (Broadcaster, 1925–)

Roy Ward Baker (Film director [*Quatermass and the Pit*], 1916–)

Sir Samuel Baker (Explorer of the upper waters of the Nile, 1821–1893)

Lady Frances Balfour (Suffragist and author, 1858–1931)

Sir Joseph Banks (Botanist, president of the Royal Society for record 41 years, 1744–1820)

Lynne Reid Banks (Author [The L-shaped Room] and playwright, 1929–)

Sir Granville Bantock (Composer [Hebridean Symphony] and Birmingham music professor for 26 years, 1868–1946)

Praise God Barebone (Preacher and parliamentarian, c.1596–1679)

Isaac Barrow (Mathematician who resigned as Cambridge professor to make way for Isaac Newton, 1630–1677)

Sir Charles Barry (Architect of Houses of Parliament, 1795–1860)

Lionel Bart (Composer [Oliver], 1930–1999)

Mollie Batten (Social reformer and campaigner for women priests, 1905–1985)

Nina Bawden [b.Mabey] (Novelist [The Ice House], 1925–)

Lilian Baylis (Theatre manager [Old Vic] and owner [Sadler's Wells], 1874–1937)

Dorothea Beale (Principal of Cheltenham Ladies College for 48 years, 1831–1906)

David Beckham (International footballer [Manchester United and England], 1975–)

Charles Tilstone Beke (Explorer of Biblical lands, 1800–1874)

Anthony Wedgwood Benn (Former politician and Cabinet Minister, 1925–)

Jill Bennett (Actor [Charge of the Light Brigade], 1931–1990)

Sir Samuel Bentham (Inventor and naval moderniser, 1757–1831)

John Peter Berger (Novelist, won 1972 Booker Prize with G, 1926–)

Annie Besant [b.Wood] (Social reformer and champion of Indian independence, 1847–1933)

Rosemary Biggs (Haematologist, researched blood-clotting mechanisms, 1912–)

Sir Henry Rowley Bishop (Composer [Home Sweet Home], 1786–1855)

Patrick Maynard Stuart Blackett (Nobel Prize-winning physicist, 1897–1974)

Sir Arthur Bliss (Composer, appointed Master of the Queen's Musick, 1891–1975)

Catherine Bliss (Educationalist, wrote The Service and Status of Women in the Churches, 1908–1989)

Claire Bloom (Actor, specialised in Shakespearean roles, 1931–)

Enid Blyton (Prolific children's author, created 'Noddy', 1897–1968)

Barbara Bodichon [b.Leigh Smith] (Suffragist, co-founded Girton College at Cambridge, 1827–1891)

Viscount Henry Bolingbroke (Foreign Secretary [1710–14], forced to flee to France because of his Jacobite sympathies, 1678–1751)

Sir Christopher Bonington (Mountaineer, took part in climbs on the Eiger and Mt Everest, 1934–)

Catherine Bramwell Booth (Salvation Army leader, 1883–1987)

Nina Boucicault (Actor, created role of Barrie's 'Peter Pan' in 1904, 1867–1950)

David Bowie [David Robert Jones] (Singer and song-writer, 1947–)

William Boyce (Composer [Hearts of Oak] and Master of the King's Musick, 1711–1779)

Mary Elizabeth Braddon (Wrote 75 novels including Ishmael, 1835–1915)

Dennis Brain (Internationally-acclaimed horn player, 1921–1957)

John Bratby (Artist, associated with 'Kitchen Sink' school, 1928–1992)

Julian Bream (Classical guitarist, 1933–)

Ebenezer Brewer (Compiler of Dictionary of Phrase and Fable, 1810–1897)

Raymond Briggs (Film animator [The Snowman, When the Wind Blows], 1934–)

Anita Brookner (Novelist [Hotel du Lac], 1928–)

Brigid Brophy (Novelist [*Hackenfeller's Ape*] and successful campaigner for Public Lending Right in the UK, 1929–1995)

Herbert Charles Brown (Nobel Prize-winning chemist, 1912–)

Sir Thomas Browne (Polymath, wrote *Religion Medici*, 1605–1682)

George [Beau] Brummell (Dandy, 1778–1840)

William John Burchell (Botanist, collected specimens in South Africa and South America, c.1782–1863)

Angela Georgina Burdett-Coutts (Philanthropist, became the first woman to be made Freeman of the City of London, 1814–1906)

Edward Burges (Architect, reconstructed Cardiff Castle, 1827–1881)

Harry Webster Burnham [1st Viscount] (Statesman, responsible for teachers' pay-scales, 1862–1933)

William Burnside (Mathematician, posed the 'Burnside problem' which went unsolved until 25 years after his death, 1852–1927)

Edward Burra (Artist and ballet designer, 1905–1976)

Montagu Burrows (Historian and co-founder of Keble College, Oxford, 1819–1905)

Sir Cyril Lodowic Burt (Educational psychologist, wrote *The Young Delinquent* and *The Backward Child*, 1883–1971)

Alan Dudley Bush (Composer and pianist, 1900–1995)

Frances Buss (Educationalist, first to describe herself as 'headmistress', 1827–1894)

Max Walter Bygraves (Entertainer, 1922–)

George Gordon Byron [Baron] (Poet ['Childe Harold's Pilgrimage'], 1788–1824)

Sir Julius Caesar (Chancellor of the Exchequer [1606–14] then Master of the Rolls for next 22 years, 1558–1636)

Michael Caine [Maurice Micklewhite] (Actor [*Zulu*, *The Cider House Rules*], 1933–)

Simon Callow (Actor [*A Room With a View*], 1949–)

William Camden (Antiquarian and historian [*Annals of the Reign of Elizabeth to 1588*], 1551–1623)

James Mark Cameron (Journalist and war correspondent, 1911–1985)

John Campbell [2nd Duke of Argyll] (Anti-Jacobite general during 1715 Rebellion, 1678–1743)

Mrs Patrick Campbell [b.Beatrice Stella Tanner] (Actor for whom Shaw created the role of Eliza in *Pygmalion*, 1865–1940)

Charles Canning [1st Earl] (Governor-General in India during Mutiny, 1812–1862)

George Canning (Foreign Secretary and briefly Prime Minister, died in office, 1770–1827)

George Leonard Carey (Archbishop of Canterbury from 1991, 1935–)

Sir Anthony Caro (Metalwork sculptor, 1924–)

John Cassell (Publisher, his firm noted for books on royalty, 1817–1865)

Lynn Russell Chadwick (Sculptor of mobiles and solid metal structures, 1914–)

Sir Charles Chaplin (The leading Hollywood actor of his time, 1889–1977)

Charles II [King of England and Scotland] (1630–1685)

Charles [Prince of Wales] (1948–)

James Hadley Chase [Rene Raymond] (Author of *No Orchids for Miss Blandish*, 1906–1985)

Chris Chataway (Olympic athlete, later a government minister, 1931–)

Geoffrey Chaucer (Poet, c.1343–1400)

Gilbert Keith Chesteron (Creator of detective 'Father Brown', 1874–1936)

Dame Harriette Chick (Nutritionist, researched childhood rickets, 1875-1977)

Erskine Childers (Novelist [*The Riddle of the Sands*] and Irish nationalist executed by the British government, 1870-1922)

Caryl Churchill (Dramatist [*Top Girls*], 1938-)

Randolph Churchill (Author and biographer [of his father Winston and Sir Anthony Eden], 1911-1968)

Susannah Cibber [b.Arne] (Actor and singer with spectacular private life, 1714-1766)

Kenneth Mackenzie Clark [Baron] (Art historian and broadcaster, 1903-1983)

Catherine Clive [b.Raftor] (Comic actor at Drury Lane Theatre, 1711-1785)

Samuel Coleridge-Taylor (Composer [*Hiawatha*] whose colour barred his acceptance as one of Britain's finest, 1875-1912)

Jackie Collins (Writer [*The World is Full of Married Men*], 1937-)

Joan Collins (Film and TV actor, 1933-)

William (Wilkie) Collins (Novelist [*The Woman in White*], 1824-1889)

Denis Compton (Footballer and Test cricketer, 1918-1997)

Fay Compton (Actor, famed as 'Peter Pan' [aged 24], 1894-1978)

Jasper Conran (Fashion designer, 1959-)

Emma Cons (Social reformer, founder of Old Vic theatre, 1838-1912)

Dame Gladys Cooper (Stage actor, also nominated three times for Hollywood Oscars, 1888-1971)

Henry Cooper (Heavyweight boxer who once memorably floored Muhammed Ali, 1934-)

Charles Cornwallis [1st Marquis] (Military commander in America, then Governor-General of India, 1738-1805)

Jessie Couvreur [b.Huybers] (Novelist based in Australia, then Belgium, 1848-1897)

Sir [Richard] Stafford Cripps (Chancellor of the Exchequer [1947-50], noted for his austerity, 1889-1952)

Thomas Cromwell [Earl of Essex] (Statesman, beheaded on order of Henry VIII, c.1485-1540)

Charles Frederick Cross (Co-inventor of nylon, 1855-1935)

George Cruikshank (Caricaturist, illustrated *Oliver Twist* in 1837, 1792-1878)

Nicholas Culpeper (Pharmacopoeia compiler, 1616-1654)

Allan Cunningham (Botanical explorer after whom many Australian tree species are named, 1791-1839)

Peter Cushing (Actor, noted for his roles in horror films [*The Curse of Frankenstein*], 1913-1996)

Sir Henry Dale (Nobel Prize-winning physiologist, 1875-1968)

Zena and Phyllis Dane (Actors, Zena 1887-1975, Phyllis 1890-1975)

John Philip William Dankworth (Jazz musician, performs with song partner and wife, Cleo Laine, 1927-)

Siobhan Davies (Choreographer active in UK and US, 1950-)

Steve Davis (Six times world snooker champion, 1958-)

Emily Davison (Suffragette martyr, trampled to death by King George V's horse in the 1913 Derby, 1872-1913)

Sir Robin Day (Broadcaster, 1923-1999)

Sir Gavin De Beer (Zoologist, director of the Natural History Museum [1950-60] and author of *Introduction to Experimental Embryology*, 1899-1972)

John Dee (Alchemist and astrologer to Mary Tudor, 1527-1608)

Daniel Defoe (Author [*Robinson Crusoe*, *Moll Flanders*] and government spy [in Scotland], 1660-1713)

Len Deighton (Author [*The Ipcress File*], 1929-)

Thomas Dekker (Playwright, wrote *The Honest Whore*, c.1570–1641)

Ethel Mary Dell (Wrote 34 novels, including *The Way of an Eagle*, 1881–1939)

Lady Gertrude Denman [b.Pearson] (Feminist, resigned as Director of the Land Army over its treatment by defence authorities, 1884–1954)

James Radcliffe Derwentwater [3rd Earl] (Jacobite, beheaded at Preston, 1689–1716)

Sir Charles Wentworth Dilke (Politician whose career was ruined by his being named in a divorce, 1843–1911)

John Donne (Poet noted for his *Elegies*, c.1572–1631)

Sir Henry Doulton (Pottery manufacturer, 1820–1897)

Sir Anthony Dowell (Dancer, 1943–)

Terry Downes (World champion middleweight boxer, 1936–)

Richard D'Oyly Carte (Impresario, commissioned operas from Gilbert and Sullivan, 1844–1901)

John Drinkwater (Playwright [*Abraham Lincoln*], 1882–1937)

Dame Daphne du Maurier (Novelist [*Jamaica Inn, Rebecca*], 1907–1989)

John George Durham [Earl] (Politician, drafted the 1832 Parliamentary Reform Bill, 1792–1840)

John Eccles (Composed Coronation music for Queen Anne, c.1650–1735)

Solomon Eccles (Musician who became a Quaker, c.1617–1682)

Amelia Edwards (Egyptologist, wrote *A Thousand Miles Up the Nile*, 1831–1892)

Sir George Edwards (Aircraft designer [of Viscount and Vanguard aircraft], 1908–)

Pierce Egan (Sporting author, established what became *Sporting Life* newspaper, 1772–1849)

Elizabeth I [Queen of England] (1533–1603)

Elizabeth (HM Queen since 1952, 1926–)

John Elliotson (Controversial physician who championed hypnotism for medicinal purposes and pioneered use of the stethoscope, 1791–1868)

Charlotte Elliott (Writer of 150 hymns, 1789–1871)

Denholm Elliott (Character actor [*Defence of the Realm*], 1922–1994)

Rowland Emett (Cartoonist and designer, associated with *Punch* magazine, 1906–1990)

Dame Edith Evans (Actor, famed as Lady Bracknell in *The Importance of Being Earnest*, 1888–1976)

Godfrey Thomas Evans (Test cricketer, played 91 times for England, 1920–)

Sir Richard Fairey (Aeronautical engineer, head of Fairey Aviation Company for 40 years, 1887–1956)

Marianne Faithfull (Singer [*As Tears Go By*], 1946–)

Eleanor Farjeon (Children's author, wrote *The Glass Slipper*, 1881–1965)

John Pascoe Fawkner (Founder of city of Melbourne, 1792–1869)

Peter Finch [George Frederick Ingle Finch] (Actor, won first posthumous Oscar for *Network*, 1916–1977)

Gerald Raphael Finzi (Composer, set poetry by Milton and Wordsworth to music, 1901–1956)

Sir Ronald Aylmer Fisher (Genetic statistician, researched human blood groups, 1890–1962)

Sir Joshua Girling Fitch (Educationalist, 1824–1903)

Michael Flanders (Song lyricist, worked with Donald Swann, 1922–1975)

Ian Lancaster Fleming (Creator of 'James Bond', 1908–1964)

Cyril Daryll Forde (Anthropologist, researched in Africa, Arizona, and New Mexico, 1902–1973)

Edward Morgan [E.M.] Forster (Novelist [*A Passage to India*], 1879-1970)

Bruce Forsyth (Entertainer, 1928-)

Charles James Fox (Three times Foreign Secretary, 1749-1806)

Celia France (Dancer, founded National Ballet of Canada, 1921-)

Rosalind Elsie Franklin (Crystallographer, her work on DNA structure never properly acknowledged, 1920-1958)

Bruce Austin Fraser [Baron] (Naval commander, victor at the Battle of North Cape in 1943, 1888-1981)

Michael Frayn (Playwright [*Noises Off*] and novelist [*A Landing on the Sun*], 1933-)

Sir Ralph Freeman (Designer of Sydney Harbour Bridge, 1880-1950)

Bernard Freyberg [1st Baron] (Soldier, won VC in World War One and commanded New Zealand forces in World War Two, 1889-1963)

Peter Racine Fricker (Composer [oratorio *The Vision of Judgement*], 1920-1990)

Mary Frith (Highwaywoman known as Moll Cutpurse, 1584-1659)

Margery Fry (Penal reformer, 1874-1958)

Christopher Gable (Dancer and actor [principally in Ken Russell films], 1940-1998)

Hugh Gaitskell (Chancellor of the Exchequer [1950-1] and later Leader of the Opposition, 1906-1963)

Elizabeth Cleghorn Gaskell [b.Stevenson] (Novelist [*Cranford*], 1810-1865)

Michael William Gatting (Test Cricketer, captained Middlesex and England, 1957-)

George III [King of Great Britain] (1738-1820)

George IV [King of Great Britain] (1762-1830)

George V [King of Great Britain] (1865-1936)

George Brown [Baron] (Foreign Secretary [1966-8], 1914-1985)

Edward Gibbon (Historian, wrote *The History of the Decline and Fall of the Roman Empire*, 1737-1794)

Stella Gibbons (Novelist [*Cold Comfort Farm*], 1902-1989)

Sir John Gielgud (Actor, 1904-1999)

Maina Gielgud (Dancer and artistic director, 1945-)

Sir William Schwenck Gilbert (Comic opera librettist, worked with Sullivan on Savoy Operettas, 1836-1911)

Carl Ronald Giles (Cartoonist with *Express* newspapers, 1916-1995)

Penelope Gilliatt (Novelist, wrote screenplay for *Sunday, Bloody Sunday*, 1932-1993)

James Gillray (Cartoonist, drew 1,500 caricatures of leading figures, 1757-1815)

James Glaisher (Meteorologist, made balloon flight to height of seven miles, 1809-1903)

Kathleen Godfree (Twice Wimbledon tennis champion, 1896-1992)

Sir Victor Gollancz (Publisher and philanthropist, 1893-1967)

Graham Alan Gooch (Test cricketer, captained Essex and England, 1953-)

Jane Goodall (Primatologist, wrote *The Chimpanzees of Gombe*, 1934-)

Sir Eugene Goossens (Composer and conductor, 1893-1962)

Charles George Gordon (Soldier, killed at Khartoum, 1833-1885)

Noele Gordon (Actor, best known for TV's *Crossroads*, 1922-1985)

Sir Edmund William Gosse (Author and poet, 1845-1928)

Kenneth Henry Grange (Industrial designer [cameras, railway locomotives], 1929-)

Harley Granville-Barker (Actor and playwright [*The Voysey Inheritance*], 1877-1946)

Robert von Ranke Graves (Poet and author of *I Claudius*, 1895-1985)

George Robert Gray (Naturalist, wrote the *Genera of Birds*, 1808–1872)

Thomas Gray (Poet ['Elegy Written in a Country Churchyard'], 1716–1771)

Jimmy Greaves (International footballer, now TV presenter, 1940–)

Lucinda Green [b.Prior-Palmer] (Equestrian, six-times winner of Badminton Horse Trials, 1953–)

Peter Greenaway (Film director [*Draughtsman's Contract*], 1942–)

Joan Greenwood (Actor [*Whisky Galore, Kind Hearts and Coronets*], 1921–1987)

Joyce Grenfell (Actor and humorist, 1910–1979)

Joseph Grimaldi (Clown whose memoirs were edited by Charles Dickens, 1779–1837)

Francis Grose (Antiquarian, 1731–1791)

Sir George Grove (Compiler of dictionary of music, 1820–1900)

Sir Alec Guinness (Actor [*The Ladykillers, Star Wars*], 1914–2000)

Thomas Guy (Philanthropist, founder of Guy's Hospital, c.1644–1724)

Quintin Hailsham [2nd Viscount] (Politician, 1907–2001)

Edmond Halley (Astronomer who correctly predicted the return of the comet named after him, 1656–1742)

Richard Hamilton ('Pop Art' painter, 1922–)

Philip Hardwick (Architect, designed Euston Station and Goldsmith's Hall, 1792–1870)

Lawrence Hargrave (Aeronautical pioneer, designed wings and engines for early aircraft, 1850–1915)

Harold Sydney Harmsworth [Viscount Rothermere] (Newspaper owner, 1868–1940)

Sir Henry Roy Harrod (Economist, 1900–1978)

John Harvard (Early American colonist, bequeathed college which became the university named after him, 1607–1638)

Edward Hawke [1st Baron] (Naval commander, victor at Quiberon Bay, 1705–1781)

Jack [John Edward] Hawkins (Actor [*The Cruel Sea*], 1910–1973)

Sir John Hawkins (Musicologist and editor of Walton's *Compleat Angler*, 1719–1789)

Johnny Haynes (International footballer [Fulham FC and England], 1934–)

Stanley William Hayter (Surrealist artist and printmaker, 1901–1988)

Eliza Haywood [b.Fowler] (Novelist [*The History of Betsy Thoughtless*], c.1693–1756)

Sir Henry Head (Neurologist, 1861–1940)

Sir Ambrose Heal (Furniture designer, 1872–1959)

Samuel Hearne (Explorer of northern Canada and the Arctic, 1745–1792)

Oliver Heaviside (Physicist, predicted discovery of ionosphere, 1850–1925)

Henry VIII [King of England] (1491–1547)

Robert Herrick (Poet, wrote 'Cherry Ripe...', 1591–1674)

Dame Myra Hess (Internationally-acclaimed pianist, 1890–1965)

Georgette Heyer (Historical novelist, author of more than 60 books, 1902–1974)

Eleanor Hibbert (Novelist best known as Victoria Holt, 1906–1993)

Graham Hill (Twice world champion racing driver, 1929–1975)

Octavia Hill (Social reformer, wrote *Homes of the London Poor*, 1838–1912)

Sir Cyril Hinshelwood (Nobel Prize-winning chemist, 1897–1967)

Sir Alfred Joseph Hitchcock (Film director [*The 39 Steps, Psycho*], 1899–1980)

Howard Hodgkin (Artist, winner of 1985 Turner Prize, 1932–)

William Hogarth (Artist ['The Rake's Progress'], 1697–1764)

Quintin Hogg (Philanthropist, founded the Regent Street Polytechnic, 1845–1903)

Thomas Holcroft (Playwright and novelist [*The Road to Ruin*], 1745–1809)

Stanley Holloway (Actor, starred as Eliza's father in *My Fair Lady*, 1890–1982)

Michael de Courcy Holroyd (Biographer noted for his work on Lytton Strachey, 1935–)

Sir Alec Douglas Home [Earl] (Prime Minister [1963–4],1903–1996)

Thomas Hood (Humorous author [*Whims and Oddities*], 1799–1845)

Gerard Manley Hopkins (Poet ['The Wreck of the Deutschland'], 1844–1889)

Annie Elizabeth Horniman (Theatre manager with interests in London, Manchester, and Dublin, 1860–1937)

John Howard (Prison reformer, after whom the League for Penal Reform is named, 1726–1790)

Richard Howe [1st Earl] (Naval commander in French Revolutionary War, 1726–1799)

Sir William Huggins (Astronomer, invented stellar spectroscope, 1824–1910)

Arthur Hughes (Pre-Raphaelite artist, 1830–1915)

James Leigh Hunt (Poet and social historian, 1784–1859)

William Holman Hunt (Artist ['The Light of the World'], 1827–1910)

Stafford Henry Iddesleigh [1st Earl Northcote] (Chancellor of the Exchequer [1874–80], 1818–1887)

William Henry Ireland (Shakespearean forger, 1777–1835)

Sir Derek Jacobi (Actor who starred in TV production of *I Claudius*, 1938–)

William Wymark Jacobs (Short story author who featured mainly nautical subjects, but also wrote *The Monkey's Paw*, 1863–1943)

James VII [of Scotland] and II [of England] (1633–1701)

Gertrude Jekyll (Horticulturist and garden designer, 1843–1932)

Niels Kai Jerne (Nobel Prize-winning immunologist, 1911–1994)

Douglas William Jerrold (Humorist author [*Black-ey'd Susan*], 1803–1857)

Pamela Hansford Johnson (Novelist [*Error of Judgement*], 1912–1981)

Sir Harold Spencer Jones (Astronomer Royal [1933–55], 1890–1960)

Inigo Jones (Architect, introduced Palladian style to England, 1573–1652)

Ben Jonson (Playwright [*Bartholomew Fair*] and Poet Laureate from 1617, 1572–1637)

Boris Karloff [William Henry Pratt] (Actor, played monster in first *Frankenstein* film, 1887–1969)

Edmund Kean (Actor whose career was ruined by adultery, 1789–1833)

John Keats (Poet ['Eve of St Agnes'], 1795–1821)

Fanny Kemble (Actor and playwright [*The Star of Seville*], 1809–1893)

Eric Henri Kennington (Artist and war memorial sculptor, 1888–1960)

Dame Kathleen Kenyon (Archaeologist, wrote *Digging up Jericho*, 1906–1978)

Anna Kingsford [b.Bonus] (Doctor and educationalist, 1846–1888)

Mary Henrietta Kingsley (Travel author who wrote about West Africa and died as a nurse in Boer War, 1862–1900)

Alan Philip Knott (Test cricketer who kept wicket for Kent and England, 1946–)

Thomas Kyd (Playwright [*The Spanish Tragedy*], 1558–1594)

Charles Lamb (Essayist and Shakespeare adaptor, 1775–1834)

Constant Lambert (Composer [*The Rio Grande*], 1905–1951)

Sir Osbert Lancaster (Cartoonist, creator of Maudie Littlehampton in *Daily Express*, 1908–1986)

Frederick William Lanchester (Engineering inventor, built UK's first motor car, 1868–1946)

Sir Edwin Henry Landseer (Animal artist ['Monarch of the Glen'], 1802–1873)

Sir Edwin Ray Lankester (Zoologist, 1847–1929)

Angela Lansbury (Actor [*The Manchurian Candidate*] and star of TV's *Murder She Wrote*, 1925–)

John Latham (Ornithologist, wrote *General History of Birds*, 1740–1837)

Gertrude Lawrence [b.Klasen] (Actor, worked with Noel Coward [*Private Lives*], 1898–1952)

Mary Douglas Leakey [b.Nicol] (Anthropologist, researched in Africa, 1913–1996)

Edward Lear (Humorist, wrote *The Owl and the Pussycat*, 1812–1888)

Thomas Letts (Diary publisher, 1803–1873)

Barnett Levey (First free Jewish settler in Australia, 1798–1837)

Matthew Gregory Lewis (Gothic novelist [*The Monk*], 1775–1818)

John Lilburne (Puritan pamphleteer, c.1614–1657)

George Lillo (Playwright [*Fatal Curiosity*], 1693–1739)

William James Linton (Engraver and printer, 1812–1898)

Joseph Lister [Lord] (Pioneer in antiseptic surgery, 1827–1912)

Joan Littlewood (Stage director [*Oh, What a Lovely War*], 1914–2002)

Margaret Davies Llewellyn [b.Davies] (Feminist, 1861–1944)

Marie Lloyd [b.Matilda Wood] (Actor, remembered for song *My Old Man Said Follow the Van*, 1870–1922)

Sir Andrew Lloyd-Webber (Musical composer [*Cats, Evita*], 1948–)

Thomas Lodge (Playwright [*Rosalynde*] and physician [*Treatise of the Plague*], c.1558–1625)

Ada, Countess of Lovelace, [b.Byron] (Computer pioneer, worked with Charles Babbage, 1815–1852)

Sir John Lubbock [1st Baron Avebury] (Politician responsible for Bank Holidays and scientist [wrote *Prehistoric Times*], 1834–1913)

Ida Lupino (Actor [*High Sierra*] and film director, 1918–1995)

Sir Edwin Landseer Lutyens (Architect, designed Cenotaph in Whitehall and Liverpool Cathedral, 1869–1944)

Elizabeth Lutyens (Operatic composer [*The Quincunx*], 1906–1983)

Dame Vera Lynn [b.Vera Welch] (Inspiring singer, 'Forces Sweetheart' in World War Two, 1919–)

Sir Joseph Lyons (Catering magnate, 1848–1917)

Edward George Lytton [1st Baron] (Novelist [*The Last Days of Pompeii*] and playwright, 1803–1873)

Edward Robert Lytton [1st Earl] (Viceroy of India [1876–80] and poet ['King Poppy'], 1831–1891)

Donald McGill [Fraser Gould] (Humorous postcard designer, 1875–1962)

Arthur Heygate Mackmurdo (Architect, member of the Arts & Crafts movement, 1851–1942)

John Ellis McTaggart (Philosopher [*The Nature of Existence*], 1866–1925)

Joseph Henry Maiden (Botanist in Australia, 1859–1925)

John Major (Prime Minister [1990–7], 1943–)

Sir Max Edgar Mallowan (Archaeologist, married Agatha Christie, 1904–1978)

Wolf Mankowitz (Author and film scriptwriter [*Casino Royale*], 1924–1998)

Ethel Mannin (Author of 40 novels, including *Red Rose*, 1900–1984)

Irene Manton (Botanist, researched plankton, 1904–1988)

Sidnie Milana Manton (Zoologist, researched arthropods [crustacea], 1902–1979)

Countess Constance Markievicz (First woman MP, 1868–1927)

Dame Alicia Markova [Lilian Alicia Marks] (Ballerina, 1910–)

Conrad Martens (Artist on Darwin's voyage round South America, 1801–1878)

Archer John Porter Martin (Nobel Prize-winning biochemist, 1910–)

Mary I [Mary Tudor] (Known as 'Bloody Mary' for her persecution of Protestants, 1516–1558)

Mary II [Queen of Britain and Ireland, wife of William of Orange] (1662–1694)

Mary of Teck [Queen Mary, married to George V] (1867–1953)

Nevil Maskelyne (Astronomer Royal who became a parish rector, 1732–1811)

Alfred Edward Mason (Novelist [At the Villa Rose], 1865–1948)

Tobias Matthay (Pianist and academic, 1858–1945)

Jessie Matthews (Dancer and actor, 1907–1981)

Reginald Maudling (Chancellor of the Exchequer [1962–4], 1917–1979)

Henry Mayhew (Author [London Labour and the London Poor] and co-founder of Punch, 1812–1887)

Sir Algernon Methuen (Publisher, 1856–1924)

Alice Meynell [b.Thompson] (Essayist and poet, 1847–1922)

Bernard Miles [Baron] (Actor and founder of Mermaid Theatre, 1907–1991)

John Stuart Mill (Philosopher and author [A System of Logic], 1806–1873)

Sir Jonathan Wolfe Miller (Doctor, actor [in Beyond the Fringe] and director, 1934–)

Alan Alexander [A.A.] Milne (Creator of 'Winnie the Pooh', 1882–1956)

Richard Monckton Milnes [1st Baron Monckton] (Reforming politician, 1809–1885)

John Milton (Poet who wrote Paradise Lost, 1608–1674)

Warren Mitchell (Actor best known as Alf Garnett, 1926–)

Sir William Molesworth [8th Baronet] (Campaigning politician, succeeded in opening Kew Gardens to public on Sundays, 1810–1855)

Edward Henry Molyneux (Fashion designer, 1891–1974)

Lionel Monckton (Light musical composer [The Country Girl], 1861–1924)

Alexander Monro ['Primus'] (Anatomist, 1697–1767)

Ashley Montagu (Anthropologist, author of UNESCO's Statement of Race, 1905–)

Charles Forbes René de Montalembert (French political author, 1810–1870)

Lady Mary Montagu (Author and traveller, campaigned for smallpox inoculation, 1689–1762)

Bernard Montgomery [Viscount] (Military commander, victor at El Alamein, 1887–1976)

Bobby [Robert] Moore (Footballer who captained England to World Cup victory in 1966, 1941–1995)

George Edward Moore (Philosopher, wrote Principia Ethica, 1873–1958)

Roger George Moore (Former 'James Bond' actor and campaigner for children's charities, 1927–)

Sir Thomas More [Saint] (Lord Chancellor who was executed after defying Henry VIII, 1478–1535)

George Morland (Artist, exhibited at Royal Academy aged 10, 1763–1804)

Henry Morley (Educational author, edited 63 volumes of literary classics, 1822–1894)

William Morris (Designer craftsman and socialist, 1834–1896)

Herbert Stanley Morrison [Baron] (Deputy Prime Minister [1945–51], 1888–1965)

John Clifford Mortimer (Author and barrister, wrote Rumpole of the Bailey, 1923–)

Malcolm Muggeridge (Broadcaster and editor of *Punch* [1953–7], 1903–1990)

Jean Muir (Fashion designer, 1928–1995)

John Middleton Murry (Author, wrote critical studies of D.H. Lawrence and Jonathan Swift, 1889–1957)

Sir Charles James Napier (Military commander in India, 1782–1853)

John Nash (Architect of Buckingham Palace, 1752–1835)

Paul Nash (War artist who painted 'Totes Meer', 1899–1946)

Dame Anna Neagle (Actor, starred in *The Lady With the Lamp*, 1904–1986)

John Mason Neale (Hymn writer [*Jerusalem the Golden*], 1818–1866)

Dame Dorothy Needham [b.Moyle] (Biochemist, researched metabolism of muscle tissue, 1896–1987)

Joseph Needham (Biochemist, wrote major study of Chinese science, 1900–1995)

Edith Nesbit (Author of *The Railway Children*, 1858–1924)

Christopher Richard Nevinson (Futuristic artist, 1889–1946)

Eric Newby (Travel author [*A Short Walk in the Hindu Kush*], 1919–)

John Henry Newman [Cardinal] (Theologian, convert to Catholicism, 1801–1890)

David Niven [James David Nevins] (Actor, star of *Around the World in 80 Days*, 1910–1983)

Joseph Nollekens (Sculptor, created likenesses of George III and Dr Johnson, 1737–1823)

Caroline Elizabeth Norton [b.Sheridan] (Campaigning author and novelist, wrote *Voice From the Factories*, 1808–1877)

Vincent Novello (Composer and publisher of music, 1781–1861)

Lawrence Edward Oates (Explorer who sacrificed his life to try to save his colleagues on Scott's expedition to the South Pole, 1880–1912)

Mary O'Brien (Singer better known as Dusty Springfield, 1939–1999)

James Edward Oglethorpe (Military commander in American colonies, 1696–1785)

Bruce Oldfield (Fashion designer, 1950–)

John James Osbourne (Playwright, author of *Look Back in Anger*, 1929–1994)

Arthur William O'Shaughnessy (Poet ['The Music-Makers'], 1844–1881)

Samuel Palmer (Artist ['Repose of the Holy Family'], 1805–1881)

Henry John Temple Palmerston [3rd Viscount] (Twice Prime Minister in the 1850s, 1784–1865)

Norman Parkinson [Ronald William Parkinson Smith] (Photographer, 1913–1990)

Sir Charles Algernon Parsons (Turbine inventor, 1854–1931)

Walter Horatio Pater (Classical scholar [*Studies in the History of the Renaissance*], 1839–1894)

John Coleridge Patteson (Bishop of Melanesia, killed by natives, 1827–1871)

Karl Pearson (Statistician, 1857–1936)

George Peele (Playwright [*The Arraignment of Paris*], c.1558–1598)

William Penn (Founder of Pennsylvania, 1621–1670)

Sir Roland Algernon Penrose (Art collector and benefactor, 1900–1984)

Samuel Pepys (Diarist, 1633–1703)

Katherine Philips [Orinda] (First English woman poet, 1631–1664)

Arthur Phillip (Australian colony governor, 1738–1814)

Sir Arthur Wing Pinero (Playwright [*The Second Mrs Tanqueray*], 1855–1934)

William Pitt [The Elder] (Twice Prime Minister in 1750s and 60s, 1708–1778)

William Pitt [The Younger] (Twice Prime Minister, for a total of 22 years, 1759–1806)

Dame Rosalind Pitt-Rivers [b.Henley] (Biochemist, researched biochemistry of the thyroid gland, 1907–1990)

Francis Place (Social and political reformer, concerned with trade union freedom, parliamentary reform, and birth control, 1771–1854)

James Robinson Planche (Playwright [The Vampire] and heraldic historian, 1796–1880)

William Henry Playfair (Edinburgh-based architect, 1789–1857)

Sir Frederick Pollock (Jurist and legal author, 1845–1937)

Alexander Pope (Poet ['The Rape of the Lock'], 1688–1744)

Sir William Jackson Pope (Chemist, 1870–1939)

Sir John Pope-Hennessy (Art historian, Director of the Victoria & Albert Museum [1967–73], 1913–1994)

Eric Richard Porter (Actor [BBC TV's The Forsyte Saga], 1928–1995)

Percival Pott (Surgeon, researched TB of the spine, 1714–1788)

Helen Beatrix Potter (Author, creator of 'Peter Rabbit', 1866–1943)

Anthony Dymoke Powell (Novelist [A Dance to the Music of Time], 1905–2000)

Frederick York Powell (Historian and Icelandic scholar, 1850–1904)

Dame Peggy van Praagh (Ballet dancer and teacher, 1910–1990)

Adelaide Ann Procter [Mary Berwick] (Poet, wrote 'The Lost Chord', set to music by Sir Arthur Sullivan, 1825–1864)

Dod Procter [b.Doris Shaw] (Artist, 1892–1972)

Richard Anthony Procter (Astronomer, wrote Saturn and His System, 1837–1888)

Margaret Millicent Prout [b.Fisher] (Artist, exhibited at Royal Academy over a 42-year period, 1875–1963)

Augustus Welby Pugin (Architect, worked on design of Houses of Parliament, 1812–1852)

Henry Purcell (Composer [Nymphs and Shepherds], 1659–1695)

Sir David Terence Puttnam (Film producer [Chariots of Fire], 1941–)

Edith Mary Pye (International aid organiser, 1876–1965)

Mary Quant (Fashion designer, popularised the mini-skirt, 1934–)

Sir Peter Courtney Quennell (Biographer of Byron and Shakespeare, 1905–1993)

Robert Herbert Quick (Educationalist, wrote Essays on Educational Reformers, 1831–1891)

Ann Radcliffe [b.Ward] (Novelist [The Mysteries of Udolpho], 1764–1823)

Sir Bertram Home Ramsay (Director of Dunkirk evacuation, 1883–1945)

Sir Terence Mervyn Rattigan (Playwright, author of The Winslow Boy, Separate Tables, 1911–1977)

Vanessa Redgrave (Oscar-winning actor [Julia], 1937–)

Sir Carol Reed (Film director [The Third Man], 1906–1976)

Ruth Rendell [Ruth Barbara Grasemann] (Author [Kissing the Gunner's Daughter], 1930–)

Viscountess Rhondda [Margaret Haig Thomas] (Feminist, survived sinking of the Lusitania to found Time and Tide magazine, 1883–1958)

David Ricardo (Economist, wrote Principles of Political Economy and Taxation, 1772–1823)

Sir Harry Ralph Ricardo (Engineer, devised octane numbering, 1885–1974)

Emile Victor Rieu (Classical translator [The Odyssey], 1887–1972)

Bridget Louise Riley (Award-winning artist, 1931–)

Lady Anne Isabella Ritchie [b.Thackeray] (Novelist [*The Village on the Cliff*], 1837–1919)

Sir William Roberts-Austen (Metallurgist, 1843–1902)

William Heath Robinson (Humorous artist and cartoonist, 1872–1944)

George Brydges Rodney [1st Baron] (Naval commander in the Caribbean, 1719–1792)

Samuel Rogers (Poet ['The Pleasures of Memory'], 1763–1855)

Charles Stewart Rolls (Car manufacturer, teamed up with Sir Henry Royce, 1877–1910)

Sir Francis Ronalds (Inventor of electrical telegraph, 1788–1873)

Sir Henry Enfield Roscoe (Chemist and MP, 1833–1915)

Archibald Philip Rosebery [5th Earl] (Prime Minister [1894–5], 1847–1929)

Sir James Clark Ross (Polar explorer, discovered Magnetic North Pole in 1831, 1800–1862)

Christina Georgina Rossetti (Poet ['Goblin Market'], 1830–1894)

Dante Gabriel Rossetti (Pre-Raphaelite artist and poet, 1828–1882)

Thomas Rowlandson (Illustrator and cartoonist [*Dr Syntax*], 1756–1827)

John Ruskin (Art author [*The Stones of Venice*], 1819–1900)

Lord John Russell [1st Earl] (Twice Prime Minister, 1792–1878)

Dame Margaret Rutherford (Oscar-winning actor [for *The VIPs*], 1892–1972)

Desmond Ryan (Irish historian and political activist, 1893–1964)

Maria Susan Rye (Feminist, campaigned for women's property rights, 1829–1903)

Alan John Sainsbury [Baron] (Grocery retailer, 1902–)

Tom Sayers (Boxer, 'Napoleon of the Prize Ring', 1826–1865)

Gerald Scarfe (Cartoonist and satirist, 1936–)

John Richard Schlesinger (Film director [*Billy Liar, Sunday, Bloody Sunday*], (1926–)

Paul Mark Scott (Novelist, author *Jewel in the Crown*, 1920–1978)

Sir Peter Markham Scott (Ornithologist and wildlife artist, 1909–1989)

William Seguier, (Artist and first Keeper of the National Gallery, 1771–1843)

Charles Gabriel Seligman (Anthropologist, researched in New Guinea, 1873–1940)

Anthony Ashley Shaftesbury [7th Earl] (Industrial reformer, 1801–1885)

Cecil James Sharp (Folk song collector, 1859–1924)

Sir Edward Sharpey-Schafer (Physiologist, predicted discovery of insulin, 1850–1935)

George John Shaw-Lefevre [Baron Eversley] (Civil rights politician, 1832–1928)

Mary Wollstonecraft Shelley (Creator of 'Frankenstein', 1797–1851)

Jack Sheppard (Thief executed for his crimes, 1702–1724)

Sir Charles Scott Sherrington (Nobel Prize-winning physiologist, 1857–1952)

Emmanuel Shinwell [Baron] (Labour leader, 1884–1986)

James Shirley (Playwright [*The Lady of Pleasure*], 1596–1666)

William Bradford Shockley (Nobel Prize-winning physicist, 1910–1989)

Nevil Shute [Nevil Shute Norway] (Novelist, wrote *A Town Like Alice*, 1899–1960)

Jean Simmons (Actor, starred in *The Robe*, 1929–)

Sir Osbert Sitwell (Author, his autobiography [*Left Hand, Right Hand!*] running to five volumes, 1892–1969)

Walter William Skeat (Philologist, compiled *Etymological English Dictionary*, 1835–1912)

George Smith (Publisher of *Dictionary of National Biography* in 63 volumes [1885–1900], 1824–1901

George Smith (Archaeologist, wrote *Assyrian Discoveries*, 1840–1876)

Sir William Smith (Lexicographer, compiled dictionaries of the Bible and of classical history, 1813–1893)

William Henry Smith (Newspaper retailer, 1825–1891)

Sir William Sidney Smith (Naval commander, victor over Turkey at Battle of Abydos [1807], 1764–1840)

Dame Ethel Mary Smythe (Composer and suffragist, 1858–1944)

Patricia Smythe (Show jumper, first woman to ride in Olympic Games, 1928–1996)

Earl of Snowdon [Anthony Armstrong Jones] (Photographer and divorced husband of Princess Margaret, 1930–)

Solomon James Solomon (Artist who pioneered wartime camouflage, 1860–1927)

Kaikhosru Shapurji Sorabji (Composer and music critic, 1892–1988)

Sir Stephen Spender (Poet, 1909–1995)

Edmund Spenser (Poet, wrote 'The Faerie Queene', c.1552–1599)

Sir Lawrence Dudley Stamp (Geographer, 1898–1966)

John Stanley (Composer [oratorio *Queen of Egypt*], 1713–1786)

Flora Annie Steel [b.Webster] (India-based social reformer and novelist [*On the Face of the Waters*], 1847–1929)

Tommy Steele [Tommy Hicks] (Singer, 1936–)

Sir Leslie Stephen (Author and first editor of *DNB*, 1832–1904)

Mary Ann Stirling [b.Kehl] (Actor whose career spanned 50 years, 1816–1895)

Dame Mary Stocks (Educationalist and broadcaster, 1891–1975)

Leopold Stokowski (US-based conductor, 1882–1977)

Nancy Storace [b.Lively] (Soprano, for whom Mozart created role of Susanna in *The Marriage of Figaro*, 1765–1817)

Giles Lytton Strachey (Biographer and historian, wrote *Eminent Victorians*, 1880–1932)

Janet Street-Porter (TV celebrity and journalist, 1944–)

Eduard Suess (Geologist and Austrian politician, 1831–1914)

Sir Arthur Seymour Sullivan (Composer, collaborated with Sir William Gilbert on the Savoy Operettas, 1842–1900)

Baroness Edith Summerskill (Doctor and Chairman of the Labour Party [1954–5], 1901–1980)

Graham Vivian Sutherland (War artist, portraitist of Churchill, 1903–1980)

Alfred Sutro (Playwright [*The Perplexed Husband*], 1863–1933)

Algernon Charles Swinburne (Poet and playwright [*Atalanta in Calydon*], 1837–1909)

James Joseph Sylvester (Mathematician, researched number theory, 1814–1897)

George James Symons (Meteorologist, organised UK-wide rainfall data, 1838–1900)

Thomas Tallis (Organist and composer, c.1505–1585)

Jessica Tandy (Oscar-winning actor [*Driving Miss Daisy*], 1907–1994)

Sir Arthur George Tansley (Ecologist and botanist, 1871–1955)

Elizabeth Taylor (Actor, star of *National Velvet* and *Cleopatra*, 1932–)

Sir Geoffrey Taylor (Mathematician and physicist, 1886–1975)

Dame Marie Tempest [b.Mary Etherington] (Actor and light-opera singer, 1864–1942)

Emma Tennant (Novelist [*The Bad Sister*], 1957–)

Sir John Tenniel (Illustrator of *Alice in Wonderland*, 1820–1914)

Angela Margaret Thirkell (Author who wrote 30 novels featuring characters from the work of Anthony Trollope, 1891–1961)

Connop Thirlwall (Historian [*History of Greece*] and educational reformer, 1797–1875)

Philip Edward Thomas (Poet, killed in battle, 1878–1917)

Emma Thompson (Oscar-winning actor [*Sense and Sensibility*], 1959–)

Sir William Hamo Thornycroft (Sculptor, created London statues to Cromwell and General Gordon, 1850–1925)

Cedric Thorpe-Davie (Scottish-based composer, 1913–1983)

Sir Michael Tippett (Composer [oratorio *Child of Our Time*], 1905–)

Thomas Frederick Tout (Mediaeval historian, 1855–1929)

Arnold Toynbee (Economics historian [*The Industrial Revolution in England*], 1852–1883)

Arnold Joseph Toynbee (Historian, wrote *The Study of History*, 1889–1975)

Ben Travers (Playwright, author of such farces as *Rookery Nook*, 1886–1980)

Sir Herbert Beerbohm Tree (Actor and theatre manager, 1853–1917)

Rose Tremain (Novelist [*The Swimming Pool Season*], 1943–)

Tommy [Thomas Edward] Trinder (Comedian whose catch-phrase was 'You lucky people', 1909–1989)

Anthony Trollope (Novelist [*Barchester Towers*], 1815–1882)

Anthony Tudor [William Cook] (Dancer and choreographer, 1908–1987)

Dame Margaret Turner-Warwick [b.Moore] (First woman President of the Royal College of Physicians [1989–92], 1924–)

Alan Mathison Turing (Mathematician and computer pioneer who committed suicide because of homophobic persecution, 1912–1954)

Colin Turnbull (Anthropologist, wrote *The Forest People*, 1924–)

Joseph Mallord Turner (Water-colour artist noted for such works as 'Rail, Steam and Speed', 1775–1851)

Twiggy [Leslie Hornby] (Model and actor, 1949–)

Louisa Twining (Social reformer, wrote *Workhouses and Pauperism*, 1820–1912)

Sir Edward Burnett Tylor (Anthropologist, wrote *Primitive Culture*, 1832–1917)

Sir Peter Alexander Ustinov (Actor and playwright, 1921–)

Sir John Vanbrugh (Architect [of Blenheim Palace] and playwright [*The Provok'd Wife*], 1664–1726)

Lucia Elizabeth Vestris [b.Bartolozzi] (Actor and opera singer, 1797–1856)

Queen Victoria [Queen of Great Britain and Empress of India] (1819–1901)

Sir Julius Vogel (Twice New Zealand Prime Minister, 1835–1899)

Charles Francis Voysey (Architect and designer, 1857–1941)

John Walker (Lexicographer [*Rhyming Dictionary*], 1732–1807)

Max Wall [Maxwell George Lorimer] (Actor and comedian, 1908–1990)

Sir Richard Wallace (Art collector, 1818–1890)

Horace Walpole [4th Earl of Oxford] (Author [*The Castle of Otranto*], 1717–1797)

Sir Spencer Walpole (Historian [*History of England From 1815 to 1856*], 1839–1907)

Peter Warlock [Philip Arnold Heseltine] (Composer [song cycle *The Curlew*], 1894–1930)

Silvia Townsend Warner (Musicologist and novelist [*Summer Will Show*], 1893–1978)

Janet Vida Watson (First woman President of the Geological Society, 1923–1985)

George Frederick Watts (Artist, presented 150 paintings to the National Portrait Gallery, 1817–1904)

Sidney James Webb [Baron Passfield] (Social reformer and President of the Board of Trade [in 1924], 1859–1947)

Arnold Weinstock [Baron] (Industrialist, 1924–)

Arnold Wesker (Playwright [Chips with Everything], 1932–)

Denis Yates Wheatley (Novelist [The Devil Rides Out], 1897–1977)

Joseph Whitaker (Publisher of the Almanac of that name, 1820–1895)

Patrick White (Australian-based author who won Nobel Prize for Literature in 1973, 1912–1990)

Alfred North Whitehead (Mathematician and philosopher, 1861–1947)

Charles Whitehead (Novelist and poet, promoted the work of Charles Dickens, 1804–1862)

June Whitfield (Comedy actress, from radio's Take It From Here to TV's Absolutely Fabulous, 1925–)

Edward Whymper (Mountaineer, first to climb Matterhorn, 1840–1911)

John Wilkes (Politician repeatedly expelled from Parliament for his outspokenness, 1727–1797)

William IV [King of Great Britain] (1765–1837)

John Williams (Missionary eaten by New Hebrides cannibals, 1796–1839)

Kenneth Williams (Actor, star of Carry On films, 1926–1987)

Harriette Wilson [b.Dubochet] (Courtesan whose memoirs caused a sensation, 1786–1855)

Sir Norman Wisdom (Comedian, 1918–)

Mary Wollstonecraft (Feminist whose ideas were too revolutionary even for the French Revolutionaries, author of A Vindication of the Rights of Women, 1759–1797)

Sir Henry Joseph Wood (Conductor, originated 'Proms' concerts, 1869–1944)

Sydney William Wooldridge (Geographer, 1900–1963)

Leonard Woolf (Author and publisher, founded the Hogarth Press, 1880–1969)

Virginia Woolf (Novelist, author of To the Lighthouse, 1882–1941)

Sir Charles Leonard Woolley (Archaeologist, wrote Digging Up the Past, 1880–1960)

William Brocklesby Wordsworth (Orchestral composer, 1908–1988)

Olive Wyon (Religious author [The Altar Fire], 1881–1966)

William Yarrell (Naturalist, founder member of the Zoological Society, 1784–1856)

John Butler Yeats (Artist and comic illustrator, 1870–1957)

Susannah York (Actor [The Killing of Sister George], 1941–)

Arthur Young (Agriculturist, founded Annals of Agriculture magazine, 1741–1820)

Dame Eileen Younghusband (Social work pioneer, 1902–1981)

Israel Zangwill (Comic author [The Bachelors' Club] and playwright, 1864–1926)

LONDONDERRY

Amanda Burton (TV actor [Silent Witness], 1956–)

Arthur Joyce Cary (Novelist [To Be a Pilgrim], 1888–1957)

George Farquhar (Playwright [The Recruiting Officer], c.1677–1707)

John Hume (Politician and Nobel Peace Prize-winner, 1937–)

LONG EATON Derbyshire
Dame Laura Knight (Artist, one of the first
    women Royal Academicians, 1877–1970)

LONG ITCHINGTON Warwickshire
Saint Wulfstan (Bishop of Worcester,
    assisted in compilation of Domesday
    Book, c.1009–1095)

LONGLEAT Wiltshire
Henry Frederick Bath [6th Marquess]
    (Stately home owner, 1905–1992)

LONG MELFORD Suffolk
Henry Wickham Steed (Author on foreign
    affairs and editor of *The Times*
    [1919–22], 1871–1956)

LONGNIDDRY East Lothian
Mollie Hunter (Award-winning children's
    author [*The Stronghold*], 1922–)

LONG SUTTON Lincolnshire
Alfred Piccaver (Operatic tenor, famed in
    Vienna for nearly 30 years, 1884–1958)

LONGTON Near Stoke-on-Trent
William Thomas Astbury (Pioneer in X-ray
    research, 1889–1961)

LONGWORTH Oxfordshire
Richard Doddridge Blackmore (Novelist
    [*Lorna Doone*], 1825–1900)
John Fell (Royal chaplain, subject of poem
    'I do not love thee Dr Fell', 1625–1686)

LOSSIEMOUTH Morayshire
James Ramsay MacDonald (First Labour
    Prime Minister, held office three times,
    1866–1937)
Malcolm MacDonald [Son of Ramsay
    Macdonald] (Minister of Health in
    wartime government, later Governor-
    General of Canada, 1901–1981)

LOSTWITHIEL Cornwall
John Westlake (International legal expert,
    Professor at Cambridge for 20 years,
    1828–1913)

LOUGHBOROUGH Leicestershire
John Cleveland (Cavalier poet released
    from prison on Cromwell's orders,
    1613–1658)
John Howe (Chaplain to Oliver Cromwell,
    1630–1705)
Walter Weldon (Industrial chemist who
    also edited literary journal *Weldon's
    Register of Facts*, 1832–1885)

LOUGHTON Essex
George Granville Barker (Poet and novelist
    [*True Confession of George Barker*],
    1913–1991)

LOW BLANTYRE Lanarkshire
David Livingstone (Explorer, first European
    to see Victoria Falls and Lake Ngami,
    1813–1873)

LOWESTOFT Suffolk
Benjamin Britten [Baron] (Composer [*Billy
    Budd, Peter Grimes*], 1913–1976)
Thomas Nashe (Playwright [*Pierce
    Penilesse*], 1567–1601)

LOW HAM Somerset
Ned [Edward George] Sherrin (Satirist and
    broadcaster, produced TV's *That Was the
    Week That Was*, 1931–)

LUDDENDEN Yorkshire
David Hartley (Doctor and philosopher,
    wrote *Observations of Man...*, 1705–1757)

LUDLOW Shropshire
Henry Peach Robinson (Photographer,
    pioneered 'High Art' style using costumed
    models, 1830–1901)

Stanley John Weyman (Novelist [*The Castle Inn, Ovington's Bank*], 1855–1928)

LUGAR Near Cumnock, Ayrshire
William Murdock (Pioneer of gas lighting, 1754–1839)

LUMSDEN Aberdeenshire
Sir William Robertson Nicoll (Author and theologian, founded *The Bookman* magazine, 1851–1923)

LURGAN County Armagh
Sir John Greer Dill (Military commander in World War Two, 1881–1944)
James Logan (Chief Justice in American colony of Pennsylvania, 1674–1751)
George William Russell (Poet ['The Candle of Vision'], 1867–1935)

LUTON Bedfordshire
John Badham (Film director [*Saturday Night Fever, Bird On a Wire*], 1939–)
Arthur Hailey (Novelist [*Airport, Wheels*], 1920–)
Paul Young (Pop singer [*Wherever I Lay My Hat*], 1956–)

LUTON Kent
William Halse Rivers (Anthropologist who treated officers suffering from 'War Trauma' in World War One, 1864–1922)

LUTTON-BOWINE Lincolnshire
Richard Busby (Headmaster of Westminster School for 57 years, 1606–1695)

LYDNEY Gloucestershire
Herbert Howells (Choral composer [*Hymnus Paradisi*], 1892–1983)

LYE Worcestershire
Sir Cedric Webster Hardwicke (Actor [*Things to Come*], 1893–1964)

LYME REGIS Dorset
Mary Anning (Discovered first fossils of plesiosaur and pterodactyl, 1799–1847)
Thomas Coram (Philanthropist, set up Foundling Hospital in London, c.1668–1751)
Percy Carlyle Gilchrist (Metallurgist, co-invented process for smelting iron ores, 1851–1935)
John Gould (Ornithological publisher, 1804–1881)

MACCLESFIELD Cheshire
Jonathan Philip Agnew (Former Test cricketer [Leicestershire and England] and broadcaster, 1960–)
Brian Houghton Hodgson (Oriental scholar, expert on Nepal and Tibet, 1800–1895)
John Mayall (Influential rock guitarist, 1933–)
Sir Arthur Smith Woodward (Geologist, wrote 650 works including *Outlines of Vertebrate Palaeontology*, 1864–1944)

MACKWORTH Derbyshire
Samuel Richardson (Novelist who used epistolary style [*Clarissa*], 1689–1761)

MADDINGHAM Kent
Denis Winston Healey [Baron] (Chancellor of the Exchequer [1974–9], 1917–)

MADELEY Staffordshire
William Bridges Adams (Engineer, improved railway track technology, 1797–1872)

MAESTEG Mid-Glamorgan
Vernon Phillips Watkins (Poet, eclipsed by Dylan Thomas in his lifetime, 1906–1967)

MAES-Y-GARNEDD Gwynedd
John Jones (Civil War leader, later executed for regicide, c.1597–1660)

MAIDEN BRADLEY Wiltshire

Edmund Ludlow (Civil War leader, fled
country to avoid arrest for regicide,
c.1617–1692)

MAIDENHEAD Berkshire

Tina Brown (Magazine editor [formerly of
Vanity Fair and *The New Yorker*], 1953–)
Hugh John Lofting (Author of *Dr Doolittle*
books, 1886–1947)
Thomas Rickman (Architect of Cambridge
University buildings, 1776–1841)

MAIDSTONE Kent

Richard Beeching [Dr and Lord]
(Administered British rail system,
reducing mileage in attempt to attain
viability, 1913–1985)
William Hazlitt (Essayist [*The Spirit of the
Age*], 1778–1830)
John Jenkins (Earliest English composer of
instrumental music, 1592–1678)
Francis Sydney Smythe (Mountaineer,
member of three Everest expeditions in
the 1930s, 1900–1949)
William Woollett (Royal engraver,
1735–1785)

MALDON Essex

John Paul Crawley (Test cricketer
[Lancashire, Hampshire and England],
1971–)
Horatio Gates (American military
commander, forced British surrender at
Saratoga, 1728–1806)
Thomas Plume (Theologian, endowed chair
of Astronomy at Cambridge, 1630–1704)

MALMESBURY Wiltshire

Thomas Hobbes (Philosopher interested in
process of government, wrote *Leviathan*,
1588–1679)

MALPAS Cheshire

Reginald Heber (Bishop of Calcutta, travelled extensively in India, 1783–1826)

MANCHESTER

*(See also ASHTON-UPON-MERSEY,
ATHERTON, FARNWORTH, SALFORD,
STOCKPORT, WIGAN)*

James Evershed Agate (Drama critic and
autobiographer [*Ego*], 1877–1947)
Caroline Aherne (TV actor and writer [*The
Royle Family*], 1963–)
Robert Ainsworth (Latin-English
lexicographer, 1660–1743)
William Harrison Ainsworth (Historical
novelist, popularised story of Dick Turpin
[*Rookwood*], 1805–1882)
Sir John Alcock (Pioneering aviator, flew
Atlantic non-stop with Brown in 1919,
shortly before his death, 1892–1919)
Michael Andrew Atherton (Former Test
cricketer [Lancashire and England] and
broadcaster, 1968–)
George Barger (Organic chemist,
1878–1939)
Lydia Becker (Suffragette who lobbied
Parliament on behalf of her cause,
1827–1890)
Eric Birley (Historian of Roman Britain,
1906–1995)
Ann Bishop (Cambridge-based biologist
who researched alternative cures for
malaria during World War Two,
1899–1990)
Robert Bolt (Playwright [*A Man For All
Seasons*] and screenwriter [*Lawrence of
Arabia, Dr Zhivago*], 1924–1995)
Matthew Brady (Convict transported to
Australia, hanged after terrorising
Tasmania, 1799–1826)
Margaret Burbridge [b.Peachey]
(Astronomer, briefly Director of Royal
Greenwich Observatory before taking
research post in US, 1923–)

Anthony Burgess (Novelist [A Clockwork Orange], 1917–)

Frances Hodgson Burnett (Author of Little Lord Fauntleroy and The Secret Garden, 1849–1924)

Nicky Butt (International footballer [Manchester United and England], 1975–)

John Byrom (Poet who copyrighted a shorthand system, 1692–1763)

Sydney Chapman (Mathematician, contributed to kinetic theory of gases, 1888–1970)

Humphrey Chetham (Philanthropic cloth manufacturer who established a Manchester hospital and public library, 1580–1653)

Samuel Clegg (Inventor who illuminated an entire London district by coal-gas in 1814, 1781–1861)

John Collier (Poet and satirist, 1708–1786)

Alfred Alistair Cooke (American broadcaster, famed for his BBC radio programme Letter From America, 1908–)

Samuel Crompton (Inventor of 'spinning mule', 1753–1827)

Sir Peter Maxwell Davies (Composer of operas [The Lighthouse] and ballets [Caroline Mathilde], 1934–)

Brenda Dean [Baroness] (Trade union leader from printing industry, 1943–)

Thomas de Quincy, (Author [Confessions of an Opium Eater], 1785–1859)

Robert Donat (Actor, starred in Hitchcock's The 39 Steps, 1905–1958)

William Hepworth Dixon (Author, campaigned for prison reform 1821–1879)

Harold Evans (Campaigning newspaper editor [Sunday Times 1967–83], 1928–)

Roger Fenton (Pioneering war photographer [in Crimea], 1819–1869)

Judy Finnigan (TV presenter [with husband Richard Madeley], 1948–)

Sir Norman Robert Foster (Architect, noted for his functional style, 1935–)

John Foulds (Composer [A World Requiem], 1880–1939)

Noel and Liam Gallagher (Brothers, members of band Oasis, 1967– and 1972– respectively)

Louis Golding (Novelist, portrayed Jewish life [Magnolia], 1895–1958)

Samuel Gorton (Colonial religious leader, banished from Massachusetts after conviction for heresy, 1592–1677)

Nathaniel Gould (Australian-based sports author, wrote novel The Double Event, 1857–1919)

William Rathbone Greg (Essayist, wrote gloomy prediction of the future in Rocks Ahead [1874], 1809–1881)

Trevor Griffiths (Playwright for stage and TV [The Party], 1935–)

Frank Hampson (Cartoonist, drew 'Dan Dare' for Eagle comic, 1918–1985)

Sir Arthur Harden (Nobel Prize-winning chemist, researched enzymes and alcohol fermentation, 1865–1940)

Harold Marsh Harwood (Playwright [The Grain of Mustard Seed], 1874–1959)

Ian Hay [John Hay Beith] (Novelist, famous for his war novels [The First Hundred Thousand], 1876–1952)

William Henry (Chemist, formulated Henry's Law concerning gas absorption by liquids, 1774–1836)

John Nicholson Ireland (Composer [The Forgotten Rite], 1879–1962)

Hewlett Johnson (Radical prelate, known as 'The Red Dean', 1874–1966)

Frederick Stanley Kipping (Chemist, founder of the silicone industry, 1863–1949)

Harold Joseph Laski (Political economist [A Grammar of Politics] and broadcaster, 1893–1950)

Marghanita Laski (Novelist, critic, and broadcaster, 1915–1988)

Ann Lee ['Mother Ann'] (Preacher and mystic, founded Shaker settlement at Niskayuna in 1776, 1736–1784)

David Lloyd-George [1st Earl] (Liberal Prime Minister [1916–22], 1863–1945)

Laurence Stephen [L.S.] Lowry (Artist who is now honoured in Salford with his own art gallery, 1887–1976)

Sir John Lyons (Linguistic theorist [*Language, Meaning and Context*], 1932–)

Ann MacBeth (Embroidery expert, member of the 'Glasgow School' of artists, 1875–1948)

William McDougall (Psychologist [*Physiological Psychology, Body and Mind*], 1871–1938)

Rosalind Mary Mitchison (Historian [*The History of Scotland*], 1919–2002)

Sir John Moores (Founder of Littlewoods retailers and football pools, 1896–1993)

Adela Constantia Pankhurst (Australian-based campaigner for women's suffrage and pacifism, 1885–1961)

Christabel Harriette Pankhurst (Suffragette, 1880–1958)

Emmeline Pankhurst (Suffragette, 1857–1928)

Sylvia Pankhurst (Suffragette, also campaigned for pacifism and socialism, 1882–1960)

John Henry Poynting (Physicist, wrote *On the Mean Density of the Earth* in 1893, 1852–1914)

Ian Thomas Ramsey (Theologian, Bishop of Durham [1966–72], 1915–1972)

Alfred Robens [Lord] (Trade unionist, government minister, and head of coal industry, 1910–1999)

Grace Robertson (Photographer, contributed to *Picture Post* and *Life* magazines, 1930–)

Sir Edwin Roe (Pioneering aircraft manufacturer, 1877–1958)

Jack Morris Rosenthal (Playwright [*Barmitzvah Boy*], 1931–)

Israel Moses Sieff [Baron] (Retail executive, Marks & Spencer, 1889–1972)

Dodie Smith (Playwright and novelist [*The 101 Dalmations*], 1896–1990)

Sir Walter Baldwin Spencer (Anthropologist, appointed Chief Protector of Australian Aboriginals in 1912, 1860–1929)

Brian Statham (Test cricketer [Lancashire and England], 1930–2000)

John Andrew Sumner [Viscount] (Judge, 1859–1934)

Mary Elizabeth Sumner (Religious activist, instrumental in founding the Mothers' Union, 1828–1921)

Elihu Thomson (US-based electrical inventor of arc lighting, 1853–1937)

Sir Joseph John Thomson (Nobel Prize-winning physicist who discovered isotopes and pioneered nuclear physics, 1856–1940)

Michael Paul Vaughan (Test cricketer [Yorkshire and England], 1974–)

Dudley Dexter Watkins (Cartoonist, creator of 'Desperate Dan', 1907–1969)

Ellen Cicely Wilkinson (Feminist, first female Minister of Education [in 1946], 1891–1947)

Sir Frederic Calland Williams (Electrical engineer, operated the first stored-program computer [in 1948], 1911–1977)

Jeanette Winterson (Novelist [*Oranges Are Not the Only Fruit*], 1959–)

MANGOTSFIELD Somerset

Francis Howard Greenway (Architect based in Australia after transportation for forgery, 1777–1837)

MANNINGTREE Essex

John Watson (Author of Scottish works

[*Days of Old Lang Syne*] who wrote as Ian MacLaren, 1850–1907)

MANORBIER CASTLE Dyfed
Giraldus Cambrensis [Gerald of Wales] (Welsh chronicler, c.1146–1223)

MANSFIELD Nottinghamshire
Robert Dodsley (Collector and publisher of plays and poems, 1704–1764)
John David Pye (Zoologist, has researched animals' use of ultrasound, e.g. bats' echolocation, 1932–)

MANSFIELD WOODHOUSE Nottinghamshire
John Andrew Ogdon (Composer for piano, 1937–1989)

MARGATE Kent
Peter Barkworth (TV actor [*Professional Foul*], 1929–)
Alfred George Deller (Singer determined to attain authentic sound of early music, 1912–1979)

MARKFIELD Leicestershire
Thomas Hooker (US-based theologian, founded Hartford [Connecticut], c.1586–1647)

MARLBOROUGH Wiltshire
Thomas Hancock (Clothing industry inventor, pioneered rubber waterproofing along with Macintosh, 1786–1865)
Douglas Richard Hurd (Foreign Secretary [1989–95], 1930–)
Henry Sacheverell (Controversial preacher who was impeached and suspended for criticising a government minister, c.1674–1724)

MARTLEY Worcestershire
Charles Stuart Calverley [b.Blayds] (Lawyer who took up poetry after a near-fatal skiing accident, 1831–1884)

MARTOCK Somerset
Thomas Southwood Smith (Physician, wrote *Treatise on Fever*, 1788–1861)

MARTON Middlesbrough
James Cook (Pacific navigator and explorer, 1728–1779)

MARTON Shropshire
Thomas Bray (Philanthropist, whose funding of libraries led to the formation of the Society for Promoting Christian Knowledge, 1656–1730)

MARYKIRK Kincardineshire
David Herd (Folklorist [*Ancient Scottish Ballads*], 1732–1810)

MATLOCK Derbyshire
Sir George Newnes (Publisher [*Tit-bits, Country Life*] and MP, 1851–1910)

MEASHAM Derbyshire
Geraldine Jewsbury (Novelist, [*Zoe, The Half Sisters*], 1812–1880)

MELBOURNE Derbyshire
Thomas Cook (Travel innovator, organised the first public excursion train journey in UK [1841], 1808–1892)

MELCOMBE REGIS Dorset
Sir James Thornhill (Artist, best remembered for the Painted Hall at Greenwich Hospital [1707–27], 1675–1734)

MELLERSTAIN Berwickshire
Lady Grisell Baillie (Philanthropist and songwriter whose domestic notebook was published as *The Household Book* in 1911, 1822–1921)

MELROSE Roxburghshire

Catherine Spence (Author and Australian traveller who was the first woman to stand for the Federal Convention [in 1897], 1825–1910)

MELTON MOWBRAY Leicestershire

John Henley (Orator and preacher [*The Complete Linguist*], caricatured by Hogarth, 1692–1756)

MEMBURY Devon

Thomas Wakeley (Surgeon, founded *The Lancet*, 1795–1862)

MENSTRIE Clackmannanshire

Sir Ralph Abercromby (Soldier, fatally wounded at Aboukir Bay, 1734–1801)

MEOPHAM Kent

John Tradescant [the younger] (Gardener whose collections from Virginia formed important part of Ashmolean Museum, Oxford, 1608–1662)

MERTHYR TYDFIL Powys

Laura Ashley (Fashion and textile designer, renowned for her romantic flair, 1925–1985)

Henry Seymour Berry Buckland [Baron] (Coal mining and newspaper executive, 1877–1928)

William Ewart Berry Camrose [1st Viscount] (Proprietor of more than 100 newspapers, including *The Sunday Times*, 1879–1954)

Samuel Walker Griffith (Legislator in Australia, three times Prime Minister of Queensland, 1845–1920)

Arthur Lewis Horner (Trade unionist and politician, co-founded the British Communist Party, 1894–1968)

James Gomer Berry Kemsley [1st Viscount] (Newspaper proprietor, including *The Sunday Times*, 1883–1968)

Joseph Parry (Orchestral and operatic composer who was also one of the most prolific hymn-writers, 1841–1903)

MERTON Surrey

Ford Madox Ford [b.Ford Hermann Hueffer] (Novelist [*The Good Soldier*], 1873–1919)

Alec James Stewart (Test cricketer [Surrey and England], 1963–)

METHLICK Aberdeenshire

George Cheyne (Physician who promoted vegetarianism, 1671–1743)

MEXBOROUGH Yorkshire

Keith Barron (TV actor [*Stand Up for Nigel Barton* and *Vote, Vote, Vote, for Nigel Barton*], 1934–)

Brian Blessed (Film and TV actor [*Z Cars*], also noted mountaineer, 1937–)

MIDDLE CHINNOCK Somerset

Victor James Marks (Former test cricketer [Somerset and England] and broadcaster, 1955–)

MIDDLESBROUGH

(See also MARTON)

Thelma Barlow (TV actor, 'Mavis' in *Coronation Street*, 1929–)

Brian Clough (Footballer and manager, guided Nottingham Forest to European Cup victories in 1979 and 1980, 1935–)

Ernest William Hornung (Novelist, creator of 'Raffles', the gentleman burglar, 1866–1921)

Chris Rea (Pop singer and songwriter, 1951–)

Jonathan Woodgate (International footballer [Leeds and England], 1980 –)

MIDDLETON Lancashire

Samuel Bamford (Weaver who became a reformer and poet, 1788–1872)

MIDDLETON Warwickshire
Francis Willughby (Pioneering naturalist, accompanied John Ray on several expeditions, 1635-1672)

MIDDLETON TYAS North Yorkshire
Sir Almroth Edward Wright (Bacteriologist who encouraged Fleming's research on penicillin, 1861-1947)

MIDDLEWICH Cheshire
John Hulse (Ecclesiastical benefactor, founded Hulsean lectures at Cambridge University, 1708-1790)

MIDSOMER NORTON Somerset
Peter Alexander (TV actor [*Emmerdale, Coronation Street, Eastenders*], 1952-)

MILBORNE ST ANDREW Dorset
John Morton [Cardinal] (Archbishop of Canterbury and Chancellor during reign of Henry VII, c.1420-1500)

MILDENHALL Suffolk
Henry William Bunbury (Sporting author and caricaturist, 1750-1811)

MILEHAM Norfolk
Sir Edward Coke (Jurist, prosecuted Sir Walter Raleigh and the Gunpowder Plotters for treason, 1552-1634)

MILFIELD Northumberland
Josephine Elizabeth Butler (Social reformer, promoted women's education, 1828-1906)

MILFORD HAVEN Dyfed
Arthur William Symons (Poet and literary critic [*The Romantic Movement in English Poetry*], 1865-1945)

MILLISLE County Down
Amy Beatrice Carmichael (Missionary in India, 1867-1971)

MILNATHORT Kinross-shire
Hugh Haliburton [Pseudonym of James Logie Robertson] (Poet who claimed to be shepherd in the Ochil Hills, 1846-1922)

MILSTON Wiltshire
Joseph Addison (Essayist, co-founded *The Spectator* in 1711, 1672-1719)

MILTON-BRYANT Bedfordshire
Sir Joseph Paxton (Architect, designed building for the 1851 Great Exhibition, 1801-1865)

MILTON KEYNES Buckinghamshire
Francis Atterbury (Dean of Westminster who was banished to France in 1723 [for his Jacobite sympathies], 1663-1732)

MILVERTON Somerset
Thomas Young (Physicist and egyptologist whose research helped in the deciphering of the Rosetta Stone, 1773-1829)

MINEHEAD Somerset
Richard John Chorley (Geomorphologist, promotes geography as human ecology, 1927-)
Arthur Charles Clarke (Science fiction author, co-wrote *2001: A Space Odyssey*, 1917-)

MINIGAFF Near Newton Stewart, Wigtownshire
John MacMillan (Ecclesiastic, founded Reformed Presbyterian Church, 1670-1753)
Alexander Murray (Self-taught language and Classics scholar, 1775-1813)

MIREHOUSE Cumbria
James Spedding (Biographer of Francis
Bacon, 1808–1881)

MITCHAM Surrey
Peter Dennis Mitchell (Nobel Prize-winning
biochemist [in 1978], 1920–1992)

MIXBURY Oxfordshire
Roundell Palmer Selbourne [1st Earl] (Twice
Attorney-General, also noted for his
hymn-writing, 1812–1895)

MOFFAT Dumfriesshire
Hugh Dowding [1st Baron] (Commander of
Fighter Command in the Battle of Britain,
1882–1970)

MONIAIVE Dumfriesshire
James Renwick (Covenanter martyr
executed in Edinburgh after refusing to
petition for a reprieve, 1662–1688)

MONKWEARMOUTH County Durham
The Venerable Bede [Saint] (Author of *The
Ecclesiastic History of the English People*,
c.673–735)

MONMOUTH Gwent
Henry V [King of England] (Victor of Battle
of Agincourt [1415], 1387–1422)

MONTROSE Angus
Robert Brown (Botanist, discoverer of
'Brownian motion', 1773–1858)
Sir Alexander Burnes (Diplomat, killed in
massacre in Afghanistan, 1805–1841)
Sir William Burnett (Physician, invented a
wood preservative, 1726–1814)
George Paul Chalmers (Artist, murdered by
thieves in Edinburgh, 1833–1878)
Joseph Hume (Enlightened politician,
campaigned for reforms,
1777–1855)

Violet Jacob (Novelist [*Flemington*] who
used Scots dialect, 1863–1946)
Willa Muir (Novelist [*Imagined Corners*]
who translated and popularised the
works of Kafka, 1890–1970)

MORECAMBE Lancashire
Dame Thora Hird (Actor in films [*Went the
Day Well?*] and on TV [*Talking Heads*],
1911–)
Eric Morecambe [b.Eric Bartholomew]
(Comedian, partnered Ernie Wise,
1926–1984)

MORETON Dorset
Tregonwell Frampton (Royal racehorse
trainer known as the 'Father of the Turf',
1641–1727)

MORETON-IN-MARSH Gloucestershire
John Sankey [Viscount] (Lord Chancellor
[1929–35], 1866–1948)

MORETONHAMPSTEAD Devon
George Parker Bidder (Engineer, designed
railway swing bridge, 1806–1878)

MORLEY Yorkshire
Herbert Asquith [1st Earl Oxford] (Prime
Minister [1908–16], 1852–1928)
Sir Titus Salt (Woollen manufacturer and
philanthropist, 1803–1876)
Craig White (Test cricketer [Yorkshire and
England], 1969–)

MORPETH Northumberland
John Urpeth Rastrick (Railway engineer,
1780–1856)
William Turner ('Father of English
botany', responsible for identifying and
naming numerous plant species,
c.1510–1568)

MORVAL Cornwall
John Mayow (Physiologist who researched
    respiration, 1641–1679)

MOSTYN Clwyd
Emlyn Williams (Actor and playwright
    [*Night Must Fall*], 1905–1987)

MOTHERWELL Lanarkshire
Sir Alexander Drummond Gibson
    (Conductor and Musical Director of
    Scottish Opera from its inception in
    1962, 1926–1995)
Liz Lochhead (Poet and playwright [*Blood
    and Ice*], 1947–)
Gary McAllister (International footballer
    [Scotland], 1964–)

MOUSEHOLE Cornwall
Dolly Pentreath (Last native Cornish
    speaker, 1685–1777)

MOY County Tyrone
John King (Explorer of Australia, first white
    man to traverse the continent from north
    to south and back again, 1838–1872)

MUNCASTER CASTLE Cumbria
Alexander William Crawford [25th Earl]
    (Nobleman author [*Sketches of the
    History of Christian Art*], 1812–1880)

MUSSELBURGH East Lothian
Rhona Cameron (TV comedian and
    presenter, 1965–)
Hugh von Halkett [Baron] (Commander of
    Hanoverian army at Waterloo,
    1783–1863)
David MacBeth Moir (Physician and poet,
    wrote *Outlines of the Ancient History of
    Medicine*, 1798–1851)

MYTHOLMROYD Yorkshire
Ted [Edward James] Hughes (Poet Laureate

[appointed in 1984] and husband of
    Sylvia Plath, 1930–1998)

NAILSEA Somerset
Mervyn John Kitchen (Test cricket umpire,
    1940–)

NAIRN Moray and Nairn
James Augustus Grant (Explorer of the Nile,
    wrote *A Walk Across Africa*, 1817–1892)
William Stephen Whitelaw [1st Viscount]
    (Statesman and cabinet minister,
    1918–1999)

NANTWICH Cheshire
David [Earl] Beatty (Admiral, commanded
    Grand Fleet after Jutland, 1871–1936)
Sir William Bowman (Physiologist,
    researched kidney functions, 1816–1892)
John Gerard (Surgeon-barber who compiled
    plant catalogue [*The Herball*], of more
    than 1,000 species, 1545–1612)

NANTYMOEL Mid-Glamorgan
Lynn Davies (Athlete, whose long-jump
    record in 1964 made him the first
    Welshman to win Olympic gold, 1942–)

NASH MILLS Hertfordshire
Sir Arthur John Evans (Archaeologist, dis-
    covered Minoan civilization, 1851–1941)

NEATH Dyfed
Hugh Dalton [Baron] (Politician who
    resigned as Chancellor in 1947 after
    accidentally leaking a Budget secret,
    1887–1962)
Henry Habberley Price (Philosopher,
    researched perception, 1899–1985)

NETHER STOWEY Somerset
Robert Parsons (Jesuit activist who briefed
    Phillip II of Spain on an invasion of
    England, 1546–1610)

NETHERBY Cumbria
Sir James Robert Graham (Home Secretary
[1841-6], 1792-1861)

**NETHERWOOD Near Bromyard, Hereford
and Worcester**
Robert Devereux Essex [2nd Earl] (Favourite
of Queen Elizabeth, 1566-1601)

NEW ABERDOUR Aberdeenshire
Andrew Findlater (Encyclopaedia editor
[*Chambers*], 1810-1885)

NEWARK-ON-TRENT Nottinghamshire
George Allen (Publisher, founded what
became Allen & Unwin, 1832-1907)
John Blow (Ecclesiastical composer who
also composed Court Masque,
1649-1708)
William Henry ['Dusty'] Hare (International
rugby player [England], 1952-)
Sir Godfrey Newbold Hounsfield (Nobel
Prize-winning physicist who developed
X-ray scanning, 1919-)
Paul Johnson (County cricketer
[Nottinghamshire] for more than 20
seasons, 1965-)
Sir William Nicholson (Artist father of Ben
Nicholson, 1872-1949)
Thomas William Robertson (Playwright
[*David Garrick, Society*], 1829-1871)
William Warburton (Bishop of Gloucester,
opposed slavery, 1698-1779)
Sir Donald Wolfit (Actor and theatre
manager, 1902-1968)

NEWBATTLE Midlothian
William Creech (Publisher [of Robert
Burns], and Lord Provost of Edinburgh,
1745-1815)

NEWBRIDGE Monmouth
Angus Rowland McBean (Theatrical
photographer, 1904-1990)

NEW BRIGHTON Merseyside
Malcolm Lowry (Novelist [*Under the
Volcano*], 1909-1957)

NEWBURGH Aberdeenshire
James McBey (Etcher who was an official
war artist in World War One,
1883-1959)

NEWBURN Northumberland
William Hedley (Early locomotive builder,
1779-1843)

NEWBURY Berkshire
Richard George Adams (Author of
Watership Down, 1920-)
Francis Baily (Astronomer, specialised in
solar astronomy, 1774-1844)
John Newport Langley (Physiologist,
nervous system specialist, 1852-1925)
Sir Alastair Pilkington (Glass manufacturer,
1920-1995)

NEWBYTH East Lothian
Sir David Baird (Military commander,
wounded at Corunna, 1757-1829)

NEWCASTLE EMLYN Dyfed
David Martyn Lloyd-Jones (Religious author
[*Studies in the Sermon on the Mount*],
1899-1981)

**NEWCASTLE-UNDER-LYME
Staffordshire**
Emma Amos (TV and film actor [*Secrets
and Lies*], 1967-)
Philip Astley (Theatre and circus manager,
1742-1814)
Vera Brittain (Author, wrote *Testament of
Youth* about World War One,
1893-1970)
Dominic Gerald Cork (Test cricketer
[Derbyshire and England], 1971-)

Thomas Harrison (Leading Roundhead, signed Charles I's death warrant, 1606–1660)

NEWCASTLE UPON TYNE
(See also DUDLEY and GATESHEAD)

Thomas Addison (Physician, researched Addison's Disease, 1793–1860)

Donna Air (TV actor and presenter [*The Big Breakfast*], 1979–)

Mark Akenside (Poet and physician whose haughty manner was satirised by Tobias Smollett, 1721–1770)

George Fife Angas (Founder of South Australia, 1789–1879)

Rowan Atkinson (Entertainer, famous for *Blackadder* and *Mr Bean*, 1955–)

Charles Freer Andrews (Missionary in India, friend of Gandhi, 1871–1940)

William Armstrong [Baron] (Industrial magnate, produced weapons and manufactures of heavy engineering, 1810–1900)

Sir Ove Arup (Engineer, worked on Coventry Cathedral and Sydney Opera House, 1895–1988)

Mary Astell (Religious author, described as England's first feminist, 1668–1731)

Charles Avison (Composer and critic, wrote *Essay on Musical Expression*, c.1710–1770)

Neil Bartlett (Professor of Chemistry at the University of California for 25 years, 1932–)

Cuthbert Collingwood [Lord] (Naval commander, took over from Nelson at Trafalgar, 1750–1819)

John Scott Eldon [1st Earl] (Politician, twice Lord Chancellor, 1751–1838)

Elizabeth Elstob (Self-taught scholar and grammarian, 1683–1756)

John Forster (Author, biographer of Dickens, 1812–1876)

Jack Higgins [b.Harry Patterson] (Author of *The Eagle Has Landed*, 1929–)

George Basil Hume [Cardinal] (Archbishop of Westminster from 1976, 1923–1999)

Thomas Joplin (Economist, specialised in banking theory, 1790–1847)

Ebenezer Landells (Wood engraver, launched *Punch* magazine, 1808–1860)

Esther Helen McCracken (Actor and playwright [*Quiet Wedding, Quiet Weekend*], 1902–1971)

Hank Marvin [b.Brian Rankin] (Guitarist [with The Shadows], 1941–)

Jimmy Nail [b.James Michael Bradford] (Actor [*Auf Wiedersehen Pet*] and singer, 1954–)

Alan Frederick Plater (Playwright [*Close the Coalhouse Door* for TV], 1935–)

Nicholas Ridley (Politician, held three cabinet posts, 1929–1993)

Anna Howard Shaw (US-based suffragist and preacher, 1847–1919)

Alan Shearer (International footballer [Newcastle United and England], 1970–)

Sting [b.Gordon Sumner] (Rock singer-songwriter, once with group The Police), 1950–)

NEWHALL Derbyshire

Jean Hanson (Physiologist, studied structure of skeletal muscle, 1919–1973)

NEWNHAM Northamptonshire

Thomas Randolph (Poet and playwright [*The Muses' Looking-Glasse*], 1605–1635)

NEWPORT Fife

Gwen Hardie (Artist, noted for abstract expressions of the female form, 1962–)

NEWPORT Isle of Wight

Marius Göring (Actor, frequently cast in Nazi roles [*Ill Met By Moonlight*], 1912–1998)

NEWPORT Monmouthshire

William Henry Davies (Itinerant poet ['What is this life if, full of care?'], 1871–1940)

John Frost (Chartist who led revolt in Newport and was transported, before being pardoned, 1784–1877)

James Henry Thomas (Locomotive fireman who became trade union steward and a Labour Minister, 1874–1949)

NEWRY County Down

Sir Joseph Barcroft (Physiologist, researched gas warfare 1872–1947)

Julia Glover (Actor, famous in the role of 'Mrs Malaprop' from The Rivals, 1779–1850)

Patrick Jennings (International footballer with Tottenham Hotspur, 1945–)

Lord Charles Russell of Killowen [1st Baron] (Twice Attorney-General, 1832–1900)

NEWSHAM Yorkshire

George Hickes (Royal Chaplain persecuted for his beliefs, 1642–1715)

NEWTON Near Rugby, Warwickshire

Edward Cave (Printer, publisher of Gentleman's Magazine for 23 years, also invented spinning machine, 1691–1754)

NEWTOWN-BY-USK Llansantffraed Powys

Henry Vaughan (Ecclesiastical poet ['Silex Scintillans'], 1622–1695)

NEWTON-LE-WILLOWS Lancashire

Rodney Robert Porter (Nobel Prize-winning biochemist, researched antibodies, 1917–1985)

NEWTON TONY Wiltshire

Celia Fiennes (Puritan travel writer, wrote Through England on a Side Saddle, 1662–1741)

NEWTOWN Powys

Robert Owen (Industrial and social reformer, established New Lanark, 1771–1858)

NISBET Roxburghshire

Samuel Rutherford (Theologian who lost religious office by opposing Restoration of Charles II, c.1600–1661)

NORBURY Shropshire

Richard Barnfield (Poet ['The Affectionate Shepherd'], 1574–1627)

NORMANSTON Suffolk

Frederick Denison Maurice (Theologian and educationalist, 1805–1872)

NORMANTON Yorkshire

Reece Dinsdale (Film actor [A Private Function, Winter Flight], 1959–)

NORTHALLERTON Yorkshire

Thomas Rymer (Historian appointed to William III, also wrote play Edgar, 1641–1713)

NORTHAM Devon

Steven Borough (Explorer, sailed first ship from England to Russia, 1525–1584)

John Henry Taylor (Champion golfer, won British Open five times, 1871–1963)

NORTHAMPTON

William Alwyn (Prolific film composer [Carve Her Name With Pride], 1905–1985)

Sir Malcolm Arnold (Composer of orchestral music, won Oscar for film music [Bridge on the River Kwai], 1921–)

Anne Bradstreet [b.Dudley] (Massachu-setts-based Puritan poet, 1612–1672)

Caroline Chisholm [b.Jones] (Australian-based philanthropist, improved conditions for transported criminals, 1808–1877)

Francis Harry Compton Crick (Nobel Prize-winning DNA scientist, 1916–)

James Rice (Co-authored novels with Sir Walter Besant, 1843–1882)

Edmund Rubbra (Composer of 11 symphonies and other works, 1901–1986)

Thomas Woolston (Ecclesiastical author imprisoned in 1729 for publishing controversial religious theory, 1670–1731)

NORTHILL Bedfordshire

Thomas Tompion ('Father of English watchmaking', 1639–1713)

NORTH SHIELDS Northumberland

Birket Foster (Wood-engraver for *Illustrated London News* who took up water-colour painting, 1825–1899)

William Wouldhave (Lifeboat inventor who lost credit for his work to Henry Greathead, 1751–1821)

NORTH STONEHAM Hampshire

Henry Parry Liddon (Theologian, defended Liberal High Church principles, 1829–1890)

NORTH TAWTON Devon

William Budd (Physician, researched zymotic diseases, 1811–1880)

NORTHWAY Gloucestershire

William Cartwright (Playwright [*The Royal Slave*], 1611–1643)

NORTHWICK PARK Northamptonshire

Lady Mary Jane Kinnaird (Philanthropist, co-founder of the YWCA, 1816–1888)

NORTHWOOD Middlesex

Roger Hilton (Artist, member of the St Ives Group, 1911–1975)

Derek Jarman (Film director [*The Garden, Edward II*], 1942–1994)

NORWICH

Peter Barlow (Physicist, compiled mathematical tables [1814] reprinted as 'Barlow's Tables' [1947], 1776–1862)

John Sherren Brewer (Scholar, principal of working man's college, 1809–1879)

Michael Brunson (TV newsreader and journalist, 1940–)

Sir Edward Crisp Bullard (Geophysicist, Director of the National Physical Laboratory [1950–5], 1907–1980)

John Caius (Physician and administrator, nine times President of the College of Physicians, 1510–1573)

Vernon Castle (Ballroom dancer, devised the Hesitation Waltz and the Turkey-trot, 1887–1918)

Samuel Clarke (Philosopher, promoted mathematical 'proof' of God's existence, 1675–1729)

John Cosin (Bishop of Durham in 1660, used militia to force Nonconformists to attend church, 1594–1672)

John Sell Cotman (Artist, drawing master at King's College, London, 1782–1842)

John Crome (Artist, helped found Norwich Society of Artists, and became its president in 1803, 1768–1821)

William Crotch (Composer, first principal of the Royal College of Music [1822–3], 1775–1847)

Rupert Everett (Film actor [*Dance With a Stranger*], 1959–)

Elizabeth Fry (Quaker prison reformer and philanthropist, 1780–1845)

Luke Hansard (Printer of parliamentary proceedings, 1752–1828)

James Hook (Composer and organist [*The Lass of Richmond Hill*], 1746–1827)

Sir William Jackson Hooker (Botanist, first Director of the Royal Botanic Garden at Kew [1841], 1785–1865)

Juliana of Norwich (Mystic [*Sixteen Revelations of Divine Love*], c.1342–c.1416)

Mary Frances Lyon (Biologist, specialises in mammalian genetics and meta-genesis, 1925–)

Harriet Martineau (Author [*The Hour and the Man*, 1839], 1802–1876)

James Martineau (Theologian, wrote *Types of Ethical Theory*, 1805–1900)

Danny Mills (International footballer [Leeds United and England], 1977–)

Thomas Morley (Composer, compiler of the *Triumphs of Oriana* [1603], 1557–1602)

Ralph Hale Mottram (Novelist [*Spanish Farm*], 1883–1971)

Beth Orton (Singer-songwriter [*Water from a vine-leaf*], 1970–)

Matthew Parker (Second Anglican Archbishop of Canterbury, 1504–1575)

Sir James Edward Smith (Botanist, purchased Linnaeus's natural history collection and became first president of Linnean Society, 1759–1828)

NORWOOD Surrey

Sir Sidney Colvin (Scholar, in charge of British Museum's prints and drawings for nearly 30 years, 1845–1927)

Charles Richardson (Lexicographer [*A New English Dictionary*, 1835–7], 1775–1865)

NOTTINGHAM (See also SNEITON)

John Bird (TV comedian [often works with John Fortune], 1936–)

Sir Jesse Boot [1st Baron Trent] (Retail chemist, opened first retail shop in 1877, 1850–1931)

William Booth (Founder of Salvation Army, 1829–1912)

Tom Browne (Children's illustrator [*Weary Willie* and *Tired Tim*], 1870–1910)

Andy Cole (International footballer [Blackburn Rovers and England], 1971–)

Betty Davies (Scottish-based textile designer, 1935–)

Christopher Dean (World and Olympic champion ice skater [with Jayne Torvill], 1958–)

Caroline Dexter (Writer and feminist, co-produced Australia's first journal published by women, 1819–1884)

Sir Alister Hardy (Marine biologist, researched plankton, 1896–1985)

John Hutchinson (Roundhead commander, imprisoned after the Restoration for having signed Charles I's death-warrant, 1615–1664)

Paul Sandby (Artist, specialised in watercolours, 1725–1809)

Alan Sillitoe (Novelist, [*Loneliness of the Long Distance Runner*], 1928–)

Jayne Torvill (World and Olympic champion ice skater [with Christopher Dean], 1957–)

Gilbert Wakefield (Controversial critic and anti-slavery campaigner, 1756–1801)

Henry Kirke White (Poet ['The Christiad'], died of overwork at Cambridge, 1785–1806)

NUN APPLETON Near Tadcaster, Yorkshire

Sir Francis Hastings Doyle (Poet, and Professor of Poetry at Oxford [1867–77], 1810–1888)

NUNCARGATE Nottinghamshire

Harold Larwood (Test cricketer, featured in 1932–3 'Bodyline series', 1904–1996)

NUNEATON Warwickshire

Ken Loach (TV and film director, [*Kes*, *Cathy Come Home*], 1936–)

Thomas Simpson (Mathematician, 1710–1761)

OAKENGATES Shropshire
Sir Gordon Richards (26 times champion jockey, 1904–1986)

OAKHAM Rutland
'Sir' Jeffrey Hudson (Court dwarf and military commander, 1619–1682)
Titus Oates (Religious 'conspirator', 1649–1705)

OBAN Argyllshire
Donald MacKenzie MacKinnon (Religious philosopher, championed Realism over Idealism, 1913–1994)

OCHILTREE Ayrshire
George Douglas [b.Brown] (Novelist, wrote *The House with the Green Shutters*, 1869–1902)
Charles Tennant (Chemical manufacturer who made bleaching more practicable, establishing world's biggest chemical works [in Glasgow], 1768–1838)

OCKHAM Surrey
William of Occam (Philosopher whose 'Occam's Razor' was seen as a classic test of parsimony, c.1285–1349)

ODCOMBE Somerset
Thomas Corygate (Court jester and traveller [on foot, reached Venice in 1608], c.1577–1617)

ODIHAM Hampshire
William Lilye (Greek and Latin scholar [*Eton Latin Grammar*], c.1466–1522)

OGBOURNE ST ANDREW Near Marlborough, Wiltshire
Sir Samuel Canning (Engineer, pioneered submarine cable-laying across the

Atlantic from the *Great Eastern*, 1823–1908)

OGMORE-BY-SEA Mid-Glamorgan
John Peter Rhys Williams (Rugby Union player, played over 50 times for Wales, 1949–)

OLANTIGH Kent
John Kemp (Archbishop of Canterbury [1452] and twice appointed Chancellor of England, c.1380–1454)

OLDHAM Lancashire
Warren Clarke (TV actor [*Nice Work, Jewel in the Crown*], 1947–)
Joseph Robert Clynes (Trade unionist who became Labour's first Lord Privy Seal, 1869–1949)
Bernard Cribbins (Actor in films [*The Railway Children*] and on TV, 1928–)
Roy Broadbent Fuller (Poet ['The Middle of the War'] and novelist [*Second Curtain*], 1912–1991)
Philip Gilbert Hamerton (Art critic, wrote *The Graphic Arts*, 1834–1894)
Audrey Henshall (Archaeologist, wrote *The Chambered Tombs of Scotland*, 1927–)
Matthew Peter Maynard (Test cricketer [Glamorgan and England], 1966–)
Eric Sykes (Comic writer and actor, 1923–)
Sir William Walton (Composer [*Belshazzar's Feast*], 1902–1983)

OLDMELDRUM Aberdeenshire
Sir Patrick Manson (Leading malaria researcher, 1844–1922)

ORMISTON East Lothian
Charles McLaren (Editor of *The Scotsman* [for 25 years] and the 6th edition of *Encyclopaedia Britannica*, 1782–1866)
Robert Moffat (African missionary in South Africa, father-in-law of David Livingstone, 1795–1883)

ORMSKIRK Lancashire

Sir James Hopwood Jeans (Physicist and astronomer, 1877–1946)

Myles Standish (Became Treasurer of first American settlement after sailing on *Mayflower*, c.1584–1656)

ORTON Cumbria

Thomas Barlow (Bodleian Librarian for 18 years and Bishop of Lincoln, 1607–1691)

OSWALDTWISTLE Lancashire

James Hargreaves (Inventor of 'Spinning Jenny', c.1720–1778)

OSWESTRY Shropshire

Sir Henry Walford Davies (Composer and Master of the King's Music, 1869–1941)

Barbara [Mary Compton] Pym (Novelist [*Quartet in Autumn*], 1913–1980)

OTLEY Yorkshire

Thomas Chippendale (Furniture designer, 1718–1779)

OTTERBOURNE Hampshire

Charlotte Yonge (Novelist [*The Heir of Redclyffe*], 1823–1901)

OTTERY ST MARY Devon

Samuel Taylor Coleridge (Poet [*The Rime of the Ancient Mariner*], 1772–1834)

Edward Davy (Physician and scientist, advanced wireless telegraphy, 1806–1885)

OULTON Yorkshire

Richard Bentley (Classical scholar, involved in controversy about authenticity of *Epistles of Phalaris*, 1662–1742)

OUNDLE Northamptonshire

Ebenezer Prout (Musicologist, introduced Wagner's work to UK, 1835–1909)

Alfred Edward Taylor (Philosopher, expert on Plato, 1869–1945)

OVINGHAM Northumberland

Thomas Bewick (Engraver whose outstanding ornithological woodcuts led to his having a species of swan named after him, 1753–1828)

OXFORD

Martin Amis (Novelist [*Money, Time's Arrow*], 1949–)

Sir Lennox Berkeley (Composer of operas *Nelson* and *Ruth*, 1903–1989)

Sir Basil Blackwell (Publisher and bookseller, 1889–1984)

Tristram Cary (Composer of electronic music, 1925–)

William Chillingworth (Theologian imprisoned during Civil Wars, 1602–1643)

Thomas Cooper (Lexicographer and Bishop of Winchester, c.1517–1594)

Sir William D'Avenant (Poet Laureate sent to the Tower during Civil Wars, 1606–1668)

Jacqueline du Pré (Cellist, 1945–1987)

Orlando Gibbons (Composer [*The Silver Swan*], 1583–1625)

Herbert Allen Giles (Sinologist, compiled *Chinese-English Dictionary*, 1845–1935)

John Richard Green (Historian, wrote *The Making of England*, 1837–1883)

Mike [Stanley Michael Bailey] Hailwood (Champion motorcyclist, 1940–1981)

John Burdon Sanderson Haldane (Biologist who adopted Indian nationality, 1892–1964)

Thomas Harriot (Mathematician and astronomer, tutor to Sir Walter Raleigh, c.1560–1621)

Stephen William Hawking (Physicist, wrote *A Brief History of Time*, 1942–)

Phyliss Dorothy [P.D.] James (Thriller writer [*Death of an Expert Witness*], 1920–)

John [King of England] (1167–1216)

Sir John Kendrew (Nobel Prize-winning biochemist, researched muscle protein, 1917–)

Martin Keown (International footballer [Arsenal and England], 1966–)

Mary Irene Levison [b.Lusk] (Religious reformer, first female chaplain to HM The Queen, 1923–)

Sue MacGregor (Broadcaster recently retired from Radio 4's *Today* programme, 1941–)

Henry [Harry] Marten (Judge and Civil War soldier, imprisoned after Civil Wars for signing Charles I's death warrant, 1602–1680)

Winifred Nicholson [b.Roberts] (Artist, adopted abstract style after husband Ben Nicholson left her, 1893–1981)

Edward Pococke (Oriental scholar, 'his learning the admiration of Europe' – *DNB*, 1604–1691)

Richard I ['Lionheart', King of England] (1157–1199)

Michael Sadleir (Author [*Fanny by Gaslight*] and publisher, 1888–1957)

Dorothy Leigh Sayers (Author, creator of 'Lord Peter Wimsey', 1893–1957)

Humphrey Searle (Composer [opera *Hamlet*], 1915–1982)

Nevil Vincent Sidgwick (Chemist, wrote *The Chemical Elements and Their Compounds*, 1873–1952)

Gertrude Mary Tuckwell (Trade union leader and one of first women JPs, 1861–1951)

Deborah Warner (Theatre and opera director, 1959–)

Anthony Wood (Historian of Oxford, expelled from university for an alleged libel, 1632–1695)

OXTON Cheshire

Cyril Meir Scott (Composer of choral and orchestral works, 1879–1970)

OXTON Nottinghamshire

Sir Kenneth George Grubb (President of the Church Missionary Society for 25 years, 1900–1980)

PADSTOW Cornwall

Humphrey Prideaux (Oriental scholar and Dean of Norwich, 1648–1724)

PAIGNTON Devon

Sue Barker (Former tennis player and TV presenter, 1956–)

PAISLEY Renfrewshire

Mary Bond (Artist inspired by Indian and Mexican cultures, 1939–)

Robert Broom (South African-based palaeontologist, pinpointed time when Man first walked upright, 1866–1951)

John Byrne (Playwright [*The Slab Boys*], 1940–)

Sir Robert Carswell (Pathologist, appointed physician to the King of Belgium in 1840, 1793–1857)

Sir Peter Coats (Textile industrialist and local benefactor, 1808–1890)

Thomas Coats (Textile industrialist and local benefactor, 1809–1883)

Margaret Caldwell Donaldson (Psychologist, wrote *Children's Minds*, 1926–)

Linda Finnie (Opera singer, specialises in Wagnerian roles, 1952–)

Pam Hogg (Fashion designer, 1958–)

Jessie Newbery (Designer, promoted embroidery as an art form, 1864–1948)

Fulton MacKay (Actor, played warder 'Mr McKay' in TV's *Porridge*, 1922–1987)

Hugh Ross MacKintosh (Theological author [*The Christian Experience of Forgiveness*], 1870–1936)

William McNaught (Engineer who invented steam-compounding technique which became known as 'McNaughting', 1813–1881)

William Sharp (Author who sometimes wrote as 'Fiona McLeod' [*The Mountain Lovers*], 1855–1905)

David Stow (Educationalist, pioneered co-education, 1793–1864)

Robert Tannahill (Folklorist and poet who drowned himself locally, 1774–1810)

Alexander Wilson (Weaver who emigrated to US where he became a leading ornithologist, 1766–1813)

John Wilson ['Christopher North'] (Critic and journalist, 1785–1854)

PANDY Gwent
Raymond Williams (Historian [*Culture and Society*] and novelist [*The Fight for Manod*], 1921–1988)

PANGBOURNE Berkshire
John Maddison Morton (Playwright [*Box and Cox*], 1811–1891)

PARKGATE Cheshire
Sir Wilfred Thomason Grenfell (Medical missionary in Labrador, 1865–1940)

PAULERSPURY Northamptonshire
William Carey (Pioneering Baptist missionary in India, 1761–1834)

PAWLETT Somerset
Peter Haggett (Geographer, wrote *The Geographer's Art*, 1933–)

PEACEHAVEN Sussex
Allison Fisher (Snooker player, professional since age 15, 1968–)

PEEBLES
Robert Chambers (Historian [*Traditions of Edinburgh*] and publisher, 1802–1871)

William Chambers (Publisher who became Lord Provost of Edinburgh, 1800–1883)

John Veitch (Philosopher, wrote *Dualism and Monism*, 1829–1894)

PELYNT Cornwall
Geoffrey Edward Grigson (Poet, founded magazine *New Verse* [1933–9], 1905–1985)

PEMBROKE
Henry VII [King of England] (1457–1509)

PENARTH South Glamorgan
Eric Linklater (Scottish-based novelist [*Private Angelo*], 1899–1974)

PENEGOES Gwynedd
Richard Wilson (Landscape artist, 1714–1782)

PENICUIK Midlothian
James Cossar Ewart (Zoologist, researched animal breeding and hybridisation, 1851–1933)

PENKHULL Staffordshire
Sir Oliver Joseph Lodge (Physicist, pioneered radio-telegraphy, 1851–1940)

PENPONT Dumfriesshire
Joseph Thomson (First European explorer to reach Lake Nyasa, 1858–1895)

PENSHURST Kent
Mary Herbert [b.Sidney, later Countess of Pembroke] (Writer, edited her brother Philip's work after his death in 1586, 1561–1621)

Algernon Sidney (Alleged regicide plotter, c.1622–1683)

Sir Philip Sidney (Poet and soldier killed in action in the Netherlands, 1554–1586)

PENZANCE Cornwall
Leonard Henry Courtney [1st Baron]

(Journalist who became Deputy Speaker
of the House of Commons, 1832–1918)
Sir Humphry Davy (Chemist and inventor
[of the Miners' Safety Lamp],
1778–1829)

PERSLEY Aberdeenshire
Sir Arthur Keith (Anthropologist involved in
Piltdown Man hoax, 1866–1955)

PERTH
John Buchan [1st Baron Tweedsmuir]
(Author [*The 39 Steps*] and statesman,
1875–1940)
Ann Heron Gloag (Co-founder of the bus
company, Stagecoach, 1942–)
Sir Patrick Geddes (Environmentalist and
town planner, 1854–1932)
David Octavius Hill (Artist and pioneering
photographer, 1802–1870)
Marjorie Kennedy-Fraser (Singer and
librettist, 1857–1930)
Charles MacKay (Songwriter [*The Good
Time Coming*], 1814–1889)
William Henry Mansfield [1st Earl] (English
Attorney-General, 1705–1793)
William Soutar (Poet, author of the
autobiographical *Diaries of a Dying Man*,
1898–1943)

PETERBOROUGH Cambridgeshire
William Paley (Theologian, author of
Natural Theology, 1743–1805)

PETERSFIELD Sussex
William Cowper (Surgeon and anatomist,
wrote *The Anatomy of Human Bodies*,
1666–1709)

PETTS WOOD Kent
Jack Dee (TV comedian and presenter,
1961–)

PETWORTH Sussex
Wilfred Scawen Blunt (Poet, imprisoned for
agitation in Ireland, 1840–1922)

PINNER Middlesex
Dame Ivy Compton-Burnett (Novelist
[*Pastors and Masters, Brothers and
Sisters*], 1892–1969)
Sir Elton John [b.Reginald Kenneth Dwight]
(Singer [*Candle in the Wind*], 1947–)

PITSCOTTIE Fife
Robert Lindsay of Pitscottie (Historian of
Stewart Kings, James I–III, c.1532–1580)

PLAXTOL Kent
Walter Turner Monckton [1st Viscount] (Cabinet minister and statesman, 1891–1965)

PLUMBLAND Cumbria
William Nicolson (Bishop of Carlisle, and
historian, 1655–1727)

PLYMOUTH Devon
George Bentham (Botanist, compiled [with
Joseph Hooker] *Genera Plantarum* over
21 years, 1800–1884)
William Bligh (Commander of HMS *Bounty*,
1754–c.1817)
Beryl Cook (Artist specialising in painting
jolly, plump ladies, 1937–)
Henry Austin Dobson (Poet and literary
biographer [of Goldsmith, Fielding, etc],
1840–1921)
Sir Charles Lock Eastlake (Artist, famed for
his portraits of Napoleon as a prisoner,
1793–1856)
Charles Lock Eastlake (Architect and
designer, his 'Eastlake' style famous in
US, 1836–1906)
Michael Mackintosh Foot (Politician, led
Labour Party [1980–3], 1913–)
Joseph Glanvill (Philosopher, argued for
freedom of thought, 1636–1680)

Robert Stephen Hawker (Poet and collector of local ballads, 1803–1875)

Sir John Hawkins (Naval commander, sailed with Drake to the Spanish Main, 1532–1595)

Benjamin Robert Haydon (Artist who, despite receiving royal patronage, shot himself in his studio, 1786–1846)

William Elford Leach (Naturalist, expert on crustacea, 1790–1836)

Sir Desmond MacCarthy (Author and literary critic [*Sunday Times*] for 24 years, 1878–1952)

Thomas James Northcote (Artist, painted 'Princes in the Tower', 1746–1831)

David Anthony Owen [Baron] (Statesman, Foreign Secretary [1977–9], 1938–)

Samuel Prout (Watercolour artist, 1783–1852)

Stuart Rendel [1st Baron] (Engineer and philanthropist in Wales, 1834–1913)

Donald Sinden (Actor [*The Cruel Sea, Doctor in the House*], 1923–)

Wayne Sleep (Dancer and choreographer, 1948–)

Sir John Collings Squire (Author and poet ['Steps to Parnassus'], 1884–1958)

Leonard Alfred Strong (Poet ['Dublin Days'] and novelist [*Deliverance*], 1896–1958)

PLYMPTON Devon
Sir Joshua Reynolds (Portrait artist, 1723–1792)

POLMONT Stirlingshire
Peter Drummond (Locomotive engineer for two Scottish railway companies, 1850–1918)

PONTNEWYNYDD Gwent
Dame Gwyneth Jones (Soprano, famed interpreter of Wagner and Strauss, 1936–)

PONTRHYDYFEN Gwynedd
Richard Burton [b.Jenkins] (Actor [*The Robe, Cleopatra*], 1925–1984)

PONTYPOOL Gwent
Thomas Barker (Artist, painted rural scenes, 1769–1847)

Joan Mary Ruddock (Peace campaigner and MP, 1943–)

PONTYPRIDD Mid-Glamorgan
Sir Geraint Llewellyn Evans (Operatic baritone, 1922–1992)

Alun Richards (Novelist [*A Woman of Experience*] and playwright [TV's *The Onedin Line*], 1929–)

Tom Jones [b.Thomas Jones Woodward] (Pop singer [*It's Not Unusual*], 1940–)

POOLE Dorset
Thomas Bell (Naturalist, researched crabs and lobsters, 1792–1880)

John Le Carré [b.David John Moore Cornwell] (Novelist [*The Spy Who Came in From the Cold*], 1931–)

Katy Hill (TV presenter [*Blue Peter, Top of the Pops*], 1970–)

James Stephen (Anti-slavery campaigner, 1758–1832)

PORTADOWN County Armagh
Anne Crawford Acheson (Sculptor, awarded CBE for her war service, 1882–1962)

PORT ELIOT Cornwall
Sir John Eliot (Statesman, died in the Tower of London for criticising royal power, 1592–1632)

PORT GLASGOW Renfrewshire
James Thomson (Poet [*The City of Dreadful Night*], 1834–1882)

PORTSEA Hampshire

Sir Henry Ayers (Australian politician after whom Ayers Rock is named, 1821–1897)

Hertha Ayrton [b.Marks] (Physicist, was refused Fellowship of the Royal Society as she was a married woman, 1854–1923)

PORT SETON East Lothian

John Bellany (Artist, 1942–)

PORTSMOUTH Hampshire

George Balfour (Civil engineer, co-founded Balfour Beatty Ltd and pioneered the National Grid, 1872–1941)

Sir Walter Besant (Novelist and social reformer, 1836–1901)

Howard Brenton (Playwright [*The Romans in Britain*], 1942–)

Isambard Kingdom Brunel (Innovative engineer, 1806–1859)

Leonard James Callaghan [Baron] (Prime Minister [1976–9], 1912–)

Barry [Barrington Windsor] Cunliffe (Archaeologist, excavated at Bath and Chichester, 1939–)

Charles Dickens (Novelist, 1812–1870)

Jonas Hanway (Philanthropist, formed Marine Society and pioneered use of the umbrella, 1712–1786)

Sir Frederic Madden (Antiquarian, edited 'Wyclif's Bible', 1801–1873)

Olivia Manning (Novelist [*Fortunes of War*], 1908–1980)

George Meredith (Novelist [*The Ordeal of Richard Feverel*], 1828–1909)

Edward Miall (Nonconformist clergyman and politician, 1809–1881)

John Pounds (Founder of 'Ragged Schools', 1766–1839)

Susannah Haswell Rowson (US-based novelist, regarded as first female to make a living out of writing, c.1762–1824)

PORT TALBOT West Glamorgan

Sir Anthony Hopkins (US-based actor [*Remains of the Day, Hannibal*], 1937–)

POTTERNE Wiltshire

Nigel Marlin Balchin (Novelist, author of *The Small Back Room*, 1908–1970)

POTTERSPURY Northamptonshire

George Claridge Druce (Botanist, produced floras of Thames Valley counties, 1850–1932)

POWDERHAM Devon

Edward Frederick Halifax [1st Earl, 2nd creation] (Foreign Secretary [1938–40] and George VI's choice to become Prime Minister in 1940, 1881–1959)

POYSTON Dyfed

Sir Thomas Picton (Military commander, killed at Waterloo, 1758–1815)

PREES HALL Cheshire

Rowland Hill [1st Viscount] (Military commander, distinguished in Napoleonic Wars, 1772–1842)

PRESCOT Cheshire

John Philip Kemble (Actor-manager [of Covent Garden Theatre], 1757–1823)

PRESTATYN Clwyd

Barry Flanagan (Modern sculptor, 1941–)

Emyr Humphreys (Novelist [*Bonds of Attachment*], 1919–)

John Leslie Prescott (Deputy Prime Minister [1997–], 1938–)

PRESTON Lancashire

Sir Richard Arkwright (Industrial inventor [spinning machines], 1732–1792)

Fiona Armstrong (TV newscaster and renowned angler, 1956–)

Roy Barraclough (TV actor ['Alec Gilroy' in *Coronation Street*], 1935–)

Angela Brazil (Author, specialised in girls' school stories, 1868–1947)

Arthur Devis (Artist and restorer, 1711–1787)

Sir Tom Finney (International footballer [England and Preston North End], 1921–)

Andrew Flintoff (Test cricketer [Lancashire and England], 1977–)

Sir John Glubb (Military commander known as 'Glubb Pasha', 1897–1986)

Sir John Eldon Gorst (Politician, MP for Cambridge University [1892–1906], 1835–1916)

Peter Purves (TV broadcaster, particularly for children [*Blue Peter*], 1939–)

Robert William Service (Canadian-based poet ['The Shooting of Dan McGrew'], 1874–1958)

Francis Thompson (Poet ['The Hound of Heaven'], 1859–1907)

PRESTONPANS East Lothian
Alexander Carlyle (Diarist and parish minister for 57 years, 1722–1805)

PRESTWICH Lancashire
Victoria Wood (Comedian [*Dinner Ladies*] and writer, 1953–)

PRILLISK County Tyrone
William Carleton (Novelist, depicted Irish rural life, 1794–1869)

PROVIDENCE GREEN North Yorkshire
John Hughlings Jackson (Neurologist, helped 'map' the human brain, 1835–1911)

PUDSEY Yorkshire
Sir Leonard Hutton (Test cricketer [England and Yorkshire], 1916–1990)

Raymond Illingworth (Test cricketer and manager [England, Yorkshire, and Leicestershire], 1932–)

PUSEY Berkshire
Edward Bouverie Pusey (Theologian, leader of the Oxford Movement, 1800–1882)

QUIDHAMPTON Wiltshire
Simon Forman ('Astrologer and quack doctor' – *DNB*, 1552–1611)

RADIPOLE Dorset
Verney Lovett Cameron (Explorer, first European to cross Africa from coast to coast, 1844–1894)

RAMPISHAM Dorset
Francis Glisson (First to describe anatomy of the liver, 1597–1677)

RAMSGATE Kent
Winifred Austen (Wildlife artist, specialised in painting marine birds, 1876–1964)

Brenda Blethyn (TV and film actor [*Secrets and Lies*], 1946–)

RAMSGILL Yorkshire
Eugene Aram (Scholar hanged for murder, 1704–1759)

RAPLOCH Stirlingshire
Dougal Graham (Jacobite balladeer, c.1724–1779)

RATHVEN Banffshire
Alexander Geddes (Biblical translator who questioned Christ's divinity, 1737–1802)

RATTRAY Perthshire
Donald Cargill (Covenanter, executed in Edinburgh for his beliefs, and for 'excommunicating' Charles II, 1619–1681)

RAWDON Yorkshire

Dennis Brian Close (Former Test cricketer [Yorkshire and England], 1931–)

READING Berkshire

Sir George Alexander (Actor, and manager of St James's Theatre from 1881, 1858–1918)

Ken [Kenneth Frank] Barrington (Cricketer, played 82 Tests for England, 1930–1981)

Sir Alec Victor Bedser (Test cricketer, played 51 times for England, 1918–)

Howard Davies (Stage director, established Royal Shakespeare Company's London studio theatre, the Warehouse, 1945–)

Tracey Edwards (Yachtswoman, captained first all-woman crew in round-the-world race, 1962–)

William Laud (Archbishop of Canterbury, executed by Roundheads, 1573–1645)

Peter Barker Howard May (Test cricketer, captained England 41 times, 1929–1994)

Arthur George Negus (TV antiques expert, 1903–1985)

Mike Oldfield (Musician whose album 'Tubular Bells' charted for five years, 1935–)

Charles Simeon (Evangelical preacher, co-founded Church Missionary Society, 1759–1836)

Sir Thomas Talfourd (Lawyer and politician, produced Copyright Acts, 1795–1854)

Elizabeth Taylor (Novelist [*The Wedding Group*], 1912–1975)

REDBRAES Berwickshire

Lady Grizel Baillie (Poet, covenanter, 1665–1746)

REDDING Near Falkirk

(See also FALKIRK)

Annie Hunter Small (Missionary, forced home from India by ill-health, 1857–1945)

REDDITCH Worcestershire

Charles Dance (Actor in films [*Gosford Park*] and TV [*Jewel in the Crown*], 1946–)

REDRUTH Cornwall

(See also ILLOGAN)

Kristen Scott Thomas (Film actor [*The English Patient, Gosford Park*], 1960–)

REIGATE Surrey

Anne Coates (Oscar-winning film editor [*Lawrence of Arabia*], 1925–)

Dame Margot Fonteyn (Ballerina, famed partner of Rudolph Nureyev, 1919–1991)

David Stuart Sheppard (Ex-cricketing Bishop of Liverpool, captained England in 1954, 1929–)

RENDCOMBE Gloucestershire

Frederick Sanger (Biochemist, first winner to receive two Nobel Prizes for chemistry [1958 and 1980], 1918–)

RENFREW

John MacQuarrie (Religious philosopher [*Principles of Christian Theology*], 1919–)

Ninian Winzet (Catholic churchman deported from Scotland after refusing to sign Protestant confession of faith, 1518–1592)

RHOSGADFAN Gwynedd

Kate Roberts (Novelist, described as 'the Welsh Chekhov', 1891–1985)

RHYL Clwyd

Ruth Ellis (Murderer, last woman to be hanged in UK, 1926–1955)

Penelope Ruth Mortimer [b.Fletcher] (Novelist [*The Pumpkin Eater*], 1918–)

RHYMNEY Mid–Glamorgan

Idris Davies (Miner, teacher, and poet, 1905–1953)

Thomas Jones (Administrator and author, founded Coleg Harlech in 1927, 1870–1955)

RHYNIE Aberdeenshire
Alexander Murdoch Mackay (Missionary in Uganda, 1849–1890)

RICHMOND Surrey
Dame Ann Elizabeth Butler-Sloss [b.Havers] (High Court judge, first woman to serve on Court of Appeal, 1933–)
Arthur Cayley (Mathematician, researched theory of matrices, 1821–1895)
Ronald Colman (Actor [*The Prisoner of Zenda*], 1891–1958)
Richard Frederick Dimbleby (Broadcaster who commentated on state occasions, 1913–1965)
Edward VIII [King of Great Britain, Duke of Windsor after 1936 Abdication] (1894–1972)
Dame Celia Johnson (Actor [*Brief Encounter*], 1908–1982)
John Mitford (Poet, edited *Gentleman's Magazine* [1834–50], 1781–1859)
Sir Clive Sinclair (Computer designer and inventor of C5, a personal transport vehicle, 1940–)
John Napier Turner (Prime Minister of Canada for short time in 1984, 1929–)

RICHMOND Yorkshire
John Laird Lawrence [1st Baron] (Governor-General of India, 1811–1879)
Conyers Middleton (Unorthodox clergyman who questioned historical accuracy of the Bible, 1683–1750)

RIDING MILL Northumberland
Thomas William Graveney (Test cricketer, made 11 centuries for England, 1927–)

RINGWOULD Kent
Sir George Gipps (Governor of New South Wales [1838–46], 1791–1847)

RIPLEY Derbyshire
Sir Barnes Neville Wallis (Aeronautical engineer, designed Wellington bomber and the 'bouncing bomb' used by 'Dam Busters', 1887–1979)

RIPLEY Surrey
Eric Clapton [b.Eric Patrick Clapp] (Rock singer and guitarist, 1945–)

RIPON Yorkshire
Frederick Orpen Bower (Professor of Botany at Glasgow University for 40 years, author of *The Ferns*, 1855–1948)

RIPPLE Kent
Sir John French [Earl of Ypres] (Military officer, replaced by Haig as commander on the Western Front in World War One, 1852–1925)

RIVENHALL Essex
Thomas Tusser (Agricultural author [*Hundreth Good Pointes of Husbandrie*], died when imprisoned for debt, c.1520–1580)

RIVERHEAD Near Sevenoaks, Kent
Baron Jeffrey Amherst (Soldier, Governor-General of British North America [1760–3], 1717–1797)

ROCHDALE Lancashire
(See also HEYWOOD)
John Bright (Radical politician who became President of the Board of Trade, 1811–1889)
Dame Gracie Fields (Singer, 1898–1979)
Sir James Phillips Kay Shuttleworth (School reformer, instituted school inspection system, 1804–1877)

ROCHESTER Kent
Enid Bagnold (Novelist [*National Velvet*],
1889–1981)
John Edensor Littlewood (Mathematician,
expert on summability theory and
Tauberian Theorems, 1885–1977)

ROCK FERRY Cheshire
May Sinclair (Author of 24 novels including
The Divine Fire, 1863–1946)

RODE Somerset
Harold Gilman (London-based artist,
1878–1919)

ROMFORD Essex
Anthony [Tony] Adams (International
footballer [Arsenal and England], 1966–)
Johnny Leach (Table tennis internationalist,
represented his country 152 times,
1922–)
Richard Madeley (TV journalist and
presenter [with wife Judy Finnigan],
1956–)

ROMSEY Hampshire
Giles Jacob (Compiler of legal dictionaries,
1686–1744)
Sir William Petty (Economist who was
appointed Surveyor-General of Ireland,
1623–1687)

ROPLEY Hampshire
Samuel Rawson Gardiner (Historian, wrote
*History of England From the Accession of
James I...* [1863], 1829–1902)

ROPSLEY Lincolnshire
Richard Foxe (Bishop of four sees and
founder of Corpus Christi College, Oxford,
in 1517, c.1448–1528)

ROSENEATH Dunbartonshire
John Anderson (Scientist, bequeathed

Anderson's College in Glasgow,
1726–1796)

ROSSALL Lancashire
William Allen [Cardinal] (Religious activist,
planned to convert England back to
Catholicism, 1532–1594)

ROTHAMSTED Hertfordshire
Sir John Bennet Lawes (Founder of the
world's first agricultural research station
[at Rothamsted], 1814–1900)

ROTHBURY Northumberland
Rowland Taylor (Religious martyr burnt to
death for his beliefs, d.1555)

ROTHERHAM Yorkshire
Sir Donald Coleman Bailey (Bailey-bridge
designer, 1901–1985)
Ebenezer Elliott (Poet who campaigned
against 'bread tax' [*Corn-Law Rhymes*],
1781–1849)
Sir Harold Hobson (Theatre critic [*Sunday
Times*, 1947–76] and radio broadcaster,
1904–1992)
David Seaman (International footballer
[Arsenal and England], 1963–)

ROTHESAY Isle of Bute
Sir William McEwen (Neurologist,
pioneered operations on the human
brain, 1848–1924)
Sheina Macalister Marshall (Zoologist,
discovered local sources of agar jelly [for
medical purposes] during World War
Two, 1896–1977)

ROTHIEMAY Banffshire
James Ferguson (Astronomer whose
writings and mechanical models of the
solar system influenced William Herschel,
1710–1776)

ROTHIEMURCHUS Inverness-shire

Duncan James Grant (London-based artist, 1885–1978)

ROTHLEY Leicestershire

Thomas Babington Macaulay [1st Baron] (Author [*Lays of Ancient Rome*] and politician [Secretary for War, 1839–41], 1800–1859)

Sir George Otto Trevelyan [2nd Baronet] (Statesman, successively secretary for both Ireland and Scotland, 1838–1928)

ROWDE Wiltshire

Sir Matthew Digby Wyatt (Architect, one of the designers of the 1851 Great Exhibition, 1820–1877)

ROWTON Shropshire

Richard Baxter (Clergyman, one-time Royal Chaplain persecuted for his beliefs, 1615–1691)

RUDSTON Yorkshire

Winifred Holtby (Novelist [*South Riding*], 1898–1935)

RUGBY Warwickshire

Rupert Brooke (Poet, died on his way to Dardanelles campaign, 1887–1915)

Sir Joseph Norman Lockyer (Astronomer, predicted discovery of helium, 1836–1920)

Dame Rose Macaulay (Novelist [*Told By an Idiot*] and travel writer [*The Pleasure of Ruins*], 1881–1958)

Lawrence Sheriff (Founder of Rugby school, d.1567)

Janice Tchalenko (Ceramic designer, 1942–)

RUISLIP Middlesex

Sue Cook (TV presenter [*Crimewatch*], 1949–)

RUNCORN Cheshire

Sir Thomas Caine (Novelist [*The Eternal City*] and Member of the House of Keys, 1853–1931)

RUSHDEN Northamptonshire

Herbert Ernest Bates (Novelist [*The Darling Buds of May*], 1905–1974)

Daniel Whitby (Bishop of Salisbury, pleaded for tolerance towards Nonconformists, 1638–1726)

RUTHERGLEN Near Glasgow

Sir Denis William Brogan (Historian of United States, 1900–1974)

Robbie Coltrane [b.Anthony Robert McMillan] (Film and TV actor [*Cracker*], 1950–)

RUTHVEN Inverness-shire

James MacPherson (Poet, creator of 'Ossian' myth, 1736–1796)

RYDE Isle of Wight

Albert Frederick Pollard (Historian, founder of Historical Association in 1906, 1869–1948)

RYE Sussex

John Fletcher (Dramatist [*The Faithful Shepherdess*], collaborated with Shakespeare, 1579–1625)

ST AGNES Cornwall

John Opie (Portrait painter known as the 'Cornish Wonder', 1716–1807)

ST ALBANS Hertfordshire

Timothy Sherwood (International footballer [Tottenham Hotspur and England], 1969–)

Sir Thomas Spencer Wells (Surgeon, specialised in ovarian surgery, 1818–1897)

ST ANDREWS Fife

Willie Auchterlonie (Champion golfer who won the British Open aged 21 and using only home-made clubs, 1872–1963)

Wilhelmina Barns-Graham (Water-colourist, 1912–)

Andrew Bell (Educationalist, advocated monitorial system, 1753–1852)

Joseph Grimond [Baron] (Politician, led Liberal Party [1956–67], 1913–1993)

Thomas ['Old Tom'] Morris (Golfer, four times winner of British championship, 1821–1908)

George John Whyte-Melville (Blood-sports novelist, died hunting accident, 1821–1878)

ST ASAPH Clwyd

Ian Rush (International footballer [Wales and Liverpool], 1961–)

ST AUSTELL Cornwall

John William Colenso (Bishop of York, accused of heresy for questioning accuracy of the Bible, 1814–1883)

Robert Duncan (TV actor [Drop the Dead Donkey] and presenter, 1952–)

Alfred Leslie Rowse (Historian [The England of Elizabeth], 1903–1997)

ST BEES Cumbria

Edmund Grindal (Archbishop of Canterbury from 1576, 1519–1583)

ST COLUMB MINOR Cornwall

William Gerald Golding (Novelist [Lord of the Flies], 1911–1993)

ST DAVID'S Dyfed

Richard Llewellyn [Richard Doyle Lloyd] (Author of How Green Was My Valley, 1907–1983)

Thomas Tomkins (Worcester Cathedral organist, composed Coronation music for Charles I in 1626, 1572–1656)

ST HELENS Isle of Wight

Sophia Dawes [Baroness of Feucheres] (Court adventuress suspected of murdering her French husband, 1790–1840)

ST HELENS Lancashire

Sir Thomas Beecham (Conductor, founded Royal Philharmonic Orchestra in 1946, 1879–1961)

John William Draper (US-based author, researched history of science, 1811–1882)

John Lyon (Amateur boxing champion, only man to win eight ABA titles, 1962–)

John Rylands (Textile manufacturer and benefactor, for whom Manchester University's library is named, 1801–1888)

ST IVES Cambridgeshire

Elizabeth Gunning (Socialite, married successively to Dukes of Hamilton and Argyll, 1734–1790)

Maria Gunning (Socialite, married Earl of Coventry, so popular she was mobbed in Hyde Park, 1733–1760)

Walter Theodore Watts-Dunton (Poet and literary critic, looked after the poet Swinburne in his later years, 1832–1914)

ST IVES Cornwall

Leonard Trelawney Hobhouse (Sociologist and one-time editor of Tribune, 1864–1929)

George Walter Selwyn Lloyd (Composer and conductor, his health and output affected by war service, 1913–)

ST LEONARDS-ON-SEA Sussex

Charles Anthony Raven [Tony] Crosland (Foreign Secretary who died in office, 1918–1977)

Sheila Kaye-Smith (Novelist [Joanna Godden], 1887–1956)

ST MARY'S HOLM Orkney

Florence Marian McNeill (Folklorist and historian, wrote *The Silver Bough*, 1885–1973)

ST NEOTS Cambridgeshire

Rula Lenska (TV actor and series presenter, 1947–)

ST PAUL'S WALDEN BURY Hertfordshire

Queen Elizabeth (Queen Consort [1936–52], then Queen Mother, 1900–2002)

ST STEPHENS Cornwall

Joseph Hocking (Ecclesiastical author [*The God That Answers By Fire*], 1855–1937)

SAFFRON WALDEN Essex

Gabriel Harvey (Satirist, who also studied poetic form, c.1550–1630)

SALFORD Adjoining Manchester

Leila Berg (Children's author [*A Box for Benny*], 1917–)

George Bradshaw (Railway timetable publisher from 1839, 1801–1853)

Shelagh Delaney (Playwright [*A Taste of Honey*], 1939–)

Albert Finney (Actor [*Tom Jones* 1963, *Miller's Crossing* 1990], 1936–)

Walter Greenwood (Author of *Love On the Dole*, 1903–1974)

James Prescott Joule (Physicist, has unit of energy named after him, 1818–1889)

Mike Leigh (Film director [*Secrets and Lies*], 1943–)

Ewan MacColl [James Miller] (Singer and author, wrote *The First Time Ever I Saw Your Face* in 1958, 1915–1989)

Paul Scholes (International footballer [Manchester United and England], 1974–)

SALISBURY Wiltshire

Michael Crawford (Film, TV, and theatre star [*Phantom of the Opera*], 1942–)

Henry Fawcett (Political economist who, as Postmaster-General, introduced parcel post and postal orders, 1833–1884)

James Harris (Grammatical scholar, 1709–1780)

John of Salisbury (Statesman and scholar, 'the most learned classical writer of the Middle Ages' – *DNB*, c.1115–1180)

Charles Viner (Legal expert, wrote *Abridgement of the Law of England* in 23 vols, 1678–1756)

John Robert Whiting (Playwright [*The Devils*], 1917–1963)

SALTASH Cornwall

Dame Moura Lympany (Concert pianist, 1916–)

SALTCOATS Ayrshire

Sir Hugh Allan (Canadian-based owner of Allan shipping line, 1810–1882)

SANDBACH Cheshire

Ivor Armstrong Richards (Literary critic, wrote *Principles of Literary Criticism*, 1893–1979)

SANDGATE Kent

Hattie [Josephine Edwina] Jacques (Comic actor, star of TV, radio, and of the *Carry On* films, 1924–1980)

SANDHOE Northumberland

Bryan Donkin (Inventor of printing and canning equipment, 1768–1855)

SANDRIDGE Devon

John Davis (Navigator, discovered the Falkland Islands and made three Arctic voyages in search of the North-West Passage, c.1550–1605)

SANDRINGHAM Norfolk
Princess Diana (1961–1997)
George VI [King of Great Britain]
(1895–1952)

SANDWICH Kent
George William Reynolds (Journalist [editor
of *Reynolds Weekly Newspaper*] and
novelist, 1814–1879)

SAWLEY Derbyshire
John Clifford (Baptist clergyman, first
President of the Baptist World Alliance,
1636–1923)

SCALEBY Cumbria
William Gilpin (Clergyman artist, wrote and
illustrated books on British scenery,
1724–1804)

SCARBOROUGH Yorkshire
Sir George Cayley (Engineer and aviator,
made man-carrying glider in 1853,
1771–1857)
John Harwood Hick (Theologian, wrote *God
and the Universe of Faiths*, 1922–)
Susan Elizabeth Hill (Novelist [*Air and
Angels*], and stage adapter [*The Woman
in Black*], 1942–)
Charles Laughton (Actor [*Mutiny on the
Bounty, Witness For the Prosecution*],
1899–1962)
Frederic Leighton [1st Baron] (Artist and
sculptor, 1830–1896)
Dame Edith Louisa Sitwell (Poet ['The
Outcasts'], 1887–1964)
Sir Sachaverell Sitwell (Poet and critic ['An
Indian Summer'], 1897–1988)
William Crawford Williamson (Surgeon
who became one of the earliest
palaeobotanists, 1816–1895)
Penelope Wilton (TV actor, 'Anne' in *Ever
Decreasing Circles*, 1946–)

SCONE Perthshire
David Douglas (Botanist and plant collector
in North America, after whom the
Douglas Fir is named, 1798–1834)

SCOTSWOOD Northumberland
Basil Bunting (Poet ['Briggflatts'],
1900–1985)

SCOURIE Sutherland
James MacKay [Baron MacKay of
Clashfern] (Lord Chancellor [1987-97],
1927–)

SCUNTHORPE Lincolnshire
Tony Jacklin (Champion golfer who won
both British and US Opens in 1969/70,
1944–)
Martin Simpson (Folk singer and guitarist,
1953–)

SEDGEFIELD County Durham
Peter Willey (Test cricketer
[Northamptonshire, Leicestershire and
England] and Test umpire, 1949–)

SEDGWICK Sussex
Sir Nevile Meyrick Henderson (Ambassador
to Hitler's Germany [1937–9],
1882–1942)

SELBORNE Hampshire
Gilbert White (Naturalist who wrote classic
work *The Natural History and Antiquities
of Selborne*, 1720–1793)

SELBY Yorkshire
Henry I [King of England] (1068–1135)
Arthur Hinsley [Cardinal] (Archbishop of
Westminster from 1935, an outspoken
enemy of fascism in Germany and Italy,
1865–1943)
Sir Jonathan Hutchinson (Surgeon,
researched syphilis, 1828–1913)

Smithson Tennant (Chemist, discovered iridium and osmium, 1761–1815)

SELKIRK
Andrew Lang (Mythological author [*Myth, Ritual and Religion*] and co-founder of Psychical Research Society, 1844–1912)

SELSEY BILL West Sussex
Keith Vaughan (Artist, work exhibited at 1951 Festival of Britain, 1912–1977)

SEMLEY Wiltshire
Robert Morley (Actor [*The Trials of Oscar Wilde, Topkapi*], 1908–1992)

SEMPRINGHAM Lincolnshire
Saint Gilbert (Founder of a religious order, c.1083–1189)

SETTLE Yorkshire
George Birkbeck (Educationalist, founded working man's institute which became Birkbeck College, 1776–1841)
Thomas Nuttall (American-based naturalist, 1786–1859)

SEVENOAKS Kent
Vita Sackville-West (Novelist and poet ['All Passions Spent'], 1892–1962)

SHAFTESBURY Dorset
James Granger (Historian [*Biographical History of England*], 1723–1776)
Richard Upjohn (US-based architect, designed Trinity Church, New York City, 1802–1878)

SHAP Cumbria
John Mill (Theologian, Chaplain to Charles II, 1645–1707)

SHEFFIELD
Gordon Banks (Footballer, goalkeeper when England won 1966 World Cup, 1937–)
Sean Bean (TV and film actor [*When Saturday Comes*], 1958–)
Sir William Bennett (Pianist and composer [*The May Queen*], 1816–1875)
Malcolm Bradbury (Novelist [*Eating People is Wrong, The History Man*], 1932–2000)
Harry Brearley (Steel metallurgist, produced stainless steel, 1871–1948)
Antonia Susan Byatt [b.Drabble] (Novelist [*Still-life, Possession*], 1938–)
Bruce Chatwin (Travel author [*In Patagonia*], 1940–1989)
Joe Cocker (Rock and soul singer, 1944–)
Margaret Drabble (Novelist [*Jerusalem the Golden*] and biographer of Arnold Bennett, 1939–)
Sir Charles Harding Firth (Historian and biographer of Cromwell, 1857–1936)
Mark Firth (Philanthropist, bequeathed Sheffield a park and Firth College, 1819–1880)
Sir John Fowler (Co-designer of Forth Railway Bridge, 1817–1898)
Joseph Gillott (Inventor of the steel pen-nib, 1799–1873)
Mary Anne Green (Historian, indexed state papers of Elizabeth I, James I, and Charles II, 1818–1895)
Sir Robert Abbot Hadfield (Metallurgist, developed manganese steel, 1858–1940)
Roy Sydney George Hattersley [Baron] (Politician and journalist, 1932–)
John Hoyland (Artist, works in abstract forms, 1934–)
Jimmy Jewel (Stage comedian, partnered Ben Warriss, 1909–1995)
Rudolph Chambers Lehmann (Newspaper editor and MP, 1856–1929)

Joseph Locke (Civil engineer, built much of West Coast main-line, 1805–1860)

Phil Oakey (Singer with group Human League, 1955–)

Michael Edward Palin (Actor [with TV's Monty Python team] and travel writer, 1943–)

John Roebuck (Pioneering chemical manufacturer, 1718–1794)

Helen Sharman (First Briton in space, occupied Mir space station for a week in 1991, 1963–)

Leonard Charles Smithers (Literary publisher of Wilde and Beardsley, later bankrupt, 1861–1907)

Alison Margaret Smithson (Architect, co-designed 'House of the Future' in 1956, 1928–1993)

Henry Clifton Sorby (Geologist who pioneered use of microscopic techniques, 1826–1908)

John Stringfellow (Aviation pioneer who experimented with steam-powered flight, 1799–1883)

Ben Warriss (Stage comedian, partnered Jimmy Jewell, 1909–1993)

SHEPPERTON Surrey

John Boorman (Film director [*The Emerald Forest, Hope and Glory*], 1933–)

SHERBORNE Dorset

St Stephen Harding (Ecclesiastic, founded Cistercian abbeys in Europe, c.1060–1134)

SHERBORNE Gloucestershire

James Bradley (Astronomer, established Greenwich meridian, 1693–1762)

SHIFNAL Shropshire

Thomas Beddoes (Physician, experimented with gas treatment of illness, 1760–1808)

SHILSTONE Devon

Thomas Savery (Mining engineer, pioneered steam-pumping of mines, c.1650–1715)

SHILTON Warwickshire

Christopher Saint Germain (Legal author, wrote *Doctor and Student*, an examination of the application of common law, c.1460–1540)

SHIPBOURNE Kent

Christopher Smart (Poet ['A Song to David'], died insane, 1722–1771)

SHIPLEY Yorkshire

Tony [Cecil Antonio] Richardson (Film director [*Tom Jones, Charge of the Light Brigade*], 1928–1991)

SHIREHAMPTON Near Bristol

Archibald Henry Sayce (Biblical scholar, wrote *Principles of Comparative Philology*, 1845–1933)

SHIRLEY Derbyshire

John Cowper Powys (Novelist [*Owen Glendower*] and poet, 1872–1963)

Theodore Francis Powys (Novelist [*Mr Weston's Good Wine*], 1875–1953)

SHOTTS Lanarkshire

Matthew Baillie (Anatomist and physiologist, wrote first English-language treatise on morbid anatomy, 1761–1823)

Margaret McCrorie Herbison (First Minister of Social Security, 1907–1996)

Andrew Keir (Actor, associated with role of 'Professor Quatermass', 1926–1997)

John Millar (Sociological and constitutional historian, opposed slave trade, 1735–1801)

SHREWSBURY Shropshire

John Benbow (Admiral, died fighting French in the West Indies, 1653–1702)

William Henry Betty (Actor, had played many Shakespearean leading roles by the age of 17, 1791–1874)

Charles Burney (Musicologist, wrote *History of Music* over 13 years, 1726–1814)

Thomas Churchyard (Soldier and author [*A Myrrour For Man*], 1520–1604)

Charles Darwin (Devised theory of evolution, 1809–1892)

Alexander [Sandy] Lyle (Golfer who won British, French and European Opens, and US Masters, 1958–)

Thomas Minton (Ceramic manufacturer, established Stoke-on-Trent as centre for quality pottery products, 1765–1836)

Ambrose Philips (MP and poet, c.1674–1749)

SHUGBOROUGH PARK Staffordshire

Baron George Anson (Sailor, circumnavigated globe in 45 months from 1740, 1697–1762)

SHUSTOKE Warwickshire

Sir William Dugdale (Antiquarian, edited *The Baronage of England*, 1605–1686)

SIDMOUTH Devon

Sir Edmund Ronald Leach (Social anthropologist [*Rethinking Anthropology*], 1910–1989)

SILLOTH Cumbria

Cecil [Charlotte Cecilia] Leitch (Golfer who won British championship four times, 1891–1977)

SITTINGBOURNE Kent

Lewis Theobald (Shakespearean scholar, was accused of substituting his own work for that of the Bard, 1688–1744)

SKIPTON Yorkshire

Ian McLeod (Chancellor of the Exchequer in 1970, died in office after one month, 1913–1970)

Henry Sidgwick (Philosopher [*Methods of Ethics*], 1838–1900)

SLAD Near Stroud, Gloucestershire

Laurie Lee (Poet and rural author [*Cider With Rosie*], 1914–1997)

SLAITHWAITE Yorkshire

Haydn Wood (Ballad composer of *Roses of Picardy*, 1882–1959)

SLEAFORD Lincolnshire

Jennifer Saunders (Comedian, famously partnered by Dawn French, also star of TV's *Absolutely Fabulous*, 1958–)

SLINFOLD Sussex

Anton Dolin [Patrick Healey Kay] (First Artistic Director of the London Festival Ballet, 1904–1983)

Sir [Charles Edward] Howard Vincent (First director of criminal investigation at Scotland Yard, 1849–1908)

SLOUGH Berkshire

Sir John Frederick William Herschel (Astronomer, pioneered celestial photography, 1792–1871)

Tracey Ullman (Singer and actor, starred in her own TV show, 1959–)

SNAINTON Near Scarborough, Yorkshire

Sir Ben Kingsley [b.Krishna Bhanji] (Actor who played Gandhi in film of that name, 1943–)

SNEINTON Near Nottingham

George Green (Self-taught mathematical scientist, responsible for Green's Theorem and Green's Functions, 1793–1841)

SNELSTON Derbyshire

Michael Thomas Sadler (Factory conditions reformer, promoted 1833 Factory Act, 1780–1835)

SNITTERFIELD Warwickshire

John Shakespeare (Merchant father of William, c.1530–1601)

SOLIHULL Warwickshire

Stephanie Cole (TV actor [*Memento Mori*], 1941–)

Rodney Hall (Arts administrator, poet and author [*Just Relations*], 1935–)

Henry Tonks (Painter who gave up medical career for his art ['Strolling Players'], 1862–1937)

SOMERBY Leicestershire

William Cheselden (Pioneering surgeon, wrote *The Anatomy of the Human Body*, 1688–1752)

SOMERSBY Lincolnshire

Alfred Tennyson [1st Baron] (Poet Laureate from 1850 ['The Lady of Shallott'], 1809–1892)

Charles Turner [b.Tennyson] (Poet, elder brother of Alfred but changed name to Turner, 1808–1879)

SOUTHALL Middlesex

Cleo Laine (Jazz singer, enjoyed long-running partnership with husband, band-leader John Dankworth, 1927–)

SOUTHAMPTON

Sir Edward Abraham (Biochemist, involved in early studies of penicillin, 1913–)

Marcus Algernon Adams (Photographer, specialised in children's studies, 1875–1959)

Darren Anderton (International footballer [Tottenham Hotspur and England], 1972–)

Emily Davies (Feminist educationalist, founded in 1873 what was to become Girton College, Cambridge, 1830–1921)

Charles Dibdin (Songwriter, best known for his nautical songs, 1745–1814)

Charlie Dimmock (TV gardening expert, 1966–)

Samuel Rolles Driver (Biblical scholar [*Introduction to the Literature of the Old Testament*], 1846–1914)

Benny Hill [Alfred Hawthorne] ('Saucy' TV and stage comedian, 1925–1992)

John Rushworth Jellicoe [1st Earl] (Admiral who commanded Grand Fleet at the Battle of Jutland in 1916, 1859–1935)

Allen Jones (Artist, sculptor, and print-maker, 1937–)

Howard [b.John Howard] Jones ('Synth' pop singer and songwriter [*What is Love*], 1955–)

Sir John Everett Millais (Artist, founder-member of the Pre-Raphaelite Brotherhood, 1829–1896)

Ken [Henry Kenneth] Russell (Film director [*Women in Love*], 1927–)

George Edward Saintsbury (Literary biographer [*A History of the French Novel*], 1845–1933)

John Thompson Stonehouse (Cabinet Minister who faked his own death, 1925–1988)

Nicholas Udall (Playwright [*Ralph Roister Doister* – reputedly England's first important stage comedy], 1504–1556)

Isaac Watts (Hymn composer [*O God, Our Help in Ages Past*], 1674–1748)

SOUTH CARLTON Lincolnshire

Sir William Monson (Naval commander in British coastal waters, 1569–1643)

SOUTHEND Essex

George Warwick Deeping (Novelist [*Sorrell and Son*], 1877–1950)

Alan David Mullally (Test cricketer [Leicestershire, Hampshire and England], 1969–)

SOUTH LEIGH Oxfordshire
James Bicheno Francis (American-based turbine designer, 1815–1892)

SOUTH MALLING Sussex
William John Courthope (Civil servant who became Professor of Poetry at Oxford, 1842–1917)

SOUTH MOLTON Devon
John Passmore Widgery [Lord] (Legal reformer who held post of Lord Chief Justice [1971–80], 1911–1981)

SOUTH PETHERTON Somerset
Sir John Harding [1st Baron] (Military commander, governed Cyprus during 1950s disturbances, 1896–1989)

SOUTHPORT Lancashire
Dora Bryan (Actor in films [*The Blue Lamp*] and TV [*Dinnerladies*], 1923–)
Miranda Richardson (Actor in films [*The Crying Game*] and TV [*Blackadder II*], 1959–)
Stanley Keith Runcorn (Geophysicist, researched Continental Drift, 1922–)
Sir Edmund Taylor Whittaker (Mathematician, wrote *A Course of Modern Analysis*, 1873–1956)

SOUTHSEA Hampshire
John Gilpin (Dancer and Artistic Director of the London Festival Ballet in 1962–5, 1930–)
Lancelot Hogben (Science writer [*Mathematics For the Million*], 1895–1975)
Peter Sellers (Actor, star of BBC radio *Goon Show*, also cinema's 'Inspector Clouseau', 1925–1980)

SOUTH SHIELDS County Durham
(See also TYNE DOCK)
Elinor Brent-Dyer (Children's author, famous for the *Chalet School* series, 1894–1969)
Dame Flora Robson (Actor, played Queen Elizabeth in *Fire Over England*, 1902–1984)
Ernest Thompson Seton (Naturalist [wrote *Wild Animals I Have Known*], and founder of Boy Scouts of America, 1860–1946)
Kathy Stobart (Saxophonist, played with Humphrey Lyttelton, 1925–)
George Frederick Stout (Philosopher, edited *Mind* magazine for 29 years, 1860–1944)
Robert Alderson Wright [Lord] (Expert on employment law, 1869–1964)

SOUTHWICK Sussex
Dame Clara Butt (Contralto, sang first performance of *Land of Hope and Glory*, 1872–1936)
Bathsua Pell Makin [b.Pell] (Educationalist, tutor to children of Charles I, 1608–1675)
John Pell (Mathematician and Cromwellian diplomat in Europe, 1610–1685)

SOWERBY Yorkshire
John Tillotson (Archbishop of Canterbury from 1691, 1630–1694)

SOWOOD Yorkshire
Christopher Saxton ('Father of English cartography', c.1542–1611)

SPALDING Lincolnshire
Frank Pick (Designer of modern London Underground system, 1878–1941)

SPENNITHORNE Yorkshire
John Hutchinson (Theologian who also collected fossils and designed timepiece in an attempt to ascertain longitude, 1674–1737)

SPENNYMOOR County Durham
Gibson Gowland (Leading actor on stage and in silent films including starring role in von Stroheim's classic *Greed*, 1872-1951)

SPILSBY Lincolnshire
Sir John Franklin (Arctic explorer, died on expedition to find North-West Passage, 1786-1847)

SPOFFORTH Yorkshire
Laurence Eusden (Poet Laureate appointed through the patronage of the Duke of Newcastle, 1688-1730)

SPRINGFIELD Essex
Joseph Strutt (Social historian [*Sports and Pastimes of the People of England*], 1742-1802)

SPRINGHEAD Near Oldham, Lancashire
Annie Kenney (Suffragette, twice arrested, but successful in campaigning for women to be allowed to work in wartime munitions' factories, 1879-1953)

STADHAMPTON Oxfordshire
John Owen (Puritan theologian, chaplain to Oliver Cromwell, 1616-1683)

STAFFORD
Thomas Brassey [1st Earl] (Statesman, published military publications, 1836-1918)
Izaac Walton (Biographer and angling author, 1593-1683)

STAINBOROUGH Yorkshire
Joseph Bramah (Inventor of safety locks and a hydraulic press, and deviser of the theory of the propeller, 1748-1814)

STAINFORTH Yorkshire
Sir George Porter (Nobel Prize-winning chemist, became Director of the Royal Institution, 1920-2002)

STAINTON South Yorkshire
Fred [Frederick Sewards] Trueman (Test cricketer [fast bowler for Yorkshire and England], 1931-)

STANDISH Gloucestershire
Beatrice Webb [b.Potter] (Social reformer, wrote *The Co-operative Movement in Britain* before marrying Sidney Webb and co-founding the London School of Economics, 1858-1943)

STANFORD Worcestershire
Mary Martha Sherwood [b.Butt] (Author of moralistic tales for children, 1775-1851)

STANFORD RIVERS Essex
Isaac Taylor (Philologist, wrote *The Alphabet*, 1829-1901)

STANMER Sussex
William Goffe (Signatory of Charles I's death warrant, fled to Massachusetts, c.1605-1679)

STAPLEFORD Nottinghamshire
Arthur Mee (Popular journalist and creator of the *Children's Encyclopaedia*, 1874-1943)

STEBBING Essex
John Patrick Stephenson (Test cricketer [Essex, Hampshire, and England], 1965-)

STEEPLE LANGFORD Wiltshire
Arthur Collier (Metaphysical philosopher, wrote *A Specimen of True Philosophy*, 1680-1732)

STEVENAGE Hertfordshire
Edward Henry Craig (Stage director and
  publisher [of *The Mask* magazine,
  1908–29], 1872–1966)
William Allen Jowitt [1st Earl] (Politician
  and Lord Chancellor [1945–51],
  1885–1957)

STEVENTON Hampshire
Jane Austen (Author [*Pride and Prejudice,
  Sense and Sensibility*], 1775–1817)

STEWARTON Ayrshire
David Dale (Industrial philanthropist,
  1739–1806)

STILLINGFLEET Yorkshire
Sir Clements Robert Markham (Geographer,
  promoted Antarctic exploration,
  1830–1916)

STILLINGTON Yorkshire
George Russell (Horticulturist, specialised
  in perfecting lupin varieties, 1857–1951)

STIRLING
Billy [William] Bremner (International
  footballer, Leeds United captain,
  1942–1997)
Willie [William] Carson (Champion jockey,
  1942–)
Henry Drummond (Theologian and
  scientist, attempted to reconcile
  Darwinism with Christianity, 1851–1897)
Duncan Ferguson (International footballer
  [Everton and Scotland], 1971–)
George Robert Gleig (Chaplain-General to
  HM Forces for 31 years, also military
  historian and biographer, 1796–1888)
Sir George Harvey (Landscape painter,
  1806–1876)
Margaret Anne Marshall (Operatic soprano,
  1949–)
Kirsty Young (TV newscaster, 1969–)

STOBHILL Perthshire
Annabella Drummond (Queen of Scotland
  from 1390 to 1401, c.1350–1401)

STOBS Roxburghshire
George Augustus Heathfield (Military
  commander, defended Gibraltar
  successfully against Spanish attack for
  four years [1779–83], 1717–1790)

STOCKPORT Near Manchester
Sir George Back (Arctic explorer, sailed
  twice with Franklin and joined search for
  Sir John Ross, 1796–1878)
Joan Dawson Bakewell (Broadcaster [TV's
  Late Night Line-Up], 1933–)
Fred Perry (First tennis player to win four
  major championships, 1909–1995)
Sir Joseph Whitworth (Engineering
  inventor, improved steel production,
  1803–1887)

STOCKSFIELD Northumberland
Dame Veronica Wedgwood (Historian,
  wrote *The 30 Years War* and biographies
  of Cromwell and Strafford, 1910–1997)

STOCKTON-ON-TEES County Durham
Ivy Close (Actor, starred in Abel Gance
  silent classic *La Roue* [1923],
  1890–1968)
Will Hay (Actor [*Oh Mr Porter*], 1888–1949)
Andrew Colin Renfrew [Baron]
  (Archaeologist, wrote *The Emergence of
  Civilization*] 1937–)
Joseph Ritson (Literary expert, exposed
  bibliographical forgeries, 1752–1803)
Thomas Sheraton (Furniture designer,
  1751–1806)
John Walker (Inventor of friction matches,
  c.1781–1859)

STOKE BISHOP Gloucestershire
Adela Florence Nicolson [b.Cory] (Poet who

wrote ['Indian Love Lyrics'] as 'Laurence Hope', 1865–1904)

STOKE FERRY Norfolk
Sir Percy Winfield (Legal scholar, edited *Cambridge Law Journal* for 20 years, 1878–1953)

STOKE GABRIEL Devon
George Jackson Churchward (Locomotive engineer, designed 'Star' class of express locomotives for the Great Western Railway, 1857–1933)

STOKE-ON-TRENT Staffordshire
Kim John Barnett (Test cricketer [Derbyshire, Gloucestershire and England], 1960–)

Glenys Barton (Internationally-acclaimed sculptor, 1944–)

Arnold Bennett (Author [*Anna of the Five Towns*], 1867–1931)

Hugh Bourne (Theologian, co-founder of the Primitive Methodists [1810], 1772–1852)

Clarice Cliff (Ceramic designer noted for bold designs and colour, 1899–1972)

William Clowes (Potter and religious activist, co-founder of the Primitive Methodists [1810], 1780–1851)

Susie Cooper (Ceramic designer, first Royal Designer for Industry [1940], 1902–1995)

Dinah Maria Craik (Novelist [*John Halifax, Gentleman*], 1826–1887)

John Lightfoot (Theologian, assisted preparation of Walton's Polyglot Bible [1657], 1602–1675)

Sir Stanley Matthews (International footballer [Blackpool, Stoke City and England], 1915–2000)

Charlotte Rhead (Ceramic designer, worked with tube lining, 1885–1947)

Josiah Spode (Manufacturer of delicate bone china, 1754–1827)

John Barrington Wain (Novelist [*Young Shoulders*], 1925–1994)

Josiah Wedgwood (Pottery manufacturer who invented unglazed blue jasper ware with white raised designs, 1730–1795)

Robbie Williams (Pop singer, at one time with group Take That, 1974–)

STONE Staffordshire
John Jervis St Vincent [Earl] (Naval commander at Cape St Vincent, where he won victory over French, Spanish, and Dutch fleets, 1735–1823)

Peter de Wint (Water-colour painter of landscapes and country life, 1784–1849)

STONEHAVEN Kincardineshire
John Charles Reith [1st Baron] (First general manager of BBC, 1889–1971)

Robert William Thomson (Inventor of pneumatic tyre, 1822–1873)

STONELEIGH Warwickshire
Sir Henry Parkes (Five times Prime Minister of New South Wales, 1815–1896)

STORNOWAY Isle of Lewis
Sir Alexander MacKenzie (Explorer, discoverer of MacKenzie River, 1764–1820)

STOUGHTON Sussex
Richard Alston (Choreographer and Artistic Director with the Rambert Dance Company [1986–92], 1948–)

STOURBRIDGE Worcestershire
Anthony Bate (TV and film character actor, 1934–)

Sir Frank Short (Artist and President of the Royal Society of Painter Etchers for nearly 30 years, 1857–1945)

STOW-CUM-QUY Cambridgeshire
Jeremy Collier (Theologian, refused to take
  Oath of Allegiance to William and Mary
  in 1689, 1650–1726)

STOW-ON-THE-WOLD Gloucestershire
Sir Frederic Charles Bartlett (First Professor
  of Experimental Psychology at
  Cambridge, 1886–1969)

STRABANE County Tyrone
Guy Carleton [1st Baron Dorchester]
  (Military commander, defeated American
  Army at Lake Champlain in 1776,
  1724–1808)
Flann O'Brien [Brian O'Nolan] (Author [At
  Swim-Two-Birds], 1911–1966)

STRACHAN Aberdeenshire
Thomas Reid (Philosopher [Essays on the
  Intellectual Powers of Man],
  1710–1796)

STRADBROKE Suffolk
Robert Grosseteste (Bishop of Lincoln who
  tried to make ecclesiastical reforms,
  c.1175–1253)

STRALOCH Perthshire
Robert Gordon (Cartographer and first
  graduate of Marischal College, Aberdeen,
  1580–1661)

STRANRAER Wigtownshire
Colin Calderwood (International footballer
  [Scotland], 1965–)

STRATFORD-ON-AVON Warwickshire
Sir Hugh Clopton (Philanthropist and Lord
  Mayor of London [1492], d.1497)
Sir William Henry Flower (Zoologist,
  Director of the Natural History Museum
  [1884–98], 1831–1899)

William Shakespeare (Playwright and
  National Bard, 1564–1616)
George Macaulay Trevelyan (Historian
  [History of England], 1876–1962)

STRATFORD ST ANDREW Suffolk
Ranulf de Glanvill (Jurist, captured King
  William the Lion [of Scotland] at Alnwick
  in 1174, d.1190)

STRATHAVEN Lanarkshire
Sir Robert Giffen (Economist, helped to
  found Economic Society in 1890,
  1837–1910)
Una McLean (Actor and comedian, 1930–)

STREET Somerset
John Xavier Merriman (Prime Minister of
  South Africa [1908–10], 1841–1926)

STREETLY Staffordshire
Janet Eveline Beat (Composer, founder-
  member of the Scottish Electro-acoustic
  Music Society 1937–)

STRENSHAM Worcestershire
Samuel Butler (Satirist poet ['Hudibras'],
  1612–1680)

STRICHEN Aberdeenshire
Nora Wilson Low (Author best known as
  Lorna Moon, her 1925 novel Dark Star
  being banned in her local library,
  1886–1930)

STROUD Gloucestershire
John Canton (Physicist, demonstrated the
  compressibility of water, 1718–1772)
Robert Charles [Jack] Russell (Test cricketer
  [Gloucestershire and England], 1963–)

STURMINSTER NEWTON Dorset
William Barnes (Poet [Poems of Rural Life
  in the Dorset Dialect], 1900–1986)

STURTON LE STEEPLE Nottinghamshire
John Robinson (Pastor to the Pilgrim
    Fathers [in Leiden], c.1576–1625)

SUDBURY Derbyshire
William Venables Vernon Harcourt
    (Chemist and ecclesiastic who helped
    organise the first meeting of the British
    Association [in 1831], 1789–1871)

SUDBURY Suffolk
Thomas Gainsborough (Artist ['The Blue
    Boy', 'The Harvest Wagon'], 1727–1788)
Margaret Hambling (Artist, 1945–)

SUNBURY-ON-THAMES Surrey
Sir Ernest Thomas Fisk (Australian-based
    radio pioneer, 1886–1965)

SUNDERLAND
Kate Adie (TV journalist, 1945–)
James Bolam (Film and TV actor [*The Likely
    Lads*], 1938–)
Sir Henry Havelock (Military commander,
    led relief of Cawnpore and Lucknow
    during the Indian Mutiny, 1795–1857)
Sir Joseph Swan (Physicist and inventor of
    electric lamp [1860], 1828–1914)
Tom Taylor (Playwright [*To Parents and
    Guardians*] and editor of *Punch*,
    1817–1880)
Graham Wallas (Political scientist, wrote
    Human Nature in Politics, 1858–1932)
Robert George Dylan Willis (Test cricketer
    and broadcaster [Warwickshire and
    England], 1949–)

SURBITON Surrey
William Heinemann (Publisher, 1863–1920)

SUTTON Bedfordshire
John Burgoyne (Military commander in
    American colonies, defeated at Saratoga,
    1722–1792)

SUTTON BENGER Wiltshire
Joseph Fry (Pottery and confectionery
    manufacturer, also typeface creator who
    published five-volume edition of the
    Bible, 1728–1787)

SUTTON COLDFIELD West Midlands
Arthur Deakin (Trade union leader [TGWU],
    1890–1955)

SWAFFHAM Norfolk
Howard Carter (Egyptologist, discovered
    the tomb of Tutankhamen, 1874–1939)

SWALWELL County Durham
William Shield (Composer and Master of
    the King's Musicians, also co-founded
    the Glee Club in 1793, 1748–1829)

SWANAGE Dorset
James Edward Meade (Nobel Prize-winning
    economist [1977], 1907–1995)

SWANBOURNE Buckinghamshire
Lady Margaret Florey (Pathologist and
    penicillin pioneer, 1904–1994)

SWANMORE Hampshire
Stephen Butler Leacock (Humorist [*The
    Garden of Folly*], 1869–1944)

SWANSEA West Glamorgan
John Charles (International footballer
    [Leeds United and Wales], 1932–)
Robert Damien Bale Croft (Test cricketer
    [Glamorgan and England], 1970–)
Sir William Robert Grove (Judge and
    physicist, created first fuel cell and first
    filament lamp, 1811–1896)
Michael Heseltine [Baron] (Politician, formerly
    President of the Board of Trade, 1933–)
Catherine Zeta Jones (Actor in films [*Mask
    of Zorro*] and TV [*Darling Buds of May*],
    1969–)

Philip Jones (Civil War soldier, later Sheriff of Glamorgan, 1618–1674)

Martyn Lewis (TV newscaster, 1945–)

Richard Nash ['Beau Nash'] (Master of Ceremonies at Bath,1674–1762)

Sir Harry Secombe (Singer and entertainer, 1921–1999)

Dylan Marlais Thomas (Poet and playwright [*Under Milk Wood*], 1914–1953)

Harri Webb (Poet and political activist, 1920–)

SWARDESTON Near Norwich

Edith Louisa Cavell (Nurse and freedom fighter, 1865–1915)

SWINDERBY Lincolnshire

Rosita [Joan] Forbes (Travel writer [*From Red Sea to Blue Nile*], 1893–1967)

SWINDON Wiltshire

Diana Dors [Diana Fluck] (Actor [*Yield to the Night*], 1931–1984)

John Francome (Seven times National Hunt champion jockey, 1952–)

Sir William Stanier (Locomotive engineer, designer of the *Princess Royal* and *Coronation* class express engines, 1876–1965)

TADCASTER Yorkshire

Elaine Maria MacDonald (Principal ballerina with Scottish Ballet for 20 years from 1969, 1943–)

TALKE Staffordshire

Reginald Joseph Mitchell (Designer of Spitfire aircraft, 1895–1937)

TAMWORTH Staffordshire

Sir Ernest William Titterton (Nuclear physicist, worked on first atomic bomb, 1916–1990)

TANTALLON CASTLE East Lothian

Gavin Douglas (Poet, wrote 'The Palice of Honour', c.1474–1522)

TANWORTH Warwickshire

Thomas Archer (Architect, designed St John's Westminster, and Roehampton House, 1668–1743)

TARDEBIGGE Worcestershire

Sir John Robert Vane (Nobel Prize-winning biochemist, 1927–)

TATSFIELD Surrey

John Surtees (Motorcycle and motor racing champion, 1934–)

TAUNTON Somerset

Jenny Agutter (Actor [*The Railway Children*, 1952–)

Edward Harper (Operatic composer [*Hedda Gabler*], 1941–)

William Ellis Metford (Ballistics engineer, designed breech-loading rifle, 1824–1899)

Hugh Montague Trenchard [1st Viscount] (Established Royal Air Force, 1873–1956)

TAVISTOCK Devon

William Browne (Poet, wrote *Britannia's Pastorals* in 3 vols, 1591–1643)

TAXAL Derbyshire

Abraham Bennet (Cleric who researched electrical science, writing *New Experiments on Electricity*, 1749–1799)

TAYPORT Fife

Douglas Young (Poet and playwright, jailed during World War Two for his political beliefs, 1913–1973)

TEDDINGTON Middlesex

Sir Noel Coward (Playwright [*Blithe Spirit*]

and actor [Our Man in Havana],
1899–1973)
Charles Harvard Gibbs-Smith (Aeronautical
historian, wrote Aviation: a Historical
Survey..., 1909–1981)

TEMPLE GUITING Gloucestershire
Richard Deane (Civil War commander,
killed at Battle of Solebay, 1610–1653)

TENBY Dyfed
Augustus John (Portrait painter,
1878–1961)
Robert Recorde (Mathematician, first to
write mathematical textbooks in English,
1510–1558)

TENTERDEN Kent
William Caxton (First English printer,
c.1422–1491)
Sir David Paradine Frost (Broadcaster,
1939–)

TERLING Essex
Robert John Rayleigh [4th Baron]
(Physicist, researched radioactivity in
rocks, 1875–1947)

TEWKESBURY Gloucestershire
Anna Ford (TV newscaster and journalist,
1943–)
Henry Green [Henry Vincent Yorke]
(Novelist [Party Going, Loving],
1905–1973)

THAME Oxfordshire
James Figg (Sporting fencer and boxer,
c.1695–1736)
Sir John Holt (Lord Chief Justice, regarded
as enlightened for his time, 1642–1710)

THAMES DITTON Surrey
Christian de Duve (Nobel Prize-winning
biochemist, for enzyme research, 1917–)

THAXTED Essex
Samuel Purchas (Travel author [Purchas,
His Pilgrimage], 1577–1626)

THEBERTON HALL Suffolk
Charles Montagu Doughty (Poet [Adam
Cast Forth] and travel author [Travels in
Arabia Deserta], 1843–1926)

THEOBALDS Sussex
John Shute Barrington [1st Viscount]
(Politician, expelled from House of
Commons, 1678–1734)

THETFORD Norfolk
Thomas Paine (Radical thinker and author,
1737–1809)

THIRSK Yorkshire
Thomas Lord (Founder of Lord's cricket
ground in London, 1755–1832)

THORNABY-ON-TEES North Yorkshire
Pat Barker (Novelist noted for her Regen-
eration trilogy dealing with the psychol-
ogical scars of World War One, 1943–)

THORNCOMBE Dorset
Samuel Hood [1st Viscount] (Naval
commander, victor over French in West
Indies in 1782, 1724–1816)

THORNHILL Dumfriesshire
Kirkpatrick MacMillan (Credited with
invention of the bicycle, 1813–1878)

THORNSETT Derbyshire
James Brindley (Engineer, built canal
between Worsley and Manchester,
1716–1772)

THORNTON Bradford, Yorkshire
Anne Brontë (Author [The Tenant of
Wildfell Hall], 1820–1849)

Charlotte Brontë (Author [*Jane Eyre*], 1816–1855)

Emily Brontë (Author [*Wuthering Heights*], 1818–1848)

Richard Rolle de Hampole (Poet and hermit, translated parts of the Bible into English, c.1290–1349)

THORNTON HEATH Surrey

Dame Jane Beverley Drew (Architect, designed Open University at Milton Keynes [1969–77], 1911–1996)

THURCASTON Leicestershire

Hugh Latimer (Religious martyr, burned at the stake, c.1485–1555)

THURLOW Suffolk

Dame Elisabeth Frink (Sculptor, worked on equestrian concepts, 1930–1993)

THURNSCOE Yorkshire

John Harry Hampshire (Test cricketer [Yorkshire, Derbyshire, and England] and Test umpire, 1947–)

THURSBY Cumbria

Sir Thomas Bouch (Builder of first Tay Bridge, 1822–1880)

TINTWISTLE Derbyshire

Vivienne Westwood (Fashion designer, 1941–)

TINWALD Dumfriesshire

William Paterson (Founder of the Bank of England, 1658–1719)

TISBURY Wiltshire

Sir John Davies (Poet and Attorney-General for Ireland [1606–19], 1569–1626)

Christopher Hinton [Baron] (Nuclear physicist, constructed UK's first large-scale commercial nuclear power station at Calder Hall in 1956, 1901–1983)

TIVERTON Devon

Derick Heathcote Amory [Viscount] (Chancellor of the Exchequer [1958–60], 1899–1981)

Peter Blundell (Manufacturer who endowed Blundell's school at Tiverton, 1520–1601)

William Buckland (Geologist, became President of the Geological Society, 1784–1856)

Richard Cosway (Miniaturist artist, c.1742–1821)

TODMORDEN Yorkshire

Dicken Ashworth (TV and film actor [*Chariots of Fire*], 1946–)

Sir John Douglas Cockcroft (Nobel Prize-winning physicist, researched nuclear energy, 1897–1967)

Sir Geoffrey Wilkinson (Nobel Prize-winning chemist, 1921–)

TOLWORTH Surrey

Muriel Box (Film writer, shared Oscar with husband Sydney for *The Seventh Veil* in 1945, 1905–1991)

TOMICH Ross and Cromarty

Simon Fraser Lovat [Lord] (Jacobite chieftain, beheaded for high treason, c.1667–1747)

TONBRIDGE Kent

Harry Andrews (Actor [*Ice Cold in Alex*], 1911–1989)

Anna Atkins (Photographer, produced one of first books illustrated with photographs, 1799–1871)

Henry Watson Fowler (Compiler of *Modern English Usage*, 1858–1933)

Cecil Frank Powell (Nobel Prize-winning physicist, 1903–1969)

Frank Woolley (Test cricketer, 1887–1978)

TONGHAM Surrey
Cyril Foster Garbett (Outspoken Archbishop
of York, 1875–1955)

TOOMEBRIDGE County Antrim
Willie John McBride (Captain of British
Lions rugby team, played 17 Tests on five
separate tours, 1940–)

TORPHICHEN West Lothian
Henry Bell (Engineer and inventor, built
Comet, Europe's first passenger-carrying
steam boat, 1767–1830)

TORQUAY Devon
Sir Richard Burton (First European to find
Lake Tanganyika, 1821–1890)
Dame Agatha Christie (Detective novelist,
creator of 'Hercule Poirot' and 'Miss
Marple', 1890–1976)
Peter Edward Cook (Actor [Bedazzled] and
satirist [TV's Not Only... But Also, with
Dudley Moore], 1937–1995)
Percy Harrison Fawcett (Explorer, lost in
Amazon jungle, 1867–c.1925)

TORRINGTON Devon
William Johnson Cory (Poet, composed
lyrics for Eton Boat Song, 1823–1892)

TORWOODLEE Selkirkshire
James Barke (Novelist, and editor of works
of Robert Burns, 1905–1958)

TOTNES Devon
Lisa Aziz (Sky TV newscaster, 1962–)

TOTON Nottinghamshire
Anne Briggs (Collector of English folk
ballads, 1944–)

TOTTERIDGE Hertfordshire
Cecil Harmsworth King (Newspaper
proprietor of Mirror newspapers,
1901–1987)
Henry Edward Manning [Cardinal]
(Ecclesiastic, 1808–1892)

TREATOR Cornwall
Sir Goldsworthy Gurney (Inventor of
steam-powered carriage, 1793–1875)

TREDEGAR Gwent
Aneurin Bevan (Politician, founder of the
National Health Service, 1897–1960)
Neil Kinnock (Politician, led Labour Party
[1983–92], 1942–)
Raymond Rearden (Six times world snooker
champion, 1932–)

TREFOREST Mid-Glamorgan
Meic Stephens (Poet and arts
administrator, compiled Oxford Companion to the Literature of Wales, 1938–)

TREGARON Dyfed
Henry Richard (Pacifist politician,
campaigned for system of arbitration for
international disputes, 1812–1888)

TREMADOC Gwynedd
Thomas Edward Lawrence ('Lawrence of
Arabia', 1888–1935)

TREMEER Cornwall
Richard Lower (Physiologist, wrote Treatise
on the Heart in 1669, 1631–1691)

TRENTHAM Staffordshire
William Theed (Sculptor, worked on Albert
Memorial, 1804–1891)

TREWARTHENICK Cornwall
William Gregor (Chemist and mineralogist,
discovered titanium locally, 1761–1817)

TRIMLEY ST MARTIN Suffolk

Thomas Cavendish (Circumnavigator of
world [1586-88], c.1555–c.1592)

TROTTON Sussex

Thomas Otway (Playwright [*The Orphan*,
Venice Preserved], 1652–1685)

TROWBRIDGE Wiltshire

Benjamin Pitman (Pioneer of shorthand in
the US, 1822–1910)
Sir Isaac Pitman (Creator of shorthand
system, 1813–1897)

TRUMPINGTON Cambridgeshire

George Alfred Henty (Author of 80 boys'
adventures [*With Clive in India*],
1832–1902)

TRURO Cornwall

Henry Charlton Bastian (Biologist, early
exponent of neurology, 1837–1915)
Henry Bone (Artist, worked in enamel,
1755–1834)
Samuel Foote (Controversial playwright
and satirist [*The Englishman in Paris*],
1720–1777)
Richard Lander (Explorer in West Africa,
1803–1834)
Henry Martyn (Missionary in India and
Persia, 1781–1812)

TULLIBODY Clackmannanshire

Robert Dick (Self-taught geologist and
botanist, 1811–1866)

TUNBRIDGE WELLS Kent

David Ivon Gower (Test cricketer
[Leicestershire and England] and
broadcaster, 1957–)
Sir William Tyrone Guthrie (Theatrical
producer, administered Old Vic and
Sadler's Wells, 1900–1971)

TURNBERRY Ayrshire

Robert the Bruce (King of Scotland, victor
at Bannockburn over England's Edward II,
1274–1329)

TURRIFF Aberdeenshire

Sir John Rose (Canadian-based diplomat,
settled British-American disputes after
American Civil War, 1820–1888)

TWEEDMOUTH Northumberland

Robert Lee (Theologian, wrote *The Reform
of the Church in Worship...*, 1804–1868)
John Mackay Wilson (Border historian
[*Tales of the Borders*], 1804–1835)

TWYNHOLM Kirkcudbrightshire

David Coulthard (Formula 1 racing driver,
1971–)

TWYWELL Northamptonshire

Hester Chapone (Poet and writer [*Letters
on the Improvement of the Mind*],
1727–1801)

TYNE DOCK County Durham

Catherine Cookson (Best-selling novelist,
1906–1998)

TYNTON West Glamorgan

Richard Price (Moral philosopher and
insurance expert, wrote *Observations on
Reversionary Payments*, 1723–1791)

UFFINGTON Lincolnshire

Lady Charlotte Schreiber (Scholar of Welsh
literature, 1812–1895)

UFFINGTON Oxfordshire

Thomas Hughes (Author of *Tom Brown's
Schooldays*, 1822–1896)

ULVERSTON Lancashire

William Norman Birkett [Baron] (Politician

and lawyer, took part in 1945-6
Nuremberg Trials, 1883-1962)
Stan [Arthur Stanley Jefferson] Laurel (of
Laurel and Hardy fame, 1890-1965)

UPAVON Wiltshire
Henry ['Orator'] Hunt (Radical activist and
politician, 1773-1835)

UPHAM Hampshire
Edward Young (Poet, wrote 'The
Complaint', 1683-1765)

UPMINSTER Essex
Ian Dury (Punk rocker, sang with group The
Blockheads, 1942-2000)

UPOTTERY Devon
Frederick Thomas Jane (Naval historian and
founder of the publishing firm which still
bears his name, 1870-1916)

UPTON Northamptonshire
James Harrington (Political economist
imprisoned for his beliefs, 1611-1677)

USK Gwent
Alfred Russel Wallace (Explorer and
naturalist whose contribution to the
debate on evolution included coining
phrase 'survival of the fittest',
1823-1913)

VIEWPARK Lanarkshire
Jimmy Johnstone (International footballer
[Celtic and Scotland], 1944-)

WAKEFIELD Yorkshire
Dame Barbara Hepworth (St Ives-based
sculptor, 1903-1975)
George Robert Gissing (Novelist [*New Grub
Street*], 1857-1903)
Kenneth Leighton (Composer [opera
Columba] and pianist, 1929-1988)

David Mercer (Playwright [*A Suitable Case
for Treatment*], also worked for cinema
and TV, 1928-1980)
John Potter (Archbishop of Canterbury
from 1737, c.1674-1747)
John Radcliffe (Royal physician and Oxford
benefactor, 1650-1714)
David Storey (Playwright and novelist [*This
Sporting Life*], 1933-)
Elaine Storkey (Christian author, wrote *God
and Sexuality* in 1966, 1944-)
William Whiteley (London-based retailer
murdered by illegitimate son, bequeathed
£1 million for the care of the elderly,
1831-1907)

WALBERTON Sussex
Sir William Anson [3rd Baronet] (Jurist,
wrote *Principles of the English Law of
Contract*, 1843-1914)

WALCOT Near Bath
Richard Debaufre Guyon (Commander in
the Hungarian, Austrian, and Turkish
armies, died of cholera at Scutari,
1803-1856)

WALESBY Lincolnshire
Daniel Waterland (Theologian, Archdeacon
of Middlesex from 1730, 1683-1740)

WALLASEY Cheshire
Walter Citrine [Baron] (Trade union leader
and General Secretary of TUC for 20
years, 1887-1983)
Harold William Tilman (Explorer and
mountaineer, led 1938 Everest
Expedition, 1898-1978)

WALLINGFORD Oxfordshire
Richard of Wallingford (Noted astronomer
and instrument maker, despite suffering
from leprosy, c.1291-1336)

WALLYFORD East Lothian
Margaret Oliphant (Author, wrote novel *The Chronicles of Carlingford*, 1828–1897)

WALMER Kent
Robert Seymour Bridges (Poet, appointed Poet Laureate in 1913, 1844–1930)
John Hassall (Artist, produced classic railway poster 'Skegness is so bracing', 1868–1948)
Philip Henry Stanhope [5th Earl] (Politician responsible for the passing of the Copyright Act [1842] and historian [*The History of England, 1713–83*], 1805–1875)

WALSALL Staffordshire
John Edward Gray (Biologist, wrote *A Handbook of British Waterweeds*, 1800–1875)
Jerome K. [Klapka] Jerome (Author [*Three Men in a Boat*], 1859–1927)

WALTHAM–ON–THE–WOLDS Lincolnshire
Augustus Charles Hobart-Hampden ['Hobart Pasha'] (Blockade-runner in American Civil War and commander in Turkish navy, 1822–1886)

WALTON Near Wakefield, Yorkshire
Charles Waterton (Naturalist and early conservationist, 1782–1865)

WALTON-LE-DALE Lancashire
Edward Baines (MP for Leeds [1834–41] and publisher of works on Lancashire and Yorkshire, 1774–1848)

WALTON ON THAMES Surrey
Julie Andrews (Actor, star of *The Sound of Music*, 1935–)

WANTAGE Oxfordshire
Alfred the Great (849–899)

Joseph Butler (Bishop of Durham who was said to have rejected appointment as Archbishop of Canterbury, 1692–1752)
Lester Keith Piggott (Eleven times champion jockey, 1935–)

WARDINGTON Oxfordshire
John Marston (Playwright [*The Malcontent*] and satirist, 1576–1634)

WARFIELD Berkshire
Edward Backhouse Eastwick (Oriental scholar, 1814–1883)

WARKWORTH Northumberland
John Rushworth (Secretary to Oliver Cromwell, wrote *Historical Collections*, c.1612–1690)

WARNHAM Sussex
Joan Eardley (Scottish-based artist, 1921–1963)

WARRINGTON Cheshire
Rick Astley (Pop singer [*Never Gonna Give You Up*], 1966–)
John Drinkwater Bethune [b.Drinkwater] (Historian of the Siege of Gibraltar, 1762–1844)
Steve [Stephen] Donoghue (Champion jockey for 10 successive years, 1884–1945)
Christopher Evans (TV and radio broadcaster, 1966–)
Neil Harvey Fairbrother (Test cricketer [Lancashire and England], 1963–)

WARWICK
John Fairfax (Australian newspaper proprietor, 1804–1877)
Walter Savage Landor (Playwright [*Imaginary Conversations*], 1775–1864)
Olivia Serres [b.Wilmot] (Self-proclaimed Princess Olive, died in prison after

alleging to be beneficiary of a royal bequest, 1772-1834)

June Tabor (Folk singer, 1947-)

WASHINGTON County Durham

Gertrude [Margaret Lowthian] Bell (Archaeologist and traveller in Middle East, 1868-1926)

John Brand (Antiquarian, wrote *History of Newcastle upon Tyne*, 1744-1806)

Bryan Ferry (Pop singer, at one time with Roxy Music, 1945-)

WATFORD Hertfordshire

Joy Batchelor (Animated cartoon producer, with John Halas produced *Animal Farm* and *Tales of Hoffnung*, 1914-1991)

Michael Bentine (Radio and TV comedian, member of the early Goon shows, 1921-1996)

Mark Christopher Ilott (Test cricketer [Essex and England], 1970-)

Gerald Moore (Outstanding piano accompanist, 1899-1987)

Gareth Southgate (International footballer [Middlesbrough and England], 1966-)

WEDNESBURY West Midlands

Henry Treece (Novelist [*The Eagles Have Flown*], 1911-1966)

WELBECK ABBEY Nottinghamshire

Lord George Bentinck (Politician who opposed Free Trade, 1802-1848)

WELBOURN Lincolnshire

Sir William Robert Robertson (Military commander who rose from the ranks to become Chief of the Imperial General Staff in World War One, 1860-1933)

WELLINGTON Shropshire

William Withering (Physician and medical botanist, promoted use of the foxglove in medicine, 1741-1799)

WELLS Somerset

George Bull (Bishop of St David's from 1705, 1634-1710)

Heathcote William Garrod (Professor of Poetry at Oxford, edited work of Keats and Wordsworth, 1878-1960)

John Keate (Headmaster at Eton [1809-34] 'remarkable for the severity of his discipline' - *DNB*, 1773-1852)

Thomas Linley (Composer and Director of Music at Drury Lane, 1732-1795)

WELLS-NEXT-THE-SEA Norfolk

Robert Ransome (Agricultural implement manufacturer, 1753-1830)

WELWYN GARDEN CITY Hertfordshire

Nick [Nicholas Alexander] Faldo (Golfer, three-times winner of the British Open, 1957-)

WENDOVER Buckinghamshire

Cecilia Payne-Gaposchkin [b.Payne] (Astronomer, co-produced *Catalogue of Variable Stars*, 1900-1979)

WESTBURY Shropshire

William Cureton (Levantine scholar and Canon of Westminster, 1808-1864)

WESTBURY Wiltshire

Penleigh Boyd (Australian-based artist, 1890-1923)

Joshua Marshman (Oriental scholar and missionary, published Chinese Bible and translated Confucius, 1768-1837)

WEST CHOBHAM Surrey

John Addison (Film music composer, won Oscar for music to *Tom Jones*, 1920-)

WEST CLANDON Surrey

Rosemary Sutcliff (Children's author, wrote *The Eagle of the Ninth*, 1920–1992)

WESTCLIFF-ON-SEA Essex

Trevor Bailey (Test cricketer and broadcaster [Essex and England], 1923–)

WESTERHAM Kent

Benjamin Hoadley (Theologian, held four bishoprics in succession, ending with that of Winchester, 1676–1761)
John Frith (Protestant martyr, 1503–1533)
James Wolfe (Military commander, victor at Quebec, 1727–1759)

WESTERKIRK Nr Langholm, Dumfriesshire

Thomas Telford (Leading civil engineer, built Menai Suspension Bridge, 1757–1834)

WEST LINTON Peeblesshire

Savourna Stevenson (Composer [*Tweed Journey*] for clarsach [Gaelic harp], 1961–)

WEST MEON Hampshire

James Edwin Rogers (Economist, wrote *History of Agriculture and Prices*, 1823–1890)

WESTON-SUPER-MARE Somerset

Albert Alexander [Earl] (Politician, rose from office-boy to First Lord of the Admiralty and Cabinet minister, 1885–1965)
John Marwood Cleese (Actor [TV's *Monty Python* and *Fawlty Towers*], 1939–)

WESTRUTHER Berwickshire

Lady Alicia Spottiswood (Poet, wrote 'Annie Laurie', 1810–1900)

WESTWARD Near Wigton, Cumbria

Sir William Henry Bragg (Nobel Prize-winning physicist, pioneer of X-ray crystallography, 1862–1942)

WEYBRIDGE Surrey

Sir Colin Davis (Conductor and composer, 1927–)
Richard Arthur Hughes (Novelist [*A High Wind in Jamaica*], 1900–1976)

WEYMOUTH Dorset

Henry Gwyn Moseley (Physicist who formulated 'Moseley's Law', killed in military action, 1887–1915)
Thomas Love Peacock (Poet and novelist, wrote *Nightmare Abbey*, 1785–1866)

WHADDON Buckinghamshire

Richard Cox (Protestant reformer, Bishop of Ely for 21 years, 1500–1581)

WHALLEY Lancashire

Sir Cyril Norwood (Educationalist, formulated new plan of secondary education adopted after 1944, 1875–1956)

WHALTON Northumberland

Sir George Pickering (Leading medical expert, researched blood pressure, 1904–1980)

WHEATHAMPSTEAD Hertfordshire

Michael George Ventris (Ancient language expert, identified Minoan script, 1922–1956)

WHITBY Yorkshire

William Bateson (Botanist who championed Mendel's previously-ignored genetics research, 1861–1926)
Arthur Brown (Pop singer renowned for album 'The Crazy World of Arthur Brown' and single *Fire*, 1944–)

Margaret Storm Jameson (Novelist [*The Voyage Home*] and autobiographer [*No Time Like the Present*], 1891-1986)

WHITCHURCH Hampshire
Alfred Thompson Denning [Baron] (Master of the Rolls and legal author, 1899-1999)

WHITCHURCH Shropshire
Sir Edward German [b.Edward German Jones] (Operatic composer [*Merrie England, Tom Jones*], 1862-1936)

WHITE WALTHAM Berkshire
Thomas Hearne (Antiquarian, researched English chronicles, 1678-1735)

WHITHORN Wigtownshire
John Ramsay McCulloch (Political economist [*Principles of Political Economy*] and Controller of the Stationery Office [1838-64], 1789-1864)

WHITLAND Dyfed
William James Matthias (Composer of opera [*The Servants*] and wedding anthem for Prince of Wales's wedding in 1981, 1934-1992)

WHITTINGHAME East Lothian
Arthur James Balfour [1st Earl] (Prime Minister, responsible for the 'Balfour Declaration' which created a Jewish homeland in Palestine, 1848-1930)

WHITTINGTON Lancashire
William Sturgeon (Electrical scientist, invented moving-coil galvanometer, 1783-1850)

WHITTLESEY Cambridgeshire
Henry Glapthorne (Playwright [*The Hollander*], 1610-c.1644)

WHITWELL Derbyshire
Christopher John Adams (Test cricketer [Derbyshire, Sussex and England], 1970-)
Joe Davis (Snooker champion, winner of every championship from 1927-46, 1901-1978)

WICK Caithness
William Barclay (Theologian [*A New Testament Wordbook*], 1907-1978)
Alexander Henry Rhind (Archaeologist, wrote *Thebes, its Tombs and its Tenants*, 1844-1863)

WICK Somerset
John Gully (Boxing champion and racehorse owner, fathered 24 children by two wives, 1783-1863)

WICKEN Cambridgeshire
Andrew Fuller (US-based theological author, wrote *An Apology For the Late Christian Missions to India*, 1754-1815)

WICKHAM Hampshire
William of Wickham (Statesman, twice Chancellor of England, 1324-1404)

WICKHAM BISHOPS Essex
Nicola France LeFanu (Composer [*The Old Woman of Beare*], 1947-)

WIDFORD Hertfordshire
John Eliot (Missionary, printed first Bible in America, translated into language of the native Americans of Massachusetts, 1604-1690)

WIDNES Cheshire
Charles Glover Barkla (Nobel Prize-winning physicist, researched X-rays, 1877-1944)

WIGAN Lancashire

George Formby (Entertainer, sang risqué
songs while accompanying himself on
the ukelele, 1904–1961)

John Leland (Presbyterian author,
1691–1766)

Pauline Tinsley (Internationally-acclaimed
soprano, 1928–)

WIGTON Cumbria

Melvyn Bragg (Novelist [*The Soldier's
Return*] and broadcaster [compère of
South Bank Show], 1939–)

WIGTOWN

James Robertson-Justice (Actor famed as
'Sir Launcelot Spratt' in the *Doctor* series
of comedy films; trained Prince Charles
in falconry, 1905–1975)

WILLINGDON Sussex

Edward Daniel Clarke (Cambridge-based
mineralogist and university librarian,
1769–1822)

**WILLINGTON QUAY Near Newcastle
upon Tyne**

Robert Stephenson (Railway engineer and
bridge-builder [designed Britannia Bridge
over the Menai Straits], 1803–1859)

WILLOUGHBY Lincolnshire

John Smith (American colonist, soldier and
author, president of Virginia [1608–9],
1580–1631)

WIMBORNE MINSTER Dorset

William Cox (Built road over the Blue
Mountains in Australia in only six
months, 1764–1837)

WIMBORNE–ST–GILES Dorset

Anthony Ashley Cooper Shaftesbury [1st
Earl] (Chancellor of the Exchequer
[1661–72] and Lord Chancellor [1672–3],
1621–1683)

WINCHBURGH West Lothian

Winifred Rushforth (Psychotherapist
pioneer, wrote *Something is Happening*
aged 96, 1885–1983)

WINCHESTER Hampshire

Prince Arthur (Eldest son of Henry VII, first
husband of Catherine of Aragon,
1486–1502)

John Ayliffe (Scholar, expelled from Oxford
for allegations made in his *Ancient and
Present State of the University of Oxford*
[1714], 1676–1732)

Richard Ford (Travel author [*Gatherings
From Spain*], 1796–1858)

Henry III [King of England] (1207–1272)

John Lingard (Historian, wrote *History of
England*, 1771–1851)

Robert Lowth (Theological author,
appointed Bishop of London in 1777,
1710–1787)

Archibald Percivall Wavell [1st Earl]
(Military commander and Viceroy of India
[1943–7], 1883–1950)

WINDERMERE Cumbria

Sir Arthur Somervell (Composer [*The
Forsaken Merman*], 1863–1937)

**WINDLESTONE HALL Near Bishop
Auckland, County Durham**

Sir Anthony Eden [Lord Avon] (Prime Minister [1955–7], committed UK to attack
on Egypt in 1956 over Suez Crisis,
1897–1977)

WINDSOR Berkshire

Sir Sydney Camm (Aircraft designer,
contributed to design of such military
aircraft as the Hurricane and the Harrier,
1893–1966)

Edward III [King of England] (Claimed the French crown, leading to Hundred Years War, 1312–1377)

Sir Ranulph Twisleton-Wykeham Fiennes (Explorer, 1945–)

Henry Hallam (Historian, wrote *State of Europe During the Middle Ages*, 1777–1859)

Henry VI [King of England] (Murdered in the Tower of London, 1421–1471)

Charles Knight (Author and publisher [of the *Penny Magazine*, 1832–45], 1791–1873)

Humphrey Lyttleton (Acclaimed jazz trumpeter and bandleader, 1921–)

Geraldine McEwan (Actor, portrayed 'Miss Jean Brodie' on TV, 1932–)

Louis Mountbatten of Burma [1st Earl] (Military commander and last Viceroy of India, murdered by the IRA, 1900–1979)

Hugh Richard Sheppard (Religious broadcaster and pacifist, co-founder of the 'Life and Liberty' movement in 1917, 1880–1937)

WINESTEAD Humberside

Andrew Marvell (Poet ['To a coy mistress'], 1621–1678)

WING Leicestershire

Sir Charles Vernon Boys (Physicist, invented radiomicrometer, 1855–1944)

WINSFORD Somerset

Ernest Bevin (Trade union official who entered Parliament and became Foreign Secretary [1945–51], 1881–1951)

Sir John Bradbury (Treasury official, replaced gold £1 and 10 shilling coins with paper notes, 1872–1950)

WINSLADE Devon

Mary Chudleigh (Poet and essayist [*The Lady's Defence*], 1656–1710)

WINSTON County Durham

Aaron Arrowsmith (London-based cartographer, original Fellow of the Royal Geographical Society, 1750–1823)

Thomas Wharton (Anatomist, discovered sub-maxillary gland which now bears his name, 1614–1673)

WINTON Cumbria

Richard Burn (Legal author [*Justice of the Peace*], 1709–1785)

John Langhorne (Poet, translator of Plutarch, 1735–1779)

WINWICK Cheshire

Sir Phipps Hornby (Naval officer, appointed Commander-in-Chief in the Pacific [1847–50], 1785–1867)

WISBECH Cambridgeshire

Thomas Clarkson (Successful anti-slavery campaigner, 1760–1846)

William Godwin (Author [*An Enquiry Concerning Political Justice*], 1756–1836)

Anton Rogers (TV actor [*Jamie on a Flying Visit*], 1933–)

WITHAM Essex

Thomas Campion (Composer and poet in both Latin and English, 1567–1620)

WITHERNSEA Near Hull

Kay Kendall (Actor [played trumpet in the film *Genevieve*], 1926–1959)

WITNEY Oxfordshire

Sir Frederick Clarke (Director of the Institute of Education in London [1936–45], 1880–1952)

Patrick Christopher Steptoe (Medical pioneer in artificial fertilisation, 1913–1988)

WIVENHOE Essex

Sir John Martin-Harvey (Actor and theatre-
manager, 1863–1944)

WOKING Surrey

Sir Laurence John Hartnett (Australian-
based car designer, 1898–1986)
Sir Samuel Morton Peto (Railway builder
and partner in firm which constructed
Nelson's Column, 1809–1889)
Delia Smith (TV cookery expert and a
director of Norwich City FC, 1941–)
Paul Weller (Pop singer, sometimes with
group The Jam, 1958–)

WOLVERHAMPTON West Midlands

Frances Barber (Actor [*Sammy and Rosie
Get Laid*], 1958–)
Sir William Maddock Bayliss (Physiologist,
discovered secretin, first known hormone,
1860–1924)
Alfred Noyes (Poet ['Drake'], 1880–1958)
Tessa Sanderson (Javelin-thrower who won
Olympic gold in 1984 and three
Commonwealth golds, 1956–)
Billy [William Ambrose] Wright
(International footballer, first Englishman
to win 100 caps, 90 of them as captain,
1924–1994)

WOLVERLEY Worcestershire

John Baskerville (Printer to Cambridge
University, typeface bears his name,
1706–1775)

WOODBRIDGE Suffolk

Brian Eno (Rock singer and producer, at
one time with group Roxy Music, 1948–)

WOODFORD Essex

Nick Berry (TV actor [*Heartbeat*], 1963–)
Coventry Kersey Patmore (Poet ['The Angel
in the House'], 1823–1896)

WOODLEY Cheshire

Hubert Henry Davies (Playwright [*Cousin
Kate, The Mollusc*], 1876–1917)

WOODSTOCK Oxfordshire

Edward the Black Prince [Prince of
England] (Victor at Battle of Poitiers,
1330–1376)
Thomas of Woodstock [Duke of
Gloucester] (Youngest son of Edward III,
1355–1397)

WOOKEY Somerset

Arthur James Cook (Miners' leader during
1926 General Strike, 1883–1931)
Sir Cyril Arthur Pearson (Newspaper and
magazine proprietor, founded *Daily
Express*, 1866–1921)

WOOLER Northumberland

Edward Dalziel (Engraver, designed
woodcut illustrations in *Bible Gallery*
[1880], 1817–1905)

**WOOLSTHORPE Near Colsterworth,
Lincolnshire**

Isaac Newton (Leading scientist,
propounded law of gravity, 1642–1717)

WOTTON-UNDER-EDGE Gloucestershire

John Biddle (Preacher, died imprisoned for
his beliefs, 1615–1662)
Sir Charles Blagden (Chemist, researched
low-temperature science, 1748–1820)

WORCESTER

Philip Henry Gosse (Naturalist, wrote
Introduction to Zoology, 1810–1888)
John Pyke Hullah (Composer [*Village
Coquettes* with lyrics by Charles Dickens],
1812–1884)
Charles John Noke (Ceramic designer,
experimented with Chinese red glaze,
1858–1941)

William Richard Morris Nuffield [1st Viscount] (Manufacturer of cheap [Morris] motor cars, 1877–1963)

Sheila Scott (Aviator, famed for long-distance solo flights, 1927–1988)

Hannah Snell (Disguised as a man, travelled world as a sailor and soldier searching for her husband, 1723–1792)

John Somers [1st Baron] (Constitutional lawyer and statesman, contributed to 1689 Declaration of Rights, 1651–1716)

Vesta Tilley [b.Matilda Powles] (Music-hall comedian and male impersonator, 1864–1952)

Mrs Henry Wood [b.Ellen Price] (Novelist [*East Lynne*], 1814–1887)

WORKINGTON Cumbria

Frankie Armstrong (Soprano folksinger, 1941–)

WORKSOP Nottinghamshire

Sir Donald Pleasance (Actor, played 'Ernst Blofeld' in *You Only Live Twice*, 1919–1995)

WORTHING Sussex

Maureen Patricia Duffy (Novelist [*The Microcosm*], 1933–)

John Selden (Historian and libertarian, wrote *Titles of Honour*, 1584–1654)

WORTLEY Yorkshire

Phil [Philip William] May (Cartoonist, contributed to *Punch*, 1864–1903)

WOTTON Surrey

John Evelyn (Celebrated diarist, 1620–1706)

WOULDHAM Kent

Henry Tracey Coxwell (Balloonist, managed Prussian balloon fleet in 1870 Franco-Prussian War, 1819–1900)

WRAWBY Lincolnshire

Joseph Shield Nicholson (Professor of Political Economy at Edinburgh for 45 years, 1850–1927)

WRENTHAM Suffolk

William Johnson Fox (Author and politician, introduced a compulsory education bill into Commons in 1850, 1786–1864)

WREXHAM Clwyd

Charles Harold Dodd (Biblical scholar, taught divinity at Cambridge for 13 years, 1884–1973)

Sir Ewart Ray Herbert Jones (Chemist who researched steroids and vitamins, and was in charge of London's anti-gas defences in World War Two, 1911–2002)

Robert Savage (International footballer [Birmingham and Wales], 1974–)

WRINGTON Somerset

John Locke (Philosopher whose *Essay Concerning Human Understanding* [1690] pioneered British empiricism, 1632–1704)

WROTHAM Kent

George Byng [Viscount] (Admiral, commanded successfully against French and Spanish navies, 1663–1733)

Henry Hardinge of Lahore [1st Viscount] (Viceroy of India [1844–8] who planned railway system and the Ganges Canal, 1785–1856)

WYE Kent

Aphra Behn (Believed to be first professional author in England, 1640–1689)

Catherine Graham Macaulay (Controversial historian [*History of England* 8 vols], 1731–1791)

WYLAM Northumberland

Timothy Hackworth (Pioneering engineer whose locomotive *Sans Pareil* challenged Stephenson's *Rocket* in 1829, 1786–1850)

George Stephenson (Engineer who built the *Rocket* in 1829 and much of the British railway system, 1781–1848)

WYMONDHAM Norfolk

Robert Kett (Campaigner against land enclosures, executed after besieging Norwich with 16,000 men, d.1549)

WYNFORD EAGLE Dorset

Thomas Sydenham (Physician known as 'The English Hippocrates', gave name to liquid opium used medicinally [Sydenham's Laudanum], 1624–1689)

YALDING Near Maidstone, Kent

Edmund Charles Blunden (Poet ['Undertones of War'], 1896–1974)

YARMOUTH Isle of Wight

Sir James Paget (Pathologist, discovered cause of trichinosis, 1814–1899)

YATE Gloucestershire

Joanne Kathleen [J.K.] Rowling (Author, creator of 'Harry Potter', 1965–)

YEOVIL Somerset

William K. Everson (Owner of largest film collection in US, 1929–)

Polly Jean Harvey (Singer-songwriter [*Sheela-na-Gig*], 1969–)

YORK

Alcuin (Scholar and member of Charlemagne's court, 737–804)

Sir John Ashton (Landscape painter, 1881–1963)

Wystan Hugh [W.H.] Auden (US-based poet, wrote 'Stop all the Clocks...', 1907–1973)

John Barry (Film composer, won Oscar for *Star Wars* music, 1933–)

Jocelyn Bell-Burnell (Radio astronomer, co-discovered first pulsar, 1943–)

St Margaret Clitherow (Martyr, crushed to death for her religious beliefs, 1556–1586)

Miles Coverdale (Biblical scholar, produced first complete Bible in English, 1488–1568)

Dame Judi [Judith Olivia] Dench (Oscar-winning actor [*Shakespeare in Love*], 1934–)

William Etty (Artist, famed for his *Cleopatra* in 1821, 1787–1849)

Guy Fawkes (Conspirator, executed and annually burned in effigy for attempting to blow up Parliament, 1570–1606)

John Flaxman (Sculptor and ceramic designer, 1755–1826)

Joseph Aloysius Hansom (Architect and inventor of Hansom cab, 1803–1882)

Frankie [Francis] Howerd (Comedian [TV's *Up Pompeii*], 1921–1992)

Elizabeth Montagu [b.Robinson] (London-based literary hostess, 1720–1800)

William Parsons Rosse [3rd Earl] (Irish-based astronomer who in 1845 built telescope with mirror six feet in diameter [and still operating], 1800–1867)

Benjamin Seebohm Rowntree (Chocolate manufacturer and philanthropist, 1871–1954)

Joseph Rowntree (Cocoa manufacturer and social reformer, 1836–1925)

John Snow (Physician who pioneered public health measures, 1813–1858)

Silvanus Phillips Thompson (Physicist, researched electricity and magnetism, 1851–1916)

Samuel Tuke (Psychiatric therapy reformer, made treatment more humane, 1784–1857)

COUNTY INDEX

Aberdeenshire
Aberdeen
Alford
Banchory
Birse
Braemar
Caskieben
Chapel of Garioch
Crathenaird
Deer
Drumoak
Fraserburgh
Fyvie
Huntly
Inverugie
Inverurie
Ironside
Keig
Lumsden
Methlick
New Aberdour
Newburgh
Oldmeldrum
Persley
Rhynie
Strachan
Strichen
Turriff

Angus
Arbroath
Auchterhouse
Benvie
Brechin
Broughty Angus
Fearn
Forfar
Glamis Castle

Kingsmuir
Kinnordy
Kirriemuir
Little Whitefield
Logie Pert
Montrose

Antrim: see County Antrim

Argyllshire
Campbeltown
Dalmally
Dunoon
Helensburgh
Inveraray
Islay
Kilninver
Kinlochleven
Oban

Armagh: see County Armagh

Ayrshire
Alloway
Ardrossan
Ayr
Blanefield
Carskeoch
Colmonell
Crosshouse
Darvel
Dreghorn
Fenwick
Irvine
Kilmarnock
Kilmaurs

Largs
Lugar
Ochiltree
Saltcoats
Stewarton
Turnberry

Banffshire
Banff
Boyndie
Rathven
Rothiemay

Bedfordshire
Bedford
Cardington
Dunstable
Edworth
Elstow
Leighton Buzzard
Little Barford
Luton
Milton Bryant
Northill
Sutton

Berkshire
Abingdon
Bucklebury
Compton Beauchamp
Cookham
Goring
Hambledon
Hungerford
Maidenhead
Newbury
Pangbourne
Pusey

Reading
Slough
Warfield
White Waltham
Windsor

Berwickshire
Bunkle
Chirnside
Cockburnspath
Coldingham
Duns
Earlston
Edrom
Kames
Ladykirk
Mellerstain
Redbraes
Westruther

Buckinghamshire
Aylesbury
Bourne End
Coleshill
Fenny Stratford
Fulmer
Gawcott
Gayhurst
Grandborough
High Wycombe
Little Missenden
Milton Keynes
Swanbourne
Wendover
Whaddon

Bute
Kingarth
Rothesay

Caithness
Dunbeath

Cambridgeshire

Alwalton
Brinkley
Cambridge
Cottenham
Denton
Grantchester
Great Shelford
Helpston
Huntingdon
Peterborough
St Ives
St Neots
Stow-cum-Quy
Trumpington

Carmarthenshire
Garnant
Hafod

Cheshire
Altrincham
Anderton
Birkenhead
Bollington
Bramhall
Buerton
Burton
Chester
Daresbury
Disley
Ellesmere
Farnworth
Gawsworth
Great Neston
Hartford
Heswall
Holmes Chapel
Hoylake
Langley
Macclesfield
Malpas
Middlewich
Nantwich
New Brighton

Oxton
Parkgate
Prees Hall
Prescot
Rock Ferry
Runcorn
Sandbach
Wallasey
Warrington
Winwick
Woodley

Clackmannanshire
Alloa
Alva
Garlet
Kincardine-on-Forth
Menstrie
Tullibody

Cornwall
Bodmin
Cambridge
Chacewater
Fowey
Godolphin Hall
Helston
Illogan
Laneast
Lelant
Lostwithiel
Morval
Mousehole
Padstow
Pelynt
Penzance
Port Eliot
Redruth
St Agnes
St Austell
St Columb Minor
St Ives
St Stephens
Saltash

Treator
Tremeer
Trewarthenick
Truro

County Antrim
Ballymoney
Glenarm
Portadown
Toomebridge

County Armagh
Keady
Lurgan

County Derry
Castledawson
Limavady
Londonderry

County Down
Annalong
Ballyroney
Bangor
Hillsborough
Holywood
Killyleagh
Millisle
Newry

County Durham
Barnard Castle
Birtley
Bishop Auckland
Bishop Middleham
Brandon
Coxhoe
Darlington
Durham
Easington
Elemore Hall
Gateshead
Hartlepool
Hebburn on Tyne

Hetton le Hole
Monkwearmouth
Sedgefield
South Shields
Stockton-on-Tees
Swalwell
Thornaby-on-Tees
Tyne Dock
Washington
Windlestone Hall
Winston

County Tyrone
Caledon
Killyclogher
Moy
Prillisk
Strabane

Cumbria
Alston
Bampton
Brampton
Bridekirk
Broughton in Furness
Carlisle
Clifton
Cockermouth
Coniston
Corney
Dalton in Furness
Dent
Docker (Westmoreland)
Eaglesfield
Hardendale
Hesket Newmarket
Heversham
Kendal
Keswick
Kirkby Lonsdale
Levens
Mirehouse
Muncaster
Netherby

Orton
Plumbland
St Bees
Scaleby
Shap
Silloth
Thursby
Westward
Wigton
Windermere
Winton
Workington

Denbighshire
Denbigh

Derbyshire
Allestree
Belper
Butterley Hall
Buxton
Chesterfield
Cromford
Denby
Derby
Dethick
Duffield
Eyam
Glossop
Hayfield
Ilkeston
Kedleston Hall
Long Eaton
Mackworth
Matlock
Measham
Melbourne
Newhall
Ripley
Sawley
Shirley
Snelston
Sudbury
Taxal

Thornsett
Tintwistle

Derry: see County Derry
Devon
Annery
Ashburton
Barnstaple
Berrynarbor
Bideford
Bridgerule
Buckland Abbey
Crediton
Dartington
Dartmouth
Devonport
Dittisham
Dodbrooke
Exeter
Great Potheridge
Hayes Barton
Holne
Ilfracombe
Ilsington
Kingsbridge
Littleham-cum-Exmouth
Membury
Moretonhampstead
Northam
North Tawton
Ottery St Mary
Paignton
Plymouth
Plympton
Powderham
Sandridge
Shilstone
Sidmouth
South Molton
Stoke Gabriel
Tavistock
Teignmouth
Tiverton
Torquay

Torrington
Totnes
Upottery
Winslade
Dorset
Blandford Forum
Blandford St Mary
Bradpole
Cranborne
Crowndale
Dorchester
East Stour
Evershot
Fifehead Magdalen
Higher Bockhampton
Lyme Regis
Melcombe Regis
Milbourne St Andrew
Moreton
Poole
Radipole
Rampisham
Shaftesbury
Sherbourne
Sturminster Newton
Swanage
Thorncombe
Weymouth
Wimbourne Minster
Wimbourne St Giles
Wynford Eagle

Down: see County Down

Dumfriesshire
Annan
Dalswinton
Dumfries
Ecclefechan
Hoddam Castle
Kirkconnel
Kirkpatrick-Fleming
Langholm
Little Duchrae

Lochrutton
Moffat
Moniaive
Penpont
Thornhill
Tinwald

Dunbartonshire
Bearsden
Cardross
Dumbarton
Kirkintilloch
Roseneath

Durham: see County Durham

East Lothian
Drem
Dunbar
Dunglass
East Linton
Gifford
Haddington
Lennoxlove
Longniddry
Musselburgh
Newbyth
Ormiston
Port Seton
Prestonpans
Tantallon Castle
Wallyford
Whittinghame

Essex
Black Notley
Braintree
Castle Hedingham
Chelmsford
Chigwell
Colchester
Dagenham
Dunmow

Earls Colne
Finchingfield
Great Harlow
Havering-at-Bower
Hempstead
Hornchurch
Ilford
Kelvedon
Leigh-on-Sea
Loughton
Maldon
Manningtree
Rivenhall
Romford
Saffron Walden
Southend
Springfield
Stanford Rivers
Stebbing
Terling
Thaxted
Westcliff-on-Sea
Wickham Bishops
Witham
Wivenhoe
Woodford

Fife
Anstruther
Auchtermuchty
Balfour
Blairhall
Carnbee
Carskerdo
Colessie
Cowdenbeath
Creich
Culross
Cults
Cupar
Dunfermline
Dysart
Earlsferry
Falkland

Inverkeithing
Kennoway
Kilmany
Kinglassie
Kirkcaldy
Largo
Limekilns
Lochgelly
Newport
Pitscottie
St Andrews
Tayport

Glamorgan
Duffryn

Gloucestershire
Alderley
Ashley
Berkeley
Bibury
Bitton
Cheltenham
Chipping Campden
Cinderford
Coleford
Down Ampney
Downend
Ebrington
Fairford
Frampton-on-Severn
Gloucester
Hatherop
Horton
Lydney
Moreton-in-Marsh
Northway
Rendcombe
Sherbourne
Slad
Standish
Stoke Bishop
Stow-on-the-Wold
Stroud

Temple Guiting
Tewkesbury
Wotton-under-Edge
Yate

Gwent
Abersychan
Blackwood

Hampshire
Aldershot
Alresford
Alton
Ashe
Barton-on-Sea
Basingstoke
Bentworth
Bishopstoke
Bournemouth
Bursledon
Elson
Fareham
Gosport
Grayshott
Hayling Island
North Stoneham
Otterbourne
Portsea
Portsmouth
Romsey
Ropsley
Selbourne
Southampton
Southsea
Steventon
Swanmore
Upham
West Meon
Whitchurch
Wickham
Winchester

Hereford & Worcester
Barnt Green
Birtsmorton

Bredwardine
Broadheath
Evesham
Fockbury
Hagley
Hawford
Hereford
Kidderminster
Kington
Ledbury
Leominster
Netherwood
Odiham

Hertfordshire
Abbots Langley
Barnet
Berkhamsted
Bishop's Stortford
Bovingdon
Broxbourne
Buntingford
Bushey
Charlton
Chorley Wood
Cumberlow Green
Dane End
Goff's Oak
Harpenden
Hatfield
Hatfield House
Hemel Hempstead
Hertford
Hitchin
Hoddesdon
Hunsdon
Little Berkhamsted
Little Hadham
Nash Mills
Potter's Bar
St Albans
St Paul's Walden Bury
Stevenage
Totteridge

Watford
Welwyn Garden City
Wheathampstead

Inverness-shire
Borlum
Bunchrew
Fort George
Inverie
Inverness
Kingussie
Rothiemurchus
Ruthven
Stornoway

Isle of Man
Douglas

Isle of Wight
East Cowes
Freshwater
Newport
Ryde
St Helens
Yarmouth

Kent
Allington
Ashford
Bearsted
Beckenham
Bekesbourne
Bexley
Boughton Malherbe
Brenchley
Broadstairs
Bromley
Canterbury
Chatham
Chislehurst
Cliftonville
Cranbrook
Dartford
Deal

Dover
Faversham
Folkestone
Gillingham
Goodnestone
Gravesend
Greenhithe
Hadlow
Herne Bay
Herne Hill
Knole
Lenham
Luton
Maidstone
Margate
Mattingham
Meopham
Olantigh
Penshurst
Petts Wood
Plaxtol
Ramsgate
Ringwould
Ripple
Riverhead
Rochester
Sandgate
Sandwich
Sevenoaks
Shipbourne
Sittingbourne
Tenterden
Tonbridge
Tunbridge Wells
Walmer
Westerham
Wouldham
Wrotham
Wye
Yalding

Kincardineshire
Laurencekirk
Marykirk

Stonehaven

Kinross-shire
Kinnesswood
Milnathort

Kircudbrightshire
Kirkbean
Twynholm

Lanarkshire
Airdrie
Bellshill
Biggar
Blantyre
Bothwell
Burnbank
Cambuslang
Cambusnethan
Coatbridge
Hamilton
Leadhills
Low Blantyre
Motherwell
Rutherglen
Shotts
Strathaven
Viewpark

Lancashire
Ainsdale
Ashton-under-Lyne
Ashton-upon-Mersey
Atherton
Bacup
Bamber Bridge
Billinge
Blackburn
Blackpool
Bolton
Bromley Cross
Burnley
Bury
Chorley

Churchtown
Crosby
Dragley Beck
Droylesden
Eccleston
Fleetwood
Halewood
Haslingden
Heywood
Higher Walton
Hurstwood
Kirkham
Knowsley Hall
Lancaster
Leigh
Middleton
Morecambe
Newton le Willows
Oldham
Ormskirk
Oswaldtwistle
Preston
Prestwich
Rochdale
Rossall
St Helens
Salford
Southport
Springhead
Stockport
Ulverston
Walton-le-Dale
Whalley
Whittington
Widnes
Wigan

Leicestershire (see also Rutland)
Arnesby
Barnwell
Bradgate
Brooksby
Burbage

Coalville
Diseworth
Dishley
Fenny Drayton
Gracedieu
Hoby
Kibworth Harcourt
Kirby Muxloe
Langham
Leicester
Loughborough
Markfield
Melton Mowbray
Rothley
Somerby
Thurcaston
Wing

Lincolnshire
Alford
Alvingham
Aswarby
Barton-upon-Humber
Boston
Bourne
Brigg
Cadeby
Claypole
Cleethorpes
Donington
Epworth
Gainsborough
Grantham
Grimsby
Hogsthorpe
Holbeach
Horncastle
Lincoln
Long Sutton
Lutton Bowine
Ropsley
Scunthorpe
Sempringham
Sleaford

Somersby
South Carlton
Spalding
Spilsby
Swinderby
Uffington
Walesby
Waltham-on-the-Wolds
Welbourn
Willoughby
Wrawby

Merioneth
Criccieth

Middlesex
Laleham
Northwood
Pinner
Ruislip
Southall
Teddington

Mid Glamorgan
Abercwmboi
Bargoed
Cwmaman
Dowlais
Nantymoel
Ogmore-by-Sea

Midlothian
Borthwick
Dalhousie Castle
Dalkeith
Eskbank
Fountainhall
Glencorse
Hawthornden
Hermiston
Lasswade
Newbattle
Penicuik

Monmouth
Monmouth
Newbridge
Newport

Morayshire
Elgin
Fochabers
Lossiemouth
Nairn

Norfolk
Baconsthorpe
Bracon Ash
Bradenham Hall
Brooke Hall
Burgh St Peter
Burnham Thorpe
Buxton
Caister-on-Sea
Catton
Cromer
Dereham
Dickleborough
Dilham
Diss
East Dereham
East Ruston
Great Snoring
Great Yarmouth
Holkham
Hoveton
Hunstanton
Ingoldsthorpe
King's Lynn
Mileham
Sandringham
Stoke Ferry
Swaffham
Swardeston
Thetford
Wells-next-the-Sea
Wymondham

Northamptonshire
Aldwincle
Appletree
Barton Seagrave
Bulwick
Collyweston
Cosgrove
Fotheringhay Castle
Hannington
Holdenby
Horton
Kettering
Kingscliffe
King's Sutton
Newnham
Northampton
Northwick Park
Oundle
Paulerspury
Rushden
Twywell
Upton

Northumberland
Alnwick
Ashington
Aynho
Bamburgh
Bedlington
Belford
Berwick-on-Tweed
Dudley
Eglingham
Embleton
Fallodon
Glanton
Haydon Bridge
Hexham
Kirkharle
Milfield
Morpeth
Newburn
Newcastle upon Tyne
North Shields

Ovingham
Riding Mill
Rothbury
Sandhoe
Scotswood
Stocksfield
Tweedmouth
Warkworth
Whalton
Willington Quay
Wooler
Wylam

Nottinghamshire
Aslockton
Attenborough
Bingham
Brackenhurst
Bulwell
Burton Joyce
East Drayton
East Retford
Eastwood
Elton
Farnsfield
Hucknall
Langar
Mansfield
Mansfield Woodhouse
Newark-on-Trent
Nuncargate
Oxton
Sneinton
Stapleford
Sturton-le-Steeple
Toton
Welbeck Abbey
Worksop

Orkney
Deerness
Kirkwall
St Mary's Holm

Oxfordshire
Bampton
Banbury
Blackbourton
Burford
Chadlington
Charlbury
Churchill
Cropredy
Crowell
Deddington
Ditchley
Dodington
Faringdon
Islip
Juniper Hill
Longworth
Mixbury
Oxford
South Leigh
Stadhampton
Thame
Uffington
Wallingford
Wantage
Wardington
Witney
Woodstock

Peeblesshire
Peebles
West Linton

Pembrokeshire
Pembroke

Perthshire
Aberdalgie
Auchterarder
Blairgowrie
Bridge of Earn
Caputh
Carpow
Cloag

Crieff
Deanston
Gask
Kilgraston
Kinclaven
Little Whitefield
Lochearnhead
Logierait
Perth
Rattray
Scone
Stobhill
Straloch

Renfrewshire
Barrhead
Eastwood
Elderslie
Greenock
Houston
Johnstone
Lochwinnoch
Paisley
Port Glasgow
Renfrew

Ross & Cromarty
Cromarty
Fearn
Gairloch
Tomich

Roxburghshire
Ancrum
Blakelaw
Denholm
Hawick
Jedburgh
Kelso
Melrose
Nisbet
Stobs

Rutland
Oakham

Selkirkshire
Ettrickhall
Foulshiels
Galashiels
Selkirk
Torwoodlee

Shetland
Lerwick

Shropshire (see also West Midlands)
Atcham
Betton
Broseley
Clive
Dawley
Dorrington
Ellesmere
Eyton
Hadley
Horsehay
Ironbridge
Kenley
Leighton
Marton
Norbury
Oakengates
Oswestry
Rowton
Shifnal
Shrewsbury
Wellington
Westbury
Whitchurch

Somerset
Alford
Aller
Ashton
Bath
Bridgwater
Chard
Clevedon
Clifton

Dulverton
East Coker
Frome
Holnicote
Huntworth
Ilchester
Ilminster
Keinton Mandeville
Kelston
Langport
Low Ham
Mangotsfield
Martock
Middle Chinnock
Midsomer Norton
Milverton
Minehead
Nailsea
Nether Stowey
Odcombe
Pawlett
Rode
South Petherton
Street
Taunton
Wells
Weston-Super-Mare
Winsford
Wookey
Wrington
Yeovil

South Glamorgan
Barry

Staffordshire (see also West Midlands)
Aston
Burton Constable
Burton-on-Trent
Cannock
Caverswall
Codsall
Congreve

Coton
Dresden
Dunston
Endon
Handsworth
Harbourne
Leek
Lichfield
Longton
Madeley
Newcastle-under-Lyme
Penkhull
Shugborough Park
Stafford
Stoke-on-Trent
Stone
Streetly
Talke
Tamworth
Trentham
Walsall

Stirlingshire
Airth
Bridge of Allan
Campsie
Elphinstone
Falkirk
Garden
Gartmore
Grangemouth
Killearn
Kinnaird
Polmont
Raploch
Redding
Stirling

Suffolk
Aldeburgh
Alderton
Barrow
Beccles
Broke Hall

Bungay
Bures
Bury St Edmunds
Creeting Mill
Drinkstone
Dunwich
East Burgholt
Felixstowe
Fressingfield
Groton
Hadleigh
Halesworth
Haverhill
Honington
Hopton
Ipswich
Laxfield
Lidgate
Long Melford
Lowestoft
Mildenhall
Normanston
Stradbroke
Stratford St Andrew
Sudbury
Theberton Hall
Thurlow
Trimley St Martin
Woodbridge
Wrentham

Surrey
Abinger
Albury
Alderstone
Camberley
Chelsham
Chertsey
Cranleigh
Croydon
Dorking
Dunsfold
Egham
Elstead

Englefield Green
Epsom
Esher
Farnham
Godalming
Guildford
Haslemere
Headley
Hersham
Horley
Kingston-on-Thames
Leatherhead
Limpsfield
Merton
Mitcham
Norwood
Ockham
Reigate
Richmond
Ripley
Shepperton
Slinfold
Sunbury on Thames
Surbiton
Tatsfield
Thames Ditton
Thornton Heath
Tolworth
Tongham
Walton on Thames
West Chobham
West Clandon
Weybridge
Woking
Worthing
Wotton

Sussex
Albourne
Amberley
Bexhill
Bognor Regis
Brighton
Chichester

Cowdray
Crowborough
Cuckfield
Eastbourne
Hastings
Henfield
Heyshott
Horsham
Hove
Hurstpierpoint
Lewes
Lindfield
Peacehaven
Petersfield
Petworth
Rye
St Leonards
Sedgwick
Selsey Bill
South Malling
Southwick
Stanmer
Stoughton
Theobalds
Trotton
Warnham
Willingdon

Sutherland
Scourie

**Tyrone (see County
Tyrone)**

**Warwickshire (see also
West Midlands)**
Arbury
Astley
Atherstone
Barford
Beauchamp Court
Hartshill
Higham-on-the-Hill
Kenilworth

Farsley
Fitzwilliam
Foulby
Fulford
Fulneck
Giggleswick
Hackforth
Halifax
Halsteads
Harewood
Harpham
Harrogate
Hatfield
Hauxwell
Heckmondwike
Helmsley
Hipperholme
Horbury
Hornby
Horsforth
Hornsea
Howden
Huddersfield
Hull
Ilkley
Keighley
Kingston-upon-Hull (see
  Hull)

Kiplin
Kirbymoorside
Kirby Wiske
Kirkheaton
Knaresborough
Luddenden
Marton
Mexborough
Middlesborough
Middleton Tyas
Morley
Mytholmroyd
Newsham
Normanton
Northallerton
Nun Appleton
Otley
Oulton
Providence Green
Pudsey
Ramsgill
Rawdon
Richmond
Ripon
Rotherham
Rudston
Scarborough
Selby

Settle
Shipley
Skipton
Slaithwaite
Snainton
Sowerby
Sowood
Spennithorne
Spofforth
Stainborough
Stainforth
Stainton
Stillingfleet
Stillington
Tadcaster
Thirsk
Thornton
Thurnscoe
Todmorden
Wakefield
Whitby
Winestead
Withernsea
Wortley
York

Zetland see Shetland

PERSONAL NAME INDEX

Allen, George (Newark)
Allen, Walter (Birmingham)
Allen, William (Rossall)
Allenby, Edmund Henry [1st
Viscount] (Brackenhurst)
Allingham, Helen (Burton-
on-Trent)
Allingham, Margery Louise
(London)
Allott, Paul John
(Altrincham)
Almond, Hely Hutchinson
(Glasgow)
Alston, Richard (Stoughton)
Alwyn, William
(Northampton)
Ambler, Eric (London)
Ames, Joseph (Great
Yarmouth)
Amherst, Baron Jeffrey
(Riverhead)
Amherst, William Pitt [Earl]
(Bath)
Amis, Sir Kingsley (London)
Amiss, Dennis
(Birmingham)
Amory, Derick Heathcote
(Tiverton)
Amos, Emma (Newcastle
under Lyme)
Anderson, Elizabeth Garrett
(London)
Anderson, Ethel
(Leamington,
Warwickshire)
Anderson, James (Hermiston)
Anderson, John (Roseneath)
Anderson, Michael (London)
Anderson, Thomas
(Edinburgh)
Andrewes, Lancelot
(London)
Andrews, Charles Freer
(Newcastle upon Tyne)

Andrews, Harry (Tonbridge)
Andrews, Julie (Walton on
Thames)
Andrews, Thomas (Belfast)
Angas, George Fife
(Newcastle upon Tyne)
Angell, Sir Norman
(Holbeach)
Anglesey, Henry [Marquis]
(London)
Angliss, Sir William
(Dudley)
Angus, Marion (Aberdeen)
Annakin, Ken (Beverley)
Anne, Queen (London)
Anning, Mary (Lyme Regis)
Anson, George, [Baron]
(Shugborough Park)
Anson, Sir William
(Walberton)
Anstey, Christopher
(Brinkley)
Appleton, Sir Edward
(Bradford)
Apted, Michael (Aylesbury)
Aram, Eugene (Ramsgill)
Arber, Agnes (London)
Arbuthnot, John
(Inverbervie)
Arch, Joseph (Barford)
Archer, Fred (Cheltenham)
Archer, Frederick Scott
(Bishop's Stortford)
Archer, Thomas (Tanworth)
Arden, John (Barnsley)
Argyll, Archibald [9th Earl]
(Dalkeith)
Argyll, John Campbell [2nd
Duke] (London)
Arkwright, Sir Richard
(Preston)
Arliss, George (London)
Armitage, Edward (London)
Armitage, Kenneth (Leeds)

Armour, Mary Nicol
(Blantyre)
Armour, Thomas Dickson
(Edinburgh)
Armstead, Henry (London)
Armstrong, Frankie
(Workington)
Armstrong, Henry (London)
Armstrong, William [Baron]
(Newcastle upon Tyne)
Arne, Thomas (London)
Arnold, Sir Edwin
(Gravesend)
Arnold, Joseph (Beccles)
Arnold, Malcolm
(Northampton)
Arnold, Matthew (Laleham)
Arnold, Thomas (East
Cowes)
Arrol, Sir William (Houston)
Arrowsmith, Aaron
(Winston)
Arthur [Prince]
(Winchester)
Arup, Sir Ove (Newcastle
upon Tyne)
Asbury, Francis
(Handsworth)
Ascham, Roger (Kirby
Wiske)
Ashbee, Charles (London)
Ashby, Sir Eric (London)
Ashcroft, Dame Peggy
(Croydon)
Ashford, Daisy (London)
Ashley, Laura (Merthyr
Tydfil)
Ashmole, Elias (Lichfield)
Ashton, Sir John (York)
Ashton, Julian (Alderstone)
Ashton, Winifred (London)
Ashworth, Dicken
(Todmorden)
Askew, Anne (Grimsby)

Askey, Arthur (Liverpool)

Aspdin, Joseph (Leeds)

Aspinall, Sir John
(Liverpool)

Asquith, Anthony (London)

Asquith, Henry (Morley)

Astbury, William Thomas
(Longton)

Astell, Mary (Newcastle
upon Tyne)

Astley, Philip (Newcastle
under Lyme)

Astley, Rick (Warrington)

Aston, Francis William
(Birmingham)

Atholl, Katherine [Duchess]
(Banff)

Atiyah, Sir Michael
(London)

Atkins, Anna (Tonbridge)

Atkins, Eileen (Birmingham)

Atkinson, Rowan
(Newcastle upon Tyne)

Atkinson, Thomas
(Cawthorne)

Attenborough, David
(London)

Attenborough, Richard
(Cambridge)

Atterbury, Francis (Milton
Keynes)

Attlee, Clement (London)

Attwell, Mabel Lucie
(London)

Atwill, Lionel (Croydon)

Auchterlonie, Willie (St
Andrews)

Auden, Wystan Hugh (York)

Audley, Thomas [Baron]
(Earls Colne)

Aungerville, Richard (Bury
St Edmunds)

Austen, Jane (Steventon,
Hampshire)

Austen, Winifred
(Ramsgate)

Austin, Alfred (Leeds)

Austin, Herbert [Baron]
(Little Missenden)

Austin, John (Creeting Mill)

Austin, John Langsham
(Lancaster)

Avison, Charles (Newcastle
upon Tyne)

Ayckbourn, Sir Alan
(London)

Ayer, Sir Alfred (London)

Ayers, Sir Henry (Portsea)

Ayers, Kevin (Herne Bay)

Ayliffe, John (Winchester)

Aylward, Gladys (London)

Ayrton, Hertha (Portsea)

Ayrton, Michael (London)

Ayrton, William Edward
(London)

Aytoun, William
(Edinburgh)

Babbage, Charles (London)

Babington, Antony
(Dethick)

Bache, Francis Edward
(Birmingham)

Back, Sir George
(Stockport)

Bacon, Francis [Baron
Verulam] (London)

Bacon, John (London)

Bacon, Sir Nicholas
(Drinkstone)

Bacon, Roger (Ilchester)

Baconthorpe, John [Doctor
Resulutus]
(Baconsthorpe)

Baddeley, Hermione
(Broseley)

Baden Powell, Robert
[Baron] (London)

Bader, Sir Douglas (London)

Badham, John (Luton)

Baffin, William (London)

Bagehot, Walter (Langport)

Bagnold, Enid (Rochester)

Baikie, William (Kirkwall)

Bailey, Bill (Bath)

Bailey, David (London)

Bailey, Sir Donald
(Rotherham)

Bailey, Trevor (Westcliff on
Sea)

Baillie, Grisell (Mellerstain)

Baillie, Grizel (Redbraes)

Baillie, Dame Isobel (Hawick)

Baillie, Joanna (Bothwell)

Baillie, John (Gairloch)

Baillie, Matthew (Shotts)

Baillie, Robert (Glasgow)

Baily, Edward (Bristol)

Baily, Francis (Newbury)

Baines, Edward (Walton le
Dale)

Bainbridge, Beryl
(Liverpool)

Bainton, Edgar (London)

Bainton, Roland (Ilkeston)

Baird, Sir David (Newbyth)

Baird, John Logie
(Helensburgh)

Baker, Sir Benjamin (Frome)

Baker, Dame Janet
(Hatfield, S. Yorkshire)

Baker, Richard [Douglas
James] (London)

Baker, Roy Ward (London)

Baker, Sir Samuel (London)

Baker, Stanley (Ferndale)

Baker, Tina (Kirby Muxloe)

Bakewell, Joan Dawson
(Stockport)

Bakewell, Robert (Dishley)

Balchin, Nigel Marlin
(Potterne)

Balcon, Sir Michael (Birmingham)

Baldwin (Exeter)

Baldwin, Peter (Chichester)

Baldwin, Stanley (Bewdley)

Balfour, Arthur James [1st Earl] (Whittinghame)

Balfour, Lady Frances (London)

Balfour, Francis Maitland (Edinburgh)

Balfour, George (Portsmouth)

Ball, Johnny (Bristol)

Ballantine, James (Edinburgh)

Ballantyne, James and John (Kelso)

Ballantyne, Robert Michael (Edinburgh)

Balnaves, Henry (Kirkcaldy)

Baltimore, George Calvert [Baron] (Kiplin)

Bamford, Samuel (Middleton)

Bancroft, Richard (Farnworth)

Banks, Gordon (Sheffield)

Banks, Sir Joseph (London)

Banks, Lynne Reid (London)

Bannatyne, George (Edinburgh)

Bannen, Ian (Airdrie)

Bannerman, Helen Brodie (Edinburgh)

Bannister, Sir Roger (London)

Bantock, Sir Granville (London)

Barbauld, Anna (Kibworth Harcourt)

Barber, Frances (Wolverhampton)

Barbirolli, Sir John (London)

Barbour, John (Aberdeen)

Barclay, Robert (Gordonstoun)

Barclay, William (Wick)

Barcroft, Sir Joseph (Newry)

Barebone, Praise God (London)

Barger, George (Manchester)

Barham, Richard Harris (Canterbury)

Baring-Gould, Sabine (Exeter)

Barke, James (Torwoodlee)

Barker, Pat (Thornaby-on-Tees)

Barker, George Granville (Loughton)

Barker, Ronnie (Bedford)

Barker, Sue (Paignton)

Barker, Thomas (Pontypool)

Barkla, Charles Glover (Widnes)

Barkworth, Peter (Margate)

Barlow, Hannah Bolton (Little Hadham)

Barlow, Jonathan (Ironbridge)

Barlow, Peter (Norwich)

Barlow, Thelma (Middlesbrough)

Barlow, Thomas (Orton)

Barmby, Nick (Hull)

Barnes, Josephine (Shorlingham)

Barnes, William (Sturminster Newton)

Barnett, Dame Henrietta (London)

Barnett, Kim John (Stoke-on-Trent)

Barnfield, Richard (Norbury)

Barns-Graham, Wilhelmina (St Andrews)

Barraclough, Roy (Preston)

Barrie, Amanda (Ashton-under-Lyne)

Barrie, Sir James (Kirriemuir)

Barrington, John Shute (Theobalds)

Barrington, Ken (Reading)

Barron, Keith (Mexborough)

Barrow, Isaac (London)

Barrow, Sir John (Dragley Beck)

Barr-Smith, Robert (Lochwinnoch)

Barry, Sir Charles (London)

Barry, John (York)

Barstow, Stanley (Horbury)

Bart, Lionel (London)

Bartholomew, Eric [Eric Morecambe] (Morecambe)

Bartholomew, John George (Edinburgh)

Bartlett, Sir Frederic (Stow on the Wold)

Bartlett, Neil (Newcastle upon Tyne)

Barton, Bernard (Carlisle)

Barton, Sir Derek (Gravesend)

Barton, Gladys (Stoke-on-Trent)

Baskerville, John (Wolverley)

Bass, George (Aswarby)

Bass, Michael Thomas (Burton-on-Trent)

Bassey, Shirley (Cardiff)

Bastedo, Alexandra (Hove)

Bastian, Henry Charlton (Truro)

Batchelor, Joy (Watford)

Bate, Anthony
(Stourbridge)

Bates, Alan (Allestree)

Bates, Henry Walter
(Leicester)

Bates, Herbert Ernest
(Rushden)

Bateson, Gregory
(Grantchester)

Bateson, William (Whitby)

Bath, Henry Frederick [6th
Marquess] (Longleat)

Batten, Mollie (London)

Batty, David (Leeds)

Bawden, Nina (London)

Bax, Sir Arnold (London)

Bax, Ernest Belfort
(Leamington)

Baxter, George (Lewes)

Baxter, Richard (Rowton)

Baylis, Lilian (London)

Bayliss, Sir William
(Wolverhampton)

Bayne, Margaret (Greenock)

Beale, Dorothea (London)

Beale, Mary (Barrow,
Suffolk)

Bean, Sean (Sheffield)

Beardsley, Aubrey
(Brighton)

Beat, Janet (Streetly, Staffs.)

Beaton, Sir Cecil (London)

Beaton, David (Balfour)

Beattie, James
(Laurencekirk)

Beatty, David [Earl]
(Nantwich)

Beaumont, Agnes (Edworth)

Beaumont, Debra
(Cuckfield)

Beaumont, Francis
(Gracedieu)

Beaumont, Sir George
(Dunmow)

Beaumont, Joseph
(Hadleigh)

Becker, Lydia (Manchester)

Beckett, Margaret (Ashton-
under-Lyne)

Beckford, William (Fonthill)

Beckham, David (London)

Beckham, Victoria
[b.Victoria Adams] (Goff's
Oak)

Beddoes, Thomas (Shifnal)

Beddoes, Thomas Lovell
(Clifton)

Bede [Saint]
(Monkwearmouth)

Bedell, William (Black Notley)

Bedloe, William (Chepstow)

Bedser, Sir Alec (Reading)

Beecham, Sir Thomas (St
Helens)

Beechey, Sir William
(Burford)

Beeching, Richard [Dr and
Lord] (Maidstone)

Beerbohm, Max (London)

Behn, Aphra (Wye)

Beilby, Sir George
(Edinburgh)

Beith, John Hay [Ian Hay]
(Manchester)

Beke, Charles Tilstone
(London)

Bell, Alexander Graham
(Edinburgh)

Bell, Alexander Melville
(Edinburgh)

Bell, Andrew (St Andrews)

Bell, Derek (Belfast)

Bell, Sir Charles
(Edinburgh)

Bell, George (Hayling Island)

Bell, Gertrude [Margaret
Lowthian) (Washington,
Co. Durham)

Bell, Henry (Torphichen)

Bell, John (Hopton)

Bell, John Stewart (Belfast)

Bell, Patrick (Auchterhouse)

Bell, Thomas (Poole)

Bell, Vanessa (London)

Bell-Burnell, Jocelyn (York)

Bellamy, Peter
(Bournemouth)

Bellany, John (Port Seton)

Benbow, John (Shrewsbury)

Benesh, Joan (Liverpool)

Benn, Anthony Neil
Wedgwood (London)

Bennet, Abraham (Taxal)

Bennett, Alan (Leeds)

Bennett, Arnold (Stoke-on-
Trent)

Bennett, Hwyel (Garnant)

Bennett, James Gordon
(Keith)

Bennett, Jill (London)

Bennett, Richard Rodney
(Broadstairs)

Bennett, Sir William
(Sheffield)

Benson, Sir Frank
(Alresford)

Bentham, George
(Plymouth)

Bentham, Jeremy (London)

Bentham, Sir Samuel
(London)

Bentinck, Lord George
(Welbeck Abbey)

Bentine, Michael (Watford)

Bentley, Richard (Oulton)

Berg, Leila (Salford)

Berger, John (London)

Berkeley, Sir Lennox
(Oxford)

Berners, Gerald Hugh
(Bridgnorth)

Berry, Nick (Woodford)

Berwick, Mary [Procter, Adelaide Ann] (London)
Besant, Annie (London)
Besant, Sir Walter (Portsmouth)
Bessemer, Sir Henry (Charlton, Herts.)
Best, George (Belfast)
Bethune, John Drinkwater (Warrington)
Betjeman, Sir John (London)
Betts, Barbara [Castle] (Chesterfield)
Betty, William Henry (Shrewsbury)
Bevan, Aneurin (Tredegar)
Bevan, Edward John (Birkenhead)
Bevin, Ernest (Winsford)
Bewick, Thomas (Ovingham)
Bickersteth, Edward (Kirkby Lonsdale)
Bickford, William (Camborne)
Bidder, George Parker (Moretonhampstead)
Biddle, John (Wotton-under-Edge)
Biffen, Sir Rowland (Cheltenham)
Biggs, Rosemary (London)
Blllington-Greig, Teresa (Blackburn)
Bindoff, Stanley Thomas (Brighton)
Binyon, Laurence (Lancaster)
Bird, Isabella (Boroughbridge)
Birkbeck, George (Settle)
Birkenhead [1st Earl] (Birkenhead)

Birkett, William [Baron] (Ulverston)
Birley, Eric (Manchester)
Birrell, Augustine (Liverpool)
Birt, John (Liverpool)
Birtwhistle, Sir Harrison (Accrington)
Bishop, Ann (Manchester)
Bishop, Sir Henry Rowley (London)
Black, Adam (Edinburgh)
Black, Cilla (Liverpool)
Black, Clementina (Brighton)
Black, Sir James Whyte (Cowdenbeath)
Black, William (Glasgow)
Blackadder, Elizabeth (Falkirk)
Blackburn, Colin (Killearn)
Blackburn, Jemima (Edinburgh)
Blackburn, Jessica (Cradley)
Blackburn, Robert (Leeds)
Blackett, Patrick Maynard Stuart (London)
Blackie, John Stuart (Glasgow)
Blacklock, Thomas (Annan)
Blackmore, Richard Doddridge (Longworth)
Blackstone, Tessa (Bures)
Blackwell, Alexander (Aberdeen)
Blackwell, Sir Basil (Oxford)
Blackwell, Elizabeth (Bristol)
Blackwell, Emily (Bristol)
Blackwood, William (Edinburgh)
Blagden, Sir Charles (Wotton-under-Edge)
Blair, Anthony [Tony] (Edinburgh)

Blair, Catherine (Bathgate)
Blake, Sir Peter (Dartford)
Blake, Robert (Bridgwater)
Blake, William (London)
Blanchflower, Danny (Belfast)
Blane, Sir Gilbert (Blanefield)
Blashford-Snell, John (Hereford)
Bleasdale, Alan (Liverpool)
Bligh, William (Plymouth)
Bliss, Sir Arthur (London)
Bliss, Catherine (London)
Blofeld, Henry Calthorpe (Hoveton)
Blomfield, Charles James (Bury St Edmunds)
Bloom, Claire (London)
Bloom, Ursula [Mrs Gower Robinson] (Chelmsford)
Bloomfield, Robert (Honington)
Blore, Edward (Derby)
Blount, Thomas (Bordesley)
Blow, John (Newark)
Blundell, Peter (Tiverton)
Blunden, Edmund Charles (Yalding)
Blunt, Wilfred Scawen (Petworth)
Blyton, Enid (London)
Bodichon, Barbara (London)
Bodley, Sir Thomas (Exeter)
Boece, Hector (Dundee)
Bogarde, Sir Dirk (London)
Bogue, David (Coldingham)
Bolingbroke, Henry [1st Viscount] (London)
Bolt, Robert (Manchester)
Bomberg, David (Birmingham)
Bond, Edward (London)
Bond, Mary (Paisley)

Bondfield, Margaret (Chard)
Bone, Henry (Truro)
Bone, Sir Muirhead (Glasgow)
Boniface (Crediton)
Bonington, Chris (London)
Boole, George (Lincoln)
Boorman, John (Shepperton)
Boot, Sir Jesse [1st Baron Trent] (Nottingham)
Booth, Charles (Liverpool)
Booth, Evangeline (London)
Booth, William (Nottingham)
Boothby, Sir Robert (Edinburgh)
Boothroyd, Betty (Dewsbury)
Borough, Steven (Northam)
Borrow, George Henry (East Dereham)
Boswell, James (Edinburgh)
Botham, Ian Terence (Heswall)
Bottomley, Gordon (Keighley)
Bottomley, Virginia (Dunoon)
Bouch, Sir Thomas (Thursby)
Boucicault, Nina (London)
Bough, Samuel (Carlisle)
Boughton, Rutland (Aylesbury)
Boult, Sir Adrian (Chester)
Boulton, Matthew (Birmingham)
Bourne, Hugh (Stoke-on-Trent)
Bowditch, Thomas (Bristol)
Bowdler, Thomas Edward (Ashley)

Bower, Frederick Orpen (Ripon)
Bowie, David (London)
Bowles, William Lisle (Kings Sutton)
Bowman, Sir William (Nantwich)
Bowring, Sir John (Exeter)
Box, Muriel (Tolworth)
Boyce, William (London)
Boycott, Charles Cunningham (Burgh St Peter)
Boycott, Geoffrey (Fitzwilliam)
Boyd, Penleigh (Westbury)
Boyd-Orr, John (Kilmaurs)
Boydell, John (Dorrington)
Boyle, James (Glasgow)
Boyle, Mark (Glasgow)
Boyle, Richard [1st Earl of Cork] (Canterbury)
Boys, Sir Charles Vernon (Wing)
Bradbury, Sir John (Winsford)
Bradbury, Malcolm (Sheffield)
Braddock, Bessie (Liverpool)
Braddon, Mary Elizabeth (London)
Bradford, Barbara Taylor (Leeds)
Bradford, James Michael [Jimmy Nail] (Newcastle upon Tyne)
Bradford, William (Austerfield)
Bradley, Andrew Cecil (Cheltenham)
Bradley, Edward (Kidderminster)
Bradley, Francis Herbert (Glasbury)

Bradley, James (Sherborne)
Bradshaw, George (Salford)
Bradstreet, Anne Dudley (Northampton)
Bradwardine, Thomas (Chichester)
Brady, Matthew (Manchester)
Bragg, Melvyn (Wigton)
Bragg, Sir William (Westward)
Braid, James (Earlsferry)
Braidwood, Thomas (Edinburgh)
Brain, Dennis (London)
Braine, John (Bradford)
Braithwaite, Lilian (Croydon)
Braithwaite, Richard Bevin (Banbury)
Bramah, Joseph (Stainborough)
Bramwell-Booth, Catherine (London)
Branagh, Kenneth (Belfast)
Brand, John (Washington)
Brassey, Thomas (Buerton)
Brassey, Thomas [1st Earl] (Stafford)
Bratby, John (London)
Bray, Thomas (Marton)
Brazil, Angela (Preston)
Breakspear, Nicolas [Adrian IV] (Abbots Langley)
Bream, Julian (London)
Brearley, Harry (Sheffield)
Bremner, Billy (Stirling)
Brent-Dyer, Elinor (South Shields)
Brenton, Howard (Portsmouth)
Brewer, Ebenezer (London)
Brewer, John Sherren (Norwich)

Brewster, Sir David (Jedburgh)
Brian, Havergal (Dresden)
Bridge, Frank (Brighton)
Bridges, Robert (Walmer)
Bridie, James (Glasgow)
Briers, Richard David (Croydon)
Briggs, Anne (Toton)
Briggs, Henry (Halifax)
Briggs, Raymond (London)
Bright, John (Rochdale)
Bright, Richard (Bristol)
Brindley, James (Thornsett)
Brisbane, Sir Thomas Makdougall (Largs)
Briscoe, Arthur John (Birkenhead)
Brittain, Vera (Newcastle-under-Lyme)
Britten, Benjamin [Baron] (Lowestoft)
Britton, Alison (London)
Broadbent, Shirley Ann [Amanda Barrie] (Ashton-under-Lyne)
Broadwood, John (Cockburnspath)
Brockhurst, Gerald Leslie (Birmingham)
Brodribb, John Henry [Sir Henry Irving] (Keinton Mandeville)
Brogan, Sir Denis William (Rutherglen)
Broke, Sir Philip (Broke Hall)
Brontë sisters (Thornton)
Brooke, Frances (Claypole)
Brooke, Rupert (Rugby)
Brookner, Anita (London)
Broom, Robert (Paisley)
Broome, David (Cardiff)
Brophy, Brigid (London)

Brougham, Henry [1st Baron] (Edinburgh)
Brown, Alexander Crum (Edinburgh)
Brown, Arthur (Whitby)
Brown, Sir Arthur Whitten (Glasgow)
Brown, George Douglas (Ochiltree)
Brown, Gordon [b.James Gordon Brown] (Glasgow)
Brown, Herbert Charles (London)
Brown, John (Biggar)
Brown, John (Bunkle)
Brown, John (Carpow)
Brown, John (Crathenaird)
Brown, Lancelot [Capability] (Kirkharle)
Brown, Robert (Montrose)
Brown, Tina (Maidenhead)
Browne, Sir Thomas (London)
Browne, Tom (Nottingham)
Browne, William (Tavistock)
Browning, Elizabeth Barrett (Coxhoe)
Browning, Robert (London)
Bruce, Christopher (Leicester)
Bruce, Frederick Fyvie (Elgin)
Bruce, James (Kinnaird House)
Bruce, Robert [King of Scotland] (Turnberry)
Bruce, Robert (Airth)
Bruce, Sir William (Blairhall)
Brudenell, James Thomas [7th Earl of Cardigan] (Hambleden)
Brummell, George Bryan [Beau] (London)

Brunel, Isambard Kingdom (Portsmouth)
Brunlees, Sir James (Kelso)
Brunner, Sir John Tomlinson (Liverpool)
Brunson, Michael (Norwich)
Bryan, Dora (Southport)
Bryce, James [1st Viscount] (Belfast)
Bryden, Bill (Greenock)
Buchan, Alexander (Kinnesswood)
Buchan, Elspeth (Banff)
Buchan, John [1st Baron Tweedsmuir] (Perth)
Buchan, William (Ancrum)
Buchanan, Claudius (Cambuslang)
Buchanan, George (Killearn)
Buchanan, Isobel (Glasgow)
Buchanan, Ken (Edinburgh)
Buchanan, Robert (Caverswall)
Buckingham, George Villiers [1st Duke] (Brooksby)
Buckland, Henry [Baron] (Merthyr Tydfil)
Buckland, William (Tiverton)
Buckle, George Earle (Bath)
Buckle, Henry Thomas (Lee)
Budd, William (North Tawton)
Budgell, Eustace (Exeter)
Bull, George (Wells)
Bullard, Sir Edward Crisp (Norwich)
Buller, Sir Redvers Henry (Crediton)
Bunbury, Henry William (Mildenhall)
Bunting, Basil (Scotswood)
Bunton, Emma (Hastings)

Bunyan, John (Elstow)

Burbridge, Margaret
(Manchester)

Burchell, William (London)

Burdett-Coutts, Angela
(London)

Burges, William (London)

Burgess, Anthony
(Manchester)

Burgess, Guy [Francis de
Moncy] (Devonport)

Burgoyne, John (Sutton,
Bedfordshire)

Burn, Richard (Winton)

Burn, William (Edinburgh)

Burnaby, Frederick
(Bedford)

Burne-Jones, Sir Edward
Coley (Birmingham)

Burnes, Sir Alexander
(Montrose)

Burnet, Thomas (Croft)

Burnett, Frances Hodgson
(Manchester)

Burnett, Sir William
(Montrose)

Burney, Charles
(Shrewsbury)

Burney, Fanny (Kings Lynn)

Burnham, Harry [1st
Viscount] (London)

Burns, Sir George (Glasgow)

Burns, Robert (Alloway)

Burnside, William (London)

Burra, Edward (London)

Burrell, Sir William
(Glasgow)

Burrows, Montagu (London)

Burt, Sir Cyril Lodowic
(London)

Burton, Amanda
(Londonderry)

Burton, Lady Isabel
(London)

Burton, John Hill (Aberdeen)

Burton, Richard
(Pontrhydfen)

Burton, Sir Richard
(Torquay)

Busby, Sir Matt (Bellshill)

Bush, Alan (London)

Bush, Kate (London)

Buss, Frances (London)

Butcher, Mark Alan
(Croydon)

Butcher, Rosemary (Bristol)

Bute, John Stuart [3rd Earl]
(Edinburgh)

Butler, Alban (Appletree)

Butler, Joseph (Wantage)

Butler, Josephine Elizabeth
(Milfield)

Butler, Reginald
(Buntingford)

Butler, Samuel (Langar)

Butler, Samuel (Strensham)

Butler-Sloss, Dame
Elizabeth (Richmond)

Butt, Dame Clara
(Southwick)

Butt, Nicky (Manchester)

Buxton, Sir Thomas (Earls
Colne)

Byatt, Antonia Susan
(Sheffield)

Bygraves, Max Walter
(London)

Byng, George [Viscount]
(Wrotham)

Byrd, William (Lincoln)

Byrne, John (Paisley)

Byrne, Patsy (Ashford)

Byrom, John (Manchester)

Byron, Lady Annabella
(Elemore Hall)

Byron, George Gordon
[Baron] (London)

Cable, Mildred (Guildford)

Cadbury, George
(Birmingham)

Cadell, Francis (Edinburgh)

Cadogan, George Henry
(Durham)

Caesar, Sir Julius (London)

Caine, Michael (London)

Caine, Sir Thomas
(Runcorn)

Caird, Edward (Greenock)

Caius, John (Norwich)

Caldecott, Randolph
(Chester)

Calder, Ritchie [Baron]
(Forfar)

Calderwood, Colin
(Stranraer)

Callaghan, Leonard James
[Baron] (Portsmouth)

Callendar, Hugh
Langbourne (Hatherop)

Callow, Simon (London)

Calverley, Charles Stuart
(Martley)

Camden, William (London)

Cameron, James Mark
(London)

Cameron, Katherine
(Glasgow)

Cameron, Rhona
(Musselburgh)

Cameron, Richard
(Falkland)

Cameron, Verney Lovett
(Radipole)

Camm, Sir Sydney
(Windsor)

Campbell, Archibald [9th
Duke of Argyll] (Dalkeith)

Campbell, Charles Arthur
(Glasgow)

Campbell, Sir Colin
(Glasgow)

Campbell, Donald Malcolm
(Horley)

Campbell, John [1st Baron
Campbell] (Cupar)

Campbell, John [2nd Duke
of Argyll] (London)

Campbell, John Francis
(Islay)

Campbell, John McLeod
(Kilninver)

Campbell, Sir Malcolm
(Chislehurst)

Campbell, Nicky
(Edinburgh)

Campbell, Mrs Patrick
(London)

Campbell, Thomas
(Glasgow)

Campbell-Bannerman, Sir
Henry (Glasgow)

Campion, Thomas (Witham)

Camrose, William [1st
Viscount] (Merthyr Tydfil)

Canning, Charles [1st Earl]
(London)

Canning, George (London)

Canning, Sir Samuel
(Ogbourne St Andrew)

Cantelupe, St Thomas
(Hambleden)

Canton, John (Stroud)

Carey, George Leonard
(London)

Carey, William
(Paulerspury)

Cargill, Donald (Rattray)

Carleton, Guy (Strabane)

Carleton, William (Prillisk)

Carlile, Richard (Ashburton)

Carlyle, Alexander
(Prestonpans)

Carlyle, Jane Baillie
(Haddington)

Carlyle, Robert (Glasgow)

Carlyle, Thomas
(Ecclefechan)

Carmichael, Amy Beatrice
(Millisle)

Carnegie, Andrew
(Dunfermline)

Caro, Sir Anthony (London)

Carpenter, Mary (Exeter)

Carpenter, William (Exeter)

Carroll, Lewis [Charles L.
Dodgson] (Daresbury)

Carson, Willie (Stirling)

Carstares, William
(Glasgow)

Carswell, Catherine
Roxburgh (Glasgow)

Carswell, Sir Robert
(Paisley)

Carter, Angela Olive
(Eastbourne)

Carter, Elizabeth (Deal)

Carter, Henry [Frank Leslie]
(Ipswich)

Carter, Howard (Swaffham)

Carthy, Martin (Hatfield)

Cartland, Barbara Hamilton
(Birmingham)

Cartwright, William
(Northway)

Cary, Arthur Joyce
(Londonderry)

Cary, Tristram (Oxford)

Caslon, William (Cradley)

Cassell, John (London)

Casson, Sir Lewis
(Birkenhead)

Castle, Barbara [b.Betts]
(Chesterfield)

Castle, Vernon (Norwich)

Catchpole, Margaret
(Ipswich)

Catesby, Robert (Lapworth)

Cattermole, George
(Dickleborough)

Cave, Edward (Newton,
Warwickshire)

Cavell, Edith Louisa
(Swardeston)

Cavendish, Margaret
(Colchester)

Cavendish, Thomas (Trimley
St Martin)

Caxton, William (Tenterden)

Cayley, Arthur (Richmond,
Surrey)

Cayley, Sir George
(Scarborough)

Cecil, Robert [3rd Marquis]
(Hatfield House)

Cecil, Robert [5th Marquis]
(Hatfield House)

Cecil, William [1st Baron
Burghley] (Bourne)

Centlivre, Susannah
(Holbeach)

Chadwick, Helen (Croydon)

Chadwick, Sir James
(Bollington)

Chadwick, Lynn Russell
(London)

Chadwick, Roy (Farnworth)

Challis, James (Braintree)

Challoner, Richard (Lewes)

Chalmers, Alexander
(Aberdeen)

Chalmers, George
(Fochabers)

Chalmers, George Paul
(Montrose)

Chalmers, James (Arbroath)

Chalmers, Thomas
(Anstruther)

Chamberlain, Arthur Neville
(Birmingham)

Chamberlain, Sir Austen
(Birmingham)

Chambers, Ephraim
(Kendal)

Chambers, John Graham
(Llanelli)

Chambers, Robert (Peebles)

Chambers, William
(Peebles)

Chance, Alexander Macomb
(Birmingham)

Chandler, Richard (Elson)

Chaplin, Charles (London)

Chapman, Sydney
(Manchester)

Chapone, Hester (Twywell)

Charles I [King of England
& Scotland]
(Dunfermline)

Charles II [King of England
& Scotland] (London)

Charles [Prince of Wales]
(London)

Charles, Craig (Liverpool)

Charles, John (Swansea)

Charlton, Sir Robert
[Bobby] (Ashington)

Charlton, Jack (Ashington)

Charnley, Sir John (Bury)

Chase, James Hadley [Rene
Raymond] (London)

Chataway, Christopher
(London)

Chatterton, Thomas
(Bristol)

Chatwin, Bruce (Sheffield)

Chaucer, Geoffrey (London)

Cheke, Sir John
(Cambridge)

Cheselden, William
(Somerby)

Cheshire, Geoffrey (Hartford)

Chesney, Francis Rawdon
(Annalong)

Chesterton, Gilbert Keith
(London)

Chetham, Humphrey
(Manchester)

Chichester, Sir Francis
(Barnstaple)

Chick, Harriette (London)

Child, William (Bristol)

Childers, Erskine (London)

Chillingworth, William
(Oxford)

Chippendale, Thomas
(Otley)

Chisholm, Caroline
(Northampton)

Chisholm, Erik (Glasgow)

Chorley, Richard John
(Minehead)

Christian, Fletcher
(Cockermouth)

Christie, Agatha (Torquay)

Christison, Sir Robert
(Edinburgh)

Chudleigh, Mary (Winslade)

Churchill, Caryl (London)

Churchill, Lord Randolph
(Blenheim Palace)

Churchill, Randolph
(London)

Churchill, Sir Winston
(Blenheim Palace)

Churchward, George
Jackson (Stoke Gabriel)

Churchyard, Thomas
(Shrewsbury)

Cibber, Susannah (London)

Citrine, Walter [Baron]
(Wallasey)

Clapp, Eric Patrick [Eric
Clapton] (Ripley)

Clapperton, Hugh (Annan)

Clapton, Eric (Ripley)

Clare, John (Helpston)

Clarendon, Edward [1st
Earl] (Dinton)

Clark, Jim (Kilmany)

Clark, Kenneth Mackenzie
[Baron] (London)

Clark, Michael (Aberdeen)

Clark, Petula (Epsom)

Clark, Sir Wilfrid (Hemel
Hempstead)

Clarke, Arthur Charles
(Minehead)

Clarke, Edward Daniel
(Willingdon)

Clarke, Sir Frederick
(Witney)

Clarke, Gillian (Cardiff)

Clarke, Samuel (Norwich)

Clarke, Warren (Oldham)

Clarke, William Branwhite
(East Bergholt)

Clarkson, Jeremy (Doncaster)

Clarkson, Thomas (Wisbech)

Cleese, John Marwood
(Weston-super-Mare)

Clegg, Samuel
(Manchester)

Clerk, Sir Dugald (Glasgow)

Cleveland, John
(Loughborough)

Cliff, Clarice (Stoke-on-
Trent)

Clifford, John (Sawley)

Clifford, William Kingdon
(Exeter)

Clitherow, St Margaret
(York)

Clive, Catherine (London)

Clopton, Sir Hugh
(Stratford on Avon)

Close, Dennis Brian
(Rawdon)

Close, Ivy (Stockton-on-
Tees)

Clough, Anne Jemima
(Liverpool)

Clough, Arthur Hugh
(Liverpool)

Clough, Brian
(Middlesbrough)

Clowes, William (Chichester)

Clowes, William (Stoke-on-Trent)

Clynes, Joseph Robert (Oldham)

Coates, Anne (Reigate)

Coates, Eric (Hucknall)

Coates, Sir Peter (Paisley)

Coates, Thomas (Paisley)

Cobbett, William (Farnham)

Cobbold, Richard (Ipswich)

Cobden, Richard (Heyshott)

Cobden-Sanderson, Thomas (Alnwick)

Cochran, Sir Charles Blake (Lindfield)

Cocker, Joe (Sheffield)

Cockcroft, Sir John Douglas (Todmorden)

Cockerell, Sir Christopher (Cambridge)

Cockerill, John (Haslingden)

Codrington, Sir Edward (Dodington)

Coke, Sir Edward (Mileham)

Coke, Thomas William [Earl of Leicester] (Holkham)

Colchester, Charles [1st Baron] (Abingdon)

Coldstream, Sir William (Belford)

Cole, Andy (Nottingham)

Cole, Sir Henry (Bath)

Cole, Dame Margaret (Cambridge)

Cole, Lloyd (Buxton)

Cole, Stephanie (Solihull)

Cole, Thomas (Bolton)

Colenso, John William (St Austell)

Coleridge, David Hartley (Clevedon)

Coleridge, Samuel Taylor (Ottery St Mary)

Coleridge, Sara (Keswick)

Coleridge-Taylor, Samuel (London)

Coles, Elizabeth [Elizabeth Taylor] (Reading)

Collier, Arthur (Steeple Langford)

Collier, Jeremy (Stow-cum-Quy)

Collier, John (Manchester)

Collings, Jesse (Littleham-cum-Exmouth)

Collingwood, Cuthbert [Lord] (Newcastle upon Tyne)

Collingwood, Robin George (Coniston)

Collingwood, William Gershom (Liverpool)

Collins, Jackie and Joan (London)

Collins, John (Galashiels)

Collins, Shirley (Hastings)

Collins, William [Wilkie] (London)

Collins, William (Chichester)

Collins, William (Eastwood)

Colman, Ronald (Richmond)

Colquhoun, Patrick (Dumbarton)

Colquhoun, Robert (Kilmarnock)

Colston, Edward (Bristol)

Colville, David (Campbeltown)

Coltrane, Robbie (Glasgow)

Colvin, Sir Sidney (Norwood)

Combe, William (Bristol)

Compton, Denis Charles Scott (London)

Compton, Fay (London)

Compton, Mary [Barbara Pym] (Oswestry)

Compton-Burnett, Dame Ivy (Pinner)

Congreve, William (Bardsey)

Connery, Sir Sean (Edinburgh)

Connolly, Cyril Vernon (Coventry)

Connolly, James (Edinburgh)

Conran, Jasper (London)

Conran, Sir Terence Orby (Esher)

Cons, Emma (London)

Constable, Archibald (Carnbee)

Constable, John (East Bergholt)

Conway, Russ [Trevor Stanford] (Bristol)

Cook, Arthur James (Wookey)

Cook, Beryl (Plymouth)

Cook, James (Marton, North Yorkshire)

Cook, Norman [Fatboy Slim] (Bromley)

Cook, Peter Edward (Torquay)

Cook, Stanley Arthur (Kings Lynn)

Cook, Sue (Ruislip)

Cook, Thomas (Melbourne)

Cook, William [Anthony Tudor] (London)

Cooke, Alfred Alistair (Manchester)

Cooke, Deryck Victor (Leicester)

Cookson, Catherine (Tyne Dock)

Cookworthy, William (Kingsbridge)

Cooper, Sir Astley (Brooke Hall)

Cooper, Eileen (Glossop)

Cooper, Dame Gladys (London)

Cooper, Henry (London)

Cooper, Jilly (Hornchurch)

Cooper, Susie (Stoke-on-Trent)

Cooper, Thomas (Leicester)

Cooper, Thomas (Oxford)

Cooper, Tommy (Caerphilly)

Copley, John Michael (Birmingham)

Coppard, Alfred Edgar (Folkestone)

Coram, Thomas (Lyme Regis)

Corbett, Ronnie [Ronald Balfour] (Edinburgh)

Cork, Dominic Gerald (Newcastle under Lyme)

Cornwall, Barry [Bryan Waller Procter] (Leeds)

Cornwallis, Charles [1st Marquis] (London)

Corrigan-Maguire, Mairead (Belfast)

Cort, Henry (Lancaster)

Cory, William Johnson (Torrington)

Coryate, Thomas (Odcombe)

Cosin, John (Norwich)

Costello, Elvis [Declan P. McManus] (Liverpool)

Cosway, Richard (Tiverton)

Cotes, Roger (Burbage)

Cotman, John Sell (Norwich)

Cotton, Sir Henry (Holmes Chapel)

Cotton, John (Derby)

Cotton, Sir Robert Bruce (Denton)

Coulson, Charles Alfred (Dudley)

Coulthard, David (Twynholm)

Coulton, George Gordon (Kings Lynn)

Couper, Archibald Scott (Kirkintilloch)

Courtney, Kathleen (Gillingham)

Courteney, Tom [Thomas Daniel] (Hull)

Courthope, William John (South Malling)

Courtney, Leonard Henry [1st Baron] (Penzance)

Cousins, Frank (Bulwell)

Cousins, Samuel (Exeter)

Coutts, Thomas (Edinburgh)

Couvreur, Jessie (London)

Coverdale, Miles (York)

Coward, Sir Noel (Teddington)

Cowell, Edward Byles (Ipswich)

Cowper, William (Berkhamsted)

Cowper, William (Petersfield)

Cox, Brian (Dundee)

Cox, Richard (Whaddon)

Cox, William (Wimborne Minster)

Coxe, Henry Octavius (Bucklebury)

Coxwell, Henry Tracey (Wouldham)

Crabbe, George (Aldeburgh)

Craig, Edward Henry Gordon (Stevenage)

Craig, James [1st Viscount Craigavon] (Belfast)

Craigie, Sir William Alexander (Dundee)

Craik, Dinah Maria (Stoke-on-Trent)

Craik, George Lillie (Kennoway)

Cram, Steve (Gateshead)

Crampton, Thomas Russell (Broadstairs)

Cranbrook, Gathorne [1st Earl] (Bradford)

Crane, Walter (Liverpool)

Cranmer, Thomas (Aslockton)

Cranston, Catherine (Glasgow)

Crawford, Michael (Salisbury)

Crawford & Balcarres [Earl] (Muncaster Castle)

Crawfurd, John (Islay)

Crawley, John Paul (Maldon)

Creasey, Sir Edward (Bexley)

Creech, Thomas (Blandford)

Creech, William (Newbattle)

Creighton, Mandell (Carlisle)

Cremer, Sir William Randal (Fareham)

Cribb, Tom (Bitton)

Cribbins, Bernard (Oldham)

Crick, Francis Harry Compton (Northampton)

Cripps, Bruce [Bruce Welch] (Bognor Regis)

Cripps, Sir [Richard] Stafford (London)

Croall, John [John Stuart] (Edinburgh)

Crockett, Samuel Rutherford (Little Duchrae)

Croft, Robert Damien (Swansea)

Croll, James (Little Whitefield)

Crome, John (Norwich)
Cromek, Robert Hartley
  (Hull)
Cromer, Evelyn Baring
  [Earl] (Cromer)
Crompton, Richmal
  [Richmal Lamburn] (Bury)
Crompton, Samuel
  (Manchester)
Cromwell, Oliver
  (Huntingdon)
Cromwell, Thomas [Earl of
  Essex] (London)
Cronin, Archibald Joseph
  (Cardross)
Crosland, Charles Anthony
  [Tony] (St Leonards)
Cross, Charles Frederick
  (London)
Crossley, Sir Francis
  (Halifax)
Crossman, Richard Howard
  Stafford (Cropredy)
Crotch, William (Norwich)
Cruden, Alexander
  (Aberdeen)
Cruickshank, Andrew
  (Aberdeen)
Cruikshank, George
  (London)
Cubitt, Thomas (Buxton)
Cubitt, Sir William (Dilham)
Cudworth, Ralph (Aller)
Cullen, William (Hamilton)
Cullis, Winifred
  (Gloucester)
Culpeper, Nicholas
  (London)
Cumberland, Richard
  (Cambridge)
Cunliffe, Barry [Barrington
  Windsor] (Portsmouth)
Cunningham, Allan
  (Dalswinton)

Cunningham, Allan
  (London)
Cunningham, John
  (Croydon)
Cunningham, William
  (Hamilton)
Cunningham, William
  (Edinburgh)
Cunninghame-Graham,
  Robert (Gartmore)
Cureton, William
  (Westbury)
Currie, James (Kirkpatrick-
  Fleming)
Curry, John Anthony
  (Birmingham)
Curtis, Tony (Carmarthen)
Curtis, William (Alton)
Curwen, John
  (Heckmondwike)
Curzon, George [Marquis]
  (Kedleston Hall)
Cushing, Peter (London)

———————————————

Dadd, Richard (Chatham)
Dahl, Roald (Llandaff)
Dale, David (Stewarton)
Dale, Sir Henry (London)
Dalgarno, George
  (Aberdeen)
Dalglish, Kenneth (Glasgow)
Dalhousie, James [Marquis]
  (Dalhousie Castle)
Dallion, Susan [Siouxsie
  Sioux] (Bromley)
Dalton, Hugh (Neath)
Dalton, John (Eaglesfield)
Dalyell, Thomas (The Binns)
Dalziel, Edward (Wooler)
Dampier, William (East
  Coker)
Dance, Charles (Redditch)
Dane, Clemence [Winifred
  Ashton] (London)

Dane, Phyllis and Zena
  (London)
Daniel, Glyn Edmund (Barry)
Dankworth, John Philip
  (London)
Darling, Charles John
  (Colchester)
Darling, Grace Horsley
  (Bamburgh)
Darusmont, Frances
  [Frances Wright] (Dundee)
Darwin, Charles Robert
  (Shrewsbury)
Darwin, Erasmus (Elton)
Dashwood, Edmee [E.M.
  Delafield] (Llandogo)
D'Avenant, Sir William
  (Oxford)
David II [King of Scotland]
  (Dunfermline)
Davids, Thomas William
  (Colchester)
Davidson, John (Barrhead)
Davidson, Randall Thomas
  [Baron] (Edinburgh)
Davidson, Thomas (Deer)
Davie, Alan (Grangemouth)
Davies, Betty (Nottingham)
Davies, Clement Edward
  (Llanfyllin)
Davies, David (Llandinam)
Davies, David [Baron]
  (Llandinam)
Davies, Sir Henry Walford
  (Oswestry)
Davies, Howard (Reading)
Davies, Hubert Henry
  (Woodley)
Davies, Idris (Rhymney)
Davies, Ivor Novello, [Ivor
  Novello] (Cardiff)
Davies, Sir John (Tisbury)
Davies, Laura (Coventry)
Davies, Lynn (Nantymoel)

Davies, Sir Peter Maxwell (Manchester)

Davies, Sarah Emily (Southampton)

Davies, Siobhan (London)

Davies, Stephen (Abercwmboi)

Davies, William Henry (Newport)

Davis, Sir Colin (Weybridge)

Davis, Joe [Joseph] (Whitwell)

Davis, John (Sandridge)

Davis, Steve (London)

Davison, Emily (London)

Davy, Edward (Ottery St Mary)

Davy, Sir Humphry (Penzance)

Dawes, Sophia (St Helens, Isle of Wight)

Dawkins, Sir William Boyd (Buttington)

Dawson, Henry (Hull)

Day, John (Dunwich)

Day, Sir Robin (London)

Deakin, Arthur (Sutton Coldfield)

Dean, Brenda (Manchester)

Dean, Christopher (Nottingham)

Dean, Dixie [William Ralph] (Birkenhead)

Deane, Richard (Temple Guiting)

De Beer, Sir Gavin (London)

De Duve, Christian (Thames Ditton)

Dee, Jack (Petts Wood)

Dee, John (London)

Dee, Kiki [Pauline Matthews] (Bradford)

Deeping, George Warwick (Southend)

Defoe, Daniel (London)

De Havilland, Sir Geoffrey (Haslemere)

Deighton, Len (London)

Dekker, Thomas (London)

Delafield, E.M. [Edmee Dashwood] (Llandogo)

Delaney, Shelagh (Salford)

Delany, Mary (Coulston)

De la Tour, Frances (Bovingdon)

Delius, Frederick (Bradford)

Dell, Ethel Mary (London)

Deller, Alfred George (Margate)

Demarco, Richard (Edinburgh)

Dench, Judi [Dame Judith Olivia] (York)

Denman, Gertrude (London)

Denness, Michael (Bellshill)

Denning, Alfred Thompson [Baron] (Whitchurch)

Dent, Joseph Mallaby (Darlington)

De Quincy, Thomas (Manchester)

Derby, Edward Geoffrey [14th Earl] (Knowsley Hall)

Derby, Edward Henry [15th Earl] (Knowsley Hall)

Derwentwater, James [3rd Earl] (London)

Devis, Arthur (Preston)

Devlin, Joseph (Belfast)

Dewar, Sir James (Kincardine-on-Forth)

Dexter, Caroline (Nottingham)

Diana, Princess of Wales (Sandringham)

Dibdin, Charles (Southampton)

Dick, James (Forres)

Dick, Robert (Tullibody)

Dickens, Charles (Portsmouth)

Dickson, Barbara (Dunfermline)

Dickson, Joan (Edinburgh)

Digby, Sir Kenelm (Gayhurst)

Dilke, Sir Charles Wentworth (London)

Dilke, Emily (Ilfracombe)

Dill, Sir John Greer (Lurgan)

Dimbleby, Richard (Richmond, Surrey)

Dimmock, Charlie (Southampton)

Dirac, Paul Adrian (Bristol)

Dinsdale, Reece (Normanton)

Disraeli, Benjamin [1st Earl Beaconsfield] (London)

Dixon, Dougal (Dumfries)

Dixon, Sir Pierson John (Englefield Green)

Dixon, William Hepworth (Manchester)

Dobell, Sydney Thompson (Cranbrook)

Dobson, Henry Austin (Plymouth)

Docherty, Tommy [Thomas Henderson] (Glasgow)

Dodd, Charles Harold (Wrexham)

Dodd, Ken (Liverpool)

Dodd, William (Bourne)

Dodgson, Charles [Lewis Carroll] (Daresbury)

Dodsley, Robert (Mansfield)

Dolin, Anton [Patrick Healey Kay] (Slinfold}

Donaldson, James (Edinburgh)

Donaldson, Sir James (Aberdeen)

Donaldson, Margaret Caldwell (Paisley)

Donat, Robert (Manchester)

Donegan, Lonnie (Glasgow)

Donkin, Bryan (Sandhoe)

Donne, John (London)

Donoghue, Steve [Stephen] (Warrington)

Donovan [b.Donovan Phillip Leith] (Glasgow)

Dors, Diana [Diana Fluck] (Swindon)

Doughty, Charles Montagu (Theberton Hall)

Douglas, David (Scone)

Douglas, Gavin (Tantallon Castle)

Douglas, Sir Howard (Gosport)

Douglas, Sir William Fettes (Edinburgh)

Douglas-Home, William (Edinburgh)

Doulton, Sir Henry (London)

Dowding, Hugh Caswell [1st Baron] (Moffat)

Dowell, Anthony (London)

Dowie, John Alexander (Edinburgh)

Dowling, Stephen (Liverpool)

Downes, Terry (London)

Dowsing, William (Laxfield)

Doyle, Sir Arthur Conan (Edinburgh)

Doyle, Sir Francis Hastings (Nun Appleton)

Doyly-Carte, Richard (London)

Drabble, Margaret (Sheffield)

Drake, Sir Francis (Crowndale)

Draper, John William (St Helens)

Drayton, Michael (Hartshill)

Dresser, Christopher (Glasgow)

Drew, Dame Jane (Thornton Heath)

Drinkwater, John (London)

Drinkwater, John Bethune (Warrington)

Driver, Samuel Rolles (Southampton)

Druce, George Claridge (Potterspury)

Drummond, Annabella (Stobhill)

Drummond, Dugald (Ardrossan)

Drummond, Henry (Albury)

Drummond, Henry (Stirling)

Drummond, James [16th Earl Perth] (Fulford)

Drummond, Peter (Polmont)

Drummond, Thomas (Edinburgh)

Drummond, William (Hawthornden)

Dryden, John (Aldwincle)

Drysdale, Russell (Bognor Regis)

Duck, Stephen (Charlton)

Duckworth, Sir John (Leatherhead)

Ducsbury, William (Cannock)

Duffy, Maureen (Worthing)

Dugdale, Sir William (Shustoke)

Du Maurier, Daphne [Dame] (London)

Duncan, Adam [Viscount] (Dundee)

Duncan, Robert (St Austell)

Dunglison, Robley (Keswick)

Dunlop, Frank (Leeds)

Dunlop, John Boyd (Dreghorn)

Dunlop, William Joseph [Joey] (Ballymoney)

Duncan, Henry (Lochrutton)

Duncan, Thomas (Kinclaven)

Dunnett, Dorothy (Dunfermline)

Duns Scotus, John (Duns)

Du Pré, Jacqueline (Oxford)

D'Urfrey, Thomas (Exeter)

Durham, John George [Earl] (London)

Dury, Ian (Upminster)

Duveen, Joseph [Baron] (Hull)

Dwight, Reginald Kenneth [Elton John] (Pinner)

Dyce, William (Aberdeen)

Dyer, Anson (Brighton)

Dyer, John (Llanfynydd)

Dyer, Kieron (Ipswich)

Dyson, Sir Frank Watson (Ashby de la Zouch)

Eadie, John (Alva)

Eadmer [Edmer] (Canterbury)

Ealham, Mark Alan (Ashford)

Eardley, Joan (Warnham)

Earle, William (Liverpool)

East, Sir Alfred (Kettering)

Eastham, George (Blackpool)

Eastlake, Sir Charles Lock (Plymouth)

Eastlake, Charles Lock (Plymouth)

Easton, Sheena (Bellshill)

Eastwick, Edward Backhouse (Warfield)

Eccles, John (London)

Eccles, Solomon (London)

Eckford, Harry (Irvine)

Eddington, Sir Arthur
(Kendal)

Ede, James Chuter [Baron]
(Epsom)

Eden, Sir Anthony [1st
Earl Avon] (Windlestone
Hall)

Edgar, David Burman
(Birmingham)

Edgeworth, Maria
(Blackbourton)

Edgeworth, Richard Lovell
(Bath)

Edmer [Eadmer]
(Canterbury)

Edmondson, Adrian
(Bradford)

Edmund, St [Edmund Rich]
(Abingdon)

Edmunds, Dave (Cardiff)

Edward The Confessor
(Islip)

Edward II [King of England]
(Caernarvon)

Edward III [King of
England] (Windsor)

Edward VIII [King of Great
Britain] (Richmond)

Edward the Black Prince
[Prince of England]
(Woodstock)

Edwards, Amelia (London)

Edwards, Gareth Owen
(Gwauncae Gurwen)

Edwards, Sir George
(London)

Edwards, Tracey (Reading)

Egan, Sir John Leopold
(Coventry)

Egan, Pierce (London)

Elder, Sir Thomas
(Kirkcaldy)

Eldon, John Scott [1st Earl]
(Newcastle upon Tyne)

Elgar, Sir Edward
(Broadheath)

Eliot, George [Marian
Evans] (Astley)

Eliot, John (Widford)

Eliot, Sir John (Port Eliot)

Elizabeth I [Queen of
England] (London)

Elizabeth II [Queen of
Great Britain] (London)

Elizabeth [Queen Mother]
(St Pauls Walden Bury)

Elkington, George Richards
(Birmingham)

Elliotson, John (London)

Elliott, Charlotte (Clapham)

Elliott, Denholm (London)

Elliott, Ebenezer
(Rotherham)

Ellis, Henry Havelock
(Croydon)

Ellis, Ruth (Rhyl)

Ellwood, Thomas (Crowell)

Elphick, Michael
(Chichester)

Elphinstone, George
[Viscount Keith]
(Elphinstone Tower)

Elphinstone, William
(Glasgow)

Elstob, Elizabeth
(Newcastle upon Tyne)

Elton, Charles Sutherland
(Liverpool)

Elvey, Maurice (Darlington)

Emett, Rowland (London)

Empson, Sir William
(Howden)

Endecott, John (Dorchester)

Eno, Brian (Woodbridge)

Enright, Dennis Joseph
(Leamington)

Erle, Sir William (Fifehead
Magdalen)

Erskine, Ebenezer
(Chirnside)

Erskine, Henry (Edinburgh)

Erskine, Mary (Garlet)

Erskine, Thomas [1st Baron]
(Edinburgh)

Ervine, St John Greer
(Belfast)

Esler, Gavin (Glasgow)

Essex, Robert Devereux
[2nd Earl] (Netherwood)

Esteve Coll, Elizabeth
(Darlington)

Etty, William (York)

Eusden, Laurence
(Spofforth)

Evans, Sir Arthur John
(Nash Mills)

Evans, Caradoc [David]
(Llanfihangelar Arth)

Evans, Christopher
(Warrington)

Evans, Dame Edith (London)

Evans, Sir Geraint Llewellyn
(Pontypridd)

Evans, Godfrey (London)

Evans, Harold (Manchester)

Evans, Lee (Bristol)

Evans, Marian [George
Eliot] (Astley)

Evans, Maurice (Dorchester)

Evans, Merlyn (Cardiff)

Evans-Pritchard, Sir Edward
(Crowborough)

Evelyn, John (Wotton)

Everett, Rupert (Norwich)

Everest, Sir George
(Gwernvale)

Everson, William (Yeovil)

Ewart, James Cossar
(Penicuik)

Ewart, William (Liverpool)

Ewing, Sir James Alfred (Dundee)

Ewing, Juliana Horatia (Ecclesfield)

Exmouth, Edward Pellew [1st Viscount] (Dover)

Eyre, Edward John (Hornsea)

Eyre, Richard Charles (Barnstaple)

Faber, Frederick William (Calverley)

Fairbairn, Andrew Martin (Inverkeithing)

Fairbairn, Sir William (Kelso)

Fairbrother, Neil Harvey (Warrington)

Fairey, Sir Richard (London)

Fairfax, John (Warwick)

Fairfax, Thomas [3rd Baron] (Denton)

Fairweather, Ian (Bridge of Allan)

Faithfull, Emily (Headley)

Faithfull, Marianne (London)

Falconer, Hugh (Forres)

Falconer, William (Edinburgh)

Faldo, Nick [Nicholas Alexander] (Welwyn Garden City)

Farjeon, Eleanor (London)

Farmer, Richard (Leicester)

Farquhar, George (Londonderry)

Farr, William (Kenley)

Farrer, Reginald John (Clapham, Yorkshire)

Farrer, William James (Docker)

Fastolf, Sir John (Caister on Sea)

Fatboy Slim [Norman Cook] (Bromley)

Fawcett, Henry (Salisbury)

Fawcett, Dame Millicent (Aldeburgh)

Fawcett, Percy Harrison (Torquay)

Fawkes, Guy (York)

Fawkner, John Pascoe (London)

Feather, Vic [Victor, Baron] (Gainsborough)

Fedden, Sir Roy [Albert Hubert] (Bristol)

Feinstein, Elaine (Bootle)

Fell, John (Longworth)

Fell, Margaret (Dalton in Furness)

Fenton, Roger (Manchester)

Ferguson, Adam (Logierait)

Ferguson, Duncan (Stirling)

Ferguson, Harry George (Hillsborough)

Ferguson, James (Rothiemay)

Ferguson, Sir Samuel (Belfast)

Fergusson, Robert (Edinburgh)

Ferranti, Sebastian Zianide (Liverpool)

Ferrier, Sir David (Aberdeen)

Ferrier, James Frederick (Edinburgh)

Ferrier, Kathleen (Higher Walton)

Ferrier, Susan (Edinburgh)

Ferry, Bryan (Washington)

Fidler, Kathleen (Coalville)

Fielding, Sarah (East Stour)

Fields, Dame Gracie (Rochdale)

Fiennes, Celia (Newton Tony)

Fiennes, Sir Ranulph (Windsor)

Figg, James (Thame)

Fildes, Sir Luke (Liverpool)

Finch, Peter [George Ingle Finch] (London)

Findlater, Andrew (New Aberdour)

Findlater, Jane and Mary (Lochearnhead)

Finlay, George (Faversham)

Finlay, Robert B. [Viscount] (Edinburgh)

Finney, Albert (Salford)

Finney, Tom (Preston)

Finnie, Linda (Paisley)

Finnigan, Judy (Manchester)

Finniston, Sir Harold Montague [Monty] (Glasgow)

Finzi, Gerald Raphael (London)

Firth, Sir Charles Harding (Sheffield)

Firth, Colin (Grayshott)

Firth, Francis (Chesterfield)

Firth, John Rupert (Keighley)

Firth, Mark (Sheffield)

Fish, Michael (Eastbourne)

Fisher, Allison (Peacehaven)

Fisher, Andrew (Crosshouse)

Fisher, Geoffrey [Baron] (Higham on the Hill)

Fisher, John [Saint] (Beverley)

Fisher, Sir Ronald Aylmer (London)

Fisk, Sir Ernest Thomas (Sunbury on Thames)

Fitch, Sir Joshua Girling (London)

Fitt, Gerry [Gerard, Baron] (Belfast)

Fitton, Mary (Gawsworth)

Fitzgerald, Penelope (Lincoln)

Fitzsimmons, Robert (Helston)

Flamsteed, John (Denby)

Flanagan, Barry (Prestatyn)

Flanders, Michael (London)

Flaxman, John (York)

Fleck, Sir Alexander [Baron] (Glasgow)

Fleming, Sir Alexander (Darvel)

Fleming, Ian Lancaster (London)

Fleming, Sir John Ambrose (Lancaster)

Fleming, Margaret (Kirkcaldy)

Fleming, Sir Sandford (Kirkcaldy)

Fleming, Tom (Edinburgh)

Fleming, Williamina (Dundee)

Fletcher, John (Rye)

Flinders, Matthew (Donington)

Flint, Sir William Russell (Edinburgh)

Flintoff, Andrew (Preston)

Flitcroft, Henry (Hampton Court)

Florey, Margaret (Swanbourne)

Flower, Sir William Henry (Stratford upon Avon)

Fludd, Robert (Bearsted)

Folkard, William [Maurice Elvey] (Darlington)

Fonteyn, Dame Margot (Reigate)

Foot, Michael Mackintosh (Plymouth)

Foote, Samuel (Truro)

Forbes, Duncan (Bunchrew)

Forbes, Edward (Douglas)

Forbes, George (Edinburgh)

Forbes, Rosita [Joan] (Swinderby)

Ford, Anna (Tewkesbury)

Ford, Ford Madox [Ford Hueffer] (Merton)

Ford, John (Ilsington, Devon)

Ford, Richard (Winchester)

Forde, Cyril Daryll (London)

Fordham, George (Cambridge)

Forman, Simon (Quidhampton)

Formby, George (Wigan)

Forster, Edward Morgan (London)

Forster, John (Newcastle upon Tyne)

Forster, Margaret (Carlisle)

Forster, William Edward (Bradpole)

Forsyth, Bill (Glasgow)

Forsyth, Brigit (Edinburgh)

Forsyth, Bruce (London)

Forsyth, Frederick (Ashford)

Forsyth, Gordon Mitchell (Fraserburgh)

Forsyth, Sir Thomas (Birkenhead)

Fortune, Robert (Edrom)

Foster, Birket (North Shields)

Foster, Sir Michael (Huntingdon)

Foster, Sir Norman Robert (Manchester)

Foulds, John (Manchester)

Fowke, Francis (Belfast)

Fowler, Graeme (Accrington)

Fowler, Henry Watson (Tonbridge)

Fowler, Sir John (Sheffield)

Fowles, John (Leigh on Sea)

Fox, Sir Charles (Derby)

Fox, Charles James (London)

Fox, George (Fenny Drayton)

Fox, William Johnson (Wrentham)

Foxe, John (Boston)

Foxe, Richard (Ropsley)

Frampton, Peter (Beckenham)

Frampton, Tregonwell (Moreton)

France, Celia (London)

Francis, James Bicheno (South Leigh)

Francome, John (Swindon)

Frankland, Sir Edward (Churchtown)

Franklin, Frederic (Liverpool)

Franklin, Sir John (Spilsby)

Franklin, Rosalind Elsie (London)

Fraser, Angus Robert (Billinge)

Fraser, Bruce Austin [Baron] (London)

Fraser, Peter (Fearn)

Frayn, Michael (London)

Frazer, Sir James George (Glasgow)

Freeman, Edward Augustus (Harborne)

Freeman, Sir Ralph (London)

French, Annie (Glasgow)

French, Dawn (Holyhead)

French, Sir John [Earl of Ypres] (Ripple)

Freyberg, Bernard [1st
  Baron] (London)
Fricker, Peter Racine
  (London)
Friel, Brian (Killyclogher)
Friese Greene, William
  (Bristol)
Frink, Elisabeth (Thurlow)
Frith, Francis (Chesterfield)
Frith, John (Westerham)
Frith, Mary (London)
Frith, William Powell
  (Aldfield)
Frobisher, Sir Martin (Altofts)
Frost, Sir David Paradine
  (Tenterden)
Frost, John (Newport)
Frost, Terry (Leamington Spa)
Froude, James Anthony
  (Dartington)
Froude, William (Dartington)
Fry, Charles Burgess
  (Croydon)
Fry, Christopher Harris
  (Bristol)
Fry, Elizabeth (Norwich)
Fry, Joseph (Sutton Benger)
Fry, Margery (London)
Fulbecke, William (Lincoln)
Fuller, Andrew (Wicken)
Fuller, John Frederick
  Charles (Chichester)
Fuller, Roy Broadbent
  (Oldham)
Fuller, Thomas (Aldwincle)
Fulton, Rikki (Glasgow)
Furnivall, Frederick James
  (Egham)

———

Gable, Christopher (London)
Gadd, Paul [Gary Glitter]
  (Banbury)
Gainsborough, Thomas
  (Sudbury)

Gairdner, William
  (Ardrossan)
Gaitskell, Hugh Todd
  (London)
Gallagher, Liam
  (Manchester)
Gallagher, Noel
  (Manchester)
Galt, John (Irvine)
Galton, Sir Francis
  (Birmingham)
Galway, James (Belfast)
Gamage, Albert Walter
  (Hereford)
Gamble, Josias Christopher
  (Enniskillen)
Garbett, Cyril Foster
  (Tongham)
Garden, Graeme (Aberdeen)
Garden, Mary (Aberdeen)
Gardiner, Samuel Rawson
  (Ropley)
Gardiner, Stephen (Bury St
  Edmunds)
Garioch, Robert [Robert
  Garioch Sutherland]
  (Edinburgh)
Garnett, Constance
  (Brighton)
Garnett, David (Brighton)
Garnett, Richard (Lichfield)
Garnett, Tony
  (Birmingham)
Garrick, David (Hereford)
Garrod, Heathcote William
  (Wells)
Garvin, James Louis
  (Birmingham)
Gascoigne, George
  (Cardington)
Gascoigne, Paul
  (Gateshead)
Gaskell, Elizabeth (London)
Gates, Horatio (Maldon)

Gatting, Michael William
  (London)
Gay, John (Barnstaple)
Geddes, Alexander
  (Rathven)
Geddes, Sir Patrick (Perth)
Geikie, Sir Archibald
  (Edinburgh)
Geikie, James (Edinburgh)
Geneen, Harold Sydney
  (Bournemouth)
George III [King of Great
  Britain] (London)
George IV [King of Great
  Britain] (London)
George V [King of Great
  Britain] (London)
George VI [King of Great
  Britain] (Sandringham)
George Brown [Baron]
  (London)
Gerald of Wales (Manorbier
  Castle)
Gerard, John (Nantwich)
German, Sir Edward
  [Edward German Jones]
  (Whitchurch)
Gibbon, Edward (London)
Gibbons, Orlando (Oxford)
Gibbons, Stella (London)
Gibbs, James (Aberdeen)
Gibbs, Sir Vicary (Exeter)
Gibbs Smith, Charles
  Harvard (Teddington)
Gibson, Sir Alexander
  Drummond (Motherwell)
Gibson, Cameron Michael
  (Belfast)
Gibson, Edmund (Bampton)
Gibson, John (Gyffin)
Gibson, Wilfrid Wilson
  (Hexham)
Gielgud, Sir Arthur John
  (London)

Gielgud, Maina (London)
Giffen, Sir Robert
  (Strathaven)
Gifford, William
  (Ashburton)
Giggs, Ryan (Cardiff)
Gilbert [Saint]
  (Sempringham)
Gilbert, Sir Joseph Henry
  (Hull)
Gilbert, William
  (Colchester)
Gilbert, William
  (Bishopstoke)
Gilbert, Sir William
  Schwenck (London)
Gilbey, Sir Walter (Bishop's
  Stortford)
Gilchrist, Percy Carlyle
  (Lyme Regis)
Giles, Annabel
  (Griffithstown)
Giles, Ashley Fraser
  (Chertsey)
Giles, Carl Ronald (London)
Giles, Herbert Allen
  (Oxford)
Giles, William [Bill]
  (Dittisham)
Giles, William Ernest
  (Bristol)
Gill, Sir David (Aberdeen)
Gill, Eric Rowton (Brighton)
Gillespie, George (Kirkcaldy)
Gillespie, James
  (Edinburgh)
Gillespie, Keith (Bangor)
Gilliatt, Penelope (London)
Gillies, Sir William George
  (Haddington)
Gillot, Joseph (Sheffield)
Gillray, James (London)
Gilman, Harold (Rode)
Gilpin, John (Southsea)

Gilpin, William (Scaleby)
Gimson, Ernest William
  (Leicester)
Gipps, Sir George
  (Ringwould)
Giraldus Cambrensis
  (Manorbier Castle)
Gissing, George Robert
  (Wakefield)
Gladstone, Herbert John
  [1st Viscount] (Dane End)
Gladstone, William Ewart
  (Liverpool)
Glaisher, James (London)
Glanvill, Joseph (Plymouth)
Glanvill, Ranulf de
  (Stratford St Andrew)
Glapthorne, Henry
  (Whittlesey)
Glas, John (Auchtermuchty)
Glazebrook, Sir Richard
  Tetley (Liverpool)
Gleig, George Robert
  (Stirling)
Glennie, Evelyn (Aberdeen)
Glisson, Francis
  (Rampisham)
Glitter, Gary [b.Paul Gadd]
  (Banbury)
Gloag, Ann (Perth)
Glover, Jane (Helmsley)
Glover, Julia (Newry)
Glover, Thomas Blake
  (Fraserburgh)
Glubb, Sir John [Glubb
  Pasha] (Preston)
Godden, Rumer
  (Eastbourne)
Godfree, Katherine
  (London)
Godolphin, Sidney [1st Earl]
  (Godolphin Hall)
Godwin, Edward William
  (Bristol)

Godwin, Francis (Hannington)
Godwin, William (Wisbech)
Goffe, William (Stanmer)
Golding, Louis (Manchester)
Golding, William Gerald (St
  Columb Minor)
Gollancz, Sir Victor
  (London)
Gonne, Maud (Aldershot)
Gooch, Sir Daniel
  (Bedlington)
Gooch, Graham Alan
  (London)
Goodall, Jane (London)
Goodrich, Sandra [Sandie
  Shaw] (Dagenham)
Goodsir, John (Anstruther)
Goodyear, Julie (Heywood)
Googe, Barnabe
  (Alvingham)
Goossens, Sir Eugene
  (London)
Goossens, Leon (Liverpool)
Gordon, Charles George
  (London)
Gordon, Hannah
  (Edinburgh)
Gordon, Sir John Watson
  (Edinburgh)
Gordon, Noele (London)
Gordon, Robert (Straloch)
Gore, Catherine (East
  Retford)
Gore, Spencer Frederick
  (Epsom)
Gorges, Sir Ferdinando
  (Ashton)
Göring, Marius (Newport)
Gorst, Sir John Eldon
  (Preston)
Gorton, Samuel
  (Manchester)
Goss, Sir John (Fareham)
Gosse, Sir Edmund (London)

Gosse, Philip Henry (Worcester)

Gosse, William Christie (Hoddesdon)

Gough, Darren (Barnsley)

Gould, Sir Francis (Barnstaple)

Gould, Fraser [Donald McGill] (London)

Gould, John (Lyme Regis)

Gould, Nathaniel (Manchester)

Gower, David Ivon (Tunbridge Wells)

Gowland, Gibson (Spennymoor)

Grace, William Gilbert (Downend)

Graham, Dougal (Raploch)

Graham, James (Edinburgh)

Graham, Sir James Robert (Netherby)

Graham, Thomas (Glasgow)

Grahame, James (Glasgow)

Grahame, Kenneth (Edinburgh)

Grahame White, Claude (Bursledon)

Grange, Kenneth Henry (London)

Granger, James (Shaftesbury)

Grant, Cary [Archibald Leach] (Bristol)

Grant, Duncan James (Rothiemurchus)

Grant, Elizabeth (Edinburgh)

Grant, James (Edinburgh)

Grant, James Augustus (Nairn)

Grant, Sir James Hope (Kilgraston)

Grant, William (Elgin)

Granville Barker, Harley (London)

Grasemann, Ruth [Ruth Rendell] (London)

Graveney, Thomas William (Riding Mill)

Graves, Robert von Ranke (London)

Gray, George Robert (London)

Gray, John Edward (Walsall)

Gray, Simon (Hayling Island)

Gray, Thomas (London)

Greaves, Jimmy (London)

Green, George (Sneinton)

Green, Henry [Henry Yorke] (Tewkesbury)

Green, John Richard (Oxford)

Green, Lucinda (London)

Green, Mary Anne (Sheffield)

Green, Robson (Dudley, Northumberland)

Green, Thomas Hill (Birkin)

Greenaway, Peter (London)

Greene, Graham Henry (Berkhamsted)

Greene, Sir Hugh Carleton (Berkhamsted)

Greene, Robert (Cambridge)

Greenway, Francis Howard (Mangotsfield)

Greenwood, Arthur (Leeds)

Greenwood, Joan (London)

Greenwood, Walter (Salford)

Greg, William Rathbone (Manchester)

Gregor, William (Trewarthenick)

Gregory, Augustus Charles (Farnsfield)

Gregory, David (Aberdeen)

Gregory, James (Aberdeen)

Gregory, James (Drumoak)

Greig, Sir Samuel (Inverkeithing)

Grenfell, Joyce (London)

Grenfell, Sir Wilfred (Parkgate)

Grenville, Sir Richard (Buckland Abbey)

Gresley, Sir Nigel (Edinburgh)

Greville, Sir Fulke [1st Baron Brooke] (Beauchamp Court)

Grew, Nehemiah (Atherstone)

Grey, Charles [2nd Earl] (Fallodon)

Grey, Lady Jane (Bradgate)

Grierson, Sir Herbert John (Lerwick)

Grieve, Christopher [Hugh McDiarmid] (Langholm)

Griffin, Bernard (Birmingham)

Griffith, Samuel Walker (Merthyr Tydfil)

Griffiths, Ann (Dolwar Fechan)

Griffiths, James (Betws)

Griffiths, Trevor (Manchester)

Grigson, Geoffrey Edward (Pelynt)

Grimaldi, Joseph (London)

Grimond, Joseph [Baron] (St Andrews)

Grimston, Margaret [Madge Kendal] (Cleethorpes)

Grimthorpe, Edmund [1st Baron] (Carlton Hall)

Grindal, Edmund (St Bees)

Grocyn, William (Colerne)

Grose, Francis (London)

Grosseteste, Robert (Stradbroke)

Grote, George (Beckenham)

Grove, Sir George (London)

Grove, Sir William Robert (Swansea)

Grub, George (Aberdeen)

Grubb, Sir Kenneth George (Oxton, Notts.)

Guest, Sir Josiah John (Dowlais)

Guinness, Sir Alec (London)

Gully, John (Wick, Somerset)

Gunn, Neil Miller (Dunbeath)

Gunn, Thomson William (Gravesend)

Gunnell, Sally (Chigwell)

Gunning, Elizabeth and Maria (St Ives)

Gurney, Edmund (Hersham)

Gurney, Sir Goldsworthy (Treator)

Gurney, Ivor (Gloucester)

Guthrie, Sir James (Greenock)

Guthrie, James (Hawick)

Guthrie, Thomas (Brechin)

Guthrie, Sir William Tyrone (Tunbridge Wells)

Guy, Thomas (London)

Guyon, Richard Debaufre (Walcot)

Gwyn, Nell (Hereford)

Habington, William (Hindlip)

Hackworth, Timothy (Wylam)

Hadfield, Sir Robert Abbot (Sheffield)

Hadley, Patrick Arthur (Cambridge)

Hadow, Sir William Henry (Ebrington)

Haggard, Sir Henry Rider (Bradenham Hall)

Haggett, Peter (Pawlett)

Haig, Douglas [1st Earl] (Edinburgh)

Hailey, Arthur (Luton)

Hailsham, Quintin Hogg [2nd Viscount] (London)

Hailwood, Mike [Stanley Michael] (Oxford)

Haldane, Elizabeth Sanderson (Edinburgh)

Haldane, John Burdon Sanderson (Oxford)

Haldane, John Scott (Edinburgh)

Haldane, Richard [1st Viscount] (Edinburgh)

Hale, Sir Matthew (Alderley)

Hales, Stephen (Bekesbourne)

Haliburton, Hugh [James Logie Robertson] (Milnathort)

Halifax, Charles Montagu [1st Earl] (Horton)

Halifax, Edward Fred [1st Earl, 2nd creation] (Powderham)

Halkett, Hugh [Baron von] (Musselburgh)

Hall, Sir Edward Marshall (Brighton)

Hall, Sir James (Dunglass)

Hall, Joseph (Ashby de la Zouch)

Hall, Marguerite Radclyffe (Bournemouth)

Hall, Sir Peter Reginald (Bury St Edmunds)

Hall, Robert (Arnesby)

Hall, Rodney (Solihull)

Hallam, Henry (Windsor)

Halley, Edmond (London)

Halliday, Michael Alexander (Leeds)

Hambling, Margaret (Sudbury)

Hamerton, Philip Gilbert (Oldham)

Hamilton, Emma (Great Neston)

Hamilton, Iain Ellis (Glasgow)

Hamilton, Patrick (Glasgow)

Hamilton, Richard (London)

Hamilton, Thomas (Glasgow)

Hamilton, William (Bangour)

Hamilton, Sir William (Glasgow)

Hamley, Sir Edward Bruce (Bodmin)

Hammond, Walter (Dover)

Hamnett, Katharine (Gravesend)

Hampole, Richard Rolle de (Thornton, Yorkshire)

Hampshire, John Harry (Thurnscoe)

Hampson, Frank (Manchester)

Hancock, Thomas (Marlborough)

Hancock, Tony [Anthony] (Birmingham)

Handley, Tommy [Thomas Reginald] (Liverpool)

Hands, Terence David (Aldershot)

Hanley, Clifford (Glasgow)

Hann, Judith (Derby)

Hannah, John (East Kilbride)

Hannington, James (Hurstpierpoint)

Hansard, Luke (Norwich)

Hansom, Joseph Aloysius (York)

Hanson, Jean (Newhall)

Hanway, Jonas (Portsmouth)

Harcourt, William Vernon (Sudbury)

Harden, Sir Arthur (Manchester)

Hardie, Gwen (Newport)

Harding, Sir John [1st Baron] (South Petherton)

Harding, Stephen [Saint] (Sherborne)

Hardinge of Lahore, Henry [1st Viscount] (Wrotham)

Hardwick, Philip (London)

Hardwicke, Sir Cedric (Lye)

Hardy, Sir Alister (Nottingham)

Hardy, Godfrey Harold (Cranleigh)

Hardy, Thomas (Higher Bockhampton)

Hare, Sir David (Bexhill)

Hare, Sir John (Giggleswick)

Hare, William ['Dusty'] (Newark-on-Trent)

Harewood, George [7th Earl] (Harewood)

Hargrave, Lawrence (London)

Hargraves, Edward Hammond (Gosport)

Hargreaves, Alison (Belper)

Hargreaves, James (Oswaldtwistle)

Harington, Sir John (Kelston)

Harmsworth, Harold [1st Viscount Rothermere] (London)

Harper, Edward (Taunton)

Harrington, James (Upton)

Harriot, Thomas (Oxford)

Harris, Sir Arthur ['Bomber'] (Cheltenham)

Harris, James (Salisbury)

Harris, John Wyndham [John Wyndham] (Knowle)

Harris, Reginald Hargreaves (Bury)

Harris, Thomas Lake (Fenny Stratford)

Harrison, George (Liverpool)

Harrison, Jane (Hull)

Harrison, John (Foulby)

Harrison, Sir Rex (Liverpool)

Harrison, Thomas (Newcastle under Lyme)

Harrison, Tony (Leeds)

Harrod, Sir Henry Roy (London)

Hart, Dame Judith (Burnley)

Hartley, David (Luddenden)

Hartley, David [The Younger] (Bath)

Hartnett, Sir Laurence (Woking)

Hartree, Douglas Rayner (Cambridge)

Harty, Sir Herbert Hamilton (Hillsborough)

Harvard, John (London)

Harvey, David (Gillingham)

Harvey, Gabriel (Saffron Walden)

Harvey, Sir George (Stirling)

Harvey, Sir John Martin (Wivenhoe)

Harvey, Polly Jean (Yeovil)

Harvey, William (Folkestone)

Harwood, Harold Marsh (Manchester)

Harwood, Elizabeth (Barton Seagrave)

Hassall, John (Walmer)

Hastings, James (Huntly)

Hastings, Warren (Churchill)

Hattersley, Roy Sydney (Sheffield)

Hatton, Sir Christopher (Holdenby)

Hatton, John Liptrot (Liverpool)

Havelock, Sir Henry (Sunderland)

Havergal, William Henry (High Wycombe)

Hawke, Edward [1st Baron] (London)

Hawker, Robert Stephen (Plymouth)

Hawkes, Jacquetta (Cambridge)

Hawking, Stephen William (Oxford)

Hawkins, Henry [1st Baron Brampton] (Hitchin)

Hawkins, Jack [John Edward] (London)

Hawkins, Sir John (London)

Hawkins, Sir John (Plymouth)

Hawkshaw, Sir John (Leeds)

Hawksmoor, Nicholas (East Drayton)

Hawkwood, Sir John de (Castle Hedingham)

Haworth, Sir Walter Norman (Chorley)

Hawthorne, Alfred [Benny Hill] (Southampton)

Hay, Ian (Manchester)

Hay, Will (Stockton-on-Tees)

Haydon, Benjamin Robert (Plymouth)

Hayley, William (Chichester)

Hayman, Francis (Exeter)

Haynes, John [Johnny] (London)

Hayter, Stanley William (London)

Haywood, Eliza (London)

Hazlitt, William (Maidstone)

Head, Sir Henry (London)

Heal, Sir Ambrose (London)

Healey, Denis Winston [Baron] (Mattingley)

Healey-Kay, Patrick [Anton Dolin] (Slinfold)

Heaney, Seamus Justin (Castledawson)

Hearne, Samuel (London)

Hearne, Thomas (White Waltham)

Heath, Sir Edward Richard (Broadstairs)

Heathcoat, John (Duffield)

Heathfield, George Augustus (Stobs)

Heaviside, Oliver (London)

Heber, Reginald (Malpas)

Hedley, William (Newburn)

Heenan, John Carmel [Cardinal] (Ilford)

Heilbron, Sir Ian Morris (Glasgow)

Heinemann, William (Surbiton)

Hemans, Felicia Dorothea (Liverpool)

Henderson, Alexander (Creich)

Henderson, Arthur (Glasgow)

Henderson, Hamish (Blairgowrie)

Henderson, Sir Nevile Meyrick (Sedgwick)

Henderson, Thomas (Dundee)

Hendry, Colin (Keith)

Henley, John Ernest (Melton Mowbray)

Henley, William (Gloucester)

Henrietta Anne [Duchess of Orléans] (Exeter)

Henry I [King of England] (Selby)

Henry III [King of England] (Winchester)

Henry V [King of England] (Monmouth)

Henry VI [King of England] (Windsor)

Henry VII [King of England] (Pembroke)

Henry VIII [King of England] (London)

Henry, Lenny (Dudley)

Henry, William (Manchester)

Henshall, Audrey (Oldham)

Henslowe, Philip (Lindfield)

Henty, George Alfred (Trumpington)

Hepworth, Barbara (Wakefield)

Herbert, Sir Alan Patrick (Elstead)

Herbert, Mary (Penshurst)

Herbert of Cherbury [1st Baron] (Eyton)

Herbertson, Andrew John (Galashiels)

Herbison, Margaret McCrorie (Shotts)

Herd, David (Marykirk)

Heriot, George (Edinburgh)

Hermes, Gertrude (Bromley)

Heron, Patrick (Leeds)

Herrick, Robert (London)

Herriot, James [James Alfred Wight] (Glasgow)

Herschel, Sir John Frederick (Slough)

Heseltine, Michael (Swansea)

Heseltine, Philip [Peter Warlock] (London)

Heskey, Emile (Leicester)

Hess, Dame Myra (London)

Hewish, Antony (Fowey)

Hewson, Sherrie (Burton Joyce)

Heyer, Georgette (London)

Heylin, Peter (Burford)

Hibbert, Eleanor (London)

Hick, John Harwood (Scarborough)

Hickes, George (Newsham)

Hicks, Sir John Richard (Leamington Spa)

Hicks, Tommy [Tommy Steele] (London)

Higgins, Alexander ['Hurricane'] (Belfast)

Higgins, Jack [Harry Patterson] (Newcastle upon Tyne)

Higson, Paddy (Belfast)

Hill, Adrian [Ronnie Hilton] (Hull)

Hill, Archibald Vivian (Bristol)

Hill, Benny [Alfred Hawthorne] (Southampton)

Hill, David Octavius (Perth)

Hill, Geoffrey William (Bromsgrove)

Hill, Katy (Poole)

Hill, Matthew Davenport (Birmingham)

Hill, Norman Graham (London)

Hill, Octavia (London)

Hill, Rowland [1st Viscount] (Prees Hall)

Hill, Sir Rowland (Kidderminster)

Hill, Susan (Scarborough)

Hiller, Dame Wendy (Bramhall)

Hilliard, Nicholas (Exeter)

Hilton, James (Leigh)

Hilton, Roger (Northwood)

Hilton, Ronnie [Adrian Hill] (Hull)

Hinshelwood, Sir Cyril (London)

Hinsley, Arthur (Selby)

Hinton, Christopher [Baron] (Tisbury)

Hislop, Joseph (Edinburgh)

Hitchcock, Sir Alfred Joseph (London)

Hoadly, Benjamin (Westerham)

Hobart-Hampden, Augustus (Waltham-on-the-Wolds)

Hobbes, Thomas (Malmesbury)

Hobbs, Sir John [Jack] (Cambridge)

Hobhouse, Leonard Trelawney (St Ives, Cornwall)

Hill, Sir Rowland (Kidderminster)

Hobson, Sir Harold (Rotherham)

Hobson, John Atkinson (Derby)

Hocking, Joseph (St Stephens)

Hockney, David (Bradford)

Hoddinott, Alun (Bargoed)

Hodgkin, Sir Alan Lloyd (Banbury)

Hodgkin, Howard (London)

Hodgkinson, Eaton (Anderton)

Hodgson, Brian Houghton (Macclesfield)

Hogarth, William (London)

Hogben, Lancelot (Southsea)

Hogg, James (Ettrickhall)

Hogg, Pam (Paisley)

Hogg, Quintin (London)

Holbrooke, Josef (Croydon)

Holcroft, Thomas (London)

Holdsworth, Sir William Searle (Beckenham)

Holland, Henry Scott (Ledbury)

Holland, Philemon (Chelmsford)

Holland, Sir Thomas Erskine (Brighton)

Holloway, Stanley (London)

Holloway, Thomas (Devonport)

Holm, Ian (Ilford)

Holman, James (Exeter)

Holmes, Arthur (Hebburn-on-Tyne)

Holroyd, Michael de Courcy (London)

Holst, Gustav Theodore (Cheltenham)

Holt, Sir John (Thame)

Holt, Victoria [Eleanor Hibbert] (London)

Holtby, Winifred (Rudston)

Holyoake, George Jacob (Birmingham)

Home, Sir Alec Douglas [Earl] (London)

Home, John (Edinburgh)

Hone, William (Bath)

Hood, Samuel [1st Viscount] (Thorncombe)

Hood, Thomas (London)

Hook, James (Norwich)

Hooke, Robert (Freshwater)

Hooker, Sir Joseph Dalton (Halesworth)

Hooker, Thomas (Markfield)

Hooker, Sir William Jackson (Norwich)

Hope, Sir Bob [Leslie Townes Hope] (London)

Hope, Laurence [Adela Florence Nicolson] (Stoke Bishop)

Hope, Thomas Charles (Edinburgh)

Hopkins, Sir Anthony (Port Talbot)

Hopkins, Sir Frederick Gowland (Eastbourne)

Hopkins, Gerard Manley (London)

Hordern, Sir Michael (Berkhamsted)

Hore-Belisha, Leslie [1st Baron] (Devonport)

Hornblower, Jonathan Carter (Chacewater)

Hornby, Albert Sidney (Chester)

Hornby, Frank (Liverpool)

Hornby, Leslie [Twiggy] (London)

Hornby, Sir Phipps (Winwick)

Horner, Arthur Lewis (Merthyr Tydfil)

Horniman, Annie Elizabeth (London)

Hornung, Ernest William (Middlesbrough)

Horrocks, Jeremiah (Liverpool)

Horsley, Sir Victor Alexander (London)

Hoskins, Bob [Robert William] (Bury St Edmunds)

Hoskins, William George (Exeter)

Hoste, Sir William (Ingoldisthorpe)

Houghton, William Stanley (Ashton-upon-Mersey)

Hounsfield, Sir Godfrey Newbold (Newark)

Housman, Alfred Edward (Fockbury)

Housman, Laurence (Bromsgrove)

Houselander, Caryll (Bath)

Houston, Renee (Johnstone)

Howard, John (London)

Howard, Trevor Wallace (Cliftonville)

Howatch, Susan (Leatherhead)

Howe, John (Loughborough)

Howe, Richard [1st Earl] (London)

Howells, Herbert (Lydney)

Howerd, Frankie (York)

How-Martyn, Edith (Cheltenham)

Hoyland, John (Sheffield)

Hoyle, Sir Fred (Bingley)

Hudd, Roy (Croydon)

Huddleston, Ernest U.T. (Bedford)

Hudson, Jeffrey ['Sir'] (Oakham)

Hudson, William (Kendal)

Hueffer, Ford Hermann [Ford Madox Ford] (Merton)

Huggins, Sir William (London)

Hughes, Arthur (London)

Hughes, Hugh Price (Carmarthen)

Hughes, Richard Arthur (Weybridge)

Hughes, Ted [Edward James] (Mytholmroyd)

Hughes, William Morris (Llandudno)

Hullah, John Pyke (Worcester)

Hulme, Thomas Ernest (Endon)

Hulse, John (Middlewich)

Hulton, Sir Edward (Harrogate)

Hume, George Basil (Newcastle upon Tyne)

Hume, David (Edinburgh)

Hume, John (Londonderry)

Hume, Joseph (Montrose)

Hume of Godscroft, David (Dunbar)

Humphreys, Emyr (Prestatyn)

Hunt, Henry ['Orator Hunt'] (Upavon)

Hunt, James Leigh (London)

Hunt, Violet (Durham)

Hunt, William Holman (London)

Hunter, John (East Kilbride)

Hunter, John (Edinburgh)

Hunter, Mollie (Longniddry)

Hunter, William (East Kilbride)

Hunter, Sir William (Glasgow)

Huntsman, Benjamin (Barton-upon-Humber)

Hurd, Douglas Richard (Marlborough)

Hurd, Richard (Congreve)

Hurst, Sir Cecil Barrington (Horsham)

Hurst, Geoffrey (Ashton-under-Lyne)

Huskisson, William (Birtsmorton)

Hutchinson, Anne (Alford)

Hutchinson, John (Nottingham)

Hutchinson, John (Spennithorne)

Hutchinson, Sir Jonathan (Selby)

Hutchison, Don (Gateshead)

Hutchison, Sir William (Collessie)

Hutton, James (Edinburgh)

Hutton, Sir Leonard (Pudsey)

Huxley, Aldous Leonard (Godalming)

Huxley, Hugh Esmor (Birkenhead)

Huxley, Thomas Henry (London)

Hyne, Charles John (Bibury)

Hyslop, James (Kirkconnel)

Iddesleigh, Stafford Henry [1st Earl Northcote] (London)

Ifield, Frank (Coventry)

Ilbert, Sir Courtenay Peregrine (Kingsbridge)

Illingworth, Raymond (Pudsey)

Illingworth, Richard (Bradford)

Ilott, Mark Christopher (Watford)

Ince, Paul (Ilford)

Inchbald, Elizabeth (Bury St Edmunds)

Inescort, Frieda (Edinburgh)

Inge, William Ralph (Crayke)

Ingelow, Jean (Boston)

Ingleby, Clement Mansfield (Birmingham)

Ingram, Herbert (Boston)

Inman, William (Leicester)

Irani, Ronald Charles
(Leigh)

Ireland, John Nicholson
(Manchester)

Ireland, William Henry
(London)

Ireton, Henry (Attenborough)

Ironside, William [1st
Baron] (Ironside)

Irvine, Andrew Robertson
(Edinburgh)

Irvine, Sir James Colquhoun
(Glasgow)

Irving, Edward (Annan)

Irving, Sir Henry [John
Henry Brodribb] (Keinton
Mandeville)

Isaacs, Alick (Glasgow)

Isaacs, Jeremy Israel
(Glasgow)

Isaacs, Susan Brierley
(Bromley Cross)

Isherwood, Christopher
William (Disley)

Islip, Simon (Disley)

Jacklin, Tony (Scunthorpe)

Jackson, Betty (Bacup)

Jackson, Frederick (Ipswich)

Jackson, Glenda (Birkenhead)

Jackson, George Holbrook
(Liverpool)

Jackson, Joe (Burton-on-
Trent)

Jackson, John Hughlings
(Providence Green)

Jackson [Baroness] [Dame
Barbara Ward] (York)

Jacob, Giles (Romsey)

Jacob, Violet (Montrose)

Jacobi, Sir Derek George
(London)

Jacobs, William Wymark
(London)

Jacques, Hattie [Josephine
Edwina] (Sandgate)

Jagger, Sir Mick [Michael
Phillip] (Dartford)

James I [King of Scotland]
(Dunfermline)

James V [King of Scotland]
(Linlithgow)

James VI [of Scotland] and
I [of England] (Edinburgh)

James VII [of Scotland] and
II [of England] (London)

James, Henry [1st Baron
Hereford] (Hereford)

James, Montague Rhodes
(Goodnestone)

James, Phyliss Dorothy
(Oxford)

Jameson, Sir Leander Starr
(Edinburgh)

Jameson, Storm [Margaret]
(Whitby)

Jamesone, George
(Aberdeen)

Jamieson, John (Glasgow)

Jane, Frederick Thomas
(Upottery)

Jarman, Derek (Northwood)

Jarvis, Charles Alfred
(Fraserburgh)

Jeans, Sir James Hopwood
(Ormskirk)

Jebb, Eglantyne (Ellesmere)

Jebb, Sir Richard
Claverhouse (Dundee)

Jefferson, Arthur Stanley
[Stan Laurel] (Ulverston)

Jeffrey, Francis [Lord]
(Edinburgh)

Jeffreys, George [1st Baron]
(Acton, Clwyd)

Jeffreys, Sir Harold (Birtley)

Jekyll, Gertrude (London)

Jellicoe, John [1st Earl]
(Southampton)

Jenkins, David Edward
(Bromley)

Jenkins, John (Maidstone)

Jenkins, Roy [Baron]
(Abersychan)

Jenner, Edward (Berkeley)

Jenner, Sir William
(Chatham)

Jennings, Patrick (Newry)

Jerne, Niels Kai (London)

Jerome, Jerome Klapka
(Walsall)

Jerrold, Douglas William
(London)

Jesse, Fryn Tennyson
(Chislehurst)

Jessop, William (Devonport)

Jevons, William Stanley
(Liverpool)

Jewel, Jimmy (Sheffield)

Jewel, John (Berrynarbor)

Jewsbury, Geraldine
(Measham)

Jex-Blake, Sophia Louisa
(Hastings)

Joad, Cyril Edwin (Durham)

Joan of Navarre (Havering-
atte-Bower)

John [King of England]
(Oxford)

John, Augustus (Tenby)

John, Barry (Cefneithin)

John, Sir Elton [Reginald
Kenneth Dwight] (Pinner)

John, Gwen (Haverfordwest)

John of Beverley [Saint]
(Harpham)

John of Salisbury
(Salisbury)

Johns, William Earl
(Hertford)

Johnson, Alexander Bryan (Gosport)

Johnson, Amy (Hull)

Johnson, Dame Celia (Richmond)

Johnson, Hewlett (Manchester)

Johnson, Lionel Pigot (Broadstairs)

Johnson, Pamela Hansford (London)

Johnson, Paul (Newark)

Johnson, Samuel (Lichfield)

Johnston, Arthur (Caskieben)

Johnstone, Dorothy (Edinburgh)

Johnstone, James (Edinburgh)

Johnstone, Jimmy (Viewpark)

Johnstone, William (Denholm)

Jolley, Elizabeth (Birmingham)

Joly, John (Holywood)

Jones, Allen (Southampton)

Jones, Catherine Zeta (Swansea)

Jones, Edward German [Sir Edward German] (Whitchurch)

Jones, Ewart Ray Herbert (Wrexham)

Jones, Gwyn (Blackwood)

Jones, Dame Gwyneth (Pontnewynydd)

Jones, Sir Harold Spencer (London)

Jones, Henry Arthur (Granborough)

Jones, Sir Henry Stuart (Leeds)

Jones, Howard (Southampton)

Jones, Inigo (London)

Jones, Jack [James Larkin] (Liverpool)

Jones, John (Maes-y-garnedd)

Jones, John Paul (Kirkbean)

Jones, Philip (Swansea)

Jones, Thomas (Rhymney)

Jones, Tom [b.Woodward] (Pontypridd)

Jonson, Ben [Benjamin] (London)

Joplin, Thomas (Newcastle upon Tyne)

Josephson, Brian David (Cardiff)

Joule, James Prescott (Salford)

Jowitt, William [1st Earl] (Stevenage)

Juliana (Norwich)

Justice, James Robertson (Wigtown)

Juxon, William (Chichester)

———————————————

Kames, Henry Home [Lord] (Kames)

Karloff, Boris [William Henry Pratt] (London)

Kay, John (Bury)

Kay-Shuttleworth, Sir James Phillips (Rochdale)

Kaye-Smith, Sheila (St Leonards)

Kean, Edmund (London)

Keate, John (Wells)

Keats, John (London)

Keble, John (Fairford)

Keegan, Kevin (Armthorpe)

Keir, James (Edinburgh)

Keith, Sir Arthur (Persley)

Keith, James (Inverugie Castle)

Kelvin [Baron] [William Thomson] (Belfast)

Kemble, Charles (Brecon)

Kemble, Fanny (London)

Kemble, John Philip (Prescot)

Kemble, Stephen (Kington)

Kemp, John (Olantigh)

Kemsley, James [1st Viscount] (Merthyr Tydfil)

Ken, Thomas (Little Berkhamsted)

Kendal, Dame Madge [Margaret Brunton Grimston] (Cleethorpes)

Kendal, Felicity (Birmingham)

Kendall, Kay (Withernsea)

Kendrew, Sir John Cowdery (Oxford)

Kennaway, James (Auchterarder)

Kennedy, Helena (Glasgow)

Kennedy, Sir Ludovic Henry (Edinburgh)

Kennedy-Fraser, Marjorie (Perth)

Kenney, Annie (Springhead)

Kennington, Eric Henri (London)

Kent, William (Bridlington)

Kentigern, St [St Mungo] (Culross)

Kenyon, Dame Kathleen (London)

Keown, Martin (Oxford)

Ker, William Paton (Glasgow)

Kerr, Deborah [Deborah Kerr Viertel] (Helensburgh)

Kerr, John (Ardrossan)

Kesson, Jessie (Inverness)

Kett, Robert (Wymondham)

Ketelbey, Albert William [Anton Vodorinski] (Birmingham)

Kettlewell, Henry Bernard (Howden)

Keyes, Sydney Arthur Kilworth (Dartford)

Keynes, John Maynard [1st Baron] (Cambridge)

Kidd, Carol (Glasgow)

Kidd, William [Captain Kidd] (Greenock)

Kilburn, Tom (Dewsbury)

Kilmuir, David Patrick [1st Earl] (Aberdeen)

King, Cecil Harmsworth (Totteridge)

King, Jessie Marion (Bearsden)

King, John (Moy)

Kingsford, Anna (Stratford)

Kingsley, Ben (Snainton)

Kingsley, Charles (Holne)

Kingsley, Mary Henrietta (London)

Kinnaird, Alison (Edinburgh)

Kinnaird, Lady Mary (Northwick Park)

Kinnock, Neil Gordon (Tredegar)

Kipping, Frederick Stanley (Manchester)

Kitchen, Mervyn John (Nailsea)

Knight, Charles (Windsor)

Knight, Dame Laura (Long Eaton)

Knott, Alan Philip (London)

Knox, John (Haddington)

Knox, Robert (Edinburgh)

Knox, Ronald Arbuthnott (Birmingham)

Knussen, Stuart Oliver (Glasgow)

Kyd, Thomas (London)

———————————————

Laine, Cleo (Southall)

Laing, Alexander Gordon (Edinburgh)

Laing, Ronald David (Glasgow)

Laird, Macgregor (Greenock)

Laithwaite, Eric Roberts (Atherton)

Laker, James Charles (Bradford)

Lamb, Charles (London)

Lambart, Constant (London)

Lambert, John (Calton)

Lamburn, Richmal [Richmal Crompton] (Bury)

Lamond, Frederic (Glasgow)

Lamont, Johann von (Braemar)

Lancaster, Sir Osbert (London)

Lanchester, Frederick William (London)

Landells, Ebenezer (Newcastle upon Tyne)

Lander, Richard (Truro)

Landor, Walter Savage (Warwick)

Landseer, Sir Edwin Henry (London)

Lane, Sir Allen (Bristol)

Lane, Edward William (Hereford)

Lane, William Arbuthnot (Fort George)

Lang, Andrew (Selkirk)

Lang, Cosmo Gordon (Fyvie)

Lang, John Dunmore (Greenock)

Langham, Simon (Langham)

Langhorne, John (Winton)

Langley, John Newport (Newbury)

Lankester, Sir Edwin Ray (London)

Lansbury, Angela (London)

La Plante, Lynda (Liverpool)

Lapworth, Arthur (Galashiels)

Lapworth, Charles (Faringdon)

Larkin, James (Liverpool)

Larkin, Philip Arthur (Coventry)

Larwood, Harold (Nuncargate)

Laski, Harold Joseph (Manchester)

Laski, Marghanita (Manchester)

Lassell, William (Bolton)

Latimer, Hugh (Thurcaston)

Latrobe, Benjamin Henry (Fulneck)

Laud, William (Reading)

Lauder, Sir Harry (Edinburgh)

Lauder, Robert Scott (Edinburgh)

Lauder, Sir Thomas Dick (Fountainhall)

Lauderdale, John Maitland [Duke of Lauderdale] (Lennoxlove)

Laughton, Charles (Scarborough)

Laughton, Sir John Knox (Liverpool)

Laurel, Stan [Arthur Stanley] (Ulverston)

Laurie, John (Dumfries)

Laver, James (Liverpool)

Lavery, Sir John (Belfast)

Law, Denis (Aberdeen)

Law, John (Edinburgh)

Law, William (Kingscliffe)

Lawes, Henry (Dinton)

Lawrence, David Herbert (Eastwood)
Lawrence, Gertrude (London)
Lawrence, John [1st Baron] (Richmond, Yorkshire)
Lawrence, Thomas Edward ['Lawrence of Arabia'] (Tremadoc)
Lawrence, Sir Thomas (Bristol)
Lawrie, Marie [Lulu] (Glasgow)
Lawton, Tommy (Bolton)
Leach, Archibald [Cary Grant] (Bristol)
Leach, Sir Edmund Ronald (Sidmouth)
Leach, Johnny (Romford)
Leach, William Elford (Plymouth)
Leacock, Stephen Butler (Swanmore)
Leakey, Mary Douglas (London)
Lean, Sir David (Croydon)
Lear, Edward (London)
Leavis, Frank Raymond (Cambridge)
Le Carré, John [David Cornwell] (Poole)
Lee, Ann ['Mother Ann'] (Manchester)
Lee, James Paris (Hawick)
Lee, Jennie [Baroness] (Lochgelly)
Lee, Laurie (Slad)
Lee, Robert (Tweedmouth)
LeFanu, Nicola (Wickham Bishops)
Lefroy, Sir John Henry (Ashe)
Le Gallienne, Richard (Liverpool)

Legge, James (Huntly)
Lehmann, Beatrix (Bourne End)
Lehmann, John Frederick (Bourne End)
Lehmann, Rosamond (High Wycombe)
Lehmann, Rudolph Chambers (Sheffield)
Leigh, Mike (Salford)
Leighton, Frederic [1st Baron] (Scarborough)
Leighton, Kenneth (Wakefield)
Leighton, Margaret (Barnt Green)
Leishman, Sir William Boog (Glasgow)
Leitch, Cecil (Silloth)
Leitch, Donovan Phillip [Donovan] (Glagow)
Leland, John (Wigan)
Lennon, John (Liverpool)
Lennox, Annie (Aberdeen)
Lenska, Rula (St Neots)
Leslie, Frank [Henry Carter] (Ipswich)
Leslie, John (Kingussie)
Leslie, Sir John (Largo)
Lessore, Therese (Brighton)
L'Estrange, Sir Roger (Hunstanton)
Lethaby, William Richard (Barnstaple)
Letts, Thomas (London)
Leverhulme, William [1st Viscount] (Bolton)
Levertov, Denise (Ilford)
Levey, Barnett (London)
Levison, Mary (Oxford)
Lewis, Agnes Smith (Irvine)
Lewis, Alun (Cwmaman)
Lewis, Cecil Day (Belfast)

Lewis, Clive Staples (Belfast)
Lewis, Hywel David (Llandudno)
Lewis, Martyn (Swansea)
Lewis, Matthew Gregory (London)
Lewis, Richard [Dic Penderyn] (Aberavon)
Lewis, Sir Thomas (Cardiff)
Lewis, Timothy Richards (Hafod)
Leyden, John (Denholm)
Liddell, Henry George (Bishop Auckland)
Liddon, Henry Parry (North Stoneham)
Lightfoot, John (Stoke-on-Trent)
Lilburne, John (London)
Lillo, George (London)
Lilly, William (Diseworth)
Lilye, William (Odiham)
Linacre, Thomas (Canterbury)
Lind, James (Edinburgh)
Lindley, John (Catton)
Lingard, Joan (Edinburgh)
Lingard, John (Winchester)
Lingen, Ralph Robert Wheeler [Baron] (Birmingham)
Linklater, Eric (Penarth)
Linley, Thomas (Wells)
Linton, Eliza Lynn (Keswick)
Linton, William James (London)
Lintot, Barnaby Bernard (Horsham)
Lipton, Sir Thomas Johnstone (Glasgow)
Lipman, Maureen Diane (Hull)
Lister, Joseph [Lord] (London)

Lister, Samuel [1st Baron
  Masham] (Bradford)
Liston, Robert (Ecclesmachan)
Littlewood, Joan (London)
Littlewood, John Edensor
  (Rochester)
Livingstone, David (Low
  Blantyre)
Llewellyn, Margaret Davies
  (London)
Llewellyn, Richard [Richard
  Doyle Lloyd] (St David's)
Lloyd, David (Accrington)
Lloyd, Frank (Glasgow)
Lloyd, George Walter (St
  Ives)
Lloyd, Marie (London)
Lloyd, Richard Doyle
  [Richard Llewellyn] (St
  David's)
Lloyd-George, David [1st
  Earl] (Manchester)
Lloyd-George of Dwyfor,
  Gwilym [1st Viscount
  Tenby] (Criccieth)
Lloyd-George of Dwyfor,
  Lady Megan (Criccieth)
Lloyd-Jones, David Martyn
  (Newcastle Emlyn)
Lloyd-Webber, Andrew
  (London)
Loach, Ken (Nuneaton)
Lochhead, Liz (Motherwell)
Lock, Graham Anthony
  (Limpsfield)
Locke, John (Wrington)
Locke, Joseph (Attercliffe)
Locke, Matthew (Exeter)
Lockhart, John Gibson
  (Cambusnethan)
Lockyer, Sir Joseph Norman
  (Rugby)
Lodge, Sir Oliver Joseph
  (Penkhull)

Lodge, Thomas (London)
Lofting, Hugh John
  (Maidenhead)
Logan, James (Lurgan)
Long, Richard (Bristol)
Longman, Thomas (Bristol)
Longuett Higgins, Hugh
  Christopher (Lenham)
Lonsdale, William (Bath)
Lord, Thomas (Thirsk)
Lorimer, James (Aberdalgie)
Lorimer, Sir Robert Stodart
  (Edinburgh)
Loudon, John Claudius
  (Cambuslang)
Loughlin, Anne (Leeds)
Lovat, Simon Fraser [Lord]
  (Tomich)
Lovelace, Ada King
  [Countess] (London)
Lovell, Sir Alfred Charles
  Bernard (Bristol)
Low, Bet (Greenock)
Low, Nora Wilson
  (Strichen)
Lowe, Arthur (Hayfield)
Lower, Richard (Tremeer)
Lowry, Clarence Malcolm
  (New Brighton)
Lowry, Laurence Stephen
  (Manchester)
Lowry, Thomas Martin
  (Bradford)
Lowth, Robert (Winchester)
Lubbock, Sir John [1st
  Baron Avebury] (London)
Lucas, Frank Lawrence
  (Hipperholme)
Lucy, Sir Henry William
  (Crosby)
Ludlow, Edmund (Maiden
  Bradley)
Lulu [Marie Lawrie]
  (Glasgow)

Lupino, Ida (London)
Lutyens, Sir Edwin Landseer
  (London)
Lutyens, Elizabeth (London)
Lydgate, John (Lidgate)
Lyell, Sir Charles (Kinnordy)
Lyle, Alexander [Sandy]
  (Shrewsbury)
Lympany, Moura (Saltash)
Lynch, Benny (Glasgow)
Lynd, Robert (Belfast)
Lyndsay, Robert (Pitscottie)
Lynn, Dame Vera (London)
Lyon, Frances (Norwich)
Lyon, John (St Helens)
Lyons, Sir John
  (Manchester)
Lyons, Sir Joseph (London)
Lyte, Henry Francis (Ednam)
Lyttleton, George [1st
  Baron] (Hagley)
Lyttleton, Humphrey
  (Windsor)
Lytton, Edward George [1st
  Baron] (London)
Lytton, Edward Robert [1st
  Earl] (London)

McAdam, John Loudon (Ayr)
McAllister, Anne (Biggar)
McAllister, Gary
  (Motherwell)
Macarthur, Elizabeth
  (Bridgerule)
MacArthur, Mary Reid
  (Glasgow)
Macartney, George [1st
  Earl] (Lissanoure)
McAteer, Jason
  (Birkenhead)
Macaulay, Catherine (Wye)
Macaulay, Dame Rose
  (Rugby)
Macaulay, Thomas

Babington [1st Baron] (Rothley)

McBean, Angus Rowland (Newbridge)

MacBeth, Ann (Manchester)

McBey, James (Newburgh)

MacBride, Maud (Aldershot)

McBride, Willie John (Toomebridge)

MacBryde, Robert (Ayr)

MacCaig, Norman Alexander (Edinburgh)

McCall, Stuart (Leeds)

MacCarthy, Sir Desmond (Plymouth)

McCartney, Sir James Paul (Liverpool)

McColl, Dugald Sutherland (Glasgow)

MacColl, Ewan [James Miller] (Salford)

McColgan, Liz (Dundee)

MacCormick, John MacDonald (Glasgow)

McCosh, James (Carskeoch)

McCracken, Esther (Newcastle upon Tyne)

McCrie, Thomas (Duns)

McCulloch, John Ramsay (Whithorn)

McCunn, Hamish (Greenock)

McDiarmid, Hugh [Christopher Grieve] (Langholm)

MacDonald, David (Helensburgh)

MacDonald, Elaine (Tadcaster)

MacDonald, Frances (Glasgow)

MacDonald, George (Huntly)

MacDonald, James Ramsay (Lossiemouth)

MacDonald, Sir John Alexander (Glasgow)

MacDonald, Malcolm (Lossiemouth)

MacDonald, Sharman (Glasgow)

McDougall, William (Manchester)

McElwee, Robert (Burton on Trent)

McEwan, Geraldine (Windsor)

McEwen, Sir John Blackwood (Hawick)

McEwen, Sir William (Rothesay)

McGill, Donald [Fraser Gould] (London)

McGill, James (Glasgow)

MacGillivray, James Pittendrigh (Inverurie)

McGrath, John Peter (Birkenhead)

McGregor, Sir Ian Kinloch (Kinlochleven)

MacGregor, John (Gravesend)

McGregor, Sue (Oxford)

MacIntosh, Charles (Glasgow)

McKail, John William (Kingarth)

MacKay, Alexander Murdoch (Rhynie)

MacKay, Charles (Perth)

MacKay, Fulton (Paisley)

MacKay, James [Baron MacKay of Clashfern] (Scourie)

McKellen, Sir Ian (Burnley)

McKenna, Siobhan (Belfast)

McKenzie, Sir Alexander (Stornoway)

MacKenzie, Alexander (Logierait)

MacKenzie, Sir Alexander Campbell (Edinburgh)

MacKenzie, Sir George (Dundee)

MacKenzie, Henry (Edinburgh)

MacKenzie, William Lyon (Dundee)

MacKinder, Sir Halford John (Gainsborough)

MacKinnon, Donald MacKenzie (Oban)

MacKintosh, Charles Rennie (Glasgow)

MacKintosh, Elizabeth [Josephine Tey] (Inverness)

MacKintosh, Hugh Ross (Paisley)

MacKintosh, William (Borlum)

Mackmurdo, Arthur Heygate (London)

Mackworth, Sir Humphrey (Betton)

McLaren, Agnes (Edinburgh)

McLaren, Charles (Ormiston)

McLaughlin, John (Doncaster)

McLean, Alistair (Glasgow)

McLean, Una (Strathaven)

Maclehose, Agnes (Edinburgh)

McLennan, John Ferguson (Inverness)

McLeod, Ian (Skipton)

McLeod, Norman (Campbeltown)

Maclure, William (Ayr)

McManus, Declan [Elvis Costello] (Liverpool)

McMenamin, Ciaran
(Enniskillen)
Macmillan, Chrystal
(Edinburgh)
Macmillan, Hugh Pattison
[Lord] (Glasgow)
Macmillan, John (Minigaff)
Macmillan, Sir Kenneth
(Dunfermline)
Macmillan, Kirkpatrick
(Thornhill)
McNair, Herbert (Glasgow)
McNaught, William
(Paisley)
MacNeice, Louis (Belfast)
McNeile, Herman Cyril
['Sapper'] (Bodmin)
McNeill, Florence (St
Mary's Holm)
McNeill, William (Bellshill)
MacNeill, John (Glenarm)
McNicol, Bessie (Glasgow)
Maconchy, Dame Elizabeth
(Broxbourne)
Macphail, Katherine
(Coatbridge)
Macpherson, Annie
(Campsie)
MacPherson, James
(Ruthven)
MacQuarrie, John
(Renfrew)
McShane, Ian (Blackburn)
McTaggart, John Ellis
(London)
Madden, Sir Frederick
(Portsmouth)
Madeley, Richard (Romford)
Mahon, Derek (Belfast)
Maiden, Joseph Henry
(London)
Mairet, Ethel (Barnstaple)
Major, John (London)
Makem, Tommy (Keady)

Makin, Bathsua Pell
(Southwick)
Mallowan, Sir Max Edgar
(London)
Malthus, Thomas Robert
(Dorking)
Mankowitz, Cyril Wolf
(London)
Mannin, Ethel (London)
Manning, Henry Edward
(Totteridge)
Manning, Olivia (Portsmouth)
Mannyng, Robert (Bourne)
Mansbridge, Albert
(Gloucester)
Mansel, Henry Longueville
(Cosgrove)
Mansfield, William Murray
[1st Earl] (Perth)
Manson, Sir Patrick
(Oldmeldrum)
Mantell, Gideon Algernon
(Lewes)
Manton, Irene (London)
Manton, Sidnie Milana
(London)
Mar, John Erskine [Earl]
(Alloa)
Margaret Rose [Princess]
(Glamis Castle)
Markham, Sir Clements
Robert (Stillingfleet)
Markievicz, Constance
[Countess] (London)
Markova, Dame Alicia
[Lilian Alicia Marks]
(London)
Marks, Lilian Alicia [Dame
Alicia Markova] (London)
Marks, Simon [Baron] (Leeds)
Marks, Victor (Middle
Chinnock)
Marlowe, Christopher
(Canterbury)

Marmion, Shackerley
(Aynho)
Marriner, Sir Neville
(Lincoln)
Marryat, Florence (Brighton)
Marsden, Samuel (Farsley)
Marshall, Sir John Hubert
(Chester)
Marshall, Margaret
(Stirling)
Marshall, Peter
(Coatbridge)
Marshall, Sheina (Rothesay)
Marshall, William
(Fochabers)
Marshall, William Calder
(Edinburgh)
Marshman, Joshua
(Westbury)
Marston, John
(Wardington)
Marston, John Westland
(Boston)
Marten, Henry [Harry]
(Oxford)
Martens, Conrad (London)
Martin, Archer John Porter
(London)
Martin, John (Haydon
Bridge)
Martin, Sir Theodore
(Edinburgh)
Martin-Harvey, Sir John
(Wivenhoe)
Martin-Spencer, Lilly
(Exeter)
Martineau, Harriet
(Norwich)
Martineau, James
(Norwich)
Martyn, Henry (Truro)
Marvell, Andrew
(Winestead)
Marvin, Hank [Brian

Rankin] (Newcastle upon Tyne)

Mary I [Mary Tudor] (London)

Mary II [Queen of Britain and Ireland] (London)

Mary Stewart [Queen of Scots] (Linlithgow)

Mary of Teck [Queen Mary] (London)

Masefield, John (Ledbury)

Masham, Damaris (Cambridge)

Maskelyne, John Nevil (Cheltenham)

Maskelyne, Nevil (London)

Mason, Alfred Edward (London)

Mason, James (Huddersfield)

Mason, Sir Josiah (Kidderminster)

Massey, William Ferguson (Limavady)

Masson, David (Aberdeen)

Matteo, Dominic (Dumfries)

Matthay, Tobias (London)

Matthews, Alfred Edward (Bridlington)

Matthews, Jessie (London)

Matthews, Pauline [Kiki Dee] (Bradford)

Matthews, Sir Stanley (Stoke-on-Trent)

Matthias, William James (Whitland)

Maudling, Reginald (London)

Maudsley, Henry (Giggleswick)

Maurice, Frederick Denison (Normanston)

Maw, John Nicholas (Grantham)

Mawson, Sir Douglas (Bradford)

Mayall, John (Macclesfield)

Maxton, James (Glasgow)

Maxwell, James Clerk (Edinburgh)

May, Peter Barker Howard (Reading)

May, Phil [Philip William] (Wortley)

Mayhew, Henry (London)

Maynard, Matthew Peter (Oldham)

Mayow, John (Morval)

Meade, James Edward (Swanage)

Meade, Richard John Hannay (Chepstow)

Mee, Arthur (Stapleford)

Meehan, Patrick Connolly (Glasgow)

Mellanby, Kenneth (Barrhead)

Mercer, David (Wakefield)

Mercer, Joseph (Ellesmere Port)

Meredith, George (Portsmouth)

Merriman, John Xavier (Street)

Metford, William Ellis (Taunton)

Methuen, Sir Algernon (London)

Meynell, Alice (London)

Miall, Edward (Portsmouth)

Michael, George (Bushey)

Mickle, William Julius (Langholm)

Micklewhite, Maurice [Michael Caine] (London)

Middleton, Conyers (Richmond, Yorkshire)

Miles, Bernard [Baron] (London)

Mill, James (Logie Pert)

Mill, John (Shap)

Mill, John Stuart (London)

Millais, Sir John Everett (Southampton)

Millar, John (Shotts)

Miller, Hugh (Cromarty)

Miller, James [Ewan McColl] (Salford)

Miller, Sir Jonathan Wolfe (London)

Miller, William (Glasgow)

Mills, Barbara (Chorley Wood)

Mills, Danny (Norwich)

Mills, Sir John Lewis (Felixstowe)

Milne, Alan Alexander (London)

Milne, Edward Arthur (Hull)

Milne, John (Liverpool)

Milnes, Richard Monckton [1st Baron Monckton] (London)

Milton, John (London)

Minton, Francis John (Cambridge)

Minton, Thomas (Shrewsbury)

Mitchell, Sir Peter Chalmers (Dunfermline)

Mitchell, Peter Dennis (Mitcham)

Mitchell, Reginald Joseph (Talke)

Mitchell, Warren (London)

Mitchell, William [Peter Finch] (London)

Mitchison, Naomi Mary Margaret (Edinburgh)

Mitford, John (Richmond)

Mitford, Mary Russell (Alresford)

Moffat, Robert (Ormiston)

Moir, David MacBeth (Musselburgh)

Molesworth, Sir William (London)

Mollison, James Allan (Glasgow)

Molyneux, Edward Henry (London)

Molyneux, Samuel (Chester)

Monckton, Lionel (London)

Monckton, Walter [1st Viscount] (Plaxtol)

Moncrieff, Sir Alexander (Edinburgh)

Mond, Alfred Moritz [Baron Melchett] (Farnsworth)

Monk, George [1st Duke Albemarle] (Great Potheridge)

Monkhouse, Bob (Beckenham)

Monro, Alexander (London)

Monro, Alexander [2nd] (Edinburgh)

Monsarrat, Nicholas (Liverpool)

Monson, Sir William (South Carlton)

Montagu, Ashley (London)

Montagu, Elizabeth (York)

Montagu, Lady Mary Wortley (London)

Montalembert, Charles René de (London)

Montgomery, Bernard [1st Viscount] (London)

Montgomery, James (Irvine)

Montgomery, Robert (Bath)

Moodie, Susanna (Bungay)

Moon, Lorna [Nora Wilson Low] (Strichen)

Moore, Bobby (London)

Moore, Brian (Belfast)

Moore, Edward (Abingdon)

Moore, Francis (Bridgnorth)

Moore, George Edward (London)

Moore, Gerald (Watford)

Moore, Henry Spencer (Castleford)

Moore, Sir John (Glasgow)

Moore, Roger George (London)

Moore, Thomas Sturge (Hastings)

Moores, Sir John (Manchester)

Morant, Harry [Breaker] (Bridgwater)

More, Hannah (Bristol)

More, Henry (Grantham)

More, Kenneth (Gerrard's Cross)

More, Sir Thomas [Saint] (London)

Morecambe, Eric [Eric Bartholomew] (Morecambe)

Morgan, Charles Langbridge (Bromley)

Morgan, Sir Henry (Llanrumney)

Morison, Robert (Aberdeen)

Morland, George (London)

Morley, Henry (London)

Morley, John [1st Viscount] (Blackburn)

Morley, Robert (Semley)

Morley, Thomas (Norwich)

Morris, Sir Lewis (Carmarthen)

Morris, Robert (Liverpool)

Morris, Thomas (St Andrews)

Morris, William (London)

Morrison, Herbert [Baron] (London)

Morrison, Van (Belfast)

Mort, Thomas Sutcliffe (Bolton)

Mortimer, John Clifford (London)

Mortimer, Penelope (Rhyl)

Morton, Alan Lauder (Glasgow)

Morton, Henry Vollam (Birmingham)

Morton, John (Milborne St Andrew)

Morton, John Maddiston (Pangbourne)

Morton, Thomas (Durham)

Moryson, Fynes (Cadeby)

Moseley, Henry Gwyn (Weymouth)

Moses, Sir Charles Joseph (Bolton)

Moss, Kate (Croydon)

Motherwell, William (Glasgow)

Mott, Sir Nevill Francis (Leeds)

Mottram, Ralph Hale (Norwich)

Mountbatten, Louis [1st Earl] (Windsor)

Mudge, Thomas (Exeter)

Muggeridge, Edward [Eadweard Muybridge] (Kingston-on-Thames)

Muggeridge, Malcolm (London)

Muir, Edwin (Deerness)

Muir, Jean Elizabeth (London)

Muir, John (Dunbar)

Muir, John (Glasgow)

Muir, Thomas (Glasgow)

Muir, Willa (Montrose)

Muir, Sir William (Glasgow)

Mullally, Alan David (Southend)

Muller, William James
(Bristol)
Mungo, Saint [St
Kentigern] (Culross)
Munro, Neil (Inveraray)
Murdock, William (Lugar)
Murison, David Donald
(Fraserburgh)
Murray, Alexander
(Minigaff)
Murray, Charles (Alford)
Murray, Sir James Augustus
(Denholm)
Murray, John (Edinburgh)
Murray, Lionel [Len]
[Baron] (Hadley)
Murray, Ruby (Belfast)
Murry, John Middleton
(London)
Musgrave, Thea (Edinburgh)
Mushet, David (Dalkeith)
Mushet, Robert Forester
(Coleford)
Muybridge, Eadweard [Edward
James Muggeridge]
(Kingston on Thames)
Myddelton, Sir Hugh (Galch
Hill)
Myers, Frederic William
Henry (Keswick)
Myles, Lynda (Arbroath)
Mylne, Robert (Edinburgh)

———

Nail, Jimmy [James Michael
Bradford] (Newcastle
upon Tyne)
Nairne, Carolina (Gask)
Napier, Sir Charles James
(London)
Napier, John (Edinburgh)
Napier, McVey (Glasgow)
Napier, Robert (Dumbarton)
Nares, Sir George Strong
(Aberdeen)

Nash, John (London)
Nash, Paul (London)
Nash, Richard ['Beau Nash']
(Swansea)
Nash, Sir Walter
(Kidderminster)
Nashe, Thomas (Lowestoft)
Nasmyth, Alexander
(Edinburgh)
Nasmyth, James
(Edinburgh)
Nathan, Isaac (Canterbury)
Naunton, Sir Robert
(Alderton)
Nayler, James (Ardsley)
Neagle, Dame Anna
(London)
Neale, Edward Vansittart
(Bath)
Neale, John Mason
(London)
Needham, Dorothy
(London)
Needham, Joseph (London)
Negus, Arthur George
(Reading)
Neill, Alexander Sutherland
(Kingsmuir)
Neill, Stephen Charles
(Edinburgh)
Neilson, James Beaumont
(Glasgow)
Nelson, Horatio [Viscount]
(Burnham Thorpe)
Nelson, Thomas (Edinburgh)
Nesbit, Edith (London)
Nettleship, Henry
(Kettering)
Nevill, Gary (Bury)
Nevill, Phil (Bury)
Nevins, James David [David
Niven] (London)
Nevinson, Christopher
Richard (London)

Nevinson, Henry Wood
(Leicester)
Newbery, Jessie (Paisley)
Newbolt, Sir Henry John
(Bilston)
Newby, Eric (London)
Newcomen, Thomas
(Dartmouth)
Newdigate, Sir Roger (Arbury)
Newman, Ernest (Liverpool)
Newman, Sir George
(Leominster)
Newman, John Henry
[Cardinal] (London)
Newnes, Sir George
(Matlock)
Newton, Sir Charles
Thomas (Bredwardine)
Newton, Isaac
(Woolsthorpe)
Newton-John, Olivia
(Cambridge)
Nicholson, Ben (Denham)
Nicholson, Joseph Shield
(Wrawby)
Nicholson, Sir William
(Newark)
Nicholson, Winifred
(Oxford)
Nicol, William (Edinburgh)
Nicolas, Sir Nicholas
(Dartmouth)
Nicoll, Sir William
Robertson (Lumsden)
Nicolson, Adela [Laurence
Hope] (Stoke Bishop)
Nicolson, William
(Plumbland)
Nilsen, Dennis (Fraserburgh)
Niven, David [James David
Nevins] (London)
Noke, Charles John
(Worcester)
Nollekens, Joseph (London)

Norris, John (Collingbourne Kingston)

Norrish, Ronald George (Cambridge)

North, Christopher [John Wilson] (Paisley)

North, Marianne (Hastings)

Northcote, Thomas James (Plymouth)

Norton, Caroline Elizabeth (London)

Norton, Mary (Leighton Buzzard)

Norway, Nevil Shute [Nevil Shute] (London)

Norwood, Sir Cyril (Whalley)

Nott, Sir John (Bideford)

Novello, Ivor [Ivor Novello Davies] (Cardiff)

Novello, Vincent (London)

Noyes, Alfred (Wolverhampton)

Nuffield, William [1st Viscount] (Worcester)

Nunn, Sir Thomas Percy (Bristol)

Nunn, Sir Trevor (Ipswich)

Nuttall, Thomas (Settle)

———————————————

Oakeshott, Michael Joseph (Harpenden)

Oakey, Phil (Sheffield)

Oastler, Richard (Leeds)

Oates, Lawrence Edward (London)

Oates, Titus (Oakham)

Oatley, Sir Charles (Frome)

O'Brien, Flann [Brian O'Nolan] (Strabane)

O'Brien, Mary [Dusty Springfield] (London)

Occam, William of (Ockham)

Ogden, Charles Kay (Fleetwood)

Ogdon, John Andrew Howard (Mansfield Woodhouse)

Ogilby, John (Edinburgh)

Ogilvie, St John (Banff)

Oglethorpe, James Edward (London)

Oldfield, Bruce (London)

Oldfield, Mike (Reading)

Oliphant, Margaret (Wallyford)

Olive, 'Princess' [Olivia Serres] (Warwick)

Olivier, Laurence Kerr [Baron] (Dorking)

Onions, Charles Talbut (Birmingham)

O'Nolan, Brian [Flann O'Brien] (Strabane)

Opie, John (St Agnes)

Orchardson, Sir William Quiller (Edinburgh)

Ordericus Vitalis (Atcham)

Orinda [Katherine Philips] (London)

Ormond, John (Dunvant)

Orton, Beth (Norwich)

Orton, Joe [John Kingsley] (Leicester)

Osbourne, John James (London)

Osbourne, Ozzy ['John'] (Birmingham)

O'Shaughnessy, Arthur William (London)

Otway, Thomas (Trotton)

Oughtred, William (Eton)

Ouida [Marie Louise de la Ramée] (Bury St Edmunds)

Outram, Sir James (Butterley Hall)

Ovett, Steve [Steven Michael] (Brighton)

Owen, David Anthony [Baron] (Plymouth)

Owen, John (Llanarmon)

Owen, John (Stadhampton)

Owen, Michael (Chester)

Owen, Sir Richard (Lancaster)

Owen, Robert (Newtown, Powys)

Owen, Robert Dale (Glasgow)

———————————————

Page, Sir Frederick Handley (Cheltenham)

Paget, Sir James (Yarmouth)

Paige, Elaine (Barnet)

Paine, Thomas (Thetford)

Paisley, Bob (Hetton le Hole)

Paley, William (Peterborough)

Palgrave, Francis Turner (London)

Palin, Michael Edward (Sheffield)

Palmer, Edward Henry (Cambridge)

Palmer, Robert (Batley)

Palmer, Samuel (London)

Palmerston, Henry [3rd Viscount] (London)

Panayioutou, Yorgas [George Michael] (Bushey)

Pankhurst, Adela Constantia (Manchester)

Pankhurst, Christabel Harriette (Manchester)

Pankhurst, Emmeline (Manchester)

Pankhurst, Sylvia (Manchester)

Paolozzi, Sir Eduardo Luigi (Edinburgh)

Pargeter, Edith (Horsehay)

Park, Mungo (Foulshiels)

Parke, Mary Winifred (Liverpool)

Parker, Agnes Miller (Irvine)

Parker, Joseph (Hexham)

Parker, Matthew (Norwich)

Parker, Richard (Exeter)

Parkes, Alexander (Birmingham)

Parkes, Sir Henry (Stoneleigh)

Parkinson, Cyril Northcote (Barnard Castle)

Parkinson, Norman (London)

Parry, Sir Charles Hubert (Bournemouth)

Parry, Joseph (Merthyr Tydfil)

Parry, Sir William Edward (Bath)

Parsons, Sir Charles Algernon (London)

Parsons, Robert (Nether Stowey)

Partington, James Riddick (Bolton)

Pasmore, Victor [Edwin John] (Chelsham)

Pater, Walter Horatio (London)

Paterson, William (Tinwald)

Patmore, Coventry Kersey (Woodford)

Paton, John (Fenwick)

Paton, Sir Joseph Noel (Dunfermline)

Patrick, James McIntosh (Dundee)

Patterson, Harry [Jack Higgins] (Newcastle upon Tyne)

Patteson, John Coleridge (London)

Pattinson, Hugh Lee (Alston)

Pattison, Dorothy Wyndlow (Hauxwell)

Pattison, Mark (Hornby, Yorkshire)

Paul, John [John Paul Jones] (Kirkbean)

Paxman, Jeremy (Leeds)

Paxton, Sir Joseph (Milton Bryant)

Payn, James (Cheltenham)

Payne-Gaposchkin, Cecilia (Wendover)

Payne-Smith, Robert (Chipping Camden)

Peacock, Thomas Love (Weymouth)

Pearce, Philippa (Great Shelford)

Pears, Sir Peter Neville Luard (Farnham)

Pearson, Sir Cyril Arthur (Wookey)

Pearson, Hesketh (Hawford)

Pearson, John (Great Snoring)

Pearson, Karl (London)

Pease, Edward (Darlington)

Pecock, Reginald (Laugharne)

Peel, Sir Robert (Bury)

Peele, George (London)

Pell, John (Southwick)

Pemberton, Sir Max (Birmingham)

Penderyn, Dic (Richard Lewis] (Aberavon)

Penn, William (London)

Pennant, Thomas (Downing)

Penrose, Sir Roland Algernon (London)

Pentreath, Dolly (Mousehole)

Peploe, Samuel John (Edinburgh)

Pepys, Samuel (London)

Percy, Thomas (Bridgnorth)

Perry, Fred [Frederick John] (Stockport)

Peters, Mary Elizabeth (Halewood)

Pethick-Lawrence, Emmeline (Clifton)

Peto, Sir Samuel Morton (Woking)

Petty, Sir William (Romsey)

Phelps, Samuel (Devonport)

Philips, Ambrose (Shrewsbury)

Philips, John (Bampton)

Philips, Katherine [Orinda] (London)

Philipson, Sir Robin (Broughton in Furness)

Phillip, Arthur (London)

Phillip, John (Aberdeen)

Phillips, Kevin (Hitchin)

Phillips, Peregrine (Bristol)

Phillpotts, Dame Bertha (Bedford)

Piccaver, Alfred (Long Sutton)

Pick, Frank (Spalding)

Pickering, Sir George (Whalton)

Picton, Sir Thomas (Poyston)

Piggott, Lester Keith (Wantage)

Pilbeam, David Roger (Brighton)

Pilcher, Rosamunde (Lelant)

Pilkington, Sir Alastair (Newbury)

Pindar, Peter [John Wolcot]
(Dodbrooke)
Pinero, Sir Arthur Wing
(London)
Pinkerton, Allan (Glasgow)
Piper, John (Epsom)
Pirie, Gordon Douglas
(Leeds)
Pitcairne, Archibald
(Edinburgh)
Pitman, Benjamin
(Trowbridge)
Pitman, Sir Isaac
(Trowbridge)
Pitman, Jenny (Hoby)
Pitscottie, Lindsay Robert
(Pitscottie)
Pitt, Thomas (Blandford St
Mary)
Pitt, William ['The Elder']
(London)
Pitt, William ['The
Younger'] (London)
Pitter, Ruth (Ilford)
Pitt-Rivers, Rosalind
(London)
Place, Francis (London)
Planche, James Robinson
(London)
Plater, Alan Frederick
(Newcastle upon Tyne)
Playfair, John (Benvie)
Playfair, William Henry
(London)
Pleasance, Sir Donald
(Worksop)
Plimsoll, Samuel (Bristol)
Plowright, Joan (Brigg)
Plume, Thomas (Maldon)
Plunket, William
Conyngham (Enniskillen)
Pococke, Edward (Oxford)
Polding, John Bede
(Liverpool)

Pole, William (Birmingham)
Pollard, Albert Frederick
(Ryde)
Pollitt, Harry (Droylesden)
Pollock, Sir Frederick
(London)
Pope, Alexander (London)
Pope, Sir William Jackson
(London)
Pope-Hennessy, Sir John
(London)
Popham, Sir John
(Huntworth)
Porson, Richard (East
Ruston)
Portal, Charles Frederick
[1st Viscount]
(Hungerford)
Porteous, John (Edinburgh)
Porter, Anna Maria
(Durham)
Porter, Eric Richard
(London)
Porter, Sir George
(Stainforth)
Porter, Helen Kemp
(Farnham)
Porter, Jane (Durham)
Porter, Rodney Robert
(Newton le Willows)
Postan, Eileen (Altrincham)
Pott, Percival (London)
Potter, Beatrix (London)
Potter, John (Wakefield)
Pounds, John (Portsmouth)
Powell, Anthony Dymoke
(London)
Powell, Cecil Frank
(Tonbridge)
Powell, Frederick York
(London)
Powell, Michael
(Bekesbourne)
Powys, John Cowper (Shirley)

Powys, Llewelyn
(Dorchester)
Powys, Theodore Francis
(Shirley)
Poynting, John Henry
(Manchester)
Praagh, Dame Peggy van
(London)
Pratt, William Henry [Boris
Karloff] (London)
Preece, Sir William Henry
(Caernarfon)
Prescott, John Leslie
(Prestatyn)
Price, Alan (Durham)
Price, Ellen [Mrs Henry
Wood] (Worcester)
Price, Henry Habberley
(Neath)
Price, Margaret
(Blackwood)
Price, Richard (Tynton)
Prideaux, Humphrey
(Padstow)
Priestley, John Boynton
(Bradford)
Priestley, Joseph (Leeds)
Prince, Henry James (Bath)
Pringle, Thomas
(Blakelaw)
Pritchett, Sir Victor Sawdon
(Ipswich)
Procter, Adelaide Ann
[Mary Berwick] (London)
Procter, Bryan Waller
[Barry Cornwall] (Leeds)
Procter, Dod (London)
Proctor, Richard Anthony
(London)
Prout, Ebenezer (Oundle)
Prout, Margaret (London)
Prout, Samuel (Plymouth)
Prout, William (Horton,
Glos.)

Prys-Jones, Arthur Glyn
(Denbigh)
Pugin, Augustus Welby
(London)
Purcell, Henry (London)
Purchas, Samuel (Thaxted)
Purves, Peter (Preston)
Pusey, Edward Bouverie
(Pusey)
Puttnam, Sir David Terence
(London)
Pye, Edith (London)
Pye, John David (Mansfield)
Pym, Barbara [Mary
Compton] (Oswestry)

Quant, Mary (London)
Quayle, Sir Anthony
(Ainsdale)
Quennell, Sir Peter
Courtney (London)
Quick, Robert Hebert
(London)
Quiller-Couch, Sir Arthur
(Bodmin)
Quilter, Roger (Brighton)

Radcliffe, Ann (London)
Radcliffe, John (Wakefield)
Radcliffe-Brown, Alfred
Reginald (Birmingham)
Rae, Barbara (Edinburgh)
Raeburn, Agnes Middleton
(Glasgow)
Raeburn, Sir Henry
(Edinburgh)
Raglan, Fitzroy James
[Baron] (Badminton)
Raikes, Robert (Gloucester)
Raleigh, Sir Walter (Hayes
Barton)
Ramée, Marie Louise de la
[Ouida] (Bury St
Edmunds)

Ramprakash, Mark
Ravindra (Bushey)
Ramsay, Allan [Father]
(Leadhills)
Ramsay, Allan [Son]
(Edinburgh)
Ramsay, Andrew ['Chevalier
de Ramsay'] (Ayr)
Ramsay, Sir Bertram Home
(London)
Ramsay, Edward
Bannerman (Aberdeen)
Ramsay, Sir William
(Glasgow)
Ramsay, Sir William
(Glasgow)
Ramsey, Sir Alfred
(Dagenham)
Ramsey, Frank Plumpton
(Cambridge)
Ramsey, Ian Thomas
(Manchester)
Ramsey, Michael [Baron]
(Cambridge)
Randolph, Thomas
(Newnham)
Rank, James Arthur [1st
Baron] (Hull)
Rankin, Brian [Hank
Marvin] (Newcastle upon
Tyne)
Rankine, William John
(Edinburgh)
Ransome, Arthur Mitchell
(Leeds)
Ransome, Robert (Wells-
next-the-Sea)
Rantzen, Esther
(Berkhamsted)
Rastell, John (Coventry)
Rastrick, John Urpeth
(Morpeth)
Rathbone, Eleanor Florence
(Liverpool)

Rattigan, Sir Terence
Mervyn (London)
Rattle, Sir Simon (Liverpool)
Raverat, Gwendolen
(Cambridge)
Rawlinson, Sir Henry
Creswicke (Chadlington)
Rawsthorne, Alan
(Haslingden)
Ray, John (Black Notley)
Rayleigh, Robert John [4th
Baron] (Terling)
Raymond, Rene [James
Hadley Chase] (London)
Rea, Chris (Middlesbrough)
Read, Sir Herbert
(Kirbymoorside)
Rearden, Raymond
(Tredegar)
Recorde, Robert (Tenby)
Redgrave, Sir Michael
(Bristol)
Redgrave, Vanessa (London)
Redknapp, Jamie (Barton
on Sea)
Redpath, Anne (Galashiels)
Redpath, James (Berwick
on Tweed)
Redpath, Jean (Edinburgh)
Reed, Sir Carol (London)
Rees-Mogg, William
[Baron] (Bristol)
Reeve, Clara (Ipswich)
Reiby, Molly (Bury)
Reid, Beryl (Hereford)
Reid, Sir George Houstoun
(Johnstone)
Reid, James Scott
Cumberland [Lord] (Drem)
Reid, Thomas (Strachan)
Reid, Thomas Mayne
(Ballyroney)
Reid, Sir William
(Kinglassie)

Reith, John [1st Baron]
(Stonehaven)
Rendel, Stuart [1st Baron]
(Plymouth)
Rendell, Ruth [Ruth
Barbara Grasemann]
(London)
Renfrew, Andrew Colin
[Baron] (Stockton-on-
Tees)
Rennie, John (East Linton)
Renshaw, William Charles
(Cheltenham)
Renwick, James (Moniaive)
Renwick, James (Liverpool)
Repton, Humphrey (Bury St
Edmunds)
Reynolds, George William
(Sandwich)
Reynolds, Sir Joshua
(Plympton)
Reynolds, Osbourne (Belfast)
Rhead, Charlotte (Stoke-
on-Trent)
Rhind, Alexander Henry
(Wick)
Rhodes, Cecil John
(Bishop's Stortford)
Rhodes, Wilfred
(Kirkheaton)
Rhodes, Zandra (Chatham)
Rhondda, Margaret Haig
[Viscountess] (London)
Ricardo, David (London)
Ricardo, Sir Harry Ralph
(London)
Rice, James (Northampton)
Rich, Edmund [St Edmund]
(Abingdon)
Richard I ['Lionheart', King
of England] (Oxford)
Richard III [King of
England] (Fotheringhay
Castle)

Richard, Henry (Tregaron)
Richard of Wallingford
(Wallingford)
Richards, Alun (Pontypridd)
Richards, Ceri (Dunvant)
Richards, Sir Gordon
(Oakengates)
Richards, Henry Brinley
(Carmarthen)
Richards, Ivor Armstrong
(Sandbach)
Richards, Keith (Dartford)
Richardson, Charles
(Norwood)
Richardson, Dorothy Miller
(Abingdon)
Richardson, Sir John
(Dumfries)
Richardson, Miranda
(Southport)
Richardson, Sir Owen
Willans (Dewsbury)
Richardson, Sir Ralph
(Cheltenham)
Richardson, Samuel
(Mackworth)
Richardson, Tony [Cecil
Antonio] (Shipley)
Rickman, Thomas
(Maidenhead)
Riddell, George [1st Baron]
(Duns)
Ridge, William Pett
(Chatham)
Ridley, Nicholas (Newcastle
upon Tyne)
Ridpath, George (Ladykirk)
Rieu, Emile Victor (London)
Rigg, Diana (Doncaster)
Riley, Bridget Louise
(London)
Ritchie, Anne Isabella
[Lady] (London)
Ritchie, Jean (Edinburgh)

Ritson, Joseph (Stockton-
on-Tees)
Rivers, William Halse
(Luton, Kent)
Rivington, Charles
(Chesterfield)
Rix, Sir Brian Norman
(Cottingham)
Roache, Linus (Burnley)
Roache, William (Ilkeston)
Robens, Alfred [Lord]
(Manchester)
Roberts, David (Edinburgh)
Roberts, Kate (Rhosgadfan)
Roberts, Thomas William
(Dorchester)
Roberts-Austen, Sir William
Chandler (London)
Robertson, Belinda (Glasgow)
Robertson, George Croom
(Aberdeen)
Robertson, Grace
(Manchester)
Robertson, James [Hugh
Haliburton] (Milnathort)
Robertson, Jeannie
(Aberdeen)
Robertson, Joseph
(Aberdeen)
Robertson, Muriel
(Glasgow)
Robertson, Thomas William
(Newark-on-Trent)
Robertson, William
(Borthwick)
Robertson, Sir William
Robert (Welbourn)
Robey, Sir George (Herne
Hill)
Robins, Benjamin (Bath)
Robinson, Gower [Ursula
Bloom] (Chelmsford)
Robinson, Henry Crabb
(Bury St Edmunds)

Robinson, Henry Peach (Ludlow)

Robinson, Jancis (Carlisle)

Robinson, Joan Violet (Camberley)

Robinson, John (Sturton-le-Steeple)

Robinson, John Arthur Thomas (Canterbury)

Robinson, Mary 'Perdita' (Bristol)

Robinson, Sir Robert (Chesterfield)

Robinson, William Heath (London)

Robson, Dame Flora (South Shields)

Rochester, John Wilmot [Earl] (Ditchley)

Roddick, Anita (Brighton)

Rodney, George Brydges [1st Baron] (London)

Roe, Sir Edwin Alliot Verdon (Manchester)

Roebuck, John (Sheffield)

Roger of Hovedon (Howden)

Rogers, Anton (Wisbech)

Rogers, James Edwin (West Meon)

Rogers, John (Aston)

Rogers, Samuel (London)

Rohmer, Sax [Arthur Sarsfield Ward] (Birmingham)

Rolle de Hampole, Richard (Thornton)

Rolls, Charles Stewart (London)

Romney, George (Dalton-in-Furness)

Ronalds, Sir Francis (London)

Rook, Jean (Hull)

Roscoe, Sir Henry Enfield (London)

Roscoe, William (Liverpool)

Rose, Iain Murray (Birmingham)

Rose, Sir John (Turriff)

Rosebery, Archibald [5th Earl] (London)

Rosenberg, Isaac (Bristol)

Rosenthal, Jack Morris (Manchester)

Ross, Sir James Clark (London)

Ross, Sir John (Balsarroch)

Ross, William [Lord] (Ayr)

Rosse, William Parsons [3rd Earl] (York)

Rossetti, Christina (London)

Rossetti, Dante Gabriel (London)

Rossiter, Leonard (Liverpool)

Rothenstein, Sir William (Bradford)

Rous, Francis (Dittisham)

Routledge, George (Brampton)

Rowbotham, Sheila (Leeds)

Rowe, Nicholas (Little Barford)

Rowlandson, Thomas (London)

Rowling, Joanne K. (Yate)

Rowntree, Benjamin Seebohm (York)

Rowntree, Joseph (York)

Rowse, Alfred Leslie (St Austell)

Rowson, Susannah (Portsmouth)

Royce, Sir Frederick Henry (Alwalton)

Royden, Agnes Maude (Liverpool)

Royds, Mabel (Little Barford)

Rubbra, Edmund

(Northampton)

Ruddiman, Thomas (Boyndie)

Ruddock, Joan (Pontypool)

Ruggles-Brise, Sir Evelyn (Finchingfield)

Runcie, Robert Alexander [Baron] (Crosby)

Runcorn, Stanley Keith (Southport)

Rush, Ian (St Asaph)

Rushforth, Winifred (Winchburgh)

Rushworth, John (Warkworth)

Ruskin, John (London)

Russell, Sir Edward (Frampton-on-Severn)

Russell, George (Stillington)

Russell, George William (Lurgan)

Russell, Jack [Robert Charles] (Stroud)

Russell, John (Guildford)

Russell, John [1st Earl] (London)

Russell, John [Jack] (Dartmouth)

Russell, Ken [Henry Kenneth] (Southampton)

Russell of Killowen, Charles [1st Baron] (Newry)

Russell, Robert Charles [Jack], (Stroud)

Russell, William Martin (Liverpool)

Rutherford, Daniel (Edinburgh)

Rutherford, Dame Margaret (London)

Rutherford, Samuel (Nisbet)

Ryan, Desmond (London)

Ryder, Sue [Baroness] (Leeds)

Rye, Maria (London)
Rylands, John (St Helens)
Ryle, Gilbert (Brighton)
Ryle, Sir Martin (Brighton)
Rymer, Thomas
  (Northallerton)

Sacheverell, Henry
  (Marlborough)
Sackville-West, Vita
  [Victoria Mary]
  (Sevenoaks)
Sadleir, Michael (Oxford)
Sadler, Flora (Aberdeen)
Sadler, Sir Michael Ernest
  (Barnsley)
Sadler, Michael Thomas
  (Snelston)
Sainsbury, Alan John
  [Baron] (London)
Saint Germain, Christopher
  (Shilton)
Saintsbury, George Edward
  (Southampton)
Saint Vincent, John Jervis
  [Earl] (Stone)
Salisbury, Sir Edward James
  (Harpenden)
Salt, Sir Titus (Morley)
Sampson, Agnes
  (Haddington)
Samuel, Herbert [1st
  Viscount] (Liverpool)
Sancroft, William
  (Fressingfield)
Sandby, Paul (Nottingham)
Sanderson, Tessa
  (Wolverhampton)
Sandwich, John Montagu
  [1st Earl] (Barnwell)
Sandys, George
  (Bishopthorpe)
Sanger, Frederick
  (Rendcombe)

Sankey, John [Viscount]
  (Moreton-in-Marsh)
Santley, Sir Charles
  (Liverpool)
'Sapper' [Herman Cyril
  McNeile] (Bodmin)
Sargent, Sir Malcolm Watts
  (Ashford)
Sassoon, Siegfried Lorraine
  (Brenchley)
Saunders, Dame Cicely
  (Barnet)
Saunders, Jennifer (Sleaford)
Savage, Robbie (Wrexham)
Savery, Thomas (Shilstone)
Savile, Sir Henry (Bradley)
Savile, Jimmy [James
  Wilson Vincent] (Leeds)
Saxton, Christopher
  (Sowood)
Sayce, Archibald Henry
  (Shirehampton)
Sayers, Dorothy Leigh
  (Oxford)
Sayers, Tom (London)
Scales, Prunella [Margaret
  Rumney] (Abinger)
Scarfe, Gerald (London)
Scargill, Arthur (Leeds)
Schlesinger, John Richard
  (London)
Scholes, Paul (Salford)
Scholes, Percy Alfred
  (Leeds)
Schreiber, [Lady] Charlotte
  (Uffington)
Scofield, [David] Paul
  (Hurstpierpoint)
Scott, Charles Prestwich
  (Bath)
Scott, Cyril Meir (Oxton)
Scott, David (Edinburgh)
Scott, Francis George
  (Hawick)

Scott, Sir George Gilbert
  (Gawcott)
Scott, Michael (Durham)
Scott, Paul Mark (London)
Scott, Sir Peter Markham
  (London)
Scott, Robert Falcon
  (Devonport)
Scott, Sheila (Worcester)
Scott, Sir Walter (Edinburgh)
Scott, William (Greenock)
Scott, William Bell
  (Edinburgh)
Scott-Thomas, Kristen
  (Redruth)
Scroggs, Sir William
  (Deddington)
Seaman, David (Rotherham)
Searle, Humphrey (Oxford)
Searle, Ronald William
  (Cambridge)
Secombe, Sir Harry
  (Swansea)
Seddon, Richard John
  (Eccleston)
Sedgwick, Adam (Dent)
Seguier, William (London)
Selbourne, Roundell [1st
  Earl] (Mixbury)
Selby, Prideaux John
  (Alnwick)
Selden, John (Worthing)
Seligman, Charles Gabriel
  (London)
Selkirk, Alexander (Largo)
Sellers, Peter (Southsea)
Selwyn-Lloyd, John [Baron]
  (Liverpool)
Senior, Nassau William
  (Compton Beauchamp)
Serres, Olivia ['Princess
  Olive'] (Warwick)
Service, Robert William
  (Preston)

Seton, Ernest Thompson (South Shields)

Settle, Elkanah (Dunstable)

Seward, Sir Albert Charles (Lancaster)

Seward, Anna (Eyam)

Sewell, Anna (Great Yarmouth)

Shaffer, Peter (Liverpool)

Shaftesbury, Anthony [1st Earl] (Wimborne St Giles)

Shaftesbury, Anthony [7th Earl] (London)

Shakespeare, John (Snitterfield)

Shakespeare, William (Stratford-on-Avon)

Sharman, Helen (Sheffield)

Sharp, Cecil James (London)

Sharp, Granville (Durham)

Sharp, James (Banff)

Sharp, William (Paisley)

Sharpe, Charles (Hoddom Castle)

Sharpey-Schafer, Sir Edward (London)

Shaw, Anna Howard (Newcastle upon Tyne)

Shaw, Richard Norman (Edinburgh)

Shaw, Sandie (Dagenham)

Shaw, Sir William Napier (Birmingham)

Shaw-Lefevre, George John [Baron Eversley] (London)

Shearer, Alan (Newcastle upon Tyne)

Shearer, Moira (Dunfermline)

Sheepshanks, John (Leeds)

Shelley, Mary Wollstonecraft (London)

Shelley, Percy Bysshe (Horsham)

Shepherd, David Robert (Bideford)

Sheppard, David Stuart (Reigate)

Sheppard, Hugh Richard (Windsor)

Sheppard, Jack (London)

Sheppard, Kate [Catherine Wilson] (Liverpool)

Sheraton, Thomas (Stockton-on-Tees)

Sherbrooke, Robert Lowe [1st Viscount] (Bingham)

Sheriff, Lawrence (Rugby)

Sherriff, Robert Cedric (Kingston on Thames)

Sherrin, Ned [Edward George] (Low Ham)

Sherrington, Sir Charles Scott (London)

Sherwood, Mary (Stanford, Worcestershire)

Sherwood, Timothy (St Albans)

Shield, William (Swalwell)

Shilton, Peter (Leicester)

Shinwell, Emmanuel [Baron] (London)

Shipton, Mother (Knaresborough)

Shirley, James (London)

Shockley, William Bradford (London)

Short, Sir Frank (Stourbridge)

Short, Nigel (Atherton)

Shorthouse, Joseph Henry (Birmingham)

Shute, Nevil [Nevil Shute Norway] (London)

Sibbald, Sir Robert (Edinburgh)

Sibley, Dame Antoinette (Bromley)

Siddons, Sarah (Brecon)

Sidgwick, Henry (Skipton)

Sidgwick, Nevil Vincent (Oxford)

Sidney, Algernon (Penshurst)

Sidney, Sir Philip (Penshurst)

Sieff, Israel Moses [Baron] (Manchester)

Siepman, Mary (Englefield Green)

Sillitoe, Alan (Nottingham)

Sim, Alastair (Edinburgh)

Simeon, Charles (Reading)

Simmons, Jean (London)

Simon, John Allsebrook [1st Viscount] (Bath)

Simpson, Sir George Clarke (Derby)

Simpson, Sir James Young (Bathgate)

Simpson, Martin (Scunthorpe)

Simpson, Myrtle (Aldershot)

Simpson, Robert Wilfred (Leamington)

Simpson, Thomas (Nuneaton)

Simpson, Tommy [Thomas] (Easington)

Sinclair, Sir Clive Marles (Richmond, Surrey)

Sinclair, John Gordon (Glasgow)

Sinclair, May (Rock Ferry)

Sinden, Donald Alfred (Plymouth)

Siouxsie Sioux [Susan Dallion] (Bromley)

Sitwell, Dame Edith (Scarborough)

Sitwell, Sir Osbert (London)

Sitwell, Sir Sacheverell (Scarborough)

Skeat, Walter William (London)

Skene, William Forbes (Inverie)

Skinner, James Scott (Banchory)

Skinner, John (Birse)

Slade, Felix (Halsteads)

Slater, Samuel (Belper)

Sleep, Wayne (Plymouth)

Slessor, Mary (Aberdeen)

Slim, William [1st Viscount] (Bristol)

Sloane, Sir Hans (Killyleagh)

Small, Annie (Redding, Falkirk)

Smart, Christopher (Shipbourne)

Smeaton, John (Austhorpe)

Smellie, William (Edinburgh)

Smiles, Samuel (Haddington)

Smillie, Robert (Belfast)

Smith, Adam (Kirkcaldy)

Smith, Alexander (Kilmarnock)

Smith, Delia (Woking)

Smith, Dodie (Manchester)

Smith, Florence [Stevie Smith] (Hull)

Smith, George (London)

Smith, Harvey [Robert] (Bingley)

Smith, James (Deanston)

Smith, Sir James Edward (Norwich)

Smith, John (Dalmally)

Smith, John (Willoughby)

Smith, John Stafford (Gloucester)

Smith, Madeleine Hamilton (Glasgow)

Smith, Maggie [Dame Margaret Natalie] (Ilford)

Smith, Sir Matthew Arnold (Halifax)

Smith, Ronald William Parkinson [Norman Parkinson] (London)

Smith, Stevie [Florence Margaret] (Hull)

Smith, Thomas Southwood (Martock)

Smith, William (Churchill)

Smith, Sir William (London)

Smith, William Henry (London)

Smith, William Robertson (Keig)

Smith, Sir William Sidney (London)

Smithers, Leonard Charles (Sheffield)

Smithson, Alison (Sheffield)

Smollett, Tobias George (Cardross)

Smyth, Dame Ethel Mary (London)

Smythe, Francis Sydney (Maidstone)

Smythe, Pat (London)

Smythe, Reginald Smith (Hartlepool)

Snell, Hannah (Worcester)

Snell, John (Colmonell)

Snow, Charles Percy [1st Baron] (Leicester)

Snow, John (York)

Snowdon, Anthony Armstrong Jones [1st Earl] (London)

Soane, Sir John (Goring)

Soddy, Frederick (Eastbourne)

Solomon, Solomon Joseph (London)

Somers, John [1st Baron] (Worcester)

Somervell, Sir Arthur (Windermere)

Somerville, Mary (Jedburgh)

Sorabji, Kaikhosru Shapurji (London)

Sorby, Henry Clifton (Sheffield)

Sorley, Charles Hamilton (Aberdeen)

Southampton, Henry [3rd Earl] (Cowdray)

Sothern, Edward Askew (Liverpool)

Soutar, William (Perth)

Southey, Robert (Bristol)

Southgate, Gareth (Watford)

Spark, Dame Muriel (Edinburgh)

Spedding, James (Mirehouse)

Speke, John Hanning (Ilminster)

Spence, Catherine Helen (Melrose)

Spence, James Lewis (Broughty Ferry)

Spence, Peter (Brechin)

Spencer, Diana [Princess of Wales] (Sandringham)

Spencer, Herbert (Derby)

Spencer, Sir Stanley (Cookham)

Spencer, Sir Walter Baldwin (Manchester)

Spender, John Alfred (Bath)

Spender, Sir Stephen (London)

Spens, Sir William (Glasgow)

Spenser, Edmund (London)

Spilsbury, Sir Bernard (Leamington Hastings)

Spode, Josiah (Stoke-on-Trent)

Spottiswood, Alicia Ann [Lady] (Westruther)

Spring, Howard (Cardiff)

Springfield, Dusty [Mary O'Brien] (London)

Spry, Constance (Derby)

Spurgeon, Charles Haddon (Kelvedon)

Squire, Sir John Collings (Plymouth)

Stabler, Harold (Levens)

Stafford-Clark, Max (Cambridge)

Stair, John Dalrymple [2nd Earl] (Edinburgh)

Stalker, James (Crieff)

Stamp, Sir Lawrence Dudley (London)

Standish, Myles (Ormskirk)

Stanford, Trevor [Russ Conway] (Bristol)

Stanhope, Philip Henry [5th Earl] (Walmer)

Stanier, Sir William Arthur (Swindon)

Stanley, Sir Henry Morton (Denbigh)

Stanley, John (London)

Stanley, Thomas (Cumberlow Green)

Stapledon, Walter de (Annery)

Stapleton, Thomas (Henfield)

Starkey, Richard [Ringo Starr] (Liverpool)

Starley, James (Albourne)

Starr, Ringo [Richard Starkey] (Liverpool)

Statham, John Brian (Manchester)

Stead, William Thomas (Embleton)

Steed, Henry Wickham (Long Melford)

Steel, Flora Annie (London)

Steele, Tommy [Tommy Hicks] (London)

Steell, Sir John (Aberdeen)

Steer, Philip Wilson (Birkenhead)

Stein, Jock (Burnbank)

Stephen, James (Poole)

Stephen, Sir Leslie (London)

Stephens, Joseph Rayner (Edinburgh)

Stephens, Meic (Treforest)

Stephenson, George (Wylam)

Stephenson, John Patrick (Stebbing)

Stephenson, Marjorie (Cambridge)

Stephenson, Robert (Willington Quay)

Steptoe, Patrick Christopher (Witney)

Stevens, Alfred (Blandford Forum)

Stevens, Williamina [Fleming] (Dundee)

Stevenson, Robert (Glasgow)

Stevenson, Robert Louis (Edinburgh)

Stevenson, Ronald (Blackburn)

Stevenson, Savourna (West Linton)

Stewart, Al (Glasgow)

Stewart, Alan James (Merton)

Stewart, Belle (Caputh)

Stewart, Dugald (Edinburgh)

Stillingfleet, Edward (Cranborne)

Sting [b.Gordon Sumner] (Newcastle upon Tyne)

Stirling, James (Garden)

Stirling, James Hutchison (Glasgow)

Stirling, Mary Ann (London)

Stirling, Patrick (Kilmarnock)

Stirling, Robert (Cloag)

Stirling, William [1st Earl] (Alva)

Stobart, Eddie [Edward] (Hesket Newmarket)

Stobart, Kathy (South Shields)

Stocks, Baroness Mary (London)

Stokesley, John (Collyweston)

Stokowski, Leopold Antonin (London)

Stonehouse, John Thompson (Southampton)

Stopes, Marie (Edinburgh)

Storace, Nancy (London)

Storey, David Malcolm (Wakefield)

Storkey, Elaine (Wakefield)

Stout, George Frederick (South Shields)

Stow, David (Paisley)

Strachan, Douglas (Aberdeen)

Strachey, Giles Lytton (London)

Strachey, John St Loe (Guildford)

Strange, Sir Robert (Kirkwall)

Strathcona, Donald [1st Baron] (Forres)

Streatfield, Noel (Amberley)

Street-Porter, Janet (London)

Stringfellow, John (Sheffield)

Strong, Leonard Alfred George (Plymouth)
Stroud, William (Bristol)
Strutt, Joseph (Springfield)
Stuart, John (Edinburgh)
Stuart, John McDouall (Dysart)
Stubbs, George (Liverpool)
Stubbs, William (Knaresborough)
Sturge, Joseph (Elberton)
Sturgeon, William (Whittington)
Such, Peter (Helensburgh)
Suess, Eduard (London)
Sugden, Samuel (Leeds)
Sullivan, Sir Arthur (London)
Sullivan, James (Cardiff)
Sully, Thomas (Horncastle)
Summerskill, Baroness Edith (London)
Sumner, Gordon [Sting] (Newcastle upon Tyne)
Sumner, John [Viscount] (Manchester)
Sumner, John Bird (Kenilworth)
Sumner, Mary (Manchester)
Surrey, Henry Howard [Earl] (Hunsdon)
Surtees, John (Tatsfield)
Surtees, Robert (Durham)
Surtees, Robert Smith (Durham)
Sutcliff, Rosemary (West Clandon)
Sutherland, Graham Vivian (London)
Sutherland, Robert Garioch (Edinburgh)
Sutro, Alfred (London)
Swainson, William (Hoylake)

Swan, Sir Joseph Wilson (Sunderland)
Swann, Donald (Llanelli)
Swettenham, Sir Frank (Belper)
Swinburne, Algernon Charles (London)
Swinburne, Sir James (Inverness)
Swinton, Alan Archibald (Edinburgh)
Sydenham, Thomas (Wynford Eagle)
Sykes, Eric (Oldham)
Sylvester, James Joseph (London)
Syme, James (Edinburgh)
Symington, William (Leadhills)
Symonds, John Addington (Bristol)
Symons, Arthur William (Milford Haven)
Symons, George James (London)
Synge, Richard Laurence (Chester)

Tabor, June (Warwick)
Tait, Archibald Campbell (Edinburgh)
Tait, Peter Guthrie (Dalkeith)
Talbot, William Henry Fox (Evershot)
Talfourd, Sir Thomas Noon (Reading)
Tallis, Thomas (London)
Tandy, Jessica (London)
Tannahill, Robert (Paisley)
Tansley, Sir Arthur George (London)
Tarleton, Sir Banastre (Liverpool)

Tassie, James (Glasgow)
Tate, Sir Henry (Chorley)
Tattersall, Richard (Hurstwood)
Taverner, John (Boston)
Taylor, Alfred Edward (Oundle)
Taylor, Elizabeth (London)
Taylor, Elizabeth [Elizabeth Coles] (Reading)
Taylor, Ernest Archibald (Greenock)
Taylor, Sir Geoffrey Ingram (London)
Taylor, Sir Henry (Bishop Middleham)
Taylor, Isaac (Stanford Rivers)
Taylor, John (Gloucester)
Taylor, John Edward (Ilminster)
Taylor, John Henry (Northam)
Taylor, Rowland (Rothbury)
Taylor, Tom (Sunderland)
Tchalenko, Janice (Rugby)
Telford, Thomas (Westerkirk)
Tempest, Dame Marie (London)
Temple, William (Exeter)
Tenison, Thomas (Cottenham)
Tennant, Charles (Ochiltree)
Tennant, Emma (London)
Tennant, Smithson (Selby)
Tennant, William (Anstruther)
Tenniel, Sir John (London)
Tennyson, Alfred [1st Baron] (Somersby)
Tenderton, Charles Abbott [1st Baron] (Canterbury)
Terry, Daniel (Bath)

Terry, Dame Ellen
(Coventry)
Tey, Josephine [Elizabeth
MacKintosh] (Inverness)
Thatcher, Margaret Hilda
(Grantham)
Theed, William (Trentham)
Theobald, Lewis
(Sittingbourne)
Thirkell, Angela Margaret
(London)
Thirlwall, Connop (London)
Thomas, Brandon
(Liverpool)
Thomas Dylan Marlais
(Swansea)
Thomas, James Henry
(Newport)
Thomas, Margaret Haig
[Viscountess Rhondda]
(London)
Thomas, Philip Edward
(London)
Thomas, Ronald Stuart
(Cardiff)
Thomas of Woodstock
(Woodstock)
Thomas the Rhymer
(Earlston)
Thompson, Alexander
[Greek] (Balfron)
Thompson, Sir D'Arcy
Wentworth (Edinburgh)
Thompson, Emma (London)
Thompson, Flora June
(Juniper Hill)
Thompson, Francis
(Preston)
Thompson, Silvanus Phillips
(York)
Thomson, Sir Charles
Wyville (Linlithgow)
Thomson, David Couper
(Dundee)

Thomson, Elihu
(Manchester)
Thomson, George
(Limekilns)
Thomson, Sir George Paget
(Cambridge)
Thomson, James (Belfast)
Thomson, James (Ednam)
Thomson, James (Port
Glasgow)
Thomson, Joseph (Penpont)
Thomson, Sir Joseph John
(Manchester)
Thomson, Robert William
(Stonehaven)
Thomson, William [Baron
Kelvin] (Belfast)
Thorburn, Archibald
(Lasswade)
Thorndike, Dame Sybil
(Gainsborough)
Thorneycroft, George
Edward [Baron] (Dunston)
Thornhill, Sir James
(Melcombe Regis)
Thornycroft, Sir William
Hamo (London)
Thorpe, Graham Paul
(Farnham)
Thorpe-Davie, Cedric
(London)
Thring, Edward (Alford)
Thring, Lord Henry (Alford)
Thurlow, Edward [1st
Baron] (Bracon Ash)
Tickell, Thomas (Bridekirk)
Tidy, Bill [William Edward]
(Liverpool)
Tillett, Benjamin (Bristol)
Tilley,Vesta [Matilda
Powles] (Worcester)
Tillotson, John (Sowerby)
Tilman, Harold William
(Wallasey)

Tilston, Steve (Liverpool)
Tinsley, Pauline (Wigan)
Tippett, Sir Michael
(London)
Titchener, Edward Bradford
(Chichester)
Titchmarsh, Alan (Ilkley)
Titmus, Frederick John
(London)
Titterton, Sir Ernest William
(Tamworth)
Tizard, Sir Henry Thomas
(Gillingham)
Todd, Alexander [Baron
Trumpington] (Glasgow)
Tomkins, Thomas (St
David's)
Tompion, Thomas (Northill)
Tonks, Henry (Solihull)
Toplady, Augustus
Montague (Farnham)
Torrence, David (Edinburgh)
Torrence, Ernest
(Edinburgh)
Torvill, Jayne (Nottingham)
Tourtel, Mary (Canterbury)
Tout, Thomas Frederick
(London)
Tovey, Sir Donald Francis
(Eton)
Townsend, Sue (Leicester)
Toynbee, Arnold (London)
Toynbee, Arnold Joseph
(London)
Tradescant, John [the
younger] (Meopham)
Traherne, Thomas (Hereford)
Travers, Benjamin (London)
Tredgold, Thomas (Brandon,
Durham)
Tree, Sir Herbert Beerbohm
(London)
Treece, Henry (Wednesbury)
Tremain, Rose (London)

Trenchard, Hugh [1st Viscount] (Taunton)

Trescothick, Marcus Edward (Bristol)

Trevelyan, George Macaulay (Stratford-on-Avon)

Trevelyan, Sir George Otto [2nd Baronet] (Rothley)

Treves, Sir Frederick (Dorchester)

Trevithick, Richard (Illogan)

Trevor-Roper, Hugh Redwald [Baron Dacre] (Glanton)

Trimmer, Sarah (Ipswich)

Trinder, Thomas Edward [Tommy] (London)

Tripp, John (Bargoed)

Tristram, Henry Baker (Eglingham)

Trollope, Anthony (London)

Trollope, Frances (Bristol)

Troughton, Edward (Corney)

Trueman, Fred [Frederick Sewards] (Stainton)

Tryon, Sir George (Bulwick)

Tuckwell, Gertrude Mary (Oxford)

Tudor, Anthony [Willliam Cook] (London)

Tufnell, Philip Clive Roderick (Barnet)

Tuke, Samuel (York)

Tulloch, John (Bridge of Earn)

Tunnicliffe, Charles Frederick (Langley)

Tunstall, Cuthbert (Hackforth)

Turing, Alan Mathison (London)

Turnbull, Colin (London)

Turnbull, William (Dundee)

Turner, Charles [Tennyson] (Somersby)

Turner, Ethel Sibyl (Doncaster)

Turner, John Napier (Richmond)

Turner, Joseph Mallord William (London)

Turner, Victor Witter (Glasgow)

Turner, William (Morpeth)

Turner-Warwick, Dame Margaret (London)

Turpin, Dick (Hempstead)

Turpin, Randolph (Leamington)

Tusser, Thomas (Rivenhall)

Twiggy [Leslie Hornby] (London)

Twining, Louisa (London)

Twort, Frederick William (Camberley)

Tylor, Sir Edward Burnet (London)

Tynan, Kenneth (Birmingham)

Tyson, Edward (Bristol)

Tyson, Frank Holmes (Farnworth)

Tytler, James (Fearn)

Udall, Nicholas (Southampton)

Ullman, Tracey (Slough)

Underhill, Evelyn (Wolverhampton)

Underwood, Derek Leslie (Bromley)

Upjohn, Richard (Shaftesbury)

Ure, Andrew (Glasgow)

Urquhart, David (Cromarty)

Urquhart, Fred (Edinburgh)

Urquhart, Sir Thomas (Cromarty)

Ustinov, Sir Peter (London)

Uttley, Alison (Cromford)

Vanbrugh, Dame Irene (Exeter)

Vanbrugh, Sir John (London)

Vanbrugh, Violet (Exeter)

Vancouver, George (King's Lynn)

Vane, Sir Henry (Hadlow)

Vane, Sir John Robert (Tardebigge)

Van Praagh, Dame Peggy (London)

Vansittart, Robert [Baron] (Farnham)

Varah, Chad [Edward] (Barton upon Humber)

Vassell, Darius (Birmingham)

Vaughan, Frankie (Liverpool)

Vaughan, Henry (Newtown-by-Usk)

Vaughan, Herbert Alfred (Gloucester)

Vaughan, Keith (Selsey Bill)

Vaughan, Michael Paul (Manchester)

Vaughan-Williams, Ralph (Down Ampney)

Veitch, John (Peebles)

Venn, John (Hull)

Ventris, Michael George (Wheathampstead)

Vestris, Lucia Elizabeth (London)

Victoria [Queen] (London)

Vincent, Sir Charles Edward (Slinfold)

Viner, Charles (Salisbury)

Vodorinski, Anton [Albert

William Ketelbey]
(Birmingham)
Vogel, Sir Julius (London)
Voysey, Charles Francis
(London)

Waddington, Conrad Hall
(Evesham)
Wade, Sarah Virginia
(Bournemouth)
Wain, John Barrington
(Stoke-on-Trent)
Waite, Terry [Terence
Hardy] (Bollington)
Wake, William (Blandford
Forum)
Wakefield, Gilbert
(Nottingham)
Wakeley, Thomas (Membury)
Walker, Dame Ethel
(Edinburgh)
Walker, Sir James (Dundee)
Walker, John (Exeter)
Walker, John (London)
Walker, John (Stockton-on-
Tees)
Wall, Max [Maxwell George
Lorimer] (London)
Wallace, Alfred Russel (Usk)
Wallace, Sir Richard
(London)
Wallace, Sir William
(Elderslie)
Wallace, William (Greenock)
Wallas, Graham
(Sunderland)
Waller, Edmund (Coleshill)
Waller, Sir William (Knole)
Wallis, Alfred (Devonport)
Wallis, Sir Barnes Neville
(Ripley)
Wallis, John (Ashford)
Walpole, Horace [4th Earl
of Orford] (London)

Walpole, Sir Spencer
(London)
Walsingham, Sir Francis
(Chislehurst)
Walters, Julie (Birmingham)
Walton, Cecile (Glasgow)
Walton, George (Glasgow)
Walton, Izaak (Stafford)
Walton, Sir William Turner
(Oldham)
Wand, John William
Charles (Grantham)
Warburton, William
(Newark-on-Trent)
Ward, Arthur Sarsfield [Sax
Rohmer] (Birmingham)
Ward, James (Hull)
Ward, Nathaniel (Haverhill)
Wardle, Elizabeth (Leek)
Wark, Kirsty (Dumfries)
Warlock, Peter [Philip
Arnold] (London)
Warner, Deborah (Oxford)
Warner, Rex Ernest
(Birmingham)
Warner, Silvia Townsend
(London)
Warren, Sir Charles (Bangor)
Warriss, Ben (Sheffield)
Warton, Joseph (Dunsfold)
Warton, Thomas
(Basingstoke)
Waterhouse, Alfred
(Liverpool)
Waterhouse, Keith Spencer
(Leeds)
Waterland, Daniel
(Walesby)
Waterston, Jane Elizabeth
(Inverness)
Waterston, John James
(Edinburgh)
Waterton, Charles (Walton,
Yorks.)

Watkins, Dudley Dexter
(Manchester)
Watkins, Vernon Phillips
(Maesteg)
Watson, Foster (Lincoln)
Watson, Janet Vida
(London)
Watson, John [Ian
McLaren] (Manningtree)
Watson, Sir John William
(Burley in Wharfedale)
Watson, Richard
(Heversham)
Watson-Watt, Sir Robert
Alexander (Brechin)
Watt, Elizabeth Mary
(Dundee)
Watt, James (Greenock)
Watts, George Frederick
(London)
Watts, Isaac (Southampton)
Watts-Dunton, Walter T.
(St Ives, Cambridgeshire)
Waugh, Alexander Raban
[Alec] (London)
Waugh, Evelyn Arthur St
John (London)
Wavell, Archibald [1st Earl]
(Winchester)
Waverley, John Anderson
[1st Viscount] (Eskbank)
Webb, Beatrice (Standish)
Webb, Harri (Swansea)
Webb, Mary Gladys
(Leighton)
Webb, Matthew (Dawley)
Webb, Sidney James [Baron
Passfield] (London)
Webster, Tom [Gilbert
Thomas] (Bilston)
Wedderburn, Joseph Henry
(Forfar)
Wedgwood, Dame Veronica
(Stocksfield)

Wedgwood, Josiah (Stoke-on-Trent)

Weinstock, Arnold [Baron] (London)

Weir, David (Falkirk)

Weir, Judith (Cambridge)

Weir, Molly (Glasgow)

Welch, Robert (Hereford)

Welch, Bruce [Bruce Cripps] (Bognor Regis)

Welch, Vera [Dame Vera Lynn] (London)

Weldon, Fay (Alvechurch)

Weldon, Walter (Loughborough)

Welland, Colin Williams (Liverpool)

Weller, Paul (Woking)

Wells, Herbert George (Bromley)

Wells, Sir Thomas Spencer (St Albans)

Wesker, Arnold (London)

Wesley, Charles (Epworth)

Wesley, John (Epworth)

Wesley, Mary (Englefield Green)

Wesley, Samuel (Bristol)

Westbrook, Kate (Guildford)

Westbrook, Mike (High Wycombe)

Westbrook, Richard [Baron] (Bradford on Avon)

Westcott, Brooke Foss (Birmingham)

Westlake, John (Lostwithiel)

Weston, Sir Richard (Sutton)

Westwood, Vivienne (Tintwistle)

Weyman, Stanley John (Ludlow)

Wheatley, Denis Yates (London)

Wheatstone, Sir Charles (Gloucester)

Wheeler, Sir Charles (Codsall)

Wheeler, Sir Robert Mortimer (Glasgow)

Whewell, William (Lancaster)

Whitaker, Joseph (London)

Whitby, Daniel (Rushden)

White, Craig (Morley)

White, Gilbert (Selborne)

White, Henry Kirke (Nottingham)

White, Patrick Victor Martindale (London)

White, William Hale (Bedford)

Whitefield, George (Gloucester)

Whitehead, Alfred North (London)

Whitehead, Charles (London)

Whitehead, William (Cambridge)

Whitelaw, Billie (Coventry)

Whitelaw, William [1st Viscount] (Nairn)

Whiteley, William (Wakefield)

Whitfield, June (London)

Whitgift, John (Grimsby)

Whiting, John Robert (Salisbury)

Whitley, John Henry (Halifax)

Whittaker, Sir Edmund Taylor (Southport)

Whittle, Sir Frank (Coventry)

Whitworth, Sir Joseph (Stockport)

Whymper, Edward (London)

Whyte, Kathleen (Arbroath)

Whyte-Melville, George John (St Andrews)

Whytt, Robert (Edinburgh)

Widgery, John Passmore [Lord] (South Molton)

Wigglesworth, Sir Vincent Brian (Kirkham)

Wight, James Alfred [James Herriott] (Glasgow)

Wightman, Frieda [Frieda Inescort] (Edinburgh)

Wilberforce, William (Hull)

Wilbye, John (Diss)

Wilkes, John (London)

Wilkes, Maurice Vincent (Dudley)

Wilkie, Sir David (Cults)

Wilkinson, Ellen Cicely (Manchester)

Wilkinson, Sir Geoffrey (Todmorden)

Wilkinson, John (Clifton)

Wilkinson, Sir John Gardner (Hardendale)

Willett, William (Farnham)

Willey, Peter (Sedgefield)

William IV [King of Great Britain] (London)

William of Ockham (Ockham)

William of Wickham (Wickham)

Williams, Betty (Belfast)

Williams, Edward (Llancarfan)

Williams, Emlyn [George] (Mostyn)

Williams, Evan James (Cwmsychbant)

Williams, Sir Frederic Calland (Manchester)

Williams, Sir George (Dulverton)

Williams, John (London)

Williams, John Peter Rhys (Ogmore-by-sea)

Williams, Kenneth (London)

Williams, Raymond (Pandy)

Williams, Robbie (Stoke-on-Trent)

Williams, Waldo (Haverfordwest)

Williamson, William Crawford (Scarborough)

Willis, Robert [Bob] (Sunderland)

Willis, Thomas (Great Bedwyn)

Willughby, Francis (Middleton, Warwickshire)

Wilson, Alexander (Paisley)

Wilson, Sir Angus Frank (Bexhill)

Wilson, Charles Thomson Rees (Glencorse)

Wilson, Colin Henry (Leicester)

Wilson, Sir Daniel (Edinburgh)

Wilson, Edward Adrian (Cheltenham)

Wilson, Ernest Henry (Chipping Campden)

Wilson, Harriette (London)

Wilson, James (Carskerdo)

Wilson, James (Hawick)

Wilson, James Harold [Baron] (Huddersfield)

Wilson, John ['Christopher North'] (Paisley)

Wilson, John Mackay (Tweedmouth)

Wilson, Richard (Greenock)

Wilson, Richard (Penegoes)

Wilson, Roy [Royston] Warner (Kettering)

Wilson, Thomas (Burton)

Wilton, Penelope (Scarborough)

Winfield, Sir Percy Henry (Stoke Ferry)

Winslow, Edward (Droitwich)

Wint, Peter de (Stone)

Winterburn, Nigel (Coventry)

Winterson, Jeanette (Manchester)

Winthrop, John [Father and son] (Groton)

Winwood, Steve (Birmingham)

Winzet, Ninian (Renfrew)

Wisdom, Norman (London)

Wise, Ernie (East Ardsley)

Wise, Thomas James (Gravesend)

Wither, George (Bentworth)

Withering, William (Wellington)

Witherspoon, John (Gifford)

Wodehouse, Sir Pelham Grenville (Guildford)

Wolcot, John [Peter Pindar] (Dodbrooke)

Wolfe, James (Westerham)

Wolfenden, John Frederick [Baron] (Halifax)

Wolfit, Sir Donald (Newark-on-Trent)

Wolfson, Sir Isaac (Glasgow)

Wollaston, William (Coton)

Wollaston, William Hyde (East Dereham)

Wollstonecraft, Mary (London)

Wolsey, Thomas [Cardinal] (Ipswich)

Wood, Sir Andrew (Largo)

Wood, Anthony (Oxford)

Wood, Haydn (Slaithwaite)

Wood, Mrs Henry [Ellen Price] (Worcester)

Wood, Sir Henry Evelyn (Braintree)

Wood, Sir Henry Joseph (London)

Wood, John (Derby)

Wood, Victoria (Prestwich)

Woodcock, George (Bamber Bridge)

Woodgate, Jonathan (Middlesbrough)

Woodward, Sir Arthur Smith (Macclesfield)

Woodward, Thomas Jones [Tom Jones] (Pontypridd)

Wooldridge, Sydney William (London)

Woolf, Arthur (Camborne)

Woolf, Leonard (London)

Woolf, Virginia (London)

Woollett, William (Maidstone)

Woolley, Sir Charles Leonard (London)

Woolley, Frank (Tonbridge)

Woolston, Thomas (Northampton)

Woolton, Frederick [1st Baron] (Liverpool)

Wootton, Baroness Barbara (Cambridge)

Wordsworth, Dorothy (Cockermouth)

Wordsworth, William (Cockermouth)

Wordsworth, William Brocklesby (London)

Worth, Charles Frederick (Bourn)

Wotton, Sir Henry (Boughton Malherbe)

Wouldhave, William (North Shields)
Wraxall, Sir Nathanael William (Bristol)
Wren, Sir Christopher (East Knoyle)
Wright, Sir Almroth Edward (Middleton Tyas)
Wright, [Billy] William Ambrose (Wolverhampton)
Wright, Fanny [Frances Darusmont] (Dundee)
Wright, Joseph (Bradford)
Wright, Joseph (Derby)
Wright, Peter (Chesterfield)
Wright, Robert Alderson [Lord] (South Shields)
Wright, Thomas (Byers Green)
Wright, William Aldis (Beccles)
Wulfstan [Saint] (Long Itchington)

Wyatt, James (Burton Constable)
Wyatt, Sir Matthew Digby (Rowde)
Wyatt, Robert (Bristol)
Wyatt, Sir Thomas (Allington)
Wycherley, William (Clive)
Wyndham, Sir Charles (Liverpool)
Wyndham, John [John Wyndham Harris] (Knowle)
Wyon, Olive (London)
Wyon, William (Birmingham)

Yarrell, William (London)
Yearsley, Ann (Bristol)
Yeats, John Butler (London)
Yonge, Charlotte (Otterbourne)
York, Michael (Fulmer)
York, Susannah (London)

Yorke, Henry [Henry Green] (Tewkesbury)
Young, Arthur (London)
Young, Douglas (Tayport)
Young, Edward (Upham)
Young, Francis Brett (Halesowen)
Young, George Malcolm (Greenhithe)
Young, James (Glasgow)
Young, Sir Jimmy (Cinderford)
Young, Kirsty (Stirling)
Young, Paul (Luton)
Young, Thomas (Milverton)
Younghusband, Dame Eileen (London)

Zangwill, Israel (London)
Zeta Jones, Catherine (Swansea)